Motion Graphics
and Effects
in Final Cut Pro

Kevin Monahan

Peachpit
Press

Motion Graphics and Effects in Final Cut Pro
Kevin Monahan

Peachpit Press
1249 Eighth Street
Berkeley, CA 94710
510/524-2178 • 800/283-9444 • 510/524-2221 (fax)

Find us on the World Wide Web at: www.peachpit.com

To report errors, please send a note to errata@peachpit.com

Peachpit Press is a division of Pearson Education

Editors	**Erfert Fenton, Geta Carlson**
Production Editor	**Hilal Sala**
Copyeditor	**Charles Koppelman**
Technical Editor	**Ned Soltz**
Compositor	**Chris Gillespie, Happenstance-Type-O-Rama**
Indexer	**Joy Dean Lee**
Cover design	**Mimi Heft**
Interior design	**Chris Gillespie and Maureen Forys, Happenstance-Type-O-Rama**

Cover images: © Digital Vision/Robin Cracknell (top), © Getty Images, Inc. (center), © Thinkstock Footage and © Getty Images/PhotoDisc (bottom)

ISBN 0-321-17915-3
9 8 7 6 5 4 3 2 1

Printed and bound in the United States of America

Dedicated to the memory of Ralph Fairweather

Acknowledgments

Like filmmaking, creating a book is a collaborative art. I'm very grateful to have had such a great team of people to assist me in bringing this book to you. (I can't fit the names of everyone who helped me onto this page; a full list of acknowledgments is provided in PDF format on the DVD, in the Chapter Extras folder.)

First of all, I'd like to thank my friends and family — especially my parents, Kevin and Sylvia Monahan and Katherine Gray — for supporting my creative endeavors over the years.

Next, I'd like to thank some very special folks who made the book what it is today: Peachpit Press editor **Marjorie Baer** made this project possible and believed in my vision from day one. My project and development editor, **Erfert Fenton** (AKA "Sarge"), turned my voice into legible text. Technical editor **Ned Soltz** provided attention to detail, insightful suggestions, and encouragement. **Lisa Brenneis** helped me get this project off the ground and offered support along the way. Thanks to **Geta Carlson**, editor and stand-in "Sarge," for her Herculean efforts during the final push. **Charles Koppelman** did a great job of copy editing much of this book. Thanks to **Hilal Sala**, the production editor, whose dedication to quality is one of the reasons this book looks so great. Senior designer **Mimi Heft** provided the behind-the-scenes efforts that resulted in the look and feel of the book. **Maureen Forys** and **Chris Gillespie** of Happenstance Type-O-Rama contributed the expert layout and design work that makes the book a pleasure to look at. **Jay Payne**, the media producer, helped make the companion DVD a truly valuable resource. **Graeme Nattress** put a lot of hard work into creating the excellent "Telly's FX" plug-ins that are included with the book.

The book could also not have been produced without help from the following people: **Olivia Cheo, Scott Clark, Ralph Fairweather, Sharon Franklin, Michele Friedman, Matt Hanson, Richard Harrington, Philip Hodgetts, Kent Kingery, Mark Leialoha, Alona Leviner, Jonathan Luskin, Steve Martin, Chris Martin, Trish and Chris Meyer, Mike Palumbo, Rob Pongi, Lugh Powers, Tom Reagan, Charles Roberts, Anongwan "Guitar" Sattrakom, Tim Serda, Wes Sewell, Mark Spencer, Billy Sheahan, Octavio Solis, Marco Solorio, Matt Silverman, Paul Stelhe, Ken Stone, Steve Tenaglia, Jim Tierney, Steven Traver, Tim Wilson, Adam Wilt, Tom Wolsky, Rick Young,** and **Yukari Yamazaki.**

There are many more who lent me a hand throughout the project; if you aren't listed here, you know who you are. Thank you!

Contents

Introduction

This book is an outgrowth of my time in the Final Cut Pro trenches since version 1 appeared on the scene in 1999 — as a filmmaker, an effects artist, and but in particular, as a teacher. I've been an Apple Certified Instructor for Final Cut Pro since 2000, and have taught the application to hundreds of people through the Bay Area Video Coalition (BAVC). In fact, it was a class I developed for BAVC, called FCP FX, which explored animation, travel mattes, compositing, transitions, generators, filters, and other techniques that provided the inspiration and much of the content for this book

My goal in writing Motion Graphics and Effects in Final Cut Pro was to introduce readers with a good working knowledge of Final Cut Pro's editing tools to the vast and exciting world of visual effects it holds in store. (To get the most out of the techniques presented here, you'll want to have completed at least a couple of Final Cut Pro editing projects. If you're completely new to Final Cut Pro, I can recommend the project-based instruction in *Apple Pro Training: Final Cut Pro 4, Editing Professional Video,* by Diana Weynand, and the comprehensive task-based reference *Final Cut Pro 4 for Macintosh: Visual QuickPro Guide,* by Lisa Brenneis, both from Peachpit Press.)

Each chapter addresses a key concept in effects creation — motion paths, for example, or composite modes — and, using files provided on the companion DVD, takes you step-by-step through a series of exercises in which you'll re-create the effects you see illustrated in the book. You'll learn dozens of valuable techniques, and acquire the skills you'll need to adapt them to your own projects. Best of all, you'll gain the confidence to experiment, which will help you grow as an effects artist, expanding your technical and aesthetic bag of tricks and developing a personal style.

The book opens by helping you set up your Final Cut Pro edit bench for producing professional-quality effects, including extra hardware, third-party applications, and plug-ins you might want to add. You'll also learn workflow strategies to help you create projects quickly and efficiently. That's good for your creative process, and it's important for your business, too. Chapter 3 reviews some essential Final Cut Pro techniques and terms that will be used throughout the rest of the book. (Advanced Final Cut Pro users: You may be tempted to breeze through these early chapters, but do keep an eye out for tips and techniques that might surprise even you veterans.)

Beginning with Chapter 4, you'll work through dozens of effects-building exercises, mastering keyframing techniques, working with multiple layers, creating transitions, and adding filters, including color-correction filters. In the later chapters you'll work with mattes, learn the intricacies of the alpha channel, and delve into composite modes. Chapter 12 offers some advanced text-animation techniques, and gives you a taste of LiveType and Title 3D effects. You'll also get some insights into FCP's time-remapping capabilities, and tips on integrating additional applications — including Adobe Photoshop — with Final Cut Pro to create jaw-dropping effects.

The DVD that comes with this book has everything you need to complete the exercises, including source clips and a master Final Cut Pro project file. But that's not all. You'll also find try-out versions of effects-related applications, and a dozen custom plug-ins that were created especially for this book. Once you've gotten your feet wet with the techniques presented here and start to gain confidence, I'm sure you'll enjoy using these filters, generators, and transitions in your own projects.

Welcome to the world of visual effects! May this guide unleash your imagination.

— KEVIN MONAHAN,
January 2004

P.S. Be sure to check my website, www.fcpworld.com, for updates, tips, and more information about creating effects with Final Cut Pro.

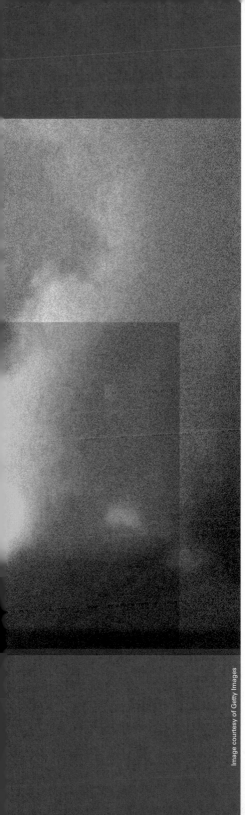

1

Setting Up Your System

Before diving headlong into creating effects, you'll need to make sure your Final Cut Pro edit bench is set up properly for video graphics production. Although you'll be tempted to start creating effects right away, spending the time setting up an efficient system from the get-go will save you countless hours later, when deadlines are looming.

Once your system is set up, you might like to try your hand at creating some effects. You'll find five warm-up exercises on a PDF file on the companion DVD, in the Chapter Extras folder. These exercises cover some basic effects-building skills, including layering, keyframing, and adding transitions. These techniques will be covered in detail throughout the book, but you might want to try the exercises to test your skill level.

Final Cut Pro 4 Effects Upgrades

Before you set up your system, you should be aware of some of the many new features and upgrades Final Cut Pro 4 offers related to effects. We'll be going over many of these new features in detail later in the book.

- **RT Extreme:** Now you can play back many effects without rendering them. Final Cut Pro 4's built-in RT Extreme architecture lets you use as many real-time effects as your Mac will allow (see Figure 1-1). In Unlimited RT mode, even many third-party plug-ins will play in real time. All filters that will play in real time are listed in bold type in the menus and the Effects tab.

- **Keyframe Editor:** In FCP 4 you can keyframe motion and filter effects directly in the Timeline (see Figure 1-2). With the Keyframes Editor, you can enable, adjust, or remove any keyframe. You can also save any Timeline layout and bring it with you when you need to work on another machine.

- **Additional Timeline improvements:** The zoom function of the Zoom Control and Zoom Slider has been upgraded to be even more intuitive. You can zoom in on a clip or a set of keyframes to do a quick adjustment, then pop back out to view the entire Timeline.

FIGURE 1-1

FCP 4's RT Extreme lets you play back many effects without rendering them. This clip is playing back in real time with two filters: Color Correction and Channel Offset.

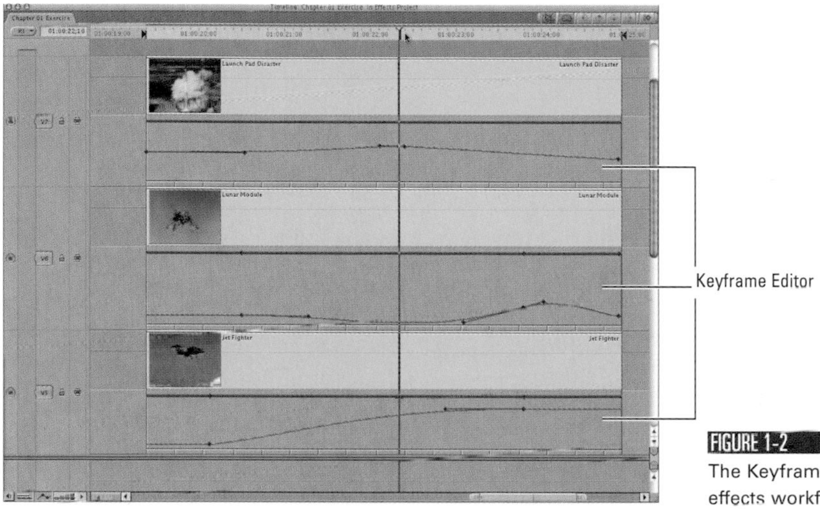

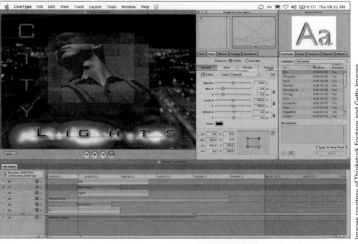

FIGURE 1-2

The Keyframe Editor improves effects workflow.

- **Time remapping:** This new feature gives you the ability to gradually slow down or speed up clips as they play, much like the "bullet time" effects in *The Matrix*. You can even make a clip play forward and then backward by adjusting a curve in the Motion tab or the new Keyframe Editor. There's a new Time Remap tool in the Tool palette and handy speed indicator tic marks at the bottom of every track.

- **LiveType:** FCP 4 includes a separate program called LiveType. At first glance you'll see that LiveType makes it easier to create motion typography. A broader view reveals that it's a full-blown compositing environment that you can use in a multitude of ways, including stacking layers, creating textures for mattes and backgrounds, harnessing objects that have built-in alpha channels, and creating templates you can save for future use. (See Figure 1-3.) LiveType also includes LiveFonts, a new kind of font that self-animates.

FIGURE 1-3

LiveType is not just a type-animation tool, but a full-blown compositing environment.

Images courtesy of Thinkstock Footage and Getty Images

■ **Improved workflow:** Workflow improvements include the following:

- Auto Select buttons allow easy application of filters across multiple tracks.

- The new Timeline patch panel allows you to target tracks where you want to (this is especially helpful for targeting multiple audio tracks).

- Auto-resizing of the interface prevents window overlap, a common performance killer.

- Mouse scrolling works in all windows, including moving the Timeline forward or backward.

- You can resize the height of individual tracks.

- Duplicate frame detection shows whether you have any duplicate frames in a composite or transition.

■ **Improved chroma keying:** Two new filters called Color Smoothing 4:1:1 and Color Smoothing 4:2:2 give FCP 4 users a hand with chroma keying. DV users, in particular, get a big improvement in edge quality.

■ **Rendering:** A brand new render engine is capable of rendering in high-quality 8- or 10-bit codecs. Auto Rendering is new as well; whenever you walk away from your Mac, FCP will automatically render files. There are a number of ways you can render a sequence's audio and video, as noted in the Sequence menu.

FIGURE 1-4

Using FCP 4's new Keyboard Layout feature, I've remapped composite mode choices to the numeric keypad when the Command and Option keys are pressed.

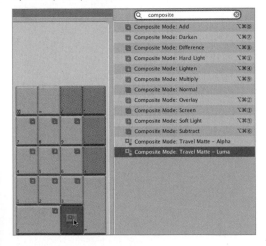

■ **Monitoring RT effects and offline RT:** With FCP 4 you can finally look at the results of your real-time effects and offline RT video on a video monitor.

■ **Playhead ganging:** With FCP 4's Playhead Sync menus, you can make the playheads in the Viewer and the Canvas move in tandem. This is great for checking a clip's effect on one video track in the Viewer while monitoring the whole multilayered effect in the Canvas.

■ **Frame Viewer:** The new Frame Viewer window offers a great way to compare frames side by side. Although this feature is primarily used for color matching in color correction, it can also be used to compare clips with and without a particular filter.

■ **Improvements to color-correction tools:** By using the new Hue Match tools, you can greatly reduce tweaking time when matching colors from one clip to the next.

■ **Dynamic trimming:** One new feature of FCP 4 is the ability to dynamically trim a cut. After it's enabled in your User Preferences, you're good to go. I use it in the Trim Edit window. Check the box and just play to the point you want to trim to and — bingo! — your edit is immediately updated.

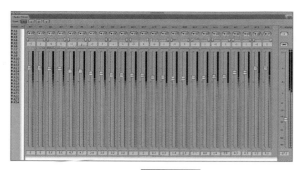

FIGURE 1-5

The Audio Mix tool lets you keyframe audio levels on the fly.

■ **Mappable keyboard and Button List:** Go to Tools → Keyboard Layout → Customize to make your own keyboard shortcuts (see Figure 1-4). The Button List offers a database of commands in the form of buttons that you can drag onto the Timeline, Viewer, Canvas, or Browser.

■ **Audio improvements:** FCP 4 includes a number of new audio filters. The new Audio Mix tool (see Figure 1-5) lets you keyframe audio levels on the fly in a process known as automation gain. The ability to keyframe audio filters on the fly, without having to render them each time you make a change, will speed up your workflow a great deal.

FIGURE 1-6

Soundtrack includes royalty-free loops that you can use to create music for your video compositions.

■ **Soundtrack:** The Soundtrack application (see Figure 1-6) allows you to create your own music from provided royalty-free loops. Effects makers will enjoy creating music to back their effects without having to search a music library. I have a hard time putting the thing down. This application is a ton of fun!

■ **Cinema Tools:** Cinema Tools lets you work with film projects, HDTV, and camcorders like the Panasonic DVX 100. You can now edit in the Timeline in the native 24p format (and several other frame speeds).

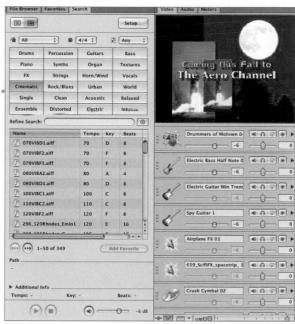

So there you have it! A roundup of the niceties added to FCP 4 for effects makers. We'll go over all of these features throughout the book, so stay tuned. For now, let's look into setting up a stable system for FCP 4 and beyond.

System Considerations

This book assumes you're working with Final Cut Pro 4 or later, so the requirements for constructing a system are based on that assumption. (You can probably do many of these effects with an earlier version of Final Cut Pro and a slower machine, but if I were in your shoes I'd get the fastest Mac I could afford with the current version of FCP and other ancillary software. Don't monkey around! Buy a system that will serve you best as an effects creator for the next few years. After booking a few jobs, you'll pay off that system in no time.) Let's look into the requirements for building a basic effects workstation.

The system requirements for FCP 4 state that you must have, at the very minimum, a G4 350 MHz Mac with an AGP PCI slot. For real-time effects, you'll need a G4 500 MHz. A dual-processor Mac is the most desirable machine for working with effects. The new dual-processor G5 Macs let you play back many tracks of real-time effects and render at blazing speed.

Your Mac should have a minimum of 512 MB of RAM to function well in OS X (10.2.5 or later), which is required for Final Cut Pro 4. You also need at least 512 MB of RAM to work with RT Extreme, which optimizes real-time effects. The G5 Macs can hold up to 8 GB of RAM, which makes FCP and the applications you use in tandem with it operate at lightning speed.

You'll need at least 1 GB of disk space to install FCP 4, with additional space available for installing material for Soundtrack and LiveType. (The audio and font materials add up to 14 GB, so plan accordingly.) To install these programs, you'll also need a DVD drive.

As of this writing, QuickTime 6.4 is recommended for FCP 4. New versions of Quick-Time are released periodically, so check Apple's website for information on the latest version, or just run the Software Updater program that comes with the OS.

tip

For the latest information on system requirements, check out the Technical Specifications section of Apple's Final Cut Pro website (www.apple.com/finalcutpro/specs.html).

REAL-TIME SYSTEMS

Most Mac G4s and G5s are capable of displaying effects in real time. With this functionality, you'll be able to work more quickly with items like transitions, filters, third-party plug-ins, and motion effects. In order for Final Cut Pro to run real-time effects using any format, you'll need a G4 with a 500 MHz or faster processor. Machines with a G4 500 MHz DP (dual-processor) or better will give you even greater performance in render speeds and overall system flexibility. For DV projects, a G4 550 MHz or better laptop will have the speed to run real-time effects.

You should be aware that there are multiple flavors of real time in FCP 4, including previews like proxy and Unlimited RT (yellow and orange bars), as well as full-resolution real time (green bar). The more powerful your computer, the more layers of proxy and Unlimited RT previews and full-resolution real-time effects will be available.

Some video capture cards offer a number of real-time effects, in varying qualities and quantities. Additional real-time effects are coming out periodically from these board manufacturers, so it pays to keep checking their websites and Apple's site (www.apple.com/finalcutpro/qualification.html). At Apple's site you can also check out the decks that are qualified to work with FCP 4.

When it comes to real-time effects, the king of video capture boards is the Pinnacle Cinewave, which offers additional support for RT Extreme.

> **note**
>
> *If you're working only with DV, you don't need a video capture card.*

HARD DRIVES

Whatever your setup, you should use good quality, name-brand hard drives. ATA or serial ATA hard drives that spin at 7200 rpm (at the very least) and are internally mounted seem to be the most reliable for working with miniDV, DVCAM, and DVC PRO25 (which I frequently refer to as *DV* throughout the book).

For DV users, FCP functions best with a second hard drive that's used exclusively for capturing audio and video. The reason for this is twofold: system performance and system maintenance. System performance is reduced when you have captured media on the same drive as your application; the system hard drive will have to work in overdrive to serve up the video and keep the system up and running. Having a second drive helps with system maintenance as well. After each major project you should erase, or initialize, the media drive. If you don't, the drive can become fragmented, eventually causing it to fail or drop frames.

With certain video capture cards — particularly the AJA Kona and the Aurora Igniter — properly configured ATA drives might give you enough speed to edit with uncompressed video. But video capture cards (as well as DVC PRO50) may require faster and more expensive SCSI drives. See what your video capture card manufacturer recommends before making any hasty decisions regarding your drive purchase. I generally err on the side of caution, which is why I suggest a fast disk array, such as a Rorke Data Array, to handle uncompressed video duties.

Inside the new generation of Mac G5s, you'll find a new breed of drive called Serial ATA. It has a faster interface that's well suited for video capture and playback. Unfortunately, the G5 is limited in the number of serial ATA drives that can be installed. If you want to purchase drives for uncompressed editing, look for external SATA drives or arrays with an internal SATA card.

FireWire hard drives

If you use FireWire hard drives for media storage and plan to capture DV, be sure to purchase only those drives and enclosures that offer the Oxford 911 or Oxford 922 Bridge set (this will be stated on the drive's packaging). Your FireWire hard drive should spin at 7200 rpm.

Current Mac towers and the newer PowerBooks offer a FireWire 800 port for connecting FireWire 800 portable hard drives (see Figure 1-7). FireWire 800 drives can handle faster data rates (up to 800 megabits per second) for dealing with higher quality video formats. More speed also means added stability for your video capture and playback tasks. FireWire 800 drives also operate more reliably over longer cable lengths (up to 100 meters, compared to FireWire 400's 4.5-meter limitation). FireWire 800 drives can be used for standard DV or, when striped together using OS X Disk Utility, are fast enough for capturing certain flavors of uncompressed video. Check out www.apple.com/firewire for late-breaking details on FireWire 800 drives.

FIGURE 1-7
This FireWire 800 drive from LaCie can handle up to 800 megabits per second.

Hard drive maintenance

Regardless of the kind of drives you have, be sure to maintain them regularly with Apple Disk Utility's Disk First Aid. Repairing Permissions frequently on your system drive is a good habit to get into to prevent those demons from cropping up at the most inopportune times. A dedicated disk utility such as Alsoft Disk Warrior is a must-have for checking the integrity of your media drives.

CONFIGURING A FINAL CUT PRO SYSTEM

Final Cut Pro is unlike most applications in that it really should be thought of as a *system*. The optimal FCP system is made up of the right hardware and software connected together logically to provide predictable results.

You've probably got your rig set up correctly, but you might want to refer to Figure 1-8 or 1-9 to be sure. All your components should be set up according to the illustrations. Information about additional components follows, including video monitor, amplified speakers, and Y-connector or audio mixer.

External video monitor

When you're working with DV and Final Cut Pro, and especially when you're working with video effects, you'll need to see how things look on a video monitor as you work (see Figure 1-10). Use an S-Video cable to hook up a calibrated NTSC or PAL monitor to your powered-up DV device (video deck, camcorder, or analog conversion box). If you don't have a professional video monitor, use the best TV set available, preferably one with an S-Video connection. Although they're not as good as professional monitors, I've seen some standard TVs do a decent job of monitoring.

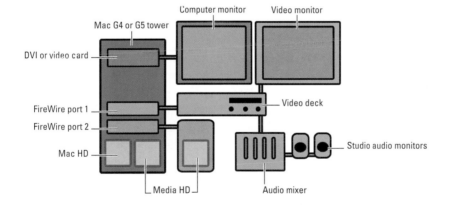

FIGURE 1-8
DV configuration.

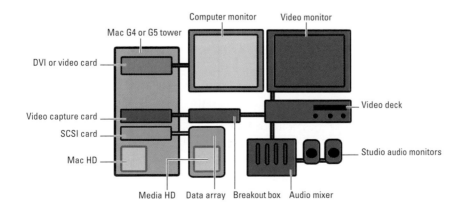

FIGURE 1-9
Uncompressed configuration.

FIGURE 1-10

I use the Sony PVM-20M2U for my video monitor.

Looking at your video effects on a monitor as you create them enables you to preview the finished results before you record your sequence to tape. You can't rely solely on what you see in the Canvas; your rendered effect will look a lot more blotchy on the Mac's screen than on the video monitor. Your effect looks so compressed on the Mac after rendering because Final Cut Pro can't display your newly rendered clip at its true resolution — it generally takes a lot of processor overhead to do so.

If you have an uncompressed capture card, you'll probably have your monitor connected through a *breakout box* — a junction box for all your audio and video cables. Check the capture card manufacturer's specs for further information.

Connecting a video deck

You'll need to have a video deck to be in business with FCP (see Figure 1-11). If you're just starting out, using a DV camcorder in your setup is fine, but after awhile you won't want to wear it out. Other reasons for upgrading to a professional DV deck are better shuttling speed and the ability to get on and off the tape heads quickly. Trust me, with a standard DV camcorder and its sluggish shuttling mechanisms, you waste precious seconds of your workday every time you use the deck. Some pro decks allow RS-422 device control, which lets you control your deck and send timecode via a separate cable, offering much snappier deck control and greater frame accuracy. A deck that can stand the rigors of shuttling, recording, and being on for long hours is what you'll want. I should mention that using a camcorder as your chief source deck in front of a seasoned client might raise questions about your level of professionalism. Don't put yourself in that position.

A bonus of a separate deck is that you can also use it to "transcode" or dub analog source material, such as that from Beta SP, through the S-Video port. (Amazingly, many camcorders do this as well.) The more expensive DV decks provide a component video or SDI interface for your dubs. Final Cut Pro works with other decks, too, such as Digital Betacam decks; you just need the right hardware to control them and the right capture cards and hard drives if you wish to acquire higher quality video. FireWire DVCPRO 50 decks from Panasonic are available now, allowing video editors to achieve outstanding image quality over FireWire at a much lower price than Sony Digital Betacam systems while offering similar quality.

---

tip

DV users: Have your DV deck or camcorder powered up at all times while working with Final Cut Pro. In a Final Cut Pro system the DV device plays a few different roles. It's not just for playing back, batch capturing, and recording; it's also for monitoring video, which is essential in effects creation. When making video effects, "what you see is what you get," so you'll want to see how your projects will look on a television screen, not a computer screen (unless your only destination is the Web).

Audio speakers

Just to get the jargon down, powered audio speakers are
also referred to as *studio audio monitors*. Your speakers
should be connected to a mixer or a Y-adapter, so you
feed audio to both the Mac and the video deck or camcorder. The speakers should be placed at ear level, not
hidden behind your computer monitors.

With the addition of Soundtrack, which offers 96 KHz
sampling, you'll want to be able to hear the quality of your creations. Good visuals should be accompanied by good sound, so spend a little extra money on good
studio audio monitors. Believe me, you'll thank yourself later. (See Figure 1-12.)

I won't lie to you; I've heard great mixes done on crummy speakers, but they're
in the minority and done by people who know their craft. In my opinion, you'll
need to spend a minimum of $300 a pair for studio audio monitors. And the more
you spend, the better off you'll be in the long run. Here's why.

Cheaper speakers that come bundled with many preconfigured systems or computer shops are "pre-EQ'd," meaning that they're typically tuned for boost in
the bass and in the high end, which is great for listening to your home stereo or
playing video games. However, you aren't doing that! When you're mixing
music, a soundtrack, or dialogue you really want to have an accurate representation of what you're working on, and this boost in the high and low end will
disguise the true mix. Not being able to hear a proper mix while you're working
is a project killer.

As a professional, what you really want are studio audio monitors that have
the "flattest" response possible, meaning that you don't want your powered
speakers to be "pre-EQ'd." This flat response signal provides extremely accurate results for any mix you can dish up. When you're talking about speaker
monitors in the Mackie or Genelec category, you're paying for a perfectly flat
response, which is guaranteed by these companies. Here are some recommen-
dations for you:

- Good : M-Audio SP-5B biamp nearfield monitors

- Better: Event PS5 biamp nearfield monitors

- Best: Genelec 1029A biamp active monitors or Mackie HR-824
  biamp active monitors

FIGURE 1-13

I use the Mackie 1202 audio mixer.

Although you might find the sticker price a little steep (typically about $800 for a pair in the "best" category), investing in quality audio gear is worthwhile. If you plan to keep working in this business, you'll learn that good audio gear lasts a long time and you'll build on your audio needs as you go. Start off with a good pair of speakers and then move towards the purchase of a matched subwoofer. If you do a lot of DVD authoring, you should also consider that you will eventually need audio monitoring for 5.1 "Stereo Surround" mixing (that's at least five speakers!).

As a final word of advice, get some decent "cans" (headphones). A good set is useful for checking your mix before output. Get a reliable brand that completely covers the ear. I like to use the AKG K240S for my own work; they're reliable, comfortable, and about $100.

Monitoring audio and video

For audio monitoring, you'll need a Y-cable audio splitter (inexpensive and available at an electronics store) or an audio mixer (see Figure 1-13). This setup allows you to switch audio output between monitoring to NTSC or PAL (audio comes out of your DV deck or DV camcorder) and not monitoring (audio comes out of your Mac).

With an audio splitter or mixer installed, you won't have to move behind your computer and DV device every time you want to switch from FireWire to Desktop monitoring. If you ever have to ask "where's my audio?" it's likely you're not monitoring properly. Here's the info you need to know:

- The keyboard shortcut Command + F12 toggles audio/video monitoring between FireWire (viewing images on your video monitor, and hearing audio from speakers attached to the deck) and the Desktop (viewing images on the Canvas only, and hearing audio from speakers connected to the Mac).

- View → External Video → All Frames also toggles monitoring between the FireWire connection and the Desktop.

With FCP 4, you probably won't switch monitoring situations very often, as you needed to do with FCP 3. In FCP 4, real-time effects play back at all times on the video monitor. It will even output OfflineRT! As far as I'm concerned, the only time you should monitor to the Desktop is when using a PowerBook to edit in the field.

note

Ideally, you should have your speakers coming out of both your Mac and your deck. However, FCP 4 lets you have your speakers hooked up to just your Mac, whether you're capturing, outputting, or monitoring. To set up your system to behave in this fashion, go to the Final Cut Pro → Audio/Video Settings → A/V Devices. From the Playback Output section, choose Audio → Built-in Controller. To choose a different output, check the box for Different Output for Edit to Tape/Print to Video, and again choose Audio → Built-in Controller.

Working with uncompressed video

As I mentioned earlier, you can purchase video capture cards that have real-time effects capability and offer higher quality output than standard DV. This is particularly useful for rendered graphics, titles, and effects.

With these cards you can take high-quality video, including standard DV, and maintain its integrity. If you do a color correction to your DV or uncompressed footage, it won't be degraded if it's rendered in the video capture card's compression scheme (codec). Rendered effects, which would normally degrade footage when rendered for FireWire DV decks, will remain pristine. Titles will also have nice, clean edges.

Photo: Mark Leialoha

FIGURE 1-14

My credo in creating effects: "The more monitor real estate, the better."

There are lots of companies offering video capture cards. All of the following are excellent choices: the AJA Kona, Aurora IgniterX SDI, DeckLink Pro from Blackmagic Design, and the Pinnacle Cinewave. Each has different advantages regarding real-time effects, scalable resolutions, ease of use, and film project or codec options. You'll have to assess your own needs regarding this often subjective issue.

AJA Video (www.aja.com) has a cool product called Io that offers the functionality of a 10-bit video capture card blended with a fully featured breakout box. This box is a real winner if you need compressed video with multiple live outputs (see Figure 1-15). Although it requires speedy drives, the Io connects to any Mac via a simple FireWire 400 connector. The Io is the solution I use for high-quality SDI output.

With many of these systems you can preview effects on your video monitor at full resolution and even record to tape without rendering to disk.

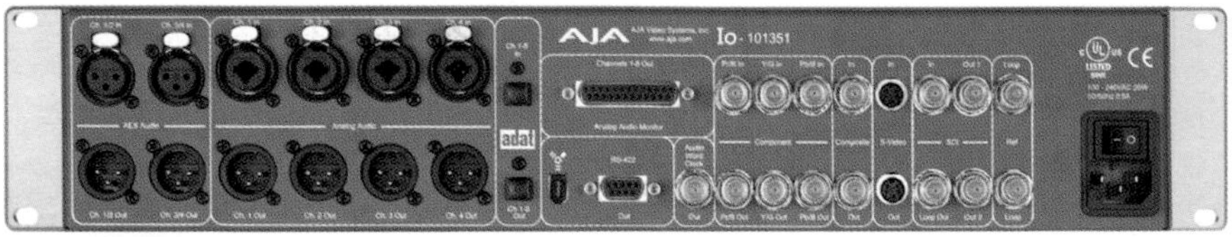

note

The AJA Io works only with FCP 4 and OS X. This works out great for me, as I do a lot of my work on FCP and will continue to do so. There are other uncompressed solutions out there that might work out better for you. Be sure to check out the discussion boards on FCP web sites like www.2-pop.com and www.creativecow.net for more opinions on uncompressed systems and other issues.

FIGURE 1-15

The AJA Io (shown from rear) can take any video source and provide uncompressed video output.

What's the Delay?

Before FCP 4.1, when you worked with DV and monitored video to NTSC or PAL via a FireWire connection, the video monitor was slightly delayed compared to what was displayed in the Canvas. The delay was about 6 to 8 frames, depending on the DV device you were using. This lag was very disconcerting, particularly to editors coming from analog systems where video capture cards took care of this lag. Fortunately, this problem has been fixed in the current version of FCP.

Now, your video monitor and computer monitor should be in sync with your sound as you monitor your effects, no matter where you choose to view your piece. If you'd like to adjust the delay time between your video monitor and Canvas, go to Final Cut Pro → System Settings → Playback Control → Frame Offset. Set your frame offset in the numeric entry box. Try 6 and see how that works.

Tools of the Electronic Edit Bench

Whether you work in a professional video facility, an office "cube," or a home studio, you'll want to set up your work environment intelligently. I call the work area around my computer my "edit bench" because that's what film editors have traditionally called the desks where they edit material. In the film world, an edit bench might include a viewer, take-up reels, an audio synchronizer, trim bins, a trash bin, china markers, and other tools of the trade. Your electronic edit bench provides the equivalents of these tools, in the form of hardware and software. If you have only a few of the tools listed below, you'll want to work toward obtaining more of them. Sooner or later, as a serious effects artist, you'll have a use for most of these items.

HARDWARE FOR EFFECTS CREATORS

Having the right hardware gives you greater latitude for importing media objects into your computer. Some of these items I would consider crucial tools; others are in the "nice to have" category.

Hardware "must-haves"

In the "must-have" category, I'd include a video deck, video monitor, and powered speakers. Now for the "nice-to-haves."

Hardware "nice-to-haves"

Here's a list of items that are nice to have, but not necessary to start creating effects using Final Cut Pro. As time goes by, you'll want to add some of these items to your arsenal.

- **DV camcorder:** Great for grabbing quick shots, backdrops, textures, and, of course, video elements. A three-chip camcorder is desirable. Camcorder hardware has made great strides in quality lately, including

DV50 (50-megabit video) and 24p options. In the professional realm, the Panasonic DVX100 leads the pack on the cheaper end (see Figure 1 16), with the many flavors of HDTV covering the higher end. It's always better to have higher quality source if you can afford it. If all you have is a one-chip DV camera, then use that, keeping in mind that for effects you're likely to alter the imagery anyway.

- **Second computer monitor or LCD display:** Although FCP's multi-tabbed environment keeps the interface very compact, there are times when you're going to need more screen real estate to spread out and expand Timelines, break off tabs, and have multiple windows open. The Apple Cinema Display or a similar monitor will give you the room you need.

- **Video capture card:** If you have quality requirements that are higher than DV, or aren't satisfied with the quality of graphics rendered in the Apple DV Codec, you'll need a high-quality capture card. When you get into purchasing a video capture card, also be sure to see what the card manufacturer recommends regarding hard drives and ancillary gear like a SCSI or IDE Controller PCI card. (If you have a G5 Mac, make sure any cards you add are compatible with this new system architecture.)

- **Scanner:** I almost put this device in the "must have" category because I find it so useful in my everyday workflow. You can scan photos, graphics, documents, and found objects to place in your compositions (see Figure 1-17). You can also scan your storyboards to create *animatics,* storyboards that you animate for previsualization. You don't need an expensive, high-resolution scanner, as the requirement for NTSC and PAL video is only 72 dpi/ppi.

- **FireWire drive:** As time goes by, FireWire drives are becoming increasingly cheaper, larger, and more reliable. There's really no reason why you shouldn't own at least one. You'll use it to move large media files around the office, take them across town, or ship them across the country. There are two flavors of FireWire drives: the regular "400" and the new faster "800" variety.

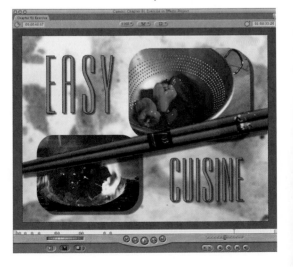

- **Color printer:** With a color printer, you can print storyboards and stills for pre-project visualization and client approval.

- **Digital still camera:** Sure, you can take video stills with your camcorder, but they'll typically be of marginal quality and limited to 720 x 480 pixels. You'll need a larger frame size for panning and zooming the stills. You can also use a digital still camera to capture textures and backgrounds to use in your video compositions. With today's digital still cameras shrinking to the size of a pack of gum and packing in more and more megapixels, you almost can't afford to be without one.

- **Pen tablet:** If you plan to do a lot of painting, matte work, or rotoscoping, you'll want a good-sized pen tablet (the bigger they are, the more control you'll have over the material). Although it's not my bag, I've even seen folks editing in FCP with one, dragging layers around with the pen. Working with a pen tablet takes a little getting used to after using a mouse, but a pen is a more natural way for artists to work (see Figure 1-18). When I'm doing a lot of graphic preparation in Boris RED, Adobe After Effects, Photoshop, or Illustrator, I often put my mouse down and reach for the pen.

- **CD/DVD burner:** CD burners are a godsend for archiving artwork, project files, and finished projects. The ability to repurpose elements from past projects is a well-kept secret among designers who work in broadcast. Having your elements cataloged and organized according to your own system will save you loads of time when you need that perfect design element in a hurry. A DVD burner offers more flexibility than a CD burner because you can store more footage or burn your show to disk. (Many Macs come with built-in CD or DVD burners. Go for a DVD burner if possible.)

FIGURE 1-18

I've cut thousands of masks with this Wacom Pen Tablet.

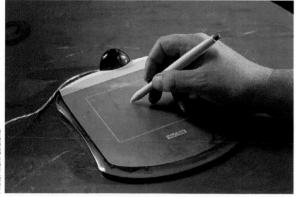

Photo: Mark Leialoha

- **Microphone:** You definitely want to have a decent microphone to make voiceover recordings and voice notes for your video compositions using FCP's Voice Over tool (Tools → Voice Over). A good all-purpose microphone, like an omnidirectional or cardioid mic, should do the trick. You might want to get a decent mic stand while you're at it. Typically, I use an inexpensive Audio Technica stereo mic (about $90) for down-and-dirty audio recordings in the field with both my DV camcorder and MD recorder.

- **USB audio adapter:** A little black box called the Powerwave, from Griffin, is useful for getting simple audio into your Mac. You can use it to record your voice into the Voice Over tool. It's also useful for recording voice or instruments into Soundtrack. The iMic, also from Griffin, is another way to get audio into your Mac (see Figure 1-19).

- **MD (MiniDisc) recorder:** Its audio quality is superior to DV's and it's conveniently small. I love this device for recording interviews, music, environments, and other audio collectables in a pinch. Look for a model with controllable inputs. (See Figure 1-20.)

- **Audio card or FireWire audio interface:** Adding a dedicated hardware PCI card, FireWire audio interface, or USB audio interface is another way to get high-quality audio into your Mac. For FireWire interfaces, the MOTU 828 mkII comes very highly recommended. PCI cards like the Delta series from M-Audio get the highest marks.

- **Audio mixer:** A mixer is useful for monitoring situations. Multiple inputs from other audio devices — like a microphone or MD recorder — can be fed into your mixer as well, and then into your Mac via a USB audio adapter box.

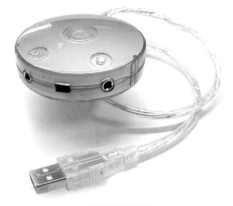

FIGURE 1-19

The Griffin iMic allows you to get simple audio into your Mac.

SOFTWARE TOOLS FOR EFFECTS CREATORS

The secret to making great-looking effects is developing a process for constructing an effect and then finding the right software tools for the job. The combination of FCP 4 and the Mac G5 is a powerhouse, but experienced video artists know that you can't do absolutely everything with FCP alone. Nowadays clients demand the latest looks they see in film, television, and — increasingly — websites. They see a fancy 3D effect and want it for their ad campaign, or want a motion-tracking move that only Apple Shake could pull off. These elements are composed outside of FCP, but in the end are brought back into FCP for integration with other elements.

Photo: Scott Clark

FIGURE 1-20

Recording cable car bells with my Sharp MD-MT831 MiniDisc recorder.

In this book I'll focus on FCP techniques whenever possible. But smart effects creators know that there are other tools and applications that can do some heavy lifting that FCP either can't do or would take too long to do. (In Chapter 14 you'll see how to integrate graphics and effects from other applications into FCP.) Here are some software applications I consider integral for effects creation in a fully equipped FCP system.

- **Still graphics application:** There are no other contenders here; you've got to have Adobe Photoshop (see Figure 1-21). Photoshop is an indispensable companion to Final Cut Pro because you can do so many things with it. Creating graphics, titles, and mattes for import into either FCP or LiveType are just a few of the things you can do in Photoshop.

- **Compositing application:** Although you can do a great deal of effects creation (sometimes referred to as *compositing*) with Final Cut Pro, there are some things you can't do. LiveType adds a pretty cool compositing environment at no extra cost, so it pays to see how far you can go with it. If you need to paint onto video, track objects over time, make complex masks, composite onto 3D layers, or use virtual cameras and lights, you'll need a program like Boris RED (see Figure 1-22), Adobe After Effects, Pinnacle Commotion Pro, Discreet Combustion, Curious gFx, or Apple Shake (see Figure 1-23).

FIGURE 1-21

Adobe Photoshop is indispensable for creating and editing still graphics.

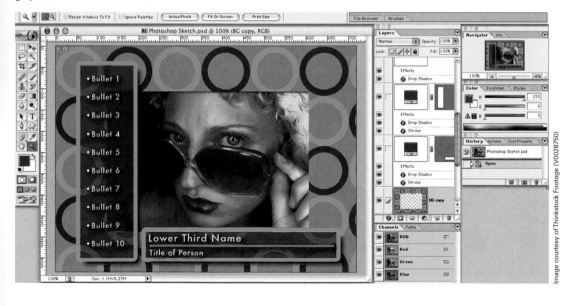

Image courtesy of Thinkstock Footage (V0028750)

These programs are also capable of *rotoscoping*, the art of cutting out a moving object from its background over time. Each compositing application has its strengths, with widely varying costs, so it's best to do a little research to see what's the best program for your needs. I'll discuss add-on applications further in Chapter 14. From here on out, when I refer to a third-party compositing application, I'm speaking of one of the above applications.

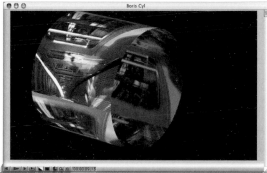

■ **Vector drawing program:** Although it's not essential, I like having a vector-based draw and paint program like Adobe Illustrator, Macromedia Freehand, or Corel Painter for sketching out ideas, laying out type, and doing illustrations. Adobe Illustrator 10 and newer will output a bitmapped file that FCP can read, so now you don't have to import files into Photoshop to rasterize your imagery. You can also create a SWF file in Macromedia Flash, a program that makes vector graphics Final Cut Pro can read.

Image: Rob Pongi (www.RobPongi.com)

FIGURE 1-22
Boris RED combines effects compositing, titling, and 3D graphics.

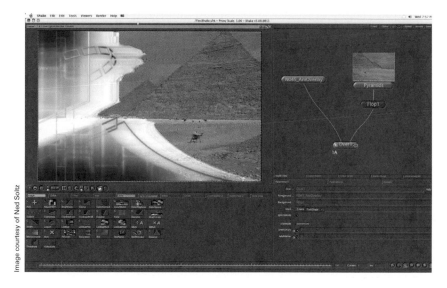

Image courtesy of Ned Soltz

FIGURE 1-23
Shake provides a robust compositing environment preferred by visual effects artists.

■ **Plug-ins:** Plug-ins are add-on effects you can purchase from various companies (see Figure 1-24). Once plug-ins are installed, they show up in FCP's Effects menu and Effects tab. Plug-ins greatly extend the functionality of existing FCP features; for example, Ultimatte or Primatte offer additional chroma-keying capabilities. Plug-in sets, such as Boris Continuum Complete or Media 100's Final Effects Complete, not only extend the functionality of FCP, but also take that concept to a whole new level with new compositing tools you won't want to live without.

Some plug-ins have other functions, such as cross-platform import. For example, Automatic Duck provides a plug-in that lets you export sequences to another NLE (like Avid Symphony) or another third-party compositing application (like Adobe After Effects). Many of the third-party plug-ins written for Adobe After Effects or Boris RED also work great with Final Cut Pro (not all of them work with FCP, however). I'll talk more about plug-ins in Chapter 14.

■ **Sound-creation program:** Getting music that fits the feel of your composition can be one of the biggest challenges a broadcast designer faces. Sifting through sound libraries can be extremely time consuming. Apple Soundtrack, which is included with FCP 4, is the killer tool for creating a quick mix on the fly. There are others out there as well, like Sonic Desktop's Sonicfire Pro, which finds, edits, and scores musical tracks from your own music or from numerous libraries produced by the product's developer. With either of these tools you can create great-sounding royalty-free tracks that precisely fit the duration of your composite. If you want to make your own music, you might like Propellerhead Software's Reason, which provides a virtual rack of electronic gear that you can patch together and play, composing in a virtual studio environment.

■ **Sound-mixing application:** To make your compositions really stand out, you're going to need a sound mixing and enhancement tool like Logic Platinum 6, Digidesign Pro Tools, or Bias Deck. You can export your FCP tracks into programs with export options in FCP's File menu. For basic audio sweetening, you can use Bias Peak Express, the free application on your FCP install disk (see Figure 1-25). Visit Bias' website (www.bias-inc.com) to get the most current version and to register your software.

note

Boris RED is the only compositing application that works within Final Cut Pro. Another plus is that Boris RED allows the use of After Effects filters, which don't run within FCP. RED's younger brother, Boris Graffiti, which is often thought of as a stand-alone titler, also works as a plug-in within FCP. Graffiti handles titling duties superbly, and also offers many features of a full-blown 2D compositing program. In addition, Graffiti does a fine job of creating 3D extruded text and making text fly on Bézier paths.

Image: Rob Pongi (RobPongi.com)

FIGURE 1-24

Plug-ins like Grain Surgery from Visual Infinity and Screen Text from Digital Anarchy lend more firepower when working inside of FCP.

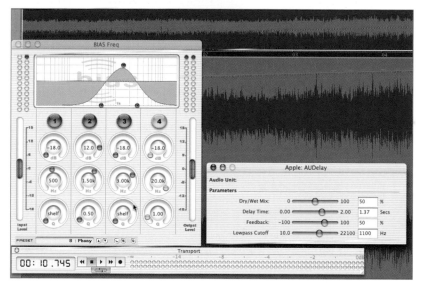

FIGURE 1-25

Sweeten your audio in Bias Peak Express, free with FCP 4.

- **3D graphics application:** After you've mastered FCP and played with some other compositing applications, you might try a 3D application to add even more tools to your bag of tricks (see Figure 1-26). 3D applications can be very complex and can take a long time to master, but don't let that stop you from striving to be at least a bit dangerous. You don't have to learn how to animate characters, but you can easily learn to do common broadcast graphics tasks such as mapping video to polygons or creating a virtual set. A lot of people, including myself, love the all-in-one interfaces of Alias' Maya and Maxon Cinema 4D XL, while others swear by Electric Image Universe or NewTek's Lightwave. Cinema 4D XL and Adobe After Effects let you share virtual camera and lighting data between the programs. This feature will surely migrate to other 3D applications in due time.

■ **DVD authoring program:** Since Final Cut Pro works seamlessly with Apple DVD Studio Pro 2, you'll want to try your hand at authoring your own DVDs. If you have even basic Photoshop skills, you can make menus with Photoshop, then author the disk with DVD Studio Pro. You can also make fodder for motion menus in DVD Studio Pro. DVD Studio Pro's younger brother, iDVD, has come a long way since its original release. In fact, you'll probably find it suitable for much of the work you do need to do in making a DVD for a client or yourself. I can personally say that iDVD rocks! It's very useful for banging out a quick demo reel. It pays to be hip to DVD output; these days, clients expect it.

■ **Compression application:** Whether your goal is creating video elements for Web pages, showing your work to clients, or sharing it with the rest of the world over the Web, you can export your work directly from Final Cut Pro into Compressor, which is included with FCP 4. Compressor provides easy integration with Final Cut Pro, DVD Studio Pro 2, QuickTime Player,

FIGURE 1-26

Cinema 4D is a 3D application that has expandable options.

and QuickTime Pro. You can batch-process jobs to repurpose content for a different delivery medium. QuickTime itself can also be used for video compression. With the Sorenson 3 Codec and MPEG 4 compressions, QuickTime offers good quality for progressive download. You can output from QuickTime for streaming video, or for downloading onto PDAs or cell phones. You may choose to use a dedicated compression application, such as Discreet Cleaner or Sorenson Squeeze, which give you access to a greater number of formats as well as more flexible parameters.

- **Other standalone programs:** There are many applications that will increase FCP's capabilities. For example, Macromedia Flash MX can shrink your video into a tiny file size and add Flash interactivity for placement on a Web page. As a "video synthesizer," Synthetik's Studio Artist adds painterly effects, real-time warping, 3D paint effects, and cool kaleidoscope effects (www.synthetik.com). I'm just scratching the surface; there are hundreds of applications that can alter the flavor of your video. Attending a digital video trade show is a good way to see and compare many of these applications.

Now that you have your system properly configured and have gathered the hardware and software tools you need for making effects, it's time to get you up to speed using effects with a "pre-flight" exercise.

Getting Started with 3D

A good way to get your feet wet in 3D design is with the 3D Toolkit from dvGarage. You'll get a working version of Electric Image as well as tutorials and sample footage. It's very reasonably priced, plus there's the added benefit of receiving instruction from visual effects master Alex Lindsay. Go to www.dvgarage.com for more information.

If you're really on a budget, then you can download Maya PLE, which is essentially a version of Maya 5 that renders files with a watermark. Maya is an outstanding 3D product that comes with plenty of help files, movies and a whole slew of folks out there willing to lend you some advice on the Web. Go to www.alias.com/eng/products-services/maya/maya_ple/index.shtml to download it.

My personal favorite is Maxon Cinema 4DXL. If you'd like to try your hand at this application, a trial version is available on the DVD that came with this book. Go to Goodies → Maxon Computer. There are loads of tutorials at www.maxoncomputer.com as well.

Exercise Set-up

This book contains over 50 step-by-step exercises and more than 250 clips you can use to create effects. There are also free plug-ins you'll need in order to complete some of the exercises. These exercises are all tied to a single Final Cut Pro project called the "Effects Project." Working through the exercises in the Effects Project will give you the vital skills you need to master motion graphics and effects with FCP.

THE EFFECTS PROJECT FILE

Before you open up the Effects Project for the first time, here's what you should know about the project and how it relates to the exercises in each chapter.

As you read through each chapter of the book, you'll be asked to work through a series of exercises. The directions for each exercise are located in the book, with the exception of the optional exercises for Chapter 1, which are located in a PDF on the DVD. (For more about the optional Chapter 1 exercises, see the section "Pre-flight Composition" later in this chapter.)

Here is the hierarchy of the Effects Project:

- Within the Browser of the Effects Project, every chapter of the book has its own bin.

- Within each chapter bin, there are more bins with audio clips, video clips, and a main chapter Exercise sequence.

- Each chapter Exercise sequence contains a series of exercises, with each one separated by a marker in the Timeline.

- The instructions for each exercise will direct you to the proper marker where the clips for the exercise have been set up for you.

To set up the project file before working through the exercises, you'll first need to copy some important items from the DVD to your Mac. You'll also need to reconnect the clips with the associated media the first time you open the Effects Project. To get this done properly, read the following sections carefully.

SETTING UP THE EFFECTS PROJECT

Let's now set up the Effects Project. First, you've got to transfer the project file and source clips into their proper folders on your hard drives. Then you've got to reconnect all of the clips and the media within the Effects Project file. Follow these steps.

1. Insert the DVD that came with this book into your DVD drive.

2. On the Desktop, double-click on the DVD icon. You'll see five folders.

   - **Effects Project files:** There are two FCP Project files inside this folder — Effects Project-NTSC and Effects Project-PAL. To do the exercises in this book, you will use the project file that is appropriate for your country's television system.

   - **Effects Project Media-NTSC:** This contains the source media for the Effects Project-NTSC project file. There are mainly QuickTime files in this folder.

   - **Effects Project Media-PAL:** This contains the source media for the Effects Project-PAL project file.

   - **Goodies:** This folder contains extras, including try-out versions of applications and plug-ins. The Goodies folder is also the location of the book's free filters.

   - **Chapter Extras:** This folder contains extra items for certain chapters, such as the PDF for the optional Chapter 1 exercises.

3. Open the Effects Project files folder and you will see two project files: Effects Project-NTSC and Effects Project-PAL. These files are identical in content. If you live in North America, drag the Effects Project-NTSC file into your Documents folder to copy it there. If you live anywhere else in the world, drag the Effects Project-PAL file into the folder instead. Close this folder after you copy the appropriate project file.

4. Prepare to copy media onto your media drive. Since the project's media folder's files take up approximately 850 megabytes on your media drive, I recommend that you clear at least 2GB of hard drive space for the media prior to copying it to your drive.

5. If you are working with the NTSC project, drag and drop the Effects Project Media-NTSC folder into your Final Cut Pro Documents → Capture Scratch folder. If you copied the PAL project file into your Documents folder, drag and drop the Effects Project Media-PAL folder into your Final Cut Pro Documents → Capture Scratch folder instead.

6. Copy the Chapter Extras folder to your Mac by dragging and dropping it from the DVD into your Documents folder.

7. In your Documents folder, double-click on the Effects Project file to open it. Once Final Cut Pro launches, have a look around in the Browser and open a bin or two. Remember: this single FCP project file contains all the clips and sequences you'll need to work through the book's exercises.

8. Right now the project's clips are offline. You'll now need to "reconnect" the Effects Project's clips to QuickTime media files. You must do this because the file path for the clips must be reestablished with the new location of the QuickTime files — your media drive. The steps are very simple.

    a. Select all bins in the project by clicking anywhere in the Name column of the Browser and then pressing Command + A.

    b. Go to File → Reconnect Media. The Reconnect Options dialog will launch.

    c. Click OK for the default setting.

    d. In the main Reconnect dialog that appears, navigate to Documents → Final Cut Pro Documents → Capture Scratch → Effects Project Media (NTSC or PAL), and then click the Choose button.

In a few seconds, your clips should be reconnected to your QuickTime source media. You can begin working on any exercise in the book.

> **note**
>
> *Since the DVD has not yet been ejected, make sure you are navigating to your Mac's media drive when reconnecting the clips and the QuickTime media files. If you mistakenly reconnect the clips back to the DVD's copies of the Quick-Time movies, the clips in FCP will go offline as soon as you eject the DVD.*

INSTALLING THE FREE PLUG-INS

On the DVD, you'll also find a set of free filters, transitions, and generators that are collectively called "Telly's FX." I'll explain them in detail in Chapter 11, but for now you'll need to install these plug-ins in your own system to complete some of the exercises and, of course, to use them in your own projects. Follow these steps to install Telly's FX:

1. Locate the filters on the DVD in the Goodies Folder → FCP World → Telly's FX.

2. Go to your system's Library → Application Support → Final Cut Pro System Support → Plug-ins folder.

3. Drag and drop the folder into the Plug-ins folder. The new plug-ins will be copied into your Plug-ins folder.

4. Restart FCP. The filters, transitions, and generators will be available in the menus and in the Effects tab. Have fun with them!

5. After the Effects Project file, Effects Project media folder, Chapter Extras, and Telly's FX plug-ins have been copied to your hard drive, eject the DVD. Store the DVD in a sleeve so you don't damage it.

Now that you have opened up your Effects Project file for the first time, reconnected all of the media, and added your new plug-ins, you're set up to work on any exercise in this book.

Pre-flight Composition

At this point in the chapter, you have a choice. For those of you who would like to get some upfront experience in making simple effects, I've made an optional series of five exercises for you to do. These are designed specifically to get you up to speed in creating effects. These exercises would also work well in an instructor-led classroom environment. More advanced users may find these exercises a bit elementary for their needs and may choose to skip them. It's up to you how you'd like to proceed.

Here's what is covered in the optional exercises:

- Basic video layering
- Picture-in-picture effects
- Tinting clips
- Basic keyframing
- Adding transitions
- System troubleshooting tips

If any of these concepts are the least bit foreign to you or you just want to fill in some gaps in your effects knowledge, you should go ahead and work through the exercises. It should not take more than 30 minutes to complete them.

If you want to do the optional exercises for Chapter 1, locate the Chapter Extras folder on the DVD and find the PDF called "Chapter 1 Exercises" right now. I suggest you print out the pages first so you won't have to take up screen real estate while you work through the steps. Printing them in color will be helpful.

If you choose not to do the optional Chapter 1 exercises and your Effects Project has all of the clips reconnected, then you can move forward in the book from here.

Wrap-up

In this chapter you've learned about the hardware and software tools that make up a video effects artist's tool set. You know what you'll need for a bare-bones setup, and what you'll need to acquire as you build your system into a more sophisticated editing platform. Now that your electronic edit bench is set up, it's time to look at some ideas for planning effects and optimizing your workflow.

WHAT'S IN THIS CHAPTER

- Ideas for harnessing your creativity
- Planning and executing effects
- Organizing your media assets
- Exporting and importing footage
- Workflow tips
- Previewing effects
- Understanding view modes and viewing options

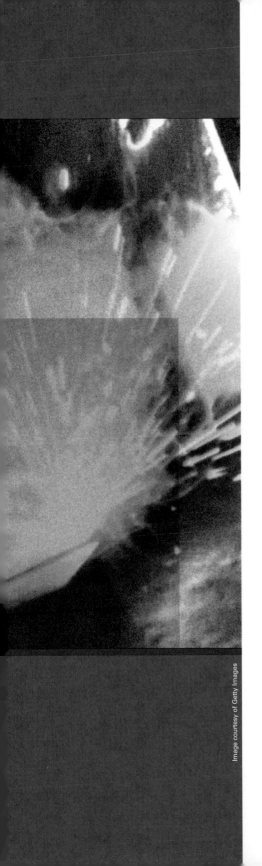

Pre-Project Considerations

2

Once you have your electronic editing bench set up and running smoothly, you might think it's time to start creating projects with Final Cut Pro. But there's one more crucial step. Before you begin creating effects, you must have a plan for getting your work done reliably, uniformly, and with no wasted effort. This chapter will give you tips on planning your projects, from coming up with ideas for effects to organizing a project's components so they'll be readily available when you delve into complex video graphics. This chapter will also show you how to work effectively with FCP's interface, including some of the new features of Final Cut Pro 4. In addition, you'll learn how to make the most of FCP's real-time effects capabilities, allowing you to preview your work as quickly as possible.

Ideas for Video Effects

Every motion graphics project begins with an idea, and your ideas have to spring from somewhere, right? Since creative ideas don't flourish in a vacuum, you can do a number of things to help bring them to life. I enjoy working at this process myself, and if you're dedicated to your work, so will you. Here are some ideas for jump-starting your creative thinking:

- **Write ideas down.** Write down questions like, "Who is this piece for?" and "What is the central message of the piece?" Soon you'll begin to get ideas. Jot them down right away, as great ideas are often fleeting.

- **Schedule some playtime.** Schedule some time each day to just play around with FCP and related applications. In my own projects, I attempt to push the limits of my own knowledge and ability. Collect these playtime projects, name them, and keep them around so you can continue to draw from them. Snippets of these projects can end up in client work, so playtime is time well spent.

- **Be a collector.** When you go out, carry at least one media-collection tool, such as a tape recorder, camcorder, or still camera. While walking around, you can collect all kinds of sounds and images. If you do this on a regular basis, you'll have source material that no one else has, which helps keep your work fresh and original.

- **Deconstruct other artists' effects.** You can often get ideas for your work by deconstructing TV commercials, movie effects, and Web sites. I get a lot of my ideas from print media as well, for composition, color, and typography. Regardless of the media source, you should note the color themes, text treatment, and so on, then write down what you like about those elements. Attempt to duplicate the look or feel of what sparked your interest. With just a little practice, you should be able to figure out — or at least intelligently guess — how someone created an effect or composite. Then you can try your hand at the same technique.

DECONSTRUCTING EXISTING EFFECTS

When you look at other artists' effects, you might see text, graphics, and other elements flying around the screen. These elements lie on separate video tracks, producing a multilayered effect. Before you begin to dissect other people's video graphics — and before you do the following exercise — you should understand how layers work in Final Cut Pro. Layered effects will be discussed in detail in Chapter 5, so for now just keep in mind that when one clip moves in front of another, it's on a higher video track (for example, track V2 is higher than track V1). With this concept in mind, you'll soon be able to look at an effect, figure out how it was done, and create a similar effect in Final Cut Pro (see Figures 2-1 and 2-2).

Clip courtesy of Thinkstock Footage (V0025313)

FIGURE 2-1

The title, "Dancebox," is in the foreground, so it must be on the highest video track.

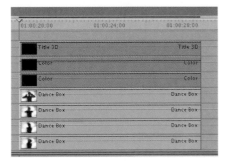

FIGURE 2-2

Note the order in which the other "Dancebox" video tracks are stacked.

The DIY Aesthetic

You can't always buy the shots you need from stock-footage providers. Perhaps commercially available clips are just not right for your idea, or maybe the shot you want just doesn't exist. In situations like that, you've got to adopt the "D.I.Y" mentality: Do It Yourself. Make a plan, do some sketches, put together a shooting schedule, and then go into the studio to create your shot. With a simple DV camcorder and a few artfully positioned lights, you can capture imagery that reflects your personal style. If you don't have a studio, you can always rent one for a day to spend time shooting other elements you may need for future projects.

Photo: Mark Leialoha

EXERCISE 2-1: DECONSTRUCTING AN EFFECT

This exercise will give you tips on how to deconstruct an effect made by another video effects artist. This skill comes in very handy when a client asks you to make an effect that's similar to one on TV or in the movies.

Important: In this exercise you are not supposed to create the effect. Instead, you'll just observe it and break it down.

Go to the Chapter 2 bin → Chapter 2 Sequences, and double-click the "Chapter 2 Exercise" sequence. Go to the marker for Exercise 1.

1. Press Command + R to render the sequence, and then press the Space Bar to play it. Watch the Canvas.

2. On a sheet of paper or some 3 × 5 cards, draw the video elements used in the composite.

3. Figure out which clips are in the foreground and which are in the background. Don't look at the Timeline yet.

4. Note any filter effects or color treatments that were used.

5. Write down any motion effects you see applied to titles or graphics.

How many layers make up these thin white lines? How many layers make up these colored rectangles? Is this layer the farthest in the background?

Images courtesy of Thinkstock Footage (V0014399 and V0014409)

MAKE | connections decisions transactions

generedex
c o n f e r e n c e

Are any of the elements animated? What kinds of effects were used on these clips? Where does this element lie in the layer hierarchy?

Now it's time to find out how well you understood the effect. Let's inspect the effect in the Timeline. Note how many layers there are and see how many you figured out.

6. As you can see, the effect was constructed with eight video tracks. However, if you look more closely, most of the items in the tracks are not clips, but similar looking items called *nests*. Nests are nothing but groups of clips (you'll learn more about nesting in Chapter 5). Nesting clips allows you to make more complex effects by placing like items together and adding effects to them as a unit.

7. Let's first consider what's on V1. It's a generator called a Color Matte. I chose an off-white color for the background. Nothing fancy here, folks.

8. In the V2 nest, called "Multi-Colored Stripes," you've got the multicolored rectangles that make up the upper half of the effect. Double-click on this nest to open it. Clicking through the Timeline within the nest, you should see two of the four rectangles moving. These rectangles were made from color mattes, then cropped, scaled, and keyframed to complete the job (you'll learn more about keyframing in Chapter 4). Click the Chapter 2 Exercise sequence tab to return to the main sequence (do this after inspecting each nest). You can see that the boxes play in front of the white background, because they're on a higher video track (V2).

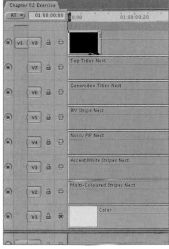

STEP 6

Note that most of the tracks contain groups of clips called *nests*. While regular clips are light blue, nests are lavender.

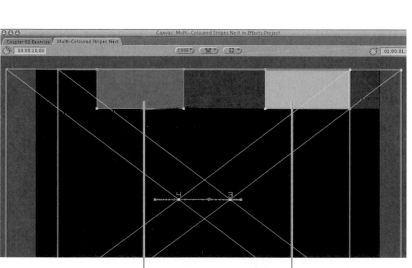

These two rectangles were animated within the nest

STEP 8

Open the nest on V2 to look at the animated rectangles.

The Replicate filter has been dragged onto the nest on V3.

9. On V3 is the "Accent White Stripes" nest. Double-click the nest to inspect its Timeline. Upon opening it, you should notice only one white stripe. This is odd, considering that there are six small stripes lying in front of the "Multi-Colored Stripes" nest. What's going on here? This is a cool trick where you can use a filter to do the tedious work for you. The filter, which is called Replicate, replicates a video frame. This filter has no effect on most generators, so I've dragged and dropped it onto the nest instead. With the filter applied to the nest, you choose exactly how many stripes you want, and how many rows of them as well. You'll learn more about adding filters in Chapter 3.

10. V4 contains the "Noisy PIP" nest. (It's called that because it has two picture-in-picture sources that are overlaid with video noise.) Double-click it to see how I constructed the sequence. You should be seeing four distinct layers. The background is the swatch of orange that dominates the middle of the Canvas. Within the orange rectangle are two video clips; both are scaled and keyframed to move across the stripe. At the top of the stack is a Noise generator. You might have noticed that the clips aren't perfectly cropped to the orange background. In the next step you'll learn how to crop a nest for a super-clean edge.

Look at the nest on V4 to see how it's constructed.

Cropping the top and bottom of a nest gives it a clean edge

11. V5 has the "BW Stripe" nest. This is a handy layer to help hide sloppy seams and provide a line of demarcation for the composition. It's made with two color mattes that are cropped: one black and one white. I often use strips of color to divide up the areas of a composition.

———— BW Stripe nest

STEP 11

A cropped color matte can hide seams or provide a way to break up a composition.

12. On V6 is the "Generedex Titles" nest. Putting titles into nests in commonplace around my shop. This is because title treatments are usually multi-layered entities, which often need to be treated as a group. In this simple nest there are two Title 3D generators, both of which are animated for position and tracking. You'll learn how to create text effects in Chapter 12.

13. V7 contains a nest called "Top Titles." Here's another good example of grouping different elements into one unit. There are two blocks of text and a vertical black line, which is a color matte that's been cropped into a tiny vertical line. The position of the word "Make" and the tracking of the three bullet points have all been animated using keyframes.

14. V8 has two small pieces of "slug" (black). I've put them there to fade in from the slug, rather than keyframing opacity for each layer. This is a common strategy for fading multiple layers to or from black.

MAKE | connections
       decisions
       transactions

STEP 13

This layer combines animated text and a vertical line made from a color matte.

Did you figure out how many layers there were in the exercise? I hope you came close to the actual number: 17 layers in all. If you didn't get very close, that's OK; counting the number of layers can be tricky when there are multiple nests. The main goal of this exercise is to give you an idea about how effects are organized in the real world. In addition, it offers a preview of some of the techniques you'll learn throughout the book.

Yet another goal of this exercise is to encourage you to study other artists' work. Of course, you don't always have the luxury of taking an effect apart to see what makes it tick. But with any luck, this exercise will help you look at other people's work with an eye toward how it's done. I enjoy learning from other artists, and look forward to trying new looks I come across. As you try more and more effects, you'll develop your own style, derived from a multitude of influences and artists.

Previsualizing Effects

tip

Record bumpers (show intros and promos) and commercials from TV, and then deconstruct them as you did in the previous exercise. I suggest you record them from popular cable networks (like MTV, E!, Comedy Central, VH-1, and The History Channel) as well as from foreign-language programs, in order to spot worldwide trends in effects and motion graphics.

Now that you've got your creative juices flowing, it's time to structure your ideas into a plan of action. That way you won't drive yourself crazy as you piece together a complex video effect. This plan of action is sometimes called *previsualization*.

A good previsualization plan should at least include a list of to-do's. For more complex projects, you might need storyboards or a flowchart to provide a visual roadmap for the various elements of your piece. Constructing to-do lists, flowcharts, spreadsheets, and storyboards can help keep you organized as you focus on completing an effects composition.

Here are some tasks you might include in a previsualization to-do list:

- **Write a treatment.** You might have already jotted down some ideas, but before you get out the sketchpad, concisely write down what you intend to do with your motion graphics composition. This can be a bullet-point list or a paragraph or two of details. Include specific information about how you plan to execute the ideas for your story. Believe me, the up-front time you spend conceptualizing your piece will pay off tenfold once you get down to actually doing the work.

- **Create storyboards.** Sketching your ideas on paper lets you quickly conceptualize your project. Although I can work like a jackrabbit with my digital tools, I feel more freedom using a simple china marker and a stack of index cards to quickly rough out my raw ideas. I can make small flipbooks of sequential drawings with these cards to help me visualize the possibilities for my piece. It's OK to use simple shapes, stick figures, and arrows; the key is to quickly envision what you want to create (see Figure 2-3). Jot down short notes on each sketch about a particular layer's properties. Storyboards are also invaluable tools for project planning because you'll know ahead of time exactly what elements are required.

■ **Acquire images.** After you've made decisions regarding the basic idea and story for an effects-oriented composition, you'll need to figure out where to get the images for the piece. What kind of footage does it need to be? Will it be created with live action, stock imagery, or software tools? Will it need to be shot? If so, how will it be shot? Will any area of the shot need to be isolated with a matte? For that, will the subject need to be shot against a blue or green screen? What should be the required quality, frame size, and compression scheme of the source? These are all questions that need to be considered before you launch into an ambitious project. Make sure that each potential element within a composition can be acquired and is within your budget and time constraints.

■ **Assess FCP's ability to do a given task.** Before launching into a complex effects project, you'll need to find out whether FCP is up to a given effects-intensive task or if additional plug-ins or applications are needed. If FCP can do the job, you can include filter information and techniques in your notes or directly on your storyboards. Similar notes can be made regarding how a third-party plug-in or application would handle an effect (complementary applications will be discussed in Chapter 14). Be realistic in your goals for an effect, and consider the cost of additional applications or plug-ins, time constraints for project completion, and your own ability to execute the effect with FCP or other applications. If there's a chance you may run into problems in creating an effect, you should assess alternatives for achieving a similar effect. Having a solid "Plan B" has spared me — and my clients — hundreds of hours of exasperation.

Photo: Mark Leialoha

Using Stock Footage

The projects in this book look so attractive because of the high-quality source imagery that was used. Thanks to Thinkstock Footage and Getty Images for providing the lion's share of the clips and images for the book and for providing you with quality material to work with when you do the exercises.

After you've tried out the clips in the Effects Project, you'll see that it's crucial to own some of this kind of footage if you want to turn first-time clients into repeat customers. Stock footage also comes in handy when you need shots of faraway places that aren't in your travel budget, archival footage, or situations that are difficult (or dangerous) to shoot on your own.

Here's a list of some of my favorite stock-footage sources:

- **Getty Images** (www.gettyimages.com/source/film) It's all under one roof here. You'll find royalty-free and rights-managed collections from the hottest stock footage providers, including Photodisc, Artbeats, Digital Vision, Rubberball, and Triangle Images.

- **Thinkstock Footage** (www.thinkstockfootage.com) The thing I like about Thinkstock's material is that there are often several shots for a given theme, allowing you to piece together a short, artful sequence. Thinkstock also supports Final Cut Pro user groups throughout the world, so they are definitely good people.

- **Artbeats** (www.artbeats.com) Artbeats is probably the best-known stock footage provider for video pros. They have one of the largest and best collections of high-quality footage I've ever seen, much of it acquired on film or HDTV.

- **Digital Juice** (www.digitaljuice.com) In addition to images of people, places, and things, you can also purchase intricate backgrounds and computer designs for your video productions. Although LiveType has a good number of backgrounds, it's always nice to have more. The Editor's Toolkit collection is massive, with matching backdrops and lower thirds.

- **12 Inch Design** (www.12inchdesign.com) This outfit offers some fantastic motion backgrounds, called ProductionBlox, which are layered backdrops with a jaw-dropping amount of intricate 3D objects.

Here are some other fine sources for stock footage:

- **ImageIcons** (www.imageicons.com)

- **Creatas** (www.creatas.com)

- **Rocketclips Stock Footage** (www.rocketclips.com)

continued

- **Blue Sky Stock Footage** (www.blueskyfootage.com)

- **Cinenet** (www.cinenet.com)

- **Bond Street Stock Footage** (www.bondstreet.com)

- **Digital Vision** (www.digitalvisiononline.com)

- **Rubberball Productions** (www.rubberball.com)

- **Film and Video Stockshots** (www.stockshots.com)

- **Buyout Footage** (www.buyoutfootage.com)

Organizing Your Media Assets

After planning your project, your next concern is bringing clips into FCP and organizing them into workable pieces. You need some footage to start making the magic happen, right? After you've imported the media, it's time to subdivide it into aptly named bins so you can easily sort through clips, graphics, and audio to find what you need.

MAKING BINS

Before capturing any media, it's a good idea to start off on the right foot by making bins where you'll capture, import, and organize footage. Let's look into a few ways to help you organize your projects.

When you're organizing captured footage, a good first step is to put the footage into primary bins for sorting. I start by capturing footage into bins marked by tape name or number. You set these primary bins, one at a time, as *logging bins* during the capturing (sometimes called *digitizing*) process. You can make any bin into a logging bin by selecting it and going to File → Set Logging Bin.

After you've captured footage into "tape number" bins, you should take the time to place the captured clips into bins with descriptive names. Here's how I organize my bins for effects projects:

- Audio Imports: I put all my imported audio in this bin.

- Captured Clips: Here's where I keep all the footage I've captured from tape. I usually have bins for both video with Sync Audio (SOT) and video-only footage.

- Imported Motion Graphics: Here's where I keep motion graphics files created in third-party applications.

- Imported Still Graphics: I use this bin to import photos from iPhoto and to import Adobe Photoshop files.

- Video Imports: This is where I keep imported stock footage and downloads from other footage sources.

Come up with your own bin naming system based on your needs.

Making bins, naming them, and organizing clips inside them is somewhat time consuming, but will pay off as you work on a project (see Figure 2-4).

Organizing clips in bins

Once you've made a number of bins for your project, you can start dragging and dropping your captured clips into them. When the clips are in appropriately named bins, you'll be able to locate them easily.

If you have a large project and your bins are becoming cluttered with clips, you can always make bins within bins. Simply make a new bin (Command + B), name it, and drag it into an existing bin. Another slick way is to Control + click on an existing bin and choose New Bin from the contextual menu. The new bin appears instantly in the existing bin. Using bins within bins, you can continue to refine your clip-organization strategy.

To further refine your clip organization, you can make copies of clips in bins and drag them into related bins. Making a copy of the clip won't take up additional space on your drive, so you're free to make as many copies as you wish. You can do this in a couple of different ways:

1. Select a clip in a bin and press Command + C to copy it.

2. Click on a new bin to select it.

3. Press Command + V to paste the copy into the new bin.

Or

1. Click on a clip to select it.

2. Hold down the Option key to drag a copy of the clip from the original bin into the new bin.

Sketching Out Ideas in Third-party Applications

When I say sketch it out, I'm advising you to put your ideas down on paper. But paper is becoming passé. Many broadcast designers prefer to sketch out their ideas in a graphics application, blurring the line between previsualization and getting right down to work. You can generate a lot of ideas in these applications before you start working on your composition. Once you choose an idea from your "sketches," you can begin refining the look and feel of your original experiment.

Effects design often begins with still layouts in a program such as Adobe Photoshop. Once you've created some layouts and type treatments, you can decide whether to bring the test layouts into yet another application, or directly to FCP. You can use your test compositions directly in your FCP project, archive them for future use, or toss them into the trash. Using other applications with FCP will be discussed in depth in Chapter 14.

The examples here show a few variations of the Photoshop illustration from Chapter 1, as well as some of the refinements that can be made quickly and easily in other applications.

Adobe Photoshop illustration

Adobe After Effects

Boris RED

A finished effect in Final Cut Pro

Image courtesy of Thinkstock Footage (V0028750)

VIEWING BIN CONTENTS

Once you've placed your clips in bins, you can organize them in either List View or Icon View. There are advantages to either method, depending on what you're trying to accomplish. You can switch between the viewing options by going to View → Browser Items and choosing As List, Small Icon, Medium Icon, or As Large Icon.

List View

In List View, clips are sorted alphanumerically by default. This view is great if you are well aware of the clips' content and need to find them by name. If you like, you can click on another column to sort by a different category. For example, if you wanted to find the longest clip in a bin, you'd sort clips by the Length column.

FIGURE 2-5

You can color-code clips in List View.

My favorite way to organize clips is to label them by color code (see Figure 2-5). The key to making this work is to customize the label names. Let's get that done first:

1. Choose User Preferences from the Final Cut Pro menu.

2. In the User Preferences dialog box, click on the Labels tab.

3. In the Labels tab, click in the respective category field and type the name you want to assign to each particular color.

You can now Control + click on any clip or group of clips and label them from one of your color-coded categories.

Icon View

Icon View is extremely useful for organizing your clips visually. For me, Large Icon mode is most useful because you can see the content of the clip more clearly. Unlike List View, which sorts clips in alphanumeric order, Icon View lets you position clips in any order you choose (see Figure 2-6). You can then select a group of clips and drag them into the Timeline, where they will fall into place in the order in which you arranged them. This technique, which is called "storyboard editing," is very useful for roughing out ideas for video composites.

1. Option + double-click a bin to open it in its own window. Repeatedly press Shift + H until the bin is in Large Icon View.

2. Arrange your clips in any order, left to right, top to bottom.

3. Select the clips by lassoing them or Command + clicking them.

4. Drag and drop the selected clips into the Timeline.

The clips will fall into the Timeline in the order you set in the bin.

FIGURE 2-6
In Icon View you can arrange your
clips in any order you like.

Poster frames

Final Cut Pro offers *poster frames*, a handy way to quickly determine the content
of a clip. A poster frame is a representative frame of a clip that is viewed in the
Browser in either List View or Icon View. In List View, the poster frame is viewed
and set within a small graphic
called a *thumbnail*. In Icon
View, the poster frame is set
directly within the icon itself
(see Figure 2-7). Setting poster
frames for a project takes only
a few minutes, and will save
you time in the long run.

FIGURE 2-7
In Icon View, you can change
which frame represents a clip's
content.

tip

In List View you can use the Selection tool to scrub through thumbnails.

FIGURE 2-8

In many cases, default poster frames don't accurately represent the contents of a clip.

FIGURE 2-9

By scrubbing through a thumbnail you can select a poster frame that gives you a good idea of what's in the clip. The poster frames here are much more useful than the default frames shown in Figure 2-8.

Thumbnails are similar to icons in every way, except that they can't be dragged into the Timeline, nor can their viewable size be changed. If you've never seen thumbnails, take a look right now.

1. Select List View (View → Browser Items → As List).

2. Control + click on any column heading and choose Show Thumbnail from the contextual menu.

A group of thumbnails appears in its own column.

By default, the poster frame is the first frame of a clip. In many cases, however, the first frame won't give you a very good idea of what's actually in the clip (see Figure 2-8). Fortunately, FCP lets you set a new poster frame for either a thumbnail in List View or an icon in Icon View.

To set a new poster frame in either List View or Icon View, follow these steps:

1. Select the Scrub tool from the Tool Palette. (The Scrub tool is a hand with left/right arrows on it; it's located right next to the regular Hand tool.)

2. Click on the thumbnail or icon and drag the mouse left to right. You'll see the contents of the clip as you drag (this is called *scrubbing*).

3. When you find a frame you'd like to use as your new poster frame, hold down the Control key.

4. Release the mouse button, then the Control key.

The new poster frame is set (see Figure 2-9).

Dragging out tabs

A great way to organize projects is to drag out FCP's various tabs and work in them individually. You can do this with bins or tabs in the Viewer or Canvas, as well as with items in the Tools menu. This is a great feature because you can spread out an element of the interface into a much larger window for detailed tasks.

In the Viewer, you can drag out the Video, Audio, Controls, Filters, and Motion tabs. You can also drag out ancillary windows from filters such as Chroma Keyer, Color Corrector 3-Way, and Color Corrector.

If you need to have two sequences open side by side, you can drag them out as tabs in the Timeline and Canvas.

Other windows operate this way as well, such as windows in the Tool Bench, QuickView, Frame Viewer, Voice Over tool, and Audio Mixer.

To drag out a bin that's been opened as a tab, drag the bin's tab out of the Browser to another part of the screen. Placing bins side by side helps you drag clips, graphics, and sequences from bin to bin or project to project (see Figure 2-10). After you finish what you're doing, you can put bins back into the Browser by clicking the button at the top-left corner of the tab or by pressing Control + W. All tabbed windows will close in this fashion.

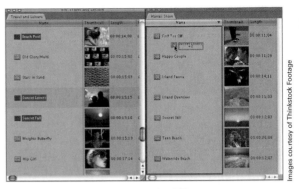

Images courtesy of Thinkstock Footage

FIGURE 2-10
Place bins side by side to easily move material from one to another.

ORGANIZING YOUR MEDIA

When I teach FCP classes, I find that many people are confused about how to organize media on their media drives, so let's briefly discuss media organization. Thankfully, when you set your Capture Scratch Disk in System Settings, Quick-Time media files are automatically put into a folder named after your project. This folder is located in the Capture Scratch folder, which is in the Final Cut Pro Documents folder. I call this the "Project Media folder." Within the Project Media folder, you can also set up a hierarchy for storing other media files, like imported stock footage or renders from third-party applications.

Strategies for media file storage

One key to staying organized is to have a system to store your rendered Quick-Time media files. These files can be hard to keep track of, as you might export them to other applications, work on them, then import them back into FCP. The type of organization scheme you use depends on how you like to work, how big your project is, and how much material you need to keep track of.

For simple projects, you can use a couple of folders inside your Capture Scratch folder → Project Media folder: one to keep track of your QuickTime exports from FCP, and another for your renders from other applications. I use this approach when I'm dealing with only a few media files and will not be using many third-party applications. If I'm working on a larger project that has similar folders, I extend this simple scenario; I just create more folders within folders for media files that will be exported from and imported to FCP.

> **tip**
>
> *You can launch bins as tabs directly from the Browser. Just Option + double-click on the bin in the Browser to open it on its own. You can then switch from List View to Icon View if you wish.*

> **note**
>
> *A Project Media folder will not show up within your Capture Scratch folder until you capture footage into a project.*

For larger and more complicated projects — for example, projects that require many applications or collaboration with other artists — you can use a more complex file-management structure. Nothing fancy here; just create more folders within folders until you're satisfied with the hierarchy.

Working this way, all related project media is in the same location, but subdivided according to application or any other criteria you choose. If I'm set up this way I can find things quickly and easily. You can also ensure a clip's smooth playback when all media is placed on a separate hard drive (sometimes referred to as a "media drive"), which is where the Capture Scratch folder should live.

Making a preset bin structure

When setting up a project, I like to make folders on the Desktop and then drag them into my FCP projects. When they're dragged into FCP, these folders become bins. After my bins are set up, I can easily import footage exactly where I wish. I've made a bin-organization template for you on the DVD. For the upcoming exercise, you'll want to copy this bin structure to your own project by doing the following:

1. Navigate to the Chapter Extras folder, and find a folder called "Project X."

2. Within the Project X folder, select the "Exports from FCP" and "Imports to FCP" folders, and drag them into your own media drive's Final Cut Pro Documents folder → Capture Scratch folder → Effects Project folder. This will copy the folders into your Capture Scratch folder.

Now you have a preset bin structure that you can build on and alter to suit your needs. Just duplicate the "Exports from FCP" and "Imports to FCP" folders by selecting them and pressing Command + D, then drag them into any new or ongoing project.

Importing a preset bin structure

After you've placed a set of folders within folders in your media drive's Capture Scratch folder, you can easily import the same structure into Final Cut Pro. This is pretty handy, as you don't have to set up another set of bins from scratch.

A quick exercise is in order here, so you can practice importing a file-management structure.

tip

When importing image sequences, be sure to set the Still/Frame Duration to :01 in your User Preferences.

tip

You can drag a copy of your Project Media folder to the Tool Bar in the Finder or to the Dock for quick access to your media assets.

EXERCISE 2-2: IMPORTING A BIN STRUCTURE

Let's import the bin structure you just copied into your Capture Scratch folder. Before you get started, make sure the Effects Project is open and that you haven't added any footage to the Imports to FCP folder.

1. Move or close some FCP windows (except the Browser) if necessary to reveal the media drive icon on the Desktop.

2. Double-click the media drive and locate the Exports from FCP and Imports to FCP folders you just copied to the Effects Project folder within the Capture Scratch folder.

3. Drag and drop the folders into the Chapter 2 bin in the Browser.

4. The folder structure comes in, with bins in place of folders.

5. Open the Imports to FCP folder and note the new bins that have come into the project.

Before I get going on each new project, I duplicate this folder structure so all the naming conventions are intact and I can manage my media assets more efficiently. I suggest you adopt this strategy as well.

tip

If you choose to make your own preset bin structure, FCP will accept only the first four folders in the hierarchy.

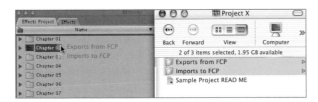

STEP 3

You can drag and drop a hierarchy of folders into any FCP project to help you manage larger projects.

Importing and Exporting QuickTime Files

When you're organizing footage for a project, exporting and importing footage is usually an unavoidable duty. I'm sure you have at least a little experience with importing and exporting QuickTime files, but FCP 4 offers a few changes, so let's quickly hit the most important scenarios.

EXPORTING FOOTAGE FROM FINAL CUT PRO

You'll want to export footage from FCP to other applications for a number of different reasons. You might want to create an effect you can't make in FCP, for example, or you might need to process a piece of footage for technical reasons. Regardless of why you're exporting a file, you have choices on how you export it. Typically, you'll want to export footage by selecting either QuickTime Movie (formerly known as a Final Cut Pro Movie) or Using QuickTime Conversion.

Exporting a QuickTime movie

To export footage from Final Cut Pro, choose File → Export → QuickTime Movie. When you're exporting a QuickTime movie, you have two additional choices to consider. The QuickTime movie can either be a "reference movie" or a "self-contained movie." A reference movie takes almost no time to process and provides an exact copy of your original footage with no recompression. You should not use a reference movie if you plan to move the file to another machine. A safer bet is to save a "self-contained" movie by checking Make Movie Self-Contained in the Save dialog box. Quality will be maintained (if you leave the Recompress All Frames option unchecked), and you'll have a file you can move or archive.

Other QuickTime options let you export to LiveType or Soundtrack. If you want to export a special movie for these applications, with markers from FCP intact, you need to choose File → Export → For LiveType or For Soundtrack. The same Save dialog will come up. You have options in the Markers pull-down menu: All Markers or Audio Scoring Markers. All Markers will bring standard FCP markers into LiveType, while Audio Scoring Markers will bring markers into Soundtrack.

Exporting using QuickTime conversion

You also have the choice of exporting with the Using QuickTime Conversion function, which is akin to exporting a self-contained movie, but with a couple of options unavailable in QuickTime Movie. For example, the only way you can export a still from FCP is by choosing Using QuickTime Conversion. Choose File → Export → Using QuickTime Conversion. The Save dialog box will open, and you'll have the choice to save to QuickTime any of the options listed in the Format menu. The Options button launches the Movie Settings dialog (see Figure 2-11), which offers advanced export functions such as changing compression schemes or frame size.

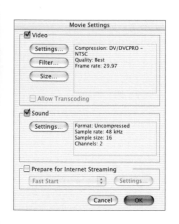

FIGURE 2-11

The Movie Settings dialog box presents advanced export functions.

Special QuickTime exports

There are some special cases for exporting QuickTime: Compressor, Audio to AIFF(s), Audio to OMF, and Cinema Tools. These items are typically used for finishing and output duties not related to project setup. Consult FCP's manual for more details.

From time to time, you may have to batch-export both batch lists and EDL (Edit Decision List) data from FCP for editing tasks handled by other machines. This is fairly rare in the case of setting up a project, and is usually a task for finishing a spot or show.

Batch exporting

When you're preparing to work on a project, having all your clips in the same compression scheme, or *codec* (such as DV-NTSC or DV-PAL), is important. Batch exporting to QuickTime is a timesaving technique to process many clips at once and have them take on a particular codec. For example, let's say you're working in the DV codec and you've imported some stock footage into FCP for a project. Since stock footage is not typically delivered in the DV codec, you'll have to process the files to conform to the DV project. Otherwise you'd have to render every frame once you brought the clips into the Timeline, which would definitely be a waste of time.

To batch-export items to QuickTime:

1. Select the items you wish to export.

2. Choose File → Batch Export.

3. In the Export Queue window, click the Settings button.

4. In the Batch dialog box, click the Set Destination button (see Figure 2-12).

5. Choose the format: QuickTime Movie or QuickTime (custom), which is identical to Using QuickTime Conversion. There are other options as well.

6. Click the Export button in the Batch Export window.

7. Import the newly converted footage back into the main project.

Your batch-processed clips are now good to go for your project.

FIGURE 2-12

Click Set Destination to batch-export files to your chosen destination.

> **tip**
>
> *If you're working with any Windows computers, you might want to do a test for possible naming-convention conflicts. Every media file that's exported from FCP must have the proper extension at the end of the file name. A simple thing like adding ".mov" to files can save you hours of frustration when working with Windows folks.*

FIGURE 2-13

Import footage directly into a bin by Control + clicking on it and then selecting Import File or Import Folder.

tip

Your imported stock footage files will have to take a "round trip" after being imported into FCP if they aren't using the same compression scheme, or codec, as your sequence. You should batch-export them to the proper codec, then re-import them.

note

If logging clips offline is something you'll want to do, check the Chapter Extras folder, where an Excel spreadsheet is already set up for you as an FCP Batch List.

IMPORTING FOOTAGE INTO FINAL CUT PRO

In addition to capturing media into FCP, you can import footage from a number of sources, including stock footage providers and footage you've made or processed in a third-party application. In either case, there's not much to it, but I'll share a few little-known tips with you. Let's begin with a quick review.

Importing from the File menu

You can bring footage into FCP in a number of ways. You typically import a single QuickTime file, several files within a folder, an entire folder of files, or several folders of files (see Figure 2-13). To get at these options, just choose File → Import, then choose either Files or Folder from the submenu. The "Choose a File" menu will then launch. Click on a media file or folder to select it. Command + click on any additional files or folders you wish to import. To select many files or folders in a row, select the first file, then Shift + click the last file in the column. You'll have footage coming into your project in no time.

Importing by dragging and dropping

You can also import footage by dragging and dropping files or folders into FCP. When you drag QuickTime files into the Browser, they'll show up as clips. To do this, locate the QuickTime files on your media drive. Select the files, then drag and drop them directly into the Browser. The technique is identical to dragging and dropping a preset bin structure, except this time there is footage already placed in the folders. I don't know of a quicker way to import footage.

Importing batch lists and EDL data

You can import a batch list of clips you logged with a tab-delimited spreadsheet program or an EDL (Edit Decision List) you created on another machine. A batch list would be only clip data, which could then be batch-captured into a logging bin. An EDL would be sequence data, which could be recaptured and then used to restore a Timeline. Either way, it's not a complex process and is well documented in FCP's manual.

Interface Workflow

As you're making effects, you'll want to use the best possible features the FCP interface has to offer. By adapting to and flowing with the interface according to the task at hand, you can get your work done more smoothly and quickly.

For starters, you should get used to the idea of adjusting FCP's windows to suit any given effects-creation task. You'll need to thoroughly understand the features and functions of the Viewer and Canvas, particularly those related to the drop-down menus.

WINDOW ARRANGEMENT

By resizing, rearranging, and moving windows, you can find ways to work more fluently. You'll need to be good at working with windows when you're creating effects, as you'll need to spread out and take up more room compared to everyday editing.

There are a number of ways you can place and resize windows around the screen to give yourself an advantage as you create effects. You can choose from a list of window arrangements in the Window menu. You can also make custom arrangements to suit your workflow, and save and restore custom window arrangements called *layouts*. You probably already know how to use the Window → Arrange menu, so let's look into custom window arrangements and saving custom layouts.

There are a few new window arrangements in FCP 4: Audio Mixing, Color Correction, Standard, and Two Up. If you have a second computer monitor, you'll have additional layouts for Color Correction, Editing, and Multiple Edits. The Audio Mixing arrangement features the Audio Mixer at the right in a "three-up" arrangement, as shown in Figure 2-14. Color Correction also gives you a third window for the Tool Bench. I prefer either the new Standard arrangement for single monitors, or one of my custom window arrangements for dual monitors. Now we'll look at how to make your own custom window arrangements.

Images courtesy of Thinkstock Footage (V0014897)

FIGURE 2-14

The Audio Mixing layout places the Audio Mixer on the right.

Custom window arrangements

You can make two custom window arrangements to suit your individual work style. Here's how:

1. Arrange FCP's windows by moving them and resizing them to suit your task.

2. After you've arranged the windows the way you'd like, hold down the Option key, then choose Window → Arrange.

3. Choose Custom Layout 1. (Repeat this process and choose Custom Layout 2 to make a second custom arrangement.)

4. Release the mouse button, then let go of the Option key. If the arrangement is still grayed out in the menu, try again, but this time let go of the Option key just a split second later than you normally would.

Your new custom window arrangement will now be available.

Saving window layouts

You can also save window layouts to disk and call them up as you need them. That way you can make as many custom arrangements as you see fit (see Figure 2-15). Having a different window arrangement for each major editing task (like pre-project

tip

If you have two computer monitors, you can devote a whole screen to the Timeline. This is handy when you're working on multiple layers.

organizing, trimming, capturing, and working with effects) gives you a great deal of flexibility. Another reason to save a window layout is to set up the interface so as not to interfere with the OS X Dock.

Here's how to save your custom window layout to disk:

1. Arrange the windows by moving them and resizing them to suit your task.

2. Go to the Window menu and choose Arrange → Save Window Layout. The Save dialog box will open, allowing you to name the arrangement. You can also choose to format the arrangement with either Auto-Aspect or Fixed Aspect behavior. Auto-Aspect will automatically fit the windows to any screen. The Fixed Aspect arrangement will cause the windows to remain the same size, regardless of the screen size.

Restoring a custom layout refers to importing a window layout you've already made and saved to disk. Any time you want to change the windows from your current setup, you can "restore" a layout by opening it.

To restore a window layout:

1. Go to the Window menu and choose Arrange.

2. Choose Restore Layout from the Arrange submenu.
   The Choose a File for Window Layouts dialog box will open.

3. Choose the layout that best suits the task at hand.

note

The custom layouts are located in User Name → Library → Preferences → Final Cut Pro User Data → Window Layouts.

tip

Control + Shift + 6, 7, 8, 9, and 0 are the keyboard shortcuts to call up your first five custom window arrangements

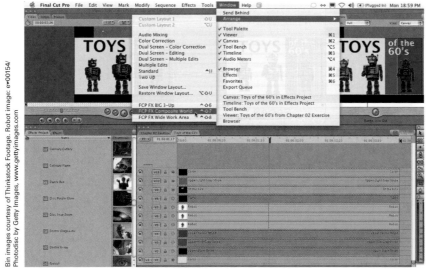

Bin images courtesy of Thinkstock Footage. Robot image: e▪00154/
Photodisc by Getty Images, www.gettyimages.com

FIGURE 2-15

Here's a custom window layout I've made, called "FCP FX Composite World." This layout lets me see many video tracks at once on a single monitor.

INTERFACE WORKFLOW EXTRAS

Final Cut Pro 4 offers some great new workflow enhancements. You can now save track layouts, add buttons to Button Bars, and customize the keyboard. These new features allow you to personalize the Final Cut Pro interface even more.

Customizing track layouts

Before starting a project, it's nice to have your tracks set up just how you want them. If you prefer to have a special layout for compositing with skinny audio tracks and thicker video tracks, you can do that by adjusting track height and then saving the track layout. Even more powerful is the ability to restore a customized track layout at any time. This means that you can call up a different track layout to suit any editing task (see Figure 2-16). Let's look at how to save and restore, or call up, customized track layouts.

To save a track layout for your Timeline:

1. Set your tracks the way you like them.

2. Click the triangle next to the Timeline's Track Height selection button to open the Track Control menu.

3. Choose Save Track Layout from the menu.

4. Name the layout and click Save.

You'll be able to call up this track layout from disk at any time:

1. Choose Restore Layout from the Track Layout menu. The Choose a File dialog box appears.

2. Choose the track layout you want, and then click the Choose button.

Cut Down on Scrolling

Effects creation is a layer-intensive process, and you'll want to see many video tracks at once without doing any time-consuming scrolling. Using Window → Arrange → Standard or a custom window arrangement gives you more space for viewing many Timeline layers, or for making your track height thicker to look at keyframe overlays or audio waveforms. If you must scroll, invest in a scrolling mouse. These work well with Final Cut Pro 4.

The Timeline's tracks will be restored to the way you originally set that custom track layout. When you have a spare moment, you'll want to make a whole slew of track layouts that you can call up for use in future projects.

Buttons and Button Bars

A new FCP 4 feature called *Button Bars* lets you display buttons that trigger common tasks that might otherwise be buried in a menu (see Figure 2-17). A Button Bar is located at the top of the Timeline, Browser, Canvas, and Viewer windows.

To add buttons to your Button Bars, all you have to do is this:

1. Press Option + J or go to Tools → Button List to open the Button List.

2. Find the task you want by typing the name of the task, such as "Speed," in the Search field. The button for speed control (or any button you searched for) appears in the Button List.

3. Drag and drop the button into the space in the top area of the Timeline, Canvas, Browser, or Viewer.

Pretty cool, isn't it?

You can also save and create more button sets according to how you like to work. Here's how:

1. Add buttons to a window's Button Bar, as described above.

2. Control + click on a button or in the Button Bar. A contextual menu will appear.

3. From the menu, choose Save Main Button Bars.

4. Name the button set something descriptive and then click Save. Your button set will now be saved to disk.

You can now have multiple button sets for your Timeline, Canvas, Viewer, and Browser, and call them up any time you need them.

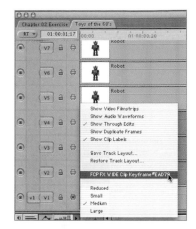

FIGURE 2-16

The new Track Layout menu allows you to change, save, and restore the appearance of a Timeline at will.

> **tip**
>
> *Control + click on a button to color-code it or add spacers between buttons.*

FIGURE 2-17

Button Bars can be customized with buttons that trigger your most common tasks.

Customizable keyboard

FCP 4 lets you customize your keyboard to suit your personal editing and compositing needs. It's very easy to do; just drag and drop the icons from the Keyboard Layout window onto any key icon in the window. Blank keys will take on the new command. Any newly dropped icon from the Keyboard Layout window will replace the icon that is currently on the button.

You can take this concept even further and make a number of special keyboard layouts that are suited for different tasks. For example, you could make a keyboard that's perfectly suited for compositing, and another that's ideally set up for trimming. Let's now explore the custom keyboard with a quick exercise.

EXERCISE 2-3: MAKING A CUSTOM KEYBOARD LAYOUT

In Chapter 1 I introduced the concept of mapping composite modes to your numeric keypad. In this exercise, we're actually going to go through the process. For this exercise you don't have to open an Exercise sequence. Just follow these steps to customize your keyboard layout:

1. Go to Tools → Keyboard Layout → Customize.
   The Keyboard Layout Window will open.

2. Click on the lock in the lower-left corner of the Keyboard Layout window to enable customizing.

3. Type the word "Composite" in the search field.
   The composite modes will display.

4. Click on the Command and Option keys in the Keyboard Layout window. By doing so, you'll see a lot of empty buttons where you can drag and drop new keyboard commands.

5. Drag and drop each composite mode onto a key you want to use. I like to use the numeric keypad. (Note that the numbers on the numeric keypad have no other function with the Command + Option buttons engaged.)

6. Go to Tools → Keyboard Layout → Export, name the keyboard "Composite Modes," and click Save.

You now have a keyboard made especially for working with composite modes. With it, you can toggle between composite modes very quickly by holding down the Command and Option keys while pressing numbers on the numeric keypad.

This saves me a lot of time when I'm comparing modes, since I don't need to keep going to the Modify or contextual menus.

When you need to, you can import any saved keyboard layout. Go to Tools → Keyboard Layout → Import.

Continue to build your custom compositing keyboard with more shortcuts as you work through the book. I think you'll find this technique extremely useful as you go forward in creating effects.

Modifier key tabs   Click and drag each mode to a different numeric key

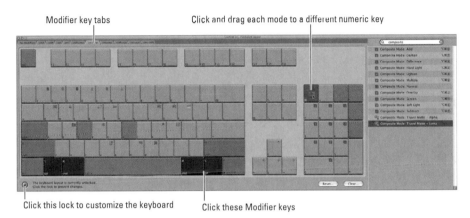

Click this lock to customize the keyboard   Click these Modifier keys

MAGNIFICATION AND VIEW MODES

The Viewer and Canvas have three pop-up menus that pertain to viewing a clip or graphic. These are the Zoom, Playhead Sync, and View Mode menus (see Figure 2-18). We'll talk more about the Playhead Sync menu in the next chapter, so let's focus on reviewing the Zoom and the View menus for now.

Zoom pop-up menu

When you look at the Zoom pop-up menu, you'll see settings for various window sizes. Note that when you make a selection from the menu, you're merely changing the viewing area of the window, not the size of the clip. As you work, you'll often change the magnification in the Canvas (less often in the Viewer).

FIGURE 2-18

The Zoom, Playhead Sync, and View Mode menus are found in the Viewer and Canvas windows.

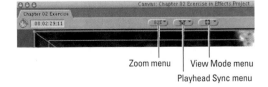

Zoom menu   View Mode menu
Playhead Sync menu

Why do you want to scale the Canvas down? Good question. You'd want to resize the Canvas below 100% to see and arrange layers in the light gray "offstage" area prior to animating them in Image + Wireframe or Wireframe mode (see Figure 2-19).

Although the Zoom menu includes a number of percentage options, it's unusual to scale either window above 100%. There's really only one good reason to do this: when you want to see your clip or composition up close. This comes in handy when doing tasks like working on the edge of a matte effect. Here's a rundown of the other options in the Zoom menu:

- **Fit to Window:** Fit to Window scales the image to fit the current size of the Canvas. This setting also refers to the largest size your Canvas or Viewer can be magnified to without experiencing performance setbacks. Shift + Z will make your Viewer or Canvas snap to the proper Fit to Window magnification.

- **Fit All:** This setting is used after you've reduced the Canvas size and then zoomed in on a particular section of the image. If you wish to view the entire image in that smaller window, choose Fit All. If you then resize the Canvas, the size of the image does not change.

- **Show as Square Pixels:** A computer can only display square pixels, while digital video uses non-square pixels. If you display a native DV on a computer monitor, it will be distorted unless you leave this option checked. I leave the Show as Square Pixels feature enabled as I work, as the distortion is distracting otherwise (see Figures 2-20 and 2-21). This function is disabled in Offline RT, as you're already working in square pixels.

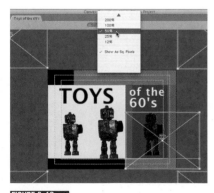

FIGURE 2-19
Scale the Canvas down to see "offstage" areas outside the Canvas.

FIGURE 2-20
This image has Show Square Pixels enabled.

FIGURE 2-21
If Show Square Pixels is not checked, the image appears "squished."

Image: ev00154/Photodisc by Getty Images, www.gettyimages.com

View Mode pop-up menu

By changing the view mode to add helpful guides and icons, you can streamline your workflow quite a bit. Note that you can also access most of the functions of this menu from the pull-down View menu. The pull-down View menu actually has a couple of features not found in the pop-up View Mode menu. We'll talk about those in a bit, but for now, let's focus on the four main categories of the View Mode menu: Boundaries, Overlays, Channels, and Backgrounds.

■ **Boundaries:** From an effects standpoint, the Boundaries section of this menu focuses on how to set the Viewer or Canvas to view, arrange, and manipulate a clip's motion properties. There are three choices here: Image, Image + Wireframe, and Wireframe. You can toggle between these modes with the keyboard shortcut W. It's vital that you understand the function of each mode so that you can select the best one for a particular task. Although it's review for most, here is a rundown of the modes:

- **Image mode** in the Canvas is primarily for watching playback of your show. I usually leave the Viewer in Image mode, as I can drag and drop clips into the Canvas or Timeline more easily. I often uncheck Show Overlays when playing back in Image mode, as overlays can be a bit distracting when stopping playback to evaluate an effect.

- **Image + Wireframe mode** is by far the most powerful mode to work with while compositing images (see Figure 2-22). Working directly in the Canvas, you can manipulate the motion properties of clips. The bonus is that you can see how a tool is affecting the image as you adjust it. You merely need to click and drag with these tools to scale, rotate, move, change the anchor point, crop, or distort clips. The mode shows any selected clip with a turquoise "bounding box" surrounding it. This bounding box represents the clip's position, scale, rotation, distortion, and cropping values at a glance. The Video Track number is conveniently attached. From time to time I use Image + Wireframe mode in the Viewer, depending on the task at hand. Image + Wireframe is so important that a good deal of Chapter 3 is dedicated to it.

FIGURE 2-22

Image + Wireframe is most useful for quickly placing and aligning clips in the Canvas.

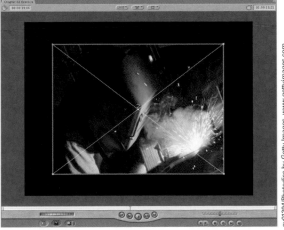

- **Wireframe mode** is useful when you have more layered effects than can be displayed in real time and need to time them to come in at a certain place or time. In this mode, only the outer boundary of each clip will play back. (If any clips are selected, you'll see the blue overlay with "X" and track number attached for each clip.) The bonus is that you can stack and animate an unlimited number of clips and never have to render them, as they'll play in real time. More powerful Macs are making Wireframe mode a bit less useful, however.

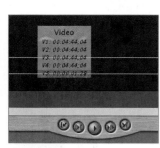

FIGURE 2-23
Timecode Overlays display the timecode for all audio and video tracks at that specific time.

- **Overlays:** The Overlays section of the View Mode menu provides helpful visual references when you're engaged in editing or compositing tasks. Overlays are only a visual aid, so don't worry about them getting recorded to tape.

Show Overlays must be checked in the menu for Title Safe and Timecode Overlays to be viewed (see Figure 2-23). There are a few other ways to enable overlays:

- In either the Viewer or the Canvas, press Control + Option + W.
- Go to the View pull-down menu and select Show Overlays.
- To toggle Timecode Overlays in either the Viewer or the Canvas, press Option + Z.
- Go to the View menu and select Show Timecode Overlays.

In the View menu there's another overlay option called Range Check. It's related to "broadcast safe" specifications. I'll hold off on discussing this option now, as we'll deal with it in depth in Chapter 7.

- **Channels:** The Channels section of the View Mode pop-up menu comes into play when you want to view a clip's RGB channels, alpha channel, or both. This comes in handy when you want to see how the alpha channel (the channel that defines the shape and level of transparency in a clip) is affecting a clip. You can view individual channels in the View menu equivalent. Go to View → Channels and select the channel you wish to view (see Figure 2-24). (The alpha channel will be discussed in detail in Chapter 8.)

- **Backgrounds:** I'm sure you've tried out some of FCP's backgrounds, so this should be nothing new. But when do you use them? In your day-to-day workflow, I suggest that you leave the Canvas background set to Black and the Viewer background set to Checkerboard. The background information for the Canvas is recorded to tape as black regardless of the background

note

You can view overlays only when a clip is paused. Overlays do not show up as you play back a clip, nor are they recorded to tape. If you need to see your Timecode overlays recorded to tape, you'll have to use the Timecode Generator filter.

choice, so black makes the most sense here. One of the checkerboards (they have opposite-colored squares) or a white background is useful for detecting transparency anomalies or problems with the edges of mattes, which you can check in the Viewer or Canvas. It's always a good idea to see how your clip is playing against one of those backgrounds before moving onto the next task. If you'd like more options for your background, head to the View menu and choose Background → Red, Green, or Blue.

Previewing Effects

Previewing is probably the single most important thing you can do as you plan and create effects. Previewing is smarter than rendering because less time is wasted in processing items that may have mistakes in them. Throughout the book I'll ask you to first preview an effect, and then render it after you're satisfied. Let's look at a few techniques commonly used in previewing effects.

PREVIEWING REAL-TIME EFFECTS

Final Cut Pro 4 has reached new heights in the ability to preview effects. With FCP 4's RT Extreme architecture, many more effects (including certain third-party plug-ins) will play in real time than in its predecessor.

Here's how I like to work:

1. Set the Timeline's RT pop-up menu to Unlimited RT and Low or Medium Quality, so that the Timeline has mostly green render bars wherever effects are applied, with some yellow and maybe a few orange render bars (see Figure 2-25). If you see lots of red render bars, then visit the next section, "Previewing Non-Real-time Effects."

2. Set In and Out points around the clip.

3. Click the Play In to Out button or use the shortcut Shift + Backslash. The clip will begin to loop in the Timeline.

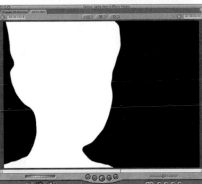

FIGURE 2-24

A still with an alpha channel as displayed in RGB, Alpha, and Alpha+RGB modes, respectively.

4. Observe the effect and decide if any changes should be made. If so, stop playback.

5. Click the Motion tab or Filters tab and adjust the errant effect's control slider or parameter.

You'll see your changes the next time you play In to Out.

FIGURE 2-25

A red render bar occurs in the Timeline when you add most effects in Safe RT mode. The same effect in Unlimited RT gives you the green render bar, indicating that it will play back in real time.

PREVIEWING NON-REAL-TIME EFFECTS

If you see the red render bar in the Timeline and you're in Unlimited RT mode and at Low Quality playback, you're going to have to either render the effect or preview it using another technique. Let me offer up some options for you.

Using the QuickView window

Use the QuickView window to preview an effect or transition. The window plays back frames that are cached in RAM, providing a mighty quick way to preview a complex effect. The coolest thing about QuickView is that it lets you change parameters or keyframes as the clip loops over its range or between In and Out points.

FIGURE 2-26

You can change the resolution in the QuickView window for faster playback.

Resolution pop-up menu

In the next loop, the new effect will load into RAM and you'll instantly see the change. As the frames continue to load, the effect will eventually play back in real time until you change another parameter.

To preview an effect using QuickView:

1. Drag and drop an effect from the Effects tab onto your chosen clip.

2. Mark In and Out points around the clip or section of a sequence you want to preview.

3. Open the QuickView window (press Option + 8) and click the Play button. Frames will begin to load, and then the effect will play back.

Stepping through an effect

The simplest and quickest way to preview an effect is to "step through" it. You're probably already doing this without realizing it. In fact, every time you move the playhead over a clip that has an effect applied to it and you note the changes in the Canvas, you're stepping through the effect. It takes at least a few clicks through the clip on the Timeline Ruler to see how an effect is working. Although you can't see an effect play back at full speed, you can get enough feedback to decide whether you want to continue refining the effect.

Scrubbing through an effect

A similar method to stepping through an effect is to "scrub through" it. To scrub through an effect, just click and drag the playhead from the Timeline Ruler across the clip and note the changes made by the newly applied effect. The faster your processor is, the better performance you'll have while scrubbing. Scrubbing should provide just enough feedback regarding how the effect worked on the clip. Next to stepping through a clip, this is one of the fastest ways to preview an effect.

The Option + P method

You can use the keyboard shortcut Option + P to preview an unrendered section of the Timeline. The processor will play back the effect as fast as it can.

To use this method, just add the effect, place the playhead slightly before the clip, and press Option + P. Note the changes in the Canvas as the playhead travels across the clip in the Timeline. A repeated pass using Option + P will provide a faster preview of the effect because the effect gets cached into the computer's RAM.

Troubleshooting

This chapter's troubleshooting issues are concerned primarily with FCP interface "gotchas." Let's look at a couple of common problems you may run into.

Playback is stuttery

Stuttery playback is a common problem, especially when you're moving and resizing windows and tabs and changing views within them.

> **tip**
>
> *You can get a more dynamic scrubbing effect that updates every frame by holding down the Option key as you scrub. I do this frequently when constructing effects.*

> **tip**
>
> *You can use the Left and Right Arrow keys to scrub one frame at a time. Holding either arrow key down will update audio and video as fast as the processor can handle it.*

To Render or Not to Render...

I'm guilty of this myself: the strong desire to render everything as I work. However, doing that is a very poor use of your time. Every time you render, you're locked out of completing your next task. In my opinion it's in your best interest to work without rendering until you're absolutely forced to — ideally just prior to recording your piece to tape. Another good time to render is when you'll be away from your Mac (god forbid!). Lunchtime is a great time to render. Home studio owners can literally render while they sleep!

FCP has a cool Auto Render function that will kick in at set intervals if you walk away from your Mac with FCP booted up. You can enable or disable Auto Render in User Preferences. Try to curb your desire to render at every turn by using previewing techniques and rendering only when absolutely necessary.

If you want to speed up rendering and can live with lower image quality, you can go to Final Cut Pro → User Preferences → Render Control tab, and change Frame Rate and Resolution to lower quality settings. You can also uncheck Motion Blur and Frame Blending to speed renders on slower machines. You'll need to make sure these settings are changed back to their defaults before outputting your piece to tape or compressing it for the Web or DVD.

Two cures for stuttery playback are keeping your Canvas in Fit to Window view and making sure your windows don't overlap.

- If the Canvas is set to a larger size, it will produce stuttery playback and won't record to tape properly. Pull down the Zoom menu in the Canvas and choose Fit to Window. You can also click on the Canvas and use the keyboard shortcut Shift + Z.

- Make sure that none of your windows are overlapping. Go to Window → Arrange and choose from one of the preset window arrangements, or drag between windows to activate FCP 4's Auto Resize function.

- If many elements of the interface are overlapping, go back to the default configuration by pressing Control + U.

Clip viewing problems

I've heard the following complaint many times: "I can't view my clip even though it's on the Timeline and the playhead is parked over it." Don't fret, as this is an easy fix.

- It's possible that you're in Wireframe mode. In this mode, you won't see a clip at all, merely the turquoise colored "bounding box." Either toggle the W key or go to the View Mode pop-up menu and choose Image or Image + Wireframe.

- If you have your Clip Overlays button enabled, it's possible that you accidentally dragged down the Opacity Level line and made your clip invisible. To fix this, either drag the line back up or double-click the clip to load it into the Viewer, and then go to the Motion tab and click the red "X" next to the control for Opacity. This will reset the clip to its original state.

Real-time previewing problems

If you're having problems previewing real-time effects on the Canvas, or are getting a dropped frames warning, you'll need to try the following:

1. In the RT pop-up menu on the Timeline, select Unlimited RT and Medium quality.

2. In the Final Cut Pro menu, go to User Preferences and uncheck Report Dropped Frames During Playback.

This way, your machine will drop frames in order to give you a real-time approximation of your effect. This is what you want to do to get more real-time effects that will play back instantaneously. You should check the Report Dropped Frames During Playback option when you're going to record to tape.

If you're having trouble seeing previews on your video monitor, check the following:

- Make sure your deck is powered up and that the video monitor is being fed from the deck's Video Out or Monitor Out jack.

- Make sure FCP is sending out a signal. Go to View → External Video → All Frames.

Wrap-up

We've covered a lot of territory in this chapter. You've learned ways to enhance your creative ideas and explored methods to stay organized as your project progresses. Finally, we touched on ways to work smarter, including strategies for previewing effects. This chapter was probably a review for many of you, but I wanted to make sure we were on the same page in our understanding of effects creation with Final Cut Pro. We have a bit more groundwork to lay in Chapter 3, so let's move forward.

WHAT'S IN THIS CHAPTER

- FCP interface and terminology overview
- Working more efficiently in the Canvas and Viewer
- Altering a clip's Motion parameters using Image + Wireframe mode

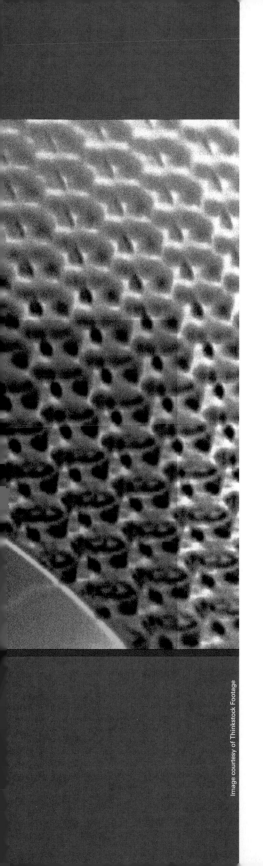

3

Adding Effects

We've spent the last two chapters preparing you for the fun that's about to begin in this chapter. Now you're ready to change the appearance of your clips. You can do small adjustments like cropping a clip's edges, or you can add a filter to radically alter a clip's appearance so it's unrecognizable compared to the original. By adding filter effects and changing Motion and Controls parameters, you can achieve some amazing results as you begin to create effects with Final Cut Pro.

After completing this chapter, you'll have mastered the basic concepts of adding effects to clips. You'll also get some good tips on effects workflow in Final Cut Pro 4, and complete some exercises that will get you primed for the remainder of the book.

Terminology Overview

Before you go into high gear making video effects, we need to make sure we're on the same page when it comes to FCP's interface and terminology. That way, when I mention a certain part of the interface you'll know exactly what I'm talking about as you try out techniques on footage in exercises and in your own projects.

EFFECTS TERMINOLOGY

Let's go over some common terms used when discussing effects. In this book, the term *video effect* or *effect* can mean any of the following:

- A motion effect, such as Scale, Rotate, or Distort. The term *motion effect* does not necessarily mean that a clip has to be in motion; it could refer to a static setting of the controls for any of the effects in the Motion tab. Changing the playback speed of a clip would also be considered a motion effect.

- A filter effect, such as Tint, Blur, or Color Correction

- A generator, such as a title

- A video transition

- A combination of any of the above

*Parameter*s are the individual controls within each video effect. These controls guide each Motion, Filters, or Controls effect. Examples of parameters include the slider for Scale in the Motion tab, an Angle Control dial in a Radial Blur filter in the Filters tab, or the Color Control swatch that picks a hue for a Text Generator in the Controls tab.

CLIP TERMINOLOGY

Throughout this book I'll toss around the term *clip*. A clip can be any of the following:

- A video or audio clip that has been captured, imported, or created in a separate program

- An imported graphic such as a layered Photoshop file

- A freeze frame

- An FCP generator like a Gradient, Color Matte, Shape, or Title 3D

- A Shockwave Flash (.SWF) file created in Adobe After Effects or Macromedia Flash MX

- Virtually anything else QuickTime can understand

SEQUENCE TERMINOLOGY

In this book, the term *layers* refers to a clip or clips on a particular video track. "Select the top three layers and move them 4 seconds down the Timeline" means to select the clips on the upper three video tracks — tracks V1, V2, and V3 — and then move them.

Another term you should be familiar with is *composition*. I use this term, (and derivatives of it, like *composite* and *comp*) to describe any video effect that displays groups of clips on various video tracks at any given point in time in a sequence. This term is widely used and understood in other video compositing applications and non-linear editing systems (*NLEs*), so that is why I favor it.

In the book, the word *composite* could also be used as a verb. "Use the Opacity slider to composite the two layers together" means to use the Opacity slider to blend the clips that are stacked up on the two video tracks.

Using the Viewer for Effects Construction

One of the first questions asked by editors coming from other platforms is "Where's the effects interface in Final Cut Pro?" In Final Cut Pro, you use the tabs of the Viewer as your effects "editor." These tabs are where you hammer out exactly how you wish the clip to look as you alter it from its default. In general, the Motion tab offers tools to shape and move a clip, the Filters tab is where you add and adjust filters to alter the look of the clip, and the Controls tab provides controls for generators such as titles and gradients.

Put in simpler terms, the Viewer has two distinct functions: you either edit with it or control effects with it. You use the Viewer for choosing In and Out points for a clip before placing it into the Timeline, and also for adding effects to it after it has been put there.

For starters, let's quickly review the Viewer's tabs.

VIEWER TAB REVIEW

If you've used FCP, you should be well acquainted with the three main tabs in the Viewer. These tabs are directly related to visual effects creation.

- **Motion tab.** This tab affects the physical properties of a clip, such as its size, position, and degree of rotation.

- **Filters tab.** This tab is blank when you first open it; you add filters to alter the look of a clip. Here you can do things like change a clip's color, add a border, or blur the image.

- **Controls tab.** This tab controls FCP and third-party generators. To bring up this tab, you'll first have to load a generator into the Viewer, as the tab remains hidden until you do so. The Generators pop-up menu, located in the lower right corner of the Viewer, allows for convenient access to all of your generators. This tab provides controls for things like titles, gradients, and graphic shapes.

Now we'll discuss some of the intricacies of the Viewer's tabs so you can feel more comfortable with how they display important information about your effects. The greatest thing about the tabs is that they generally behave in the same way. Rather than providing redundant information on each tab, let's go over the features the tabs have in common.

Viewer tab columns

In each Viewer tab you'll find three columns: Name, Parameters, and Nav (short for Navigation); see Figure 3-1. The columns subdivide the names of the effects from the controls and navigational portion of the interface.

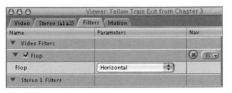

FIGURE 3-1
Each Viewer tab has a Name, Parameters, and Nav column.

- **Name:** The Name column displays the name of a particular motion effect or filter. It also lists the names of the parameters you can view once you click any disclosure triangle. In the case of the Controls tab, only the parameters of that particular generator are displayed.

  In the Motion tab, some parameters have only one control, like Opacity's single slider, while others have several, like Drop Shadow's three sliders, Angle Control, and Color Control swatch.

  Motion tab parameters are always in the same order. Controls tab parameters are in an order dictated by the chosen generator. Filters are listed in the order in which they were added, but you can change the order by clicking and dragging them to a new place in the list.

- **Parameters:** This column refers to a slider, angle control dial, numeric field, menu, or the like attributed to a specific effect. The various controls you'll find throughout each tab are discussed below.

- **Nav:** This column includes some very important controls used for keyframing and navigating through effects.

  - **Insert/Delete Keyframe button:** You click the Insert/Delete Keyframe button to make a new keyframe for a particular parameter at the playhead's position in the Keyframe Graph (keyframing will be covered in the next chapter). You can also use it to remove a keyframe. Click this button when the playhead is parked on the keyframe and it will be removed precisely at that point in time.

  - **Reset button:** The Reset button (a red "X") resets each parameter to its default. When the going gets tough, the tough start over from scratch.

note

Changing the order of the filter stack is a technique I'll share with you in Chapter 11, "Filter Techniques."

- **Keyframe navigation arrows:** Once you have keyframes set, you can navigate to the next one by clicking on the right arrow. If you'd like to get to the previous keyframe, click the left arrow. You'll want to navigate directly to keyframes to alter or delete them.

- **Clip Keyframes pop-up menu:** This menu, found in the Motion tab, dictates which keyframes you'll see in the Motion bar when you select the Clip Keyframes button on the Timeline. This menu is discussed in the sidebar called "Clip Keyframes and Keyframe Button Techniques." You'll learn more about keyframes in the next chapter.

Figure 3-2 shows the elements found in the Viewer tabs.

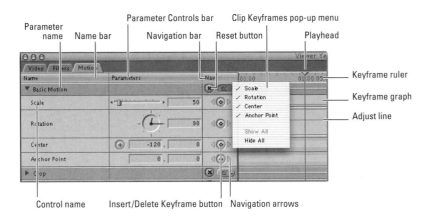

FIGURE 3-2

Click any Viewer tab and you'll see these elements.

Parameter controls

tip

Sliders have tiny arrows at either side of the tic-mark scale. If you click these you can change the parameter by single values, which is exceedingly valuable for fine-tuning an effect.

Although I'm sure you're already familiar with the controls found in the Viewer tabs, here are some details you might not know. These parameters are the ones you'll find in the various tabs of the Viewer.

- **Sliders:** The most prevalent control in FCP is the slider. Sliders are really intuitive to use; just click and drag to the right to increase a value, or drag to the left to decrease a value. Note that there are three kinds of sliders:

  - **Regular sliders** have tic marks equally spaced across the parameter controls area. Regular sliders provide even and balanced results when keyframing.

Clip Keyframes and Keyframe Button Techniques

Many people are confused about how to use the Clip Keyframes pop-up menu (see Figure 3-2), and therefore avoid using it altogether. This menu is located in the Motion and Filters tabs, next to every Reset button. Understanding this menu can save you time and frustration when you want to move keyframes to a different place on the Timeline using the Motion or Filters bar.

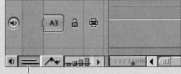

Clip Keyframes button

The Clip Keyframes menu is tied to the Clip Keyframes function in the Timeline. You enable Clip Keyframes by clicking the Clip Keyframes button in the lower-left portion of the Timeline.

- Any Motion keyframes that are set are represented as small blue diamonds on a blue line below the clip called the Motion bar.

- Any Filters keyframes that are set are blue-green diamonds on a line called the Filters bar.

- Controls keyframes are not visible on the Timeline in this mode.

You can click and drag only those set keyframes that are checked in the Clip Keyframes menu.

In adjusting the placement of keyframes in the Timeline, your goal is to move only the keyframes that you intend to work with. The most common scenario is when you click the Add Keyframe button in the Canvas, which sets keyframes for almost all the motion parameters, when perhaps you wanted to affect only one or two. Excess keyframes are set, so if you want to move just one keyframe, you can't tell which one it is! You'll have to move many keyframes that aren't affecting the clip, wasting precious time. The Clip Keyframes menu will tell you which keyframes are showing and which are not. By enabling only the ones you want to see, you will tame this time-draining behavior. You'll also have much more control when tweaking the effect.

In the menu, first choose to Hide All keyframes. Once all keyframes are hidden, you can return to the menu to choose only those parameters you want displayed in the Clip Keyframes area. A single check next to each parameter shows this. Moving keyframes in the Clip Keyframes area of the Timeline is a lot easier because you've got fewer of them to move.

Related to this technique is Control + clicking on the Add Motion Keyframe button in the Canvas. By doing so, you'll engage a pop-up menu that offers you control over which parameters you wish to keyframe.

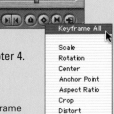

If you don't know how to make keyframes yet, you may wish to return to this sidebar after reading Chapter 4. Clip Keyframes will be discussed later in this chapter, in "The Timeline's New Functionality."

Add Keyframe
shortcut menu

- **Logarithmic sliders** take off from zero and increase in value exponentially, rather than in linear fashion. Scale is a good example of a logarithmic slider. Logarithmic sliders tend to have most of their usable function nearest to the first 20% of the graph.

- **Double-sided logarithmic sliders** have negative values attributed to them as well, so the tic marks get closer together as they approach and leave zero. Aspect Ratio is a good example of a double-sided logarithmic slider. When tic marks are closer together, the overall change in the parameter's value will progressively slow down.

■ **Angle Control:** This is the clock-like feature you see throughout the FCP interface for any parameter control that requires an angle, like Rotation in the Motion tab. The longer black hand indicates the distance a given clip moves in degrees. The shorter red hand shows the number of revolutions if you keyframe the effect.

By the way, in the Basic Motion area of the Motion tab, the Angle Control has a limit of 24 revolutions for the Rotation parameter, so go easy. I doubt you'll ever need that many anyway.

■ **Point Control:** Most FCP'ers refer to this as the "crosshairs," so go figure. Point Controls are buttons that specify a coordinate on the X,Y axis. Your first experience with Point Controls is likely to be with the Center parameter, located in the Motion tab. To work with this parameter, you first click the Point Control button in the tab, then click and drag the corresponding crosshairs in the Canvas. Once you let go of the mouse button, the point stays at the location to which you dragged. If you need to make any adjustments to the placement of the crosshairs, you'll have to click on the Point

"Gear Down" for Precise Control

When you're adjusting a control such as a slider, you might find that you can't precisely control that parameter. Don't worry; there's a simple way to get finer control over items such as sliders and dials.

When you're adjusting a control and are close to the value you want, hold down the Command key to engage "gear down" behavior. Gear down slows down the increments to let you easily choose precisely the value you want. For example, as you slide the Scale slider, hold down the Command key to scale in smaller increments. Once you've used gear down, it will become second nature as you work.

Control again, something that takes a bit of getting used to. If you click and drag the crosshairs in the Canvas with the Command key held down, the numbers will continually update in the Viewer.

- **Numeric fields:** Numeric fields define a clip's relationship to the center (0,0) of the Canvas. Although the fields certainly aren't too flashy looking or click-and-draggable, the power is in the precise placement only numerical calculation can bring. You'll find numeric fields for controlling the clip's Center, Anchor Point, and Distort properties in the Motion tab. They're also found in several filters, such as the 4-point and 8-point Garbage Mattes.

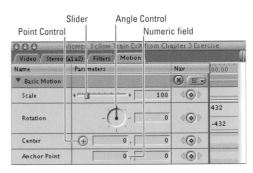

FIGURE 3-3

Here are the parameter controls for Basic Motion.

Figure 3-3 shows some parameter controls.

- **Color Control:** The Color Control, which some people call a *color swatch,* is a convenient way to pick colors for your effects. You have the ability to keyframe your effect to move from one color to another. A single click to the swatch brings up the Apple Color Picker. At the top of the Color Picker are several variations of the tool; choose the one most suitable for you.

  Here are some added features of the Color Control swatch that are hidden underneath a disclosure triangle:

  - **HSB sliders:** By turning down the disclosure triangle you can see the HSB sliders, which are controllable but not individually keyframable.

  - **Eyedropper button:** This is for picking a color for your effect. You pick colors from somewhere on the Canvas or in the Video tab. If you need to grab a color from somewhere else, such as from another document or from the Desktop, click the color swatch to launch the Apple Color Picker and use its Eyedropper tool, which works systemwide.

  - **Hue Direction button:** This button comes into play when you're keyframing an effect to move from one color to another (see Figure 3-4). The business behind the button is to choose the path it takes around the RGB color wheel: the long route or the short route. If you aren't sure what I'm talking about, check out the RGB Color Picker. If you wanted a tint to change from blue to purple, it could change directly from blue to purple if you traveled clockwise on the wheel. Or, it could change from blue to cyan, to green, to yellow, to red, to magenta, and then finally to purple if you traveled counterclockwise. The key to controlling the Hue Direction button is to make sure that it is set the same way at each keyframe. If you don't do this, it won't work predictably.

note

The Anchor Point's numeric fields refer to its relationship to the center of the clip itself, not the absolute center of the Canvas.

note

The Eyedropper tool in the Color Picker is different in OS X. It's a good-sized crosshairs in the shape of a magnifying glass. The bonus is that it will help you pick colors from anywhere in the interface. Clicking the green button at the top of the Color Picker makes it quite large and easy to see, a plus that has not been possible in past operating systems.

HSB sliders
Eyedropper
Hue Direction button
Color Control

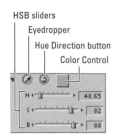

FIGURE 3-4
The Hue Direction button controls which way colors travel around the RGB Color Wheel when keyframed to change over time.

Parameter checkboxes   Clip control well

FIGURE 3-5
The Clip Control well and parameter checkboxes.

tip

If a parameter's Enable checkbox is not checked, then that effect will not show up in any final render. Be sure to check all necessary checkboxes prior to rendering if you intend to include that particular filter, motion blur, or drop shadow in the final product.

■ **Enable checkbox:** All filters and a couple of parameters in the Motion tab (Motion Blur and Drop Shadow) offer checkboxes. When a box is checked, it indicates that an effect is enabled. Clicking the box on and off repeatedly allows you to quickly make decisions regarding the look of an effect.

■ **Menu:** You'll see menus throughout the FCP interface. Note that parameters that offer menus are never keyframable. Check one out in Motion Blur.

These next fields are specific to the Filters and Controls tabs:

■ **Clip Control:** The Clip Control "well" (see Figure 3-5) is for dragging and dropping clips to form a matte or to blend with the source clip. For FCP's native effects, only first frame will register in a blended effect. However, clips dropped into the well will play back in full motion with certain third-party plug-ins.

■ **Parameter checkboxes:** These are a bit different than the checkboxes for enabling an effect. These are actually on/off buttons that control a parameter (see Figure 3-5).

■ **Text fields:** In the standard Text generators — like Text, Outline Text, and Crawl — and in FCP's View Finder filter, you'll find a field where you can add your own text. For generators, the text field is located in the Controls tab.

■ **Specialty controls:** There are specialty controls for the Title 3D and Title Crawl generators, as well as the Color Correction and Chroma Keyer filters. I'll describe those controls when we cover those topics in depth.

THE KEYFRAME GRAPH

Although we won't be talking about keyframing in depth until the next chapter, you should reacquaint yourself with the Keyframe Graph to the right of the columns in the Viewer tabs. We'll soon be using the graph to precisely place keyframes for the purpose of changing parameters over time, but for now you can work on changing the values of parameters by clicking and dragging the thin green lines, called *adjust lines,* in the Keyframe Graph.

As you approach the parameter adjust line, an incarnation of the Selection tool automatically becomes the Adjust Line Segment pointer, which looks like a double arrow pointing up and down (see Figure 3-6).

In addition to moving the parameter controls (sliders, for example), you can use the Adjust Line Segment pointer to control effects by dragging the thin green adjust lines up and down.

To vertically expand the Keyframe Graph's work area, click the dividing line between parameters and drag upward.

To review:

- Clicking and dragging the adjust line upward with the Adjust Line Segment pointer increases the value for a parameter.

- Clicking and dragging the adjust line downward with the Adjust Line Segment pointer decreases the value for a parameter.

Keyframe Graph area

Playhead

Keyframe ruler

Drag here to expand the work area

Adjust Line Segment pointer

Adjust line

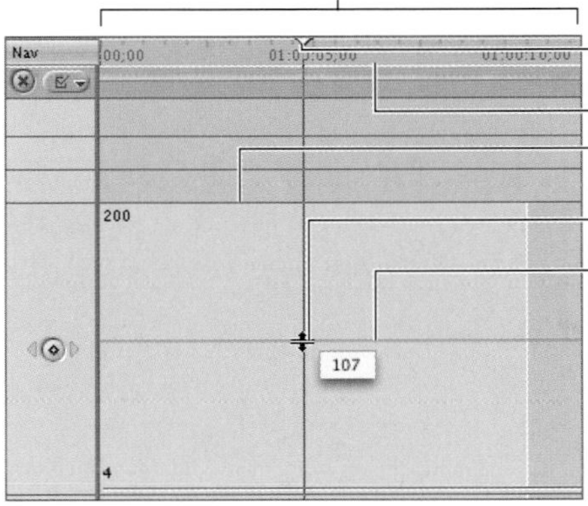

FIGURE 3-6

Note that the Adjust Line Segment pointer turns into the Selection tool when you click on the adjust line.

Filter Start and End points

In the Filters tab, after you've added a filter to a clip you'll see small, black vertical lines along the top of each filter parameter in the Keyframe Graph. These lines, the *Filter Start and End points* (see Figure 3-7) , show the limits of the filter effect. You can change these limits by clicking and dragging on them wherever you see fit. Doing this can be an effects strategy to make a filter effect "pop on" (or off) in an instant.

Another use for filter Start and End points is related to workflow. By shifting the filter Start and End points to a section of a clip you want to affect, you won't have to render the entire clip, only the section between the filter Start and End points. Although this is less of a concern with real-time effects and with FCP 4, moving filter Start and End points to only the place where the filter is needed creates less work for the computer and will free up more real-time functionality elsewhere in that particular section of a multilayered effect.

As you approach the newly set filter Start and End points with the Selection tool, the Slide tool will appear. Click and drag with it to slide the Start and End points to a new spot in the clip.

Clip In and Out points

The light-gray section of the Keyframe Graph is the active area of the clip that you'll work on when keyframing it (see Figure 3-7). It is actually the area defined by your In and Out points from the Timeline. The dark-gray section of the Keyframe Graph indicates the area of the clip outside the duration of your set In and Out points. There are certain cases where you would set keyframes before your set In point or after your set Out point, such as keyframing a motion effect so it plays through a transition.

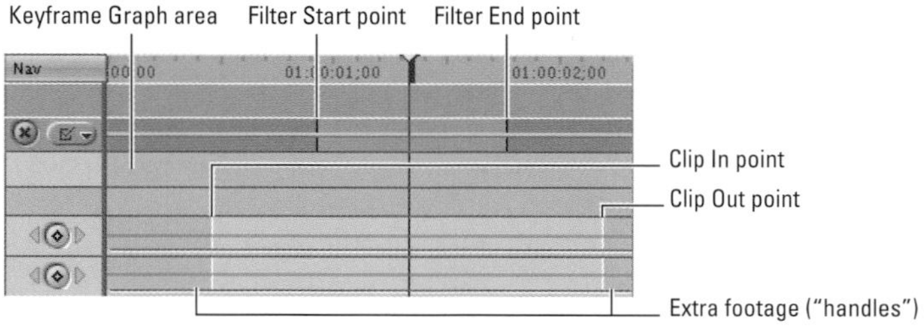

FIGURE 3-7

The Keyframe Graph in the Filters tab is the place to change the duration of a static filter effect.

Zoom Control

You use the Zoom Control and Zoom slider (see Figure 3-8) to zoom in on a section of keyframes in the Keyframe Graph, or into a clip or group of clips on the Timeline. You can also zoom out quickly to see all of your keyframes or clips at once.

The Zoom Control works the same way in the Viewer as it does in the Timeline. You click and drag it to the left to zoom in on the playhead or the selected clip or clips. Click and drag to the right to zoom out.

Zoom slider

This slider has two functions: to zoom in or out and to slide left or right in the Keyframe Graph or Timeline. Click either thumb tab (located at either end of the slider) and drag left or right to zoom in or out on the playhead. If you have a clip or a group of selected clips, it will zoom in on them.

tip

If you hold down the Shift key and drag on one of the thumb tabs, you'll zoom in or out from that side of the slider.

The sliding function comes into play when you've zoomed in on an area of the Keyframe Graph or Timeline. Once you're zoomed in, you can move where you wish in either interface by clicking and dragging the center part of the slider to a new area. You can also click in the area next to the slider to move the bar one full length of the Timeline window. You can also move the slider by clicking on the scroll arrows at either end of the Timeline. There are helpful overlays to assist you in navigation. You can see both In and Out points, as well as a small purple line indicating the location of the playhead, which is where you typically want to navigate to.

Timecode navigation

The small box at the lower left of every Viewer tab (except the Video tab, where it's located on the upper right) is a Timecode field. If you're working on the Timeline copy of a clip, it will display the current sequence timecode right in the tab. This field also indicates how much you move the playhead forward or backward when you enter numbers with the keypad or the number keys on your keyboard. For example, if you wanted to move the playhead forward 5 seconds, you'd type +500 and press Enter, because that 500 means 5 seconds and zero frames. You could also enter a precise timecode value from your sequence, and then press Enter to go directly to that frame.

Figure 3-8 shows Zoom Controls and Timecode navigation fields.

Now that you know all about the Viewer tabs, let's look at how to ensure that you're working on the proper copy of the clip, which is crucial to your effects workflow.

note

Because I type a lot of numeric values when I'm working in Final Cut Pro, I like to use the Enter key next to the numeric keypad. If you prefer, you can press the Return key instead.

tip

Once a particular window is chosen, pressing the Tab key will move you to the various numeric fields so that you can enter timecode values. Don't bother adding colons for your Timecode values; FCP adds them automatically.

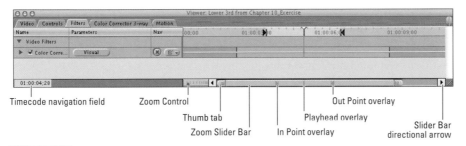

FIGURE 3-8

You'll find Zoom Controls and Timecode navigation fields on the bottom of each tab.

Zoom Control Shortcuts

These keyboard shortcuts quickly and precisely zoom you to where you want to go, right on the playhead:

- To zoom in, use the Command and + keys. While holding down the Command key, tap repeatedly on the + key to continue zooming in on the playhead.

- To zoom out, use the Command and − keys. While holding down the Command key, tap repeatedly on the − key to continue zooming out from the playhead.

- To fit all keyframes in the Keyframe Graph at once, press Shift + Z.

> **tip**
>
> *In Open mode there's a catch related to working on sequences that have more than one track. With multiple tracks, which clip will open into the Viewer? Good question. Just make sure the Auto Select control for that track is highlighted. Open mode will automatically open that clip in the Viewer.*

> **tip**
>
> *Once you switch Playhead Sync modes in the Canvas or Viewer, the newly set mode will automatically engage in the opposite window. If you're not sure which mode you're working in, note that each mode has an icon that shows up inside the pop-up button, telling you which mode you're currently in.*

PLAYHEAD GANGING

Things have changed in a big way in Final Cut Pro 4 regarding playhead behavior. There's now an advanced function called *ganging*. With ganging enabled, the playhead in the Viewer moves in lockstep with the playhead in the Canvas and Timeline.

A new menu has been added to both the Canvas and Viewer to address ganging behavior: the Playhead Sync pop-up menu (see Figure 3-9). The menu is located between the Zoom and View Mode pop-up menus. In this new menu you'll find four different ways the playhead will react regarding ganging: Off, Follow, Open, and Gang.

When playheads are ganged you can scrub through a clip in the Viewer and the playhead will follow in all of the other windows. If you drag the playhead 15 frames forward in the Viewer, for example, the Canvas's playhead will move forward the same amount. There are a number of reasons why you'd want to do this, so let's look at the available options and come up with scenarios for each selection.

Playhead Sync modes

Here's a brief introduction to the new playhead ganging modes.

- **Off:** In the default off position, playhead ganging is disengaged, allowing you to move the playheads independently of each other.

- **Follow:** In Follow mode the playheads in the Viewer and the Canvas will be ganged only when a clip is loaded into the Viewer from the Timeline. This means ganging will be engaged only when you're working on clips. When you go back to working in the Timeline, the ganging behavior won't distract you. If you're working on the Browser copy of the clip and attempt to gang in Follow mode, the menu command will be ignored.

- **Open:** This mode does it all! It not only gangs the playheads together, it also automatically opens the Timeline copy of the clip as soon as the playhead touches it. This is great news for those of us who forget to open a clip in the Viewer before adding or adjusting effects. The cool thing is that the selected tab stays open from clip to clip as the playhead moves, making it easy to make quick adjustments to filter or motion settings from clip to clip.

■ **Gang:** This mode is similar to Open mode, but doesn't automatically open the Timeline copy of the clip. This is useful in certain situations where you want ganging but don't want to have the Timeline copy of the clip continually opening, as it does in Open mode. Perhaps you want to gang a filtered copy of a clip with the original Master clip for comparison purposes. Similarly, if you were working on a show with multiple camera angles, you could load up a synched shot from another camera and go into Gang mode. That way, as you scrub you could easily find the best place to make the cut. Gang mode has additional implications for trimming, aligning keyframes, and other functions.

Understanding Clips

When you're dealing with effects in Final Cut Pro, there's a strategy for working in the Viewer. It involves understanding which copy of a clip you're adding effects to. To avoid mistakes and confusion later on, you must master this core concept. Read on.

WORKING ON THE PROPER COPY OF A CLIP

When it's added to the Timeline, a clip from the Browser changes behavior. The clip that's placed into the Timeline becomes a "copy" of the master clip from the Browser. That Timeline "copy" of the master clip is the clip you'll want to add effects to.

Once you know that you're working on the Timeline copy of a clip — and can verify it — you'll have far fewer problems when troubleshooting your effects. How do you know when you're not working with the right copy? If you're making some adjustments to motion control parameters, for example, or have added a filter to a clip, and don't immediately see changes in the Canvas, you're probably working on the master clip. In the next section you'll learn how to work on the proper copy of a clip.

By learning how to load the Timeline copy of the clip into the Viewer, you're set up for properly creating effects. After you develop this habit, you'll have little trouble and have more fun making cool effects with Final Cut Pro. Let's do that right now with our first exercise.

> **note**
>
> *From my experience as an instructor, I can tell you that students who have trouble controlling effects are usually working on the wrong copy of a clip, using the original master clip instead of the copy they placed in the Timeline.*

Why Not Add an Effect to a Master Clip?

You're probably wondering why you wouldn't add an effect to a master clip before placing the clip into the Timeline. The main reason is related to workflow.

For example, let's say you add a motion effect and drop a filter or two onto a lengthy clip in the Viewer, set In and Out points, and then place the clip in the Timeline. A bit later, you wish to use a different part of the same master clip in the Timeline. The effects would remain on that part of the master clip, so you'd have to remove or reset them, which would waste time. In fact, you might not even be able to play the master clip back in the Viewer to set new In and Out points, since it would have a pile of effects bogging it down.

EXERCISE 3-1: CREATING A PICTURE-IN-PICTURE EFFECT

This exercise will prepare you for working on the proper copy of a clip when adding effects to it. The first several steps will be repeated in upcoming exercises, so make sure you're comfortable with them. Locate the Chapter 3 bin in the Browser, and then open the Chapter 3 Sequences bin and find the sequence called "Chapter 3 Exercise." Double-click the sequence to open it. Move to the marker called Exercise 1 at the beginning of the Timeline. You'll find two clips stacked up there, "Optical Lens" and "Eye Chart."

1. Place the playhead on the clips in the Timeline so you can see them as you work.

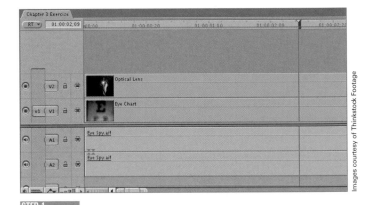

STEP 1

Place the playhead on the clips in the Timeline.

2. Load the Optical Lens clip from the Timeline into the Viewer using one of the following methods:

   ■ With the Selection tool, double-click on the clip in the Timeline.

   ■ Select the clip in the Timeline and press Enter or Return.

   ■ In Image + Wireframe mode, double-click the clip on the wireframe in the Canvas.

Images courtesy of Thinkstock Footage

- Control + click the clip and select Open 'Optical Lens' from the contextual pop-up menu.

- From the Playhead Sync pop-up menu in the Canvas, choose Open mode and park the playhead directly on the clip, with the Auto Select button enabled for V2.

3. Look for the "sprocket holes" in the Scrubber Bar of the Viewer to make sure you're working on the right copy of the clip. Viewing these double dots in the Scrubber Bar is the easiest way to verify that you're working on the Timeline copy of the Optical Lens clip.

STEP 3
Look for "sprocket holes" in the Viewer's Scrubber Bar.

4. Click the Viewer's Motion tab. Go to the Scale parameter and slide the slider a bit to the left. You should see the Optical Lens clip scaling down in the Canvas as you do this. Set scale at 70% to reveal the background (in this case, the Eye Chart clip). As you can see, by scaling down clips that are on upper tracks, you can create a very simple static picture-in-picture effect.

5. Drag the Scale slider to the right. Although you could scale up a clip as much as 1000%, you will never want to go that high. See what happens when you begin to slide the slider to that level. Note that the image quality will begin to degrade when you go past 100%, so take care in choosing any value higher than 100% for finished work. For now, return the scale setting to 70% and then save the Effects Project by pressing Command + S.

Any time you're having trouble with your Filters, Motion, or Controls tab effects, check to see if you've followed the steps just presented. If you're still having a tough time, head for the Troubleshooting section.

Images courtesy of Thinkstock Footage (V0017555)

STEP 4
Scale down the clip on the upper track to reveal the clip on the lower track.

"What you see is what you what you get"

One reason for working on the Timeline copy of the clip is the ability to adjust an effect and then get immediate feedback. If you can't see what you're doing as you're doing it, you can't work effectively.

Once you see what you expect to see in the Canvas and on your video monitor, you'll have the confidence to make changes or adjustments to a given clip.

USING THE CANVAS FOR EFFECTS

The Canvas provides the visual palette where you can compose and approve your work. It provides visual updates of your effects as you make adjustments to clips in the Motion, Filters, and Controls tabs in the Viewer.

Here you can also manipulate the wireframes of clips and motion paths with tools from the Tool palette when you're in Image + Wireframe mode (see Figure 3-10). Use the View Mode pop-up menu to get into Image + Wireframe mode, or select the Canvas and toggle the W key until you're in Image + Wireframe mode.

Because you're working on the Timeline copy of a clip, you can leave the Viewer's tabs open for adjusting parameters of the Motion, Filters, or Controls tabs as you check the Canvas and your video monitor. You should get pretty fast feedback in all interfaces if the effect is not too render-intensive. This back-and-forth checking between Canvas and video monitor is something you'll have to get used to, as it's important to check your work in both places.

Images courtesy of RobPongi.com

FIGURE 3-10

You can manipulate the aspect ratio of a clip's wireframe in the Canvas.

THE TIMELINE'S NEW FUNCTIONALITY

In Final Cut Pro 4 you have a brand new way to work with effects: directly in the Timeline. An expanded Clip Keyframes area called the *Keyframe Editor* lets you adjust any keyframe right in the Timeline. You can even smooth the keyframes with Bézier handles offered by the Pen Smooth tool and other methods that will be discussed later.

In addition to the new Keyframe Editor and the Motion and Filter bars from previous versions of FCP, Clip Keyframes mode also includes a Speed Indicator area to monitor speed effects (these will be discussed in Chapter 13).

We'll be hitting keyframing in the Timeline in the next chapter, but it's a good idea to get acquainted with the new functionality of the Timeline up front.

Setting up the Keyframe Editor

To work comfortably in the Keyframe Editor, you must first expand it in the Timeline. You have control over how wide to make the work area, much like you do when you're expanding the Keyframe Graph area in a Viewer tab.

note

I rarely adjust wireframes in the Viewer, choosing instead to do that in the Canvas with the Timeline copy of the clip. For me, it's too time consuming to click back and forth from the Video tab to the Motion or Filters tab to monitor a quick adjustment.

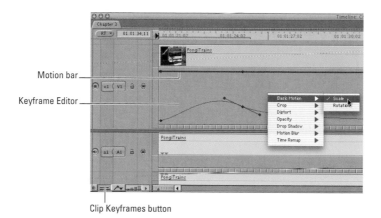

Motion bar

Keyframe Editor

Clip Keyframes button

FIGURE 3-11
With the Keyframe Editor, you
can control effects directly in the
Timeline.

1. To open the Keyframe Editor, click the Clip Keyframes button or press Option + T (see Figure 3-11).

2. Click and drag to make the Keyframe Editor under all tracks expand upward (see Figure 3-12).

3. Move the Selection tool to the Keyframe Editor column, located to the right of a track's Auto Select button. Click and drag upward. A dark gray line will replace the Selection tool as you drag in the Keyframe Editor column. Stop dragging when your tracks are wide enough (see Figure 3-13).

4. Control + click in the Keyframe Editor and note the menu and submenus. You'll be able to add, delete, move, and adjust any keyframe here, including time remap. The Pen tool will also assist you with the same tasks you can do in the Viewer tabs.

tip

Toggling the Q Key will change your selection between the Canvas and the Viewer. This is a very handy keyboard shortcut, as you'll free yourself from having to click on the windows to select them. Sometimes you might wonder why you aren't seeing your effect update; a quick refresh of the Canvas will often be the solution.

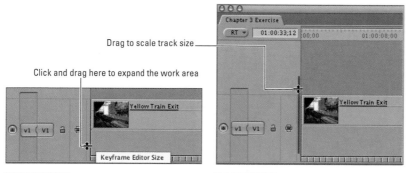

Drag to scale track size

Click and drag here to expand the work area

FIGURE 3-12
The Keyframe Editor can be expanded.

FIGURE 3-13
You can expand the track size within the Keyframe Editor.

tip

When using the Keyframe Editor, you can save vertical space in the Timeline if you collapse the audio portion of the interface. Control + click on the Clip Keyframes button and choose Audio → Select None to do this.

New Time Remap tool

There's a new tool in the Clip Keyframes area called the Time Remap tool. This little baby makes time-remap keyframes denoting a clip's original "source frames." These source frames can be moved to other areas of the clip, allowing you to make unique speed effects in FCP 4.

We'll be working with the Time Remap tool in Chapter 13, "Speed Effects," but for now just note that it's used for working with time-remap keyframes directly in the Timeline, and is even more useful when you've got the Keyframe Editor open.

Changing Parameters and Adding Effects

When you add filter effects to a clip or change Motion or Controls tab parameters, the clip changes in some way. This change can be subtle, radical, or somewhere in between. If you can dream it up, you should be able to make it. Before we get into advanced concepts, let's first lay the groundwork for creating effects. Some of the exercises in this chapter might seem elementary, but bear with me. Once you learn these fundamentals, you'll feel comfortable about the steps you need to take in creating any effect, simple or complex. And you'll be much less likely to get caught by any of the "gotchas" that trip up even the pros from time to time.

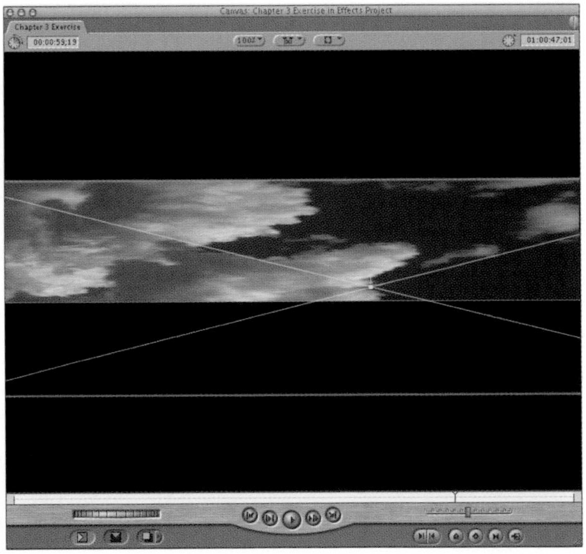

Image courtesy of Artbeats Starter Kit, wc101, www.Artbeats.com

FIGURE 3-14

Setting up a static effect: Rotation, Aspect Ratio, Crop, and a color correction filter combine to give a new look to some clouds.

STATIC EFFECTS

A *static effect* can be a filter effect, motion effect, or generator setting — or any combination thereof — that does not change over time (see Figure 3-14). We'll make effects change over time in the next chapter, but for now we're setting up the effect's starting or ending "look."

Setting up a static effect is your first step towards making a multilayered video composite, which is often made up of many clips.

ADJUSTING A CLIP'S MOTION PARAMETERS

You can alter the shape of a clip by resetting the Basic Motion parameters in the Motion tab. Here I'll cook up some ideas on how to use each parameter. I'll also preview some concepts regarding moving these parameters over time, so you'll be ready to work with keyframing when we get to the next chapter.

- **Scale:** Scale is at the top of the list of things you'll want to do when you're creating motion graphics. You'll scale clips when you construct effects like picture-in-picture or flying title effects. Almost every multilayered video composite will involve some sort of scaling. To simulate 3D space, for example, you'll use scaling plus keyframing to make an object grow larger over time so it looks like it's coming toward you.

- **Rotation:** The Rotation parameter rotates a clip around its given anchor point to a new angle. By changing the rotation angle of a clip, you can turn it on its side or even upside down. Clicking and dragging the black handle changes the angle of the clip by degrees. When you get around to keyframing the effect, you can make your clip turn around in circles as it plays. For example, if you imported a graphic of a wheel, you could make the wheel turn.

- **Center:** By modifying the Center parameter, you can place a clip in a different position in the Canvas. Repositioning and scaling a clip often go hand in hand, especially for something like a picture-in-picture effect. When you add keyframing to the mix, you can fly your clip around the Canvas or even to or from the unseen area of the Canvas, as if it were coming on or off a stage. It's easiest to position a clip in the Canvas in Image + Wireframe mode. However, I urge you to check out the X,Y positioning and round them off to whole numbers, which gives a cleaner look and makes it easier to calculate movements when you start flying the clip around.

- **Anchor Point:** This parameter provides a "pivot point" around which you can move a clip. You can alter the behavior of other parameters such as Scale, Position, Rotate, or Distort when you change the anchor point from its familiar resting place at (0,0). However, this behavior is not detectable at this point; things don't start getting interesting until the keyframing starts. Anchor Point in its static state acts almost like the Center parameter, affecting a clip's position. It's easiest to set a new anchor point position in the Canvas. As you drag out the anchor point handle using the

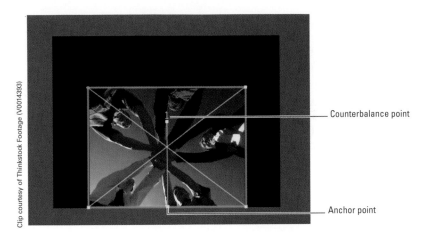

Clip courtesy of Thinkstock Footage (V0014393)

Counterbalance point

Anchor point

FIGURE 3-15

The anchor point and counterbalance point come into play
in tandem with other motion
parameters. Here the clip is
scaled from the bottom, rather
than the center.

FIGURE 3-16

The clip is distorted on the upper-
and lower-right side. It has also
been scaled down a bit.

Distort tool

FIGURE 3-17

Use the Distort tool to reshape
images in the Canvas.

Distort Tool, a "counterbalance" point with the layer number on it is displayed (see Figure 3-15). You can reposition the anchor point at any place
you wish, on or off the Canvas.

■ **Crop:** This parameter allows you to remove areas of a clip. Sometimes
you'll want to crop out unsightly things, like the little black lines on the
sides of a clip when you scale it down (called *blanking lines*), or a person or
thing that you don't want to include in the frame. In addition to hiding
things, you can also look at cropping as a way to highlight a person or
object in a multilayered composite. You can also use Crop to help you
shape a clip. Crop includes a slider for Edge Feather, which is a nice option
for scaled-down clips and graphics. When keyframed, crop can reveal or
hide clips, titles, and graphics over time. This trick is widely used in video
graphics.

■ **Distort:** This parameter provides the illusion of perspective. You can independently control each point to distort a clip (see Figure 3-16). I like the
flexibility of that method, but in the real world you'll be looking for the
perfect mathematical coordinates. The best way to work with this motion
effect is in the Canvas, where you can drag a clip to the distortion of your
choice with the Distort tool (see Figure 3-17), typically with a keyboard
modifier. With Distort, you have the nifty option of an Aspect Ratio slider,
which gives a nice 3D illusion to a clip floating in space. Distort, like
Anchor Point, has both numeric fields and a Canvas tool to control it. Setting up a good-looking distort will usually involve roughing it in with the
Distort tool and then checking the numerical values in the Motion tab to
make it look nice and even. When keyframed, you can create some wicked
3D effects with Distort.

Clip on V1 track

Clip courtesy of Thinkstock Footage (V0019940)

Clip on V2 track

Opacity is lowered on V2 to blend the two clips

FIGURE 3-18
Using the Opacity parameter, you can superimpose one clip over another.

- **Opacity:** This parameter allows you to adjust the transparency of a clip. Adjusting the opacity of a clip is a common task you'll become very familiar with as you fade clips, titles, and graphics up and down in the Timeline. Keyframing Opacity, you could fade a clip up from black, fade a title up from invisible, or fade up a superimposition or blending of two clips (see Figure 3-18).

- **Drop Shadow:** Adding an offset edge to a clip using a drop shadow creates the illusion of depth or perspective (see Figure 3-19). A drop shadow is best used to offset a title or a picture-in-picture effect. Controls allow you to soften or harden the shadow, influencing the perception of light and distance. You can also choose the color, offset, angle, and opacity of the shadow.

- **Motion Blur:** This parameter will not only affect the motion within a frame, but will also be influenced by keyframe motion. Motion Blur creates a smoother effect as you crank up the sample values. (*Samples* are the number of frames prior to the current frame that are mixed into the blend created by a blur percentage.) I prefer to use between 16 and 32 samples and vary the blur percentage, depending on the task. As far as keyframing goes, in the Motion tab, the percentage of Motion Blur can't change over time; it's either on or off, depending on whether the checkbox is checked. However, if you open the effect into the Keyframe Editor, you can do this by adding and altering keyframes on the adjust line.

- **Time Remap:** Time remapping will be discussed in detail in Chapter 13.

tip

In its default setting, Drop Shadow's offset is set a bit too high for typical drop shadows. An offset of 2 or 3 is a better place to start for most situations.

FIGURE 3-19
Here a drop shadow has been added to a scaled-down clip.

ADJUSTING MULTIPLE MOTION PARAMETERS

note

The more samples there are, the smoother a Motion Blur will be. The number of samples is related to the number of images from surrounding frames that are used in the blend. With 32 samples, 32 individual areas of the surrounding frames are blended.

You don't need to stop at adjusting just one parameter in the Motion tab. On many occasions you'll need to adjust several motion parameters within a single clip. For example, in the next exercise you'll scale down a clip and then crop some pixels off the left and right edges. Both of these motion parameters affect the clip, and you need to adjust each one to set up the picture-in-picture effect.

As you've probably discovered already, you can adjust multiple parameters in a clip by altering parameters in the Viewer's Motion tab, by manipulating a wireframe in the Canvas, or both. As you work more and more with FCP, you'll find yourself using both of these windows to get your work done. I like to first rough in the manipulation with the wireframe in the Canvas, then fine-tune the numbers in the Motion tab.

In the next exercise you'll learn how to adjust multiple parameters.

EXERCISE 3-2: STYLIZING A PICTURE-IN-PICTURE EFFECT

In this exercise you'll be making another picture-in-picture effect. This won't be your standard picture-in picture effect, however. It will be an offset clip to provide some graphic interest. You'll also be twisting some knobs and sliding some sliders to get more familiar with the parameters in the Motion tab.

Go to the Chapter 3 bin and locate the Chapter 3 Exercise sequence. Double-click the sequence to open it. Move to the marker called "Exercise 2." You'll find two clips edited into place for you: "Optical Rig" and the "Eye Chart" clip we saw in the last exercise. This time the Eye Chart clip is on the V2 video track, so it's now in the foreground and will be the subject of the picture-in-picture effect.

tip

Motion Blur is one of the more render-intensive tasks you're asked to do in FCP, so updating even one frame may take quite awhile. If you're making changes, engage the Caps Lock key to prevent the Canvas from updating.

1. Double-click the Eye Chart clip to load it into the Viewer. As you did in Exercise 1, look for the sprocket holes in the Scrubber Bar.

2. Park the playhead on the clip in the Timeline so that you can see changes as they occur.

3. Click the Viewer's Motion tab to bring it forward.

4. Scale down the Eye Chart clip using the Scale slider. (Press the Command key if you want to "gear down" the adjustment, percentage by percentage.) Click the small arrows to the left and right of the slider to achieve a 75% size for your clip. (Or enter 75 in the numeric field if you prefer.)

STEP 4
Scale the Eye Chart clip to 75%.

STEP 5
Rotate the Eye Chart clip 90 degrees.

STEP 6
Adjust the Center parameter to move the clip to the left side of the screen.

5. Hold down the Shift key and use the Angle Control to achieve a reading of 90 degrees for Rotation.

6. Enter a value of –120 into the left numeric field of the Center parameter.

7. Click open the disclosure triangle for Distort. Change the aspect ratio to –60 using the Two-sided Logarithmic Scale slider. Click the small arrows to aid you in your task. Changing the aspect ratio has drastically distorted the clip.

8. Opacity is the next motion parameter to adjust. Turn down the disclosure triangle to adjust the slider. Set the slider to 70, and the Eye Chart will be partially transparent (or semi-opaque). You can now see the patient underneath the Eye Chart clip.

9. Place the playhead at the beginning of the clips and play back this effect. If you set the RT pop-up menu to Unlimited RT, it will be a real-time effect.

10. Now let's add a drop shadow by first checking the Drop Shadow checkbox, and then clicking the disclosure triangle. Set the Softness slider to 80 and the Opacity slider to 30. There — that's a better-looking drop shadow.

STEP 7
Distort the clip by changing its aspect ratio.

STEP 8
Adjust the clip's opacity to make it semitransparent.

STEP 10
Adjust a drop shadow's Softness and Opacity to create a realistic-looking shadow.

If you add a lot of effects, you may see the red render bar.

When working in Image + Wireframe mode, click on the Motion tab to bring it forward in the Viewer. Image + Wireframe is great for roughing in layouts, while the Motion tab is the place for fine-tuning and numerical alignment. You'll be using both interfaces, depending on your task or preference.

When you're adjusting parameters in the Motion tab or the Filters tab, it doesn't matter which tab you use first. Work in the order that makes the best sense for your workflow.

11. Drat! Now that you've added a drop shadow, the render bar may be red. You might not be able to play the clip back on some systems. This means that you've got to render.

12. Select the Eye Chart clip and then press Command + R to render the effect. If your Render Status window does not pop up and start rendering, your render settings are amiss. To fix this:

    a. Go to Sequence→ Render Selection (or Render In to Out, which may be the case if you've marked edit points).

    b. Ensure that Needs Render is checked. It's the red bar, just like in your Timeline's render bar.

    c. Make sure that Item Level is unchecked so you can see the time and percentage of completion estimate in the Render Status window.

13. Now that you've got your render settings in order, press Command + R once more to render the effect with the drop shadow. When it's done, play back the results of the rotated, semi-opaque picture-in-picture effect with a drop shadow.

14. Save your project by pressing Command + S.

You've now gone through almost every control in the Motion tab. With these fundamentals under your belt, you're ready to take on the rest of the motion effects in this book.

ALTERING MOTION PARAMETERS USING IMAGE + WIREFRAME MODE

You'll be able to adjust a good number of the Motion parameters in the Canvas using Image + Wireframe mode, especially for roughing in basic motion effects. I'm a big fan of Image + Wireframe mode because it gives me the freedom to change the shape of a clip at any time by merely clicking and dragging it.

I can scale down a clip, crop it, reposition it, and add a drop shadow in less time than it takes to write this sentence. No kidding!

When you're familiar with the FCP toolset and its modifiers, you can really start flying when it comes to manipulating wireframes. I should mention that if you want to work in ordinary Wireframe mode instead, no worries; everything works the same way.

By the way, some Motion tab effects, like Drop Shadow, Motion Blur, and Opacity, aren't available in the Canvas in Image + Wireframe mode; you'll have to adjust those parameters directly in the Motion tab. That said, you can have fun and work quickly by manipulating the shape of the clip's wireframe. If you need to speed along when working with motion parameters, you can use the techniques you'll learn in the following exercise.

STEP 2

Scale and squeeze the White house clip to reveal part of the Capitol clip.

EXERCISE 3-3: CREATING A SPLIT SCREEN

There are a couple of ways to make a split-screen effect. One way is to scale down two clips and place them side by side. This exercise demonstrates another way to make a split-screen effect: by distorting the aspect ratio of two clips. Let's get started; you know the drill. Locate the Chapter 3 bin and double-click on the Chapter 3 Exercise sequence. Move to the marker labeled Exercise 3. You'll see a couple of clips — "White House" and "Washington Capitol" — in the Timeline.

1. Select the White House clip. Make sure the playhead is parked on the clips so you can see what's going on with the wireframe in the Canvas.

2. In Image + Wireframe mode, scale down the White House clip in the Canvas.

   As you drag a corner of the wireframe with the Selection tool (it will turn into the small crosshairs), hold down the Shift key to alter the Aspect Ratio parameter. While holding down the Shift key, click on the lower-right corner of the White House clip and drag horizontally to "squeeze" it inward, revealing roughly 25% of the Washington Capitol clip on either side of it.

3. Move the White House clip to the left side of the Canvas by clicking and Shift + dragging it.

4. Select the Washington Capitol clip and repeat what you just did to the White House clip, but move the Capitol clip to the right side of the Canvas. You now have a split-screen effect.

5. Preview the effect; it should play in real-time. Render it and save your project.

STEP 3

Shift + drag the White House clip to the left side of the Canvas.

STEP 4

Scale and squeeze the Washington Capitol clip and Shift + drag it to the right side of the Canvas.

Clips courtesy of Thinkstock Footage (V0025438 and V0025783)

Now that you know how to adjust a motion parameter, either by manipulating the controls in the Motion tab or by clicking and dragging on the clip's wireframe in the Canvas, it's time to explore the concept of adding filters to clips so we can really alter their appearance.

ADDING A FILTER TO A CLIP

Now we can have some real fun! We're going to learn how to add filter effects to clips (see Figure 3-20). Final Cut Pro includes a multitude of filters, and you can also purchase third-party filters called plug-ins to add more functionality to your arsenal of effects. (We'll talk more about third-party plug-ins in Chapter 14.) When you add a filter, you'll see your clip change radically right away. Don't be afraid to tweak some parameter controls to taste; FCP is non-destructive in its nature, so you can play around here as much as you like.

I should mention that some effects look great as static effects and you'll want to leave them that way. Others don't seem to gather steam until they're keyframed.

Let's first look at the two methods of putting a filter onto a clip: the Effects tab and the Effects menu.

Adding a filter using the Effects tab

The most intuitive way to add a filter is to drag and drop it from the Effects tab. Just locate the filter you want in the Effects tab, then click and drag the filter's icon directly onto the clip in the Timeline. Believe it or not, you can even drag and drop filters directly to the image in the Canvas or into the Viewer's Video or Filters tab if the clip has been loaded into the Viewer from the Timeline.

FIGURE 3-20

Here's an example of a static effect. The clip on the right has the Invert filter applied to it.

In the following exercise we're going to do an effect called a flop. A flop is useful for solving problems when a shot has mistakenly crossed the imaginary camera line on the set, and will demonstrate the use of a static filter effect quite nicely.

EXERCISE 3-4: DRAGGING AND DROPPING A FILTER ONTO A CLIP

It's easy enough to drag and drop a filter onto a given clip. The real purpose of this exercise is to help you develop good workflow habits and confidence when dealing with filter effects.

Start the exercise by opening the Chapter 3 bin, and double-click on the Chapter 3 Exercise sequence. Navigate to the marker called Exercise 4. This time, we'll use the "Cell Phone Woman" clip.

1. The Cell Phone Woman clip has already been added to the Timeline for you. You should look at your clip in the Canvas as you work on it. Make sure you park the playhead on the clip if you don't see it in the Canvas right away.

2. Click on the Effects tab to bring it forward, or drag it out to another area of your monitor(s).

3. Click open the disclosure triangle for Video Filters.

4. Open the Perspective bin and locate Flop.

5. Drag and drop Flop onto the clip in the Timeline. Alternatively, you can drag it right onto the image in the Canvas. The clip will reverse direction in the Canvas when you apply the filter.

6. IMPORTANT: Double-click the clip in the Timeline to load it back into the Viewer. You can also select the clip and press Enter or go to Open mode in the Playhead Sync menu. Look for the sprocket holes in the Scrubber Bar of the Viewer's Video tab.

STEP 5

Drop the Flop filter onto the clip in the Timeline.

7. Click on the Filters tab in the Viewer. If you wish, change the effect by pulling down its menu. You have the choice of Horizontal, Vertical, or Both in the pull-down menu. Try each one on for size. Note that no keyframes are available for this effect; it's meant to be a static effect. A classic Flop is horizontal; leave it that way when you're through experimenting.

The shot is now flopped. If you had a person on the right side of the screen, for example, that person is now on the left.

Clip courtesy of Thinkstock Footage (V0020002)

STEP 7

The original image (on left) is now flopped horizontally.

8. You can preview the effect with Unlimited RT mode selected in the Timeline or in the QuickView window. If you have the time, you may want to render it to disk by pressing Command + R.

9. Save the project.

Although it was pretty simple, I hope this exercise demonstrated the advantages of having a workflow strategy when working with effects. I'm trying to get you into the habit of always loading your clip into the Viewer prior to adding or adjusting its effects parameters.

Adding a filter using the Effects menu

Dragging and dropping from the Effects tab is intuitive, but it can take time to drill down to the filter you're looking for. That's why using the Effects menu is a favorite of those who like a more direct route to their filters. Which method you use is up to you. Let's run through this common task with another exercise.

EXERCISE 3-5: ADDING A FILTER FROM THE EFFECTS MENU

Start by double-clicking on the Chapter 3 Exercise sequence. Go to the marker called Exercise 5. Again, we'll use the "Cell Phone Woman" clip.

1. The clip is already edited into the Timeline, so park the playhead on the clip before moving on to the next step.

2. Make sure you double-click on the clip in the Timeline to load it back into the Viewer (or select the clip and press Enter).

3. From the Effects menu, choose Video Filters → Image Control → Desaturate. The clip will turn black-and-white.

4. Click the Filters tab and play with the effect by adjusting the Desaturate filter's Amount slider. Note how some of the color returns as you slide it to the left. Bring it to 50% for a washed out, desaturated look.

5. Play through your effect and adjust it until you're satisfied with it. This will be a real-time effect in Unlimited RT mode.

6. Save the project.

You should now have a good idea about how to add effects using the Effects menu. I've found myself using this menu as my method of choice for filter delivery, but you can make up your own mind: Effects tab or Effects menu.

ADDING MULTIPLE FILTER EFFECTS TO A SINGLE CLIP

As with adjusting multiple motion parameters for a clip, you can also add multiple filters to the Filters tab. There are certain filter effects that complement each other as you stack them up to combine their effects. It follows that there are probably thousands of combinations of FCP filters that work well together, so you'll want to experiment.

note

You can add a single filter to multiple clips as well. Just select them in the Timeline prior to following the steps in Exercise 3-5.

STEP 4

Adjust the Desaturate filter's Amount slider to achieve the effect you want.

tip

When you're creating filter effects, you don't have to settle for using a filter's default setting. Instead, alter the sliders, menus, and numeric fields to suit your taste.

Adding multiple effects to a clip

A nice combination of filters would be Flop and Desaturate. By adding the two filters to the Filters tab, you can adjust both of them at the same time.

Use one of the following methods to add two filters to a clip. (You can add more filters if you like, but we'll use two in this example.)

The Effects tab drag-and-drop method has two options:

note

You can also add multiple filters to multiple clips, all at the same time. Do this by first selecting the clips in the Timeline and then using one of the above methods. When you drag multiple filters by Command + clicking them, the one you drag carries a ghosted image of a "+" and the number of filters you're dragging and dropping (see Figure 3-21).

- Option A: Drag and drop both of the filters from the Effects tab onto the clip in the Timeline or directly onto the Canvas one by one.

    or

- Option B: Command + click on the two filters in the Effects tab, then drag both of them onto the clip in the Timeline in one fell swoop (see Figure 3-21). This power move will save you time if you already know how the filters will affect the clip (and each other).

In either case, since you've double-clicked the clip, you're also free to drag and drop multiple filters into the Filters tab. You can also drag and drop into the Video tab if you like, after a clip has been loaded into the Viewer.

FIGURE 3-21

You can drag several filters directly onto a clip in the Timeline.

As long as the clip is selected, you can keep adding filters from the Effects menu. You'll see your efforts update in your Canvas and video monitor as you continually add filter effects.

You now know that you can change multiple motion parameters of a clip. You just learned that you can also add multiple filters to a clip or group of clips. With the right combination of motion parameters and the perfect blend of filters, you can create some powerful effects. This book is structured to not only show you filter combinations, but also to give you ideas for making your own combinations. In finding these ideal combinations of Filters, Motion, and Controls parameters, you'll always have new ways to communicate your vision.

Dragging and dropping an existing filter onto clips

If you already have at least one filter in a clip's Filters tab, you can either drag and drop it or copy and paste it onto other clips in the Timeline (see Figure 3-22). Try this technique-building tip by following these steps:

1. Double-click the clip that has the filter(s) you want to use. Select the filter (or filters) in the Filters tab. Command + click non-contiguous filters if you wish.

2. Select the clip or clips you want to apply the filter (or filters) to.

3. Drag and drop the filter(s) onto the selected clips.

The filter or filters are applied to all the selected clips.

You can also copy and paste existing filters onto clips, but this method works only if you're pasting the filters into a single clip.

1. Double-click the clip that has the filter(s) you want to use. Select the filter (or filters) in the Filters tab. You can Command + click non-contiguous filters if you wish.

2. Select the clip you want to apply the filter (or filters) to.

3. Copy the filters using Command + C.

4. Double-click the new clip to load it into the Viewer, and then click the Filters tab.

5. Paste the filters into the new clip's Filters tab.

The new clip will now have the filters from the original.

Now that you know a number of different ways to add filters to a clip, what happens if you've gone overboard and need to remove some filters? We'll look into that in the next section.

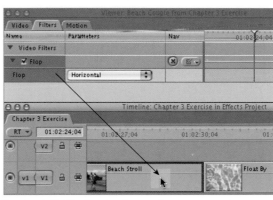

Drag an existing filter from one clip to another

FIGURE 3-22

Drag and drop filters from an existing clip's Filters tab to duplicate their effect in selected clips in the Timeline.

REMOVING FILTER EFFECTS

I've been encouraging you to experiment with adding and combining filters. But any experiment can go awry. Don't worry. You can remove filters if they aren't working out for you. Believe me, you'll want to learn to remove them almost as soon as you learn to add them. Here are some methods for removing errant filters:

- In the Filters tab, click on an unwanted filter and press Delete to remove it. Repeat the process for each filter you want to remove.

- To remove several filters at once, select the first one, then Command + select additional filters and press Delete (see Figure 3-23).

- To remove all filters from a clip, click the Filters tab, press Command + A to select all filters, then press Delete.

- If you need to remove multiple filters from multiple clips, that's a function of Remove Attributes. Select a clip or group of clips and go to Edit → Remove Attributes. The dialog box for Remove Attributes will appear. You can also launch this dialog box by Control + clicking on a clip in the Timeline and choosing Remove Attributes from there. From that dialog box, click in the Filters checkbox, and then click OK. The filters will be removed.

By now you've gained a lot of experience in adding filters and changing Motion and Controls parameters within a clip or group of clips. We'll continue to build on these concepts as we go forward. In the next chapter we're going to talk about animating Motion, Filters, and Controls tab parameters through keyframing, which is great fun and a very satisfying skill to have as a visual artist.

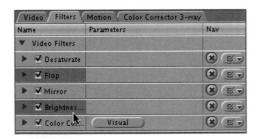

FIGURE 3-23

You can select a group of filters and
remove them at the same time.

Troubleshooting

I'd venture to say that almost any trouble you have with this chapter's exercises stems from not working on the proper copy of the clip. I'll highlight a few scenarios where this would cause problems.

After making a change to a Motion parameter, you don't see the change

You're changing a motion parameter control in the Motion tab, but you don't see it moving or changing in the Canvas and video monitor as you work. What went wrong?

You're probably altering the controls from the master clip, not the Timeline copy of the clip. As much as you try to change a master clip's parameters, it won't change it in the Timeline. This is because any clip changes behavior once it is added to the Timeline.

You can solve any problem that's related to working on the wrong copy of the clip by loading it into the Viewer and working on it there. Check for the sprocket holes (a double row of dots) in the Viewer's Scrubber Bar before making any adjustments to any Filter, Motion, or Controls parameter.

Saving Favorites

Any time you make a great motion path, motion effect, or filters effect, you should save it as a Favorite so you can use it again at any time. Favorites are effects that you create and store in the Favorites bin in the Effects tab.

To save a Favorite motion effect, for example, follow these steps:

1. Select the clip and go to Effects → Make Favorite Motion.

2. Check the Favorites bin to make sure your effect was saved there.

3. Name the effect something pertinent.

Now that you know how to save a motion effect as a Favorite, you should know how to save a filter effect as a Favorite, as well:

1. Select the filter in the Filters tab.

2. Press Option + F. Now, your filter effect will be saved in the Favorites bin.

To use these Favorites, just drag and drop them onto clips, as you would with any other effect.

You don't see any changes in the Canvas after you've added a filter

Filter-application problems can stem from working on the wrong copy of a clip. The problems here are usually related to how you added your Filter, as well as how you attempted to adjust it.

If a clip shows no change, even after you add a filter effect from the Effects menu, you probably added a filter from the Effects menu in the Viewer *before* editing it into the Timeline, and then were attempting to control the master clip from the Filters tab, rather than the proper Timeline copy of the clip.

If you've dragged and dropped a filter on to a clip in the Timeline, but you don't see any changes in the Canvas when you make changes to a parameter, you may have made one of the following mistakes:

■ You forgot to load the clip after you dragged and dropped the filter,

or

■ You double-clicked on a filter straight from the Effects tab. Since it wasn't attached to the proper copy of the clip (or any clip, for that matter), you would not see any change in the Canvas or video monitor.

To remedy this problem, double-click the clip to load it into the Viewer before adding or changing filter effects.

Wrap-up

Now that you've completed this chapter, you should understand how to work with effects using the FCP interface. You should also know that video effects in FCP are made by changing the default parameters of the Motion or Controls tabs or by adding filters to clips and adjusting them. Changing single or multiple parameters in any of the tabs is also something you should feel comfortable with. You even have a method to add multiple filters to a single clip or a group of clips.

Last but not least, you've learned — I hope — that working on the Timeline copy of the clip can solve most problems you have with adding effects. Double-click the clip and find those sprocket holes in the Scrubber Bar, and you'll be OK.

We'll build on these concepts as we go on to learn more advanced techniques for effects creation with Final Cut Pro.

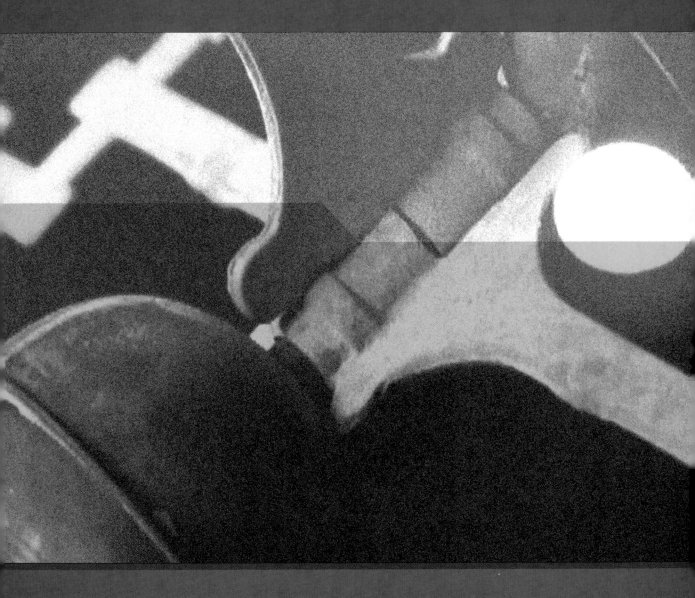

Animating Effects

Now that you have your system set up, your media organized, and the basics of adding and adjusting effects fresh in your mind, you're about to do some very ambitious things. In this chapter you'll learn how to make filter and motion effects animate over time, which is a fundamental part of video effects creation. You'll also learn how to make clips move on motion paths, allowing them to change size, position, or orientation on the screen.

Controlling Animation with Keyframes

Without keyframes, life as a video compositor would be pretty boring. A clip would not change its appearance over time. In a world without keyframes, you could rotate a clip 90 degrees and add a blue tint, and it would stay rotated 90 degrees and tinted blue for the duration of the clip. For that, you probably wouldn't win any awards at your local film festival. But with the techniques you'll learn in this chapter you'll be able to make the clip tumble across the screen, change from blue to red, and engage in all sorts of eye-catching effects.

WHAT ARE KEYFRAMES?

When you set values in Motion, Filters, and Controls tab parameters, a clip takes on certain characteristics. You can mark these values with keyframes. A keyframe represents a precise value for an effect at a particular point in time. To change the value over time, you can add another keyframe. The clip will then change its appearance between the two keyframes.

To make keyframes in Final Cut Pro, you click the diamond-shaped Insert/Delete Keyframe button next to a parameter in the Keyframe Graph of one of the Viewer tabs. (I sometimes call this the Keyframe button for short.) When the button lights up, you're setting a value for that effect at that point in time (see Figure 4-1). You then specify a point later in time and set a different value.

You can also add keyframes in the Canvas to move your clips on curved or straight lines called motion paths. More about these in just a bit.

With FCP 4, many effects will play in real time on your video monitor, so you can adjust the effect's values and then immediately play back the clip with its new settings. In many cases you can adjust keyframes as you preview a clip by checking it in the QuickView window or using some other preview method. Finding the

FIGURE 4-1

When you click the diamond-shaped Insert/Delete Keyframe button, it lights up green to show that a keyframe has been created.

proper adjustment as you preview is a smart way to work, as you'll spend less time rendering keyframed effects that aren't timed quite right.

Now that you know what keyframes are, let's look at the two different types of keyframes.

TYPES OF KEYFRAMES

In the Keyframe Graph in the tabs of the Viewer, and in the new Keyframe Editor in the Timeline, you'll see two kinds of keyframes: one- and two-dimensional keyframes. Note that the naming convention seems backwards, but take my word for it that two-dimensional keyframes have only one value while one-dimensional keyframes have two values (see Figure 4-2). Allow me to explain so that we're all on the same page when discussing particular keyframes:

- **Two-dimensional keyframes** have only one value attached to them. Most filter, motion, and controls effects in FCP (Scale and Rotation, for example) use two-dimensional keyframes. These keyframes are green in the Keyframe Graph. In the Keyframe Editor and Filters and Motion bars, filter keyframes are green and motion keyframes are blue. The best thing about two-dimensional keyframes is that you can "smooth" a keyframe right in the Keyframe Graph or Keyframe Editor. When a keyframe is smoothed, it will offer Bézier handles to make the change between keyframes accelerate or decelerate over time. (More about smoothing in a bit.)

- **One-dimensional keyframes** have multiple values attached to them. For example, Center keyframes are one-dimensional because they have to display values for both the X and the Y axis. One-dimensional keyframes can be smoothed only in the Canvas in Image + Wireframe mode. These keyframes are black in the Keyframe Graph and blue in the Motion bar. Their values can't be adjusted in the Keyframe Editor. You can move them to a different time in the Motion bar, however.

I'll talk more about smoothing these two kinds of keyframes as you work through the rest of this chapter. For now, just remember that there are two kinds of keyframes and that you work with them differently.

tip

Just because you can animate something, that doesn't mean that you should. For example, some filter effects offer a dizzying array of controls, numeric fields, and combinations thereof. You have to make the decision whether to animate certain parameters, while leaving others in an ideally set position.

note

Keyframes can control Motion, Filters, and Controls parameters over multiple video layers, not just those on Video 1. This ability is one of the more powerful features FCP shares with hard-core compositing applications. You'll learn more about compositing clips on various video tracks in Chapter 5.

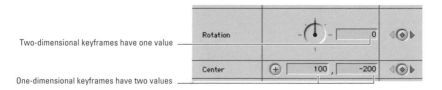

Two-dimensional keyframes have one value

One-dimensional keyframes have two values

FIGURE 4-2

Bear with me on the terminology: two-dimensional keyframes have one value, and one-dimensional keyframes have two values.

HOW TO KEYFRAME EFFECTS

Keyframing isn't hard to do once you have a foolproof method for doing it. After you've loaded the clip into the Viewer, you're ready to move those parameters over time with some basic keyframe techniques.

The best way to demonstrate how to keyframe filter and motion parameters is to jump right into an exercise, so let's get going.

EXERCISE 4-1: KEYFRAMING FILTER AND MOTION PARAMETERS

In this exercise you'll animate filter and motion parameters within a clip. You're going to do some very basic effects here; the goal is to stay focused on the methodology of keyframing, not necessarily the artfulness of your creation.

Open the Chapter 4 bin, and then the Chapter 4 Sequences bin, and double-click the Chapter 4 Exercise sequence. Move to the marker for Exercise 1 to begin this exercise.

A clip has already been edited into the Timeline for you.

1. Load the Timeline copy of the clip into the Viewer. (If you are in Open mode in the Playhead Sync menu, your clip will automatically open in the Viewer if the video track has Auto Select enabled.)

2. Move the playhead to precisely 1:00. To do so, type 100 in the Timeline's Timecode field and press Enter. The playhead will snap to 1:00. (Alternatively, you can drag the playhead to 1:00 in the Timeline Ruler.)

3. Here at 1:00, you'll set the first keyframe for your motion parameters. You're going to keyframe two motion parameters (Scale and Crop) and one filter parameter (Color Correction → Color Control).

   a. Click the Motion tab and enter the following values:

   Basic Motion → Scale: 0

   Crop → Left: 100

   b. Click the diamond-shaped Insert/Delete Keyframe buttons for Scale and Crop; the button turns green for each parameter. (Don't be alarmed when your clip disappears from the Canvas. It's going to scale up from zero and therefore shouldn't be visible at this point.)

4. Drag and drop the Color Corrector 3-Way filter (Effects tab → Video Filters → Color Correction → Color Corrector 3-Way) onto your clip.

    a. Click the Filters tab. Click the disclosure triangle to access the filter's parameters (but don't click the Visual button). You're going to set the first keyframe for one of the parameters of your newly added color-correction effect.

    b. Click the Keyframe button for Color Controls → Saturation. The button turns green. It should be already set to 100, so leave it be.

STEP 4
Drop the Color Corrector 3-Way filter onto the clip.

5. Move the playhead where you want the next keyframe to be. For this exercise, move it to 5:00 by typing 500 and pressing Enter.

6. With the playhead in its new position, change the values of the filter's parameters. New keyframes will be automatically set after the values are changed.

    a. In the Motion tab, enter the following values:

    Scale: 100

    Crop Left: 0

    b. In the Filters tab, enter the following:

    Color Correction → Color Controls → Saturation: 0

STEP 6b
In the Filters tab, set Saturation to 0.

tip

If the Canvas is selected, you can use timecode entry for navigating to a specific timecode, or enter values using your keypad, whether or not the clip is selected. The Q key will quickly toggle between the Viewer and the Canvas.

tip

The keyboard shortcut for Add Motion Keyframe is Control + K.

tip

When you click the Add Keyframe button, you add a keyframe to several motion parameters at once, which is a fast way to work.

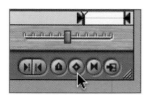

FIGURE 4-3

Click the Add Motion Keyframe button to simultaneously set key-frames for Scale, Rotation, Center, Anchor Point, Crop, and Distort.

7. Press the Home key and then review your effect by pressing the L key or the Space Bar. This is a real-time effect for most systems.

8. Render the effect by selecting the clip and choosing Sequence → Render Selection → Video.

You should now see your clip scaling up, revealing, and turning black-and-white. If it's not doing all three of these things, carefully follow the steps and try again. This is a fairly basic combination of effects, but it should give you a glimpse of what you can pull off with FCP.

Using the Add Motion Keyframe button

The Add Motion Keyframe button is located underneath the Scrubber bars in both the Canvas and the Viewer. The button is used for simultaneously setting keyframes for Scale, Rotation, Center, Anchor Point, Crop, and Distort. I call this setting a *global keyframe*. (See Figure 4-3.)

When using the Add Motion Keyframe button, make sure you're working on the Timeline copy of the clip. Usually, by force of habit, I click the button in the Canvas, as it's unavailable when working in the Keyframe Graph.

If you don't want to keyframe every parameter at once, there's a technique you can use with the Add Motion Keyframe button. If you Control + click directly on the button, a shortcut menu will pop up, giving you access to individual motion parameters rather than the whole group of basic motion effects. (See Figure 4-4.) This is great for avoiding unnecessary keyframing. You can also use the shortcut menu to remove keyframes. Just remove the checkmark next to an item on the menu by clicking it.

Instead of using the Add Motion Keyframe button to make motion keyframes, you can open the Motion tab to access the individual parameters. You also have access to motion parameters in the Keyframe Editor, right in the Timeline.

DELETING KEYFRAMES

If you're in the business of making keyframes, you'll need to know how to remove them as well. It's really quite easy to remove a keyframe, be it in the Motion tab, Filters tab, Controls tab, Keyframe Editor, or in the case of Center keyframes, right in the Canvas. FCP offers a number of methods for removing keyframes, so let's check them out.

To delete a keyframe from a clip in the Viewer, follow these steps:

1. Navigate to the keyframe you wish to delete in the Keyframe Graph or Keyframe Editor.

2. Once the playhead is parked on the keyframe, click the Insert/Delete Keyframe button.

   When the green light is off, the keyframe has been removed at that location for that parameter.

   You can also delete a keyframe from the Keyframe Graph or the Keyframe Editor in one of the following ways:

   - Click the keyframe and drag it away with a flicking motion.

   - Control + click the keyframe and select Clear from the pop-up menu.

   - Click the keyframe with the Pen Minus Tool (PP is the keyboard shortcut).

To delete a keyframe from a clip in the Canvas:

   - Control + click on the keyframe and choose Clear. (We'll be keyframing in the Canvas a bit later in the chapter.)

To delete multiple keyframes of an individual parameter:

   - Click the Reset button (the red "X") next to each parameter for Motion, Controls, or Filters.

Workflow Strategies for Keyframes

Working with keyframes can be cumbersome if you don't have a system in place. In this section I'll show you how to work more effectively with Keyframe Overlays and with the Pen tool in the Keyframe Graph and the new Keyframe Editor. I'll also give you tips on how to navigate to your keyframes quickly and easily. Before we get into those topics, let's tackle the larger subject of keyframe behavior.

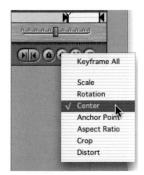

FIGURE 4-4

Control + clicking the Add Motion Keyframe button brings up a menu that lets you add a keyframe to a particular parameter.

note

Clicking the Add Motion Keyframe button will not add keyframes for a filter effect; it's only for motion parameters. With filters, you have to individually click every keyframable parameter you want to change.

tip

If you approach any green Adjust Line in the Keyframe Graph with the Selection tool and hold down the Option key, it will turn into the Pen tool. After a keyframe is set, approaching it once more with the Option key held down will produce the Pen Minus tool.

KEYFRAME BEHAVIOR

Now that you know the basics of how keyframes work, it's necessary to refine your understanding of how keyframes influence effects. Keyframes behave predictably if you keep a few simple rules in mind:

- The farther apart you place your keyframes, the slower an effect will develop over time. The closer they're spaced, the faster an effect will develop.

- An effect can accelerate, decelerate, or move at a constant speed as it leaves or approaches any keyframe. These changes are made with Bézier handles, which will be discussed a bit later in this chapter.

- An effect can change sharply or smoothly, depending on whether a keyframe has been smoothed by Bézier handles or is left as a standard "corner point" keyframe.

- When a clip has many closely spaced keyframes in a parameter, you can add an energetic or even frenzied look to your composition (see Figure 4-5). Conversely, when you've got an effect moving smoothly between two keyframes, you can create a calmer feeling.

You'll get the hang of adjusting keyframe spacing as we continue to work with them throughout the book.

tip

Adjust your keyframes as you're previewing an effect in the QuickView window. That way you can get an idea of how the effect is working before you commit to rendering it.

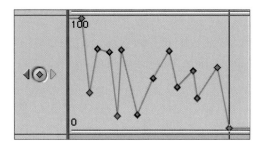

FIGURE 4-5
Closely spaced keyframes can create a frenzied effect.

Keyframe smoothing

When you animate an effect in Final Cut Pro, the default movements of the sliders make the effects move at a constant rate. You can make the changes more gradual by *smoothing* the keyframe (also called *interpolation*). FCP averages the values between keyframes and decides how the picture will look for a particular frame in the Canvas.

Interpolation is also represented visually in the Keyframe Graph and the Keyframe Editor. In both graphs, the keyframe's adjust lines can be either straight (linear) or curved (Bézier). Keyframes use linear interpolation by default. Here are the highlights of the two methods of interpolation:

- **Linear interpolation** means the parameters you keyframe will change at a constant rate. The adjust line between two keyframes in the Keyframe Graph symbolizes this; it goes from point to point at a sharp angle.

- **Bézier interpolation** means effects will change in an accelerated or decelerated manner, according to the curve you make in the Keyframe Graph or Keyframe Editor with Bézier handles.

APPLYING BÉZIER HANDLES TO KEYFRAMES

It's a snap to apply a Bézier curve to keyframes for any parameter in the Keyframe Graph or the Keyframe Editor. (By the way, the following pertains only to applying Bézier curves to two-dimensional keyframes. We'll cover applying the curves to one-dimensional keyframes in the next section.)

To apply Bézier curves to two-dimensional keyframes, follow these steps:

1. Control + click on any two-dimensional keyframe (recall that they are the green ones). A contextual menu appears.

2. Choose Smooth to apply Bézier interpolation. (See Figure 4-6.) The linear keyframe will turn into a Bézier keyframe. Adjustable handles will sprout from that point. Adjusting the curve changes the velocity of the effect.

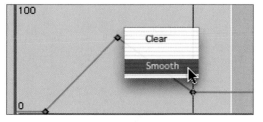

FIGURE 4-6

Control + click a keyframe and choose Smooth from the pop-up menu to turn it into a Bézier curve with adjustable handles.

Once you convert a linear keyframe to a Bézier keyframe, you may want to preview the effect right then. In the default setting, Bézier interpolation will make the values change more smoothly. Often, smoothing is the only thing you need to do to make an effect look attractive.

Adjusting Bézier curves

You can click on a keyframe's Bézier handles and drag them to suit your tastes. Drag the handles up or down, or stretch them away from or toward the keyframe.

Bézier handles behave in the following ways:

- The first and the last keyframe for any parameter has only one handle, called a *velocity handle*. This handle is most useful for accelerating out of and decelerating into the first and last keyframes.

- Keyframes between the first and last keyframes have two-sided Bézier handles. These handles are locked together until you "break" them (more on that in the next section). The locked behavior is useful for making very smooth transitions as the clip plays through the keyframe.

tip

Expand the work area for the Keyframe Graph or Keyframe Editor to work more easily with Bézier handles for keyframes.

- In their default state, the handles behave like a seesaw. If you drag down on the handle of a two-sided Bézier, the other side of the handle will move up by an equal amount (see Figure 4-7).

- By stretching Bézier handles, you can vastly alter the steepness of the curve. If you stretch the handle on one side, the other will stretch an equal amount.

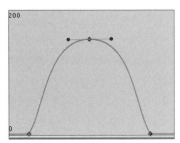 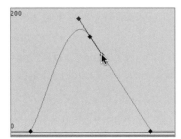

FIGURE 4-7

When you drag down on a Bézier handle, the other side of the handle will move up an equal amount, reshaping the curve (right).

Altering Bézier handles

By using a combination of keyboard modifiers and clicking and dragging, you can "break" the Bézier handles from their default state. You can then create curves in the Keyframe Graph or Keyframe Editor that offer a variety of ways to affect motion, controls, and filters.

tip

You can use both positive and negative numeric values in almost every parameter of all the Viewer tabs. However, each parameter has a limit to the values you can apply.

- Hold down the Shift key to change one side of a Bézier curve independently of the other. Release the Shift key to lock the handles back together. Using the new, unequal lengths you set, you can alter the newly shaped handle by clicking and dragging it. (See Figure 4-8.)

- To change the angle of the Bézier handle, click and drag on one side while holding down the Command key. Release the Command key to set the shape of the handle, then click and drag the handle to adjust the new curve.

- The Shift + Command key combination will allow you to do both of these things at the same time.

FIGURE 4-8

The handle on the left is a standard Bézier handle; the one on the right has been "broken."

When you alter the Bézier handles as just described, you can adjust the original curve to make your control parameters change gradually or wildly. Take some time to experiment with Bézier handles.

Returning keyframes to linear interpolation

If you find that an experiment with a keyframe's Bézier curve didn't work out, you can return the curve to linear interpolation and start over. Here's how:

1. Control + click on the keyframe in the Keyframe Graph of your chosen parameter.

2. Choose Corner from the pop-up menu. The keyframe returns to linear interpolation. (See Figure 4-9.)

or

1. Get the Pen Smooth Tool (PPP is the keyboard shortcut).

2. Click on the keyframe with the tool. The keyframe returns to linear interpolation.

You can then switch back to Bézier keyframes and try your effect again. Choose Smooth in the contextual menu to return to Bézier interpolation.

tip

The Scale parameter has a logarithmic slider that will prevent you from scaling something up evenly — unless you Control + click on a keyframe and choose Smooth. As odd as it sounds, if you adjust the Bézier handle so the curve is sagging just a bit, a clip will scale more evenly.

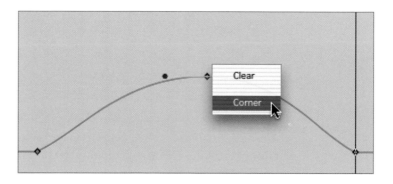

FIGURE 4-9

To return a keyframe to linear interpolation, Control + click on the keyframe and choose Corner from the pop-up menu.

The Case for Navigation

Keyframe navigation not only gets you where you want to go in a hurry, but also helps assure that you have the playhead parked precisely on a particular keyframe. There are two main reasons why you want to position the playhead precisely: to make and monitor changes to a keyframe and to prevent placing unintended keyframes.

Being parked on a keyframe gives you the ability to alter the parameters of an effect while seeing the results in the Canvas and on your video monitor. This process is called *monitoring an effect*. When you've visually reached a suitable setting for that keyframe, you're free to move on to your next task. You might also want to park on a keyframe to delete it easily.

Being parked directly on a keyframe also helps prevent you from adding any unwanted keyframes. If the playhead isn't parked directly on a keyframe, you'll add another keyframe at the playhead's current location if you adjust a parameter. This can produce less than desirable results, usually a "hiccup" in movement or a filter misbehaving.

KEYFRAME NAVIGATION

You'll want to navigate quickly between keyframes so you can make adjustments to them. You can navigate between keyframes directly in the Motion, Filters, and Controls tabs. The Keyframe Editor requires a different technique, which I'll describe a bit later.

Navigating in the Keyframe Graph

In Chapter 3 we briefly discussed the keyframe navigational triangles (which you can think of as "arrows"). Now you'll see just how they're used. These triangles are for navigating precisely between keyframes in the tabs of the Viewer. To review, you'll find these small navigational triangles in the Nav bar of the Motion, Filters, and Controls tabs. They help you move quickly between keyframes so that you can adjust or remove them.

It's helpful to know the location of other keyframes in the Keyframe Graph when you're zoomed too close or too far to see the surrounding keyframes. You can use the triangles to reveal whether there are other keyframes for that parameter: before it, after it, or in both directions. (See Figure 4-10.)

Keyframe navigation shortcuts

The following keyboard shortcuts are very useful for navigating to keyframes for Motion, Filters, and Controls tab parameters. The shortcuts are also the key to navigating from keyframe to keyframe in the Keyframe Editor.

- Shift + K takes you to the next keyframe
- Option + K takes you to the previous keyframe

Changing keyframe values at a different location

So far I've stressed the importance of navigating the playhead to a keyframe if you want to change its value without adding an errant keyframe. This is not the only way to change a parameter that's already been set, however. You can also change a keyframe value without worrying where the playhead is parked. Here's how:

- In the Keyframe Graph or the Keyframe Editor, use the Selection tool to click and drag the keyframe up or down. (The tool should turn into a small crosshairs as you drag the keyframe.) You're on the right track when a pop-up helper tells you the precise value of how much you're changing the keyframe.

note

If you want the playhead to move from keyframe to keyframe in the Timeline without the Keyframe Editor open, you'll have to select the clip or clips first. The Tracks Forward tools are handy for this task.

If there's an arrow to the right of a parameter's Insert/Delete Keyframe button, you'll find one or more keyframes later in the Timeline.

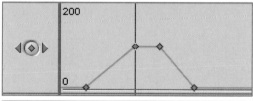

If there are arrows on both sides of a Insert/Delete Keyframe button, and the diamond is lit, there are keyframes both before and after the current playhead position, including a keyframe set for that point in time.

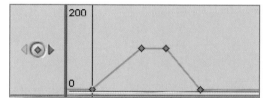

If there are arrows on both sides of a Insert/Delete Keyframe button, but the diamond is not lit, there are keyframes both before and after the current playhad position, but there is no keyframe set for that point in time.

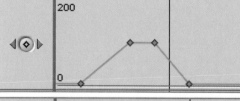

If there's an arrow to the left of the Insert/Delete Keyframe button, there are one or more keyframes earlier in the Timeline.

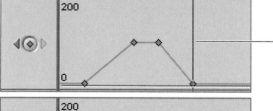

Playhead

If the arrows are grayed out, there are no keyframes set for that parameter.

FIGURE 4-10

The navigation triangles in the Keyframe Graph can help you determine where keyframes are located.

tip

If you think you'll have many parameters to change across multiple tabs, making a marker (by pressing the M key) while working in the Keyframe Graph is always a good idea. That way you can stay focused on a point in time when scrolling up and down the interface. It's also a good idea to add a marker in the Timeline, so that when you're working in the Keyframe Editor you can stay focused on creating keyframes in different parameters at the same point in time.

This technique is helpful if you want to monitor how a parameter is affecting a clip at a different point in time, rather than how it looks after it has finished animating. In other words, if you're previewing another frame of the effect, this can be an excellent way to see the intensity of your effect at a time other than at a keyframe.

The only "gotcha" here is that you need to be sure you're dragging and adjusting directly on the keyframe itself in the Keyframe Graph or Keyframe Editor, rather than manipulating the sliders or numeric fields. Doing the latter will make a new keyframe if the playhead is not parked on the keyframe you want to adjust.

KEYFRAME OVERLAYS

In the bottom-left corner of the Timeline are five buttons. The one that looks like a line graph is called *Keyframe Overlays*. Click the button to enable it. (See Figure 4-11.)

Keyframe overlays allow you to adjust opacity levels and audio levels, and give you the ability to keyframe these two parameters directly on the clip in the Timeline.

In the Timeline, opacity is represented by a black line in the video portion of the clip. Pink lines in the audio portion of the clip represent audio levels. (See Figure 4-12.) As you approach the lines representing these parameters, the Selection tool turns into the Adjustment Line Segment pointer. You use this tool to drag a clip's audio or video adjust lines up or down. More often than not, you'll want to keyframe these parameters right in the Timeline. It's easy enough to do; just use the Pen tool, which we'll look into next.

tip

With Keyframe Overlays enabled, you can Control + click an opacity keyframe in the Timeline to turn it into a Bézier curve.

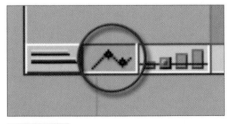

FIGURE 4-11
Click the Keyframe Overlays button to enable it.

FIGURE 4-12
The black line represents opacity.
The pink line represents audio level.

USING THE PEN TOOL IN THE VIEWER AND TIMELINE

With the Pen tool, you can click precisely where you want to add a keyframe. By using the Pen tool in the Timeline, you can fade a clip's opacity or audio level up or down at the beginning or end of the clip. You can also ramp opacity and audio levels up or down in the middle of a clip. Opacity and audio levels are real-time effects, so you can easily tweak the keyframes to quickly adjust your blends and fades. You can work with the Pen tool in the Keyframe Graph, Timeline, or — in the case of Center keyframes from the Motion tab — directly in the Canvas.

The Pen tool and Keyframe Overlays

You can use the Pen tool to adjust opacity and audio levels directly in the Timeline.

To create a fade effect in the Timeline, follow these steps:

1. Click the Keyframe Overlays button to enable it.

2. Click the Pen tool in the Tool Palette (or press the P key).

To fade up opacity at the beginning of a clip, follow these steps:

1. With the Pen tool, click on the black opacity line where you want the effect to be fully faded up. (See Figure 4-13.) For example, you may want to be fully faded up from black at 1:00. A keyframe is set at that point.

2. Click at the beginning of the clip to add that important second keyframe (see Figure 4-14).

3. Click and drag the keyframe at :00 in a downward motion to fade the opacity level down to 0 (see Figure 4-15). You should see the small black opacity line ramping up to 100 at 1:00 on the Timeline.

Keyframes in Other Applications

Most programs for motion graphics designers offer some form of advanced keyframing. For example, keyframing capabilities not found in FCP are available in programs like Adobe After Effects, Boris RED, Cinema 4D, and Maya. You can include LiveType with this crowd as well, because it offers some advanced keyframing stunts.

The difference between Final Cut Pro keyframes and those in some of the other motion graphics applications is that the latter provide an array of behavior-specific keyframes and keyframe "assistants." Keyframes in those applications can make effects hold in a constant pattern, reverse an action, loop events, rush to the next keyframe at the last minute, and perform other tricks that you can't typically do in FCP.

Boris RED plugs into Final Cut Pro, so you can use its advanced keyframe techniques without leaving FCP. You'll be working within the RED timeline as you do the advanced work, though.

LiveType's keyframing is fantastic, but I still recommend having an additional application for advanced keyframing. Programs like Boris RED and After Effects are essential for serious motion graphics artists.

FIGURE 4-13

Click the black opacity line with the Pen tool.

FIGURE 4-14

Set a keyframe for Opacity to fade up.

FIGURE 4-15

Drag the keyframe downward to make the Opacity level fade up.

To fade down opacity at the end of a clip, follow these steps:

1. With the Pen tool, click the black opacity line where you want the effect to begin fading down. A keyframe is set at that point.

2. To add the second keyframe, click where the effect should be fully faded down.

3. Click and drag the keyframe in a downward motion to fade the opacity level down to 0.

Adding Keyframes in the Keyframe Graph using the Pen tool

The great thing about the Pen tool is that you can add keyframes at precise points in time without worrying about the position of the playhead. To add keyframes:

1. In the Motion, Filters, or Controls tab, approach the keyframe adjust line in the Keyframe Graph with the Pen tool. (You can also use the Selection tool; just hold down the Option key and it will temporarily turn into the Pen tool.)

2. With the Pen tool, click in the location where you'd like a keyframe for that parameter. A keyframe is added at that point.

3. Adjust the keyframe if necessary, and preview your effect.

Adding Keyframes in the Keyframe Editor using the Pen tool

When you've got the Clip Keyframes button engaged, you can add keyframes right in Keyframe Editor. Here's how:

1. Engage the Line Graph for the parameter you want to work on by Control + clicking in the work area of the Keyframe Editor. In the contextual menu that appears, choose the parameter you want to adjust.

2. Click on the adjust line with the Pen tool to add keyframes to the animation.

Rubberbanding using the Pen tool

The term *rubberbanding* refers to fading certain parameters down for a time, then back up. You can easily achieve rubberbanding using the Pen tool. This technique works in the Timeline with opacity and audio keyframes, and in the Keyframe Graph and Keyframe Editor with any keyframes.

It's easy to visualize this with an example from the audio world. You'd probably want to fade down a backing music track for a short time to make it softer during a voiceover, and then fade the audio back up after the VO was complete. For video opacity, you could introduce a superimposed image for a period of time, and then fade it out.

For this operation, you'll need to set four keyframes: one to hold the starting value of the parameter in place, another placed quite close to the first to ramp the effect up or down, a third (usually equal in value to the second keyframe) to keep the parameter locked into place, and a final keyframe to ramp the effect back to its original value. (See Figure 4-16.)

tip

Adding keyframes with the Pen tool could come in handy for making keyframes for a music video. You could align FCP Timeline markers (keyboard shortcut M) with audio waveforms, and then go back with the Pen tool and add some keyframes at those marked points.

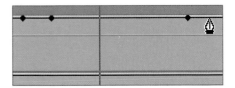 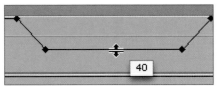

FIGURE 4-16
To use the rubberbanding technique you'll first need to set four keyframes. Next, drag the adjust line to fade the parameter up or down.

Motion Paths

Motion paths provide the "flight plans" for clips. You might say they put the "motion" in motion graphics, the very essence of this book.

Motion paths are visible on the Canvas when you engage Image + Wireframe or Wireframe mode. The clip moves on the lines and curves of the motion paths that are created with two (or more) Center keyframes. If there are only two keyframes set, then the motion path is called a *simple motion path*. If many keyframes are used, then it is deemed a *complex motion path*.

CREATING A MOTION PATH

You can think of keyframes in the Canvas as points that create a curve or a line. Motion paths can be very simple, or can have lots of twists and turns. You can change the shape of the motion path from a straight line to a curve by clicking and dragging on Bézier handles, much as you've already seen with two-dimensional keyframes. These handles are enabled by Control + clicking directly on the keyframes in the Canvas, not the Keyframe Graph or Keyframe Editor. We'll practice working with motion paths shortly.

There are two flavors of Center keyframes that create the paths: *linear* and *corner point* keyframes. Linear keyframes create a curved path, while corner point keyframes create a path with angles. Regardless of whether the Center keyframe is a linear or corner point keyframe, it's a one-dimensional keyframe, meaning that it has two values and can be smoothed in the Canvas.

The Bézier control handle for Center keyframes

The Bézier handles that emanate from Center keyframes control both the shape and velocity of a motion path. You will deal with these Bézier control handles only in the Canvas. When a Center keyframe is set as Ease In/Ease Out or Linear, it will carry a two-sided Bézier handle that's a bit different than the Bézier handle you manipulated for two-dimensional keyframes. The handle appears as a purple bar extending from the keyframe with a large purple dot at either end of it (see Figure 4-17). These handles control not only the shape of a motion path, but also the clip's velocity as it flies along the path.

Keep the following points in mind when you're working with Bézier handles for Center keyframes:

- You control the shape of the path by moving Bézier handles.

- You control the velocity by clicking and dragging small purple velocity-control "dots" on the bar of the Bézier handle.

Moving a Bézier handle

Controlling Bézier handles in the Canvas for a Center keyframe is identical to dealing with them in the Keyframe Graph or the Keyframe Editor. Dragging one side of the handle causes the other side to move as well, altering the shape of the curve.

Bézier handle   Velocity tic marks

Velocity handle
(Velocity dot)

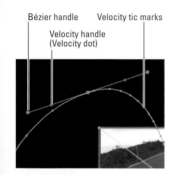

FIGURE 4-17

Center keyframes have a large purple dot at each end of the Bézier handle.

Altering a Bézier handle

By using a combination of keyboard modifiers and clicking and dragging, you can "break" Center keyframes' Bézier handles from their default state. Once they're broken, you can create complex, asymmetrical shapes.

- As with Keyframe Graph Bézier handles, you can stretch one side of a curve independently of the other by holding down the Shift key. Release the Shift key to lock the handles back together using the new, unequal lengths you set.

- Change the angle of the Bézier handle by clicking and dragging on one side with the Command key held down. Release the Command key to set the shape of the handle.

- The Shift + Command key combination allows you to do both of these things at the same time.

- By stretching the Bézier handles, you can vastly alter the steepness of the curve.

When you alter the Bézier handles in the ways just described, you can bend a motion path into new and interesting shapes.

Controlling the velocity of a motion path

You should be aware of a couple of additional features of these Center-parameter Bézier handles.

Look closely and check out the small purple dots about halfway down the bar. I refer to these as *velocity dots* because they alter the velocity of a clip as it travels on a motion path. Let's see how these velocity dots work.

Clicking and dragging the velocity dots on the Bézier handle makes the small purple tic marks in the motion path "bunch up" toward or spread out away from the keyframe. This gives you a visual representation of the clip's speed (see Figure 4-17).

You can do this in a couple of ways:

- Click and drag the velocity dots on the Bézier handle. Doing so adjusts the tic marks.

or

- Control + click the keyframe in the Canvas and select Ease In/Ease Out. This will give you a nice velocity change from the default linear keyframe setting. You can return to the purple dot if you need to tweak it a bit.

> **tip**
>
> *To quickly create a loop in a motion path, twist the Bézier handle 180 degrees. The linear keyframe you loop must be next to a corner point keyframe. The size of the loop is determined by how far you stretch the Bézier handle.*

Rules of thumb for velocity

Keep an eye on the tic marks on the motion path as you adjust the velocity dots on the Bézier handle. Getting immediate visual feedback of the clip moving on the motion path is definitely a power move, so preview your clip as you adjust it.

As you adjust the velocity dots, keep the following in mind:

- The closer the tic marks are to each other, the slower the clip will accelerate as it leaves a keyframe or decelerate as it reaches a keyframe. The further apart the tic marks are, the faster a clip will accelerate or decelerate.

- To reset a clip's velocity to a constant speed, Control + click on the keyframe and choose Linear. This will return a linear keyframe's velocity to its default state.

- You can adjust one side of a curve's velocity. By holding down the Shift key as you adjust the velocity dots on the Bézier handle, you'll see the tic marks move on only one side of the curve.

- If you zoom in on the Canvas and tweak the dots just a little, you can control the velocity with much more precision as you preview the effect in the QuickView window.

Now you have the information you need to make motion paths and precisely control the velocity of the clips moving on them.

FIGURE 4-18

Simple motion paths provide elegant movement and are easy to control.

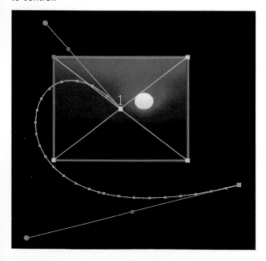

SIMPLE MOTION PATHS

Almost all the motion paths you make should be simple, two-keyframe motion paths, as they are the most elegant and the easiest to control. In my opinion, if you're tempted to add a third keyframe, you probably aren't trying hard enough. (See Figure 4-18.) That said, we'll be creating complex motion paths later in the chapter — but you definitely should master simple motion paths before you go down that road.

EXERCISE 4-2: MOVING A CLIP IN IMAGE + WIREFRAME MODE

A simple motion path is in almost every case an open path, meaning that it starts in one place and ends in a different place, on or off the Canvas. In this exercise, we'll create the simplest of all motion paths, a straight line.

Locate the Chapter 4 Exercise sequence. Double-click the sequence to open it, and then move to the Exercise 2 marker. A clip has already been edited into the Timeline for you.

1. Load the Timeline copy of the clip into the Viewer by double-clicking it.

2. Ensure that you're in Image + Wireframe mode by pulling down the View Mode menu and selecting it (or toggle the W key).

3. In the Timeline, move the playhead near the beginning of the clip. Click the Motion tab so you can view the clip's motion parameters.

4. Scale down the wireframe by clicking and dragging on a corner of a clip with the Selection tool in the Canvas. Drag toward the center point of the clip to scale it to approximately 30% of its original size. Click and drag the clip to the lower-right corner of the Canvas.

5. Next to the Center parameter, click on the diamond-shaped Keyframe button in the Nav column. It should turn green. You've now set the first keyframe.

6. In the Timeline, move the playhead ahead 4:00.

7. Hold down the Shift key and click and drag the scaled-down wireframe horizontally to the other side of the Canvas. You should see a path of dots trailing from the clip as you drag in a straight line. Once you've moved the clip to where you want it, let go of the mouse button and then the Shift key. (If you don't see a motion path, you probably forgot to move the playhead in the previous step.)

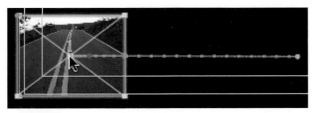

STEP 7

You should see a line of dots trailing from the clip as you drag it in the Canvas.

tip

Did you know you can move an entire motion path all at once? Park the playhead on a Center keyframe, and then click and drag the path to a new area of the Canvas while holding down the Shift and Command keys.

8. Preview your effect until you're satisfied with the movement. Render the effect if you like.

9. Save the motion path as a Favorite by pressing Control + F. Locate it in the Favorites bin in the Effects tab and name it "Straight Line."

Now that you're warmed up when it comes to keyframing motion paths, you're set to tackle more complex duties. But for now, since we'll be dealing with adjusting and manipulating keyframes directly on the Canvas, let's get a few details straight about Center keyframe behavior.

KEYFRAME BEHAVIOR ON MOTION PATHS

When a clip is moving on a motion path, you can expect keyframes to exhibit the following characteristics:

■ Between two Center keyframes, clips can travel either in straight lines or curves.

■ By changing the arrangement of the dots on a motion path with the purple velocity-control dot, you can make a clip accelerate, decelerate, or remain constant in velocity as it leaves or approaches a Center keyframe.

■ A Center keyframe can behave as either a sharp corner point or a smooth curve.

■ The closer together two Center keyframes are placed on the Canvas, the more slowly a clip will move between them. The farther apart two Center keyframes are placed, the more quickly a clip will move between them.

EXERCISE 4-3: MODIFYING A SIMPLE MOTION PATH

In this exercise we'll take the "Straight Line" motion path you just created and change it into a graceful arc. Here, the goal is to make your sharp-edged corner-point keyframes change into smoothly curving linear keyframes.

Double-click the Chapter 4 Exercise sequence to open it, and go to the Exercise 3 marker. A clip has been placed in the Timeline for you.

1. Load the Timeline copy of the clip into the Viewer by double-clicking it. Look for the double dots in the Scrubber Bar. You should still be in Image + Wireframe mode.

2. Locate your saved Favorite called "Straight Line." Drag and drop the Favorite icon onto the clip in the Timeline.

3. We'll now modify the motion path of the straight line to form an arc on which to fly your clip.

   a. With the clip selected in the Timeline, Control + click the clip's keyframe (the green dot) on the right in the Canvas.

   b. Choose Linear from the contextual menu.

   c. Do the same for the keyframe on the left. The motion path should look a bit different; there will be a couple of purple dots near each keyframe. (You could also choose Ease In/Ease Out from the contextual menu to induce Bézier handles from Center keyframes; we'll discuss that a bit later.)

4. Select the Zoom tool from the Tool Palette (or use the keyboard shortcut Z) and lasso one of the keyframes in the Canvas to inspect the area more closely.

5. Switch back to the Selection tool and approach the large purple dot along the line. The tool will turn into small crosshairs. Click and drag the purple dot upward. Note that it's actually a Bézier handle that "pulls" up or down on the motion path like a rubber band. Leave the handle set pointing upward.

6. While you're still zoomed in, click the Hand tool in the Tool Palette (or use the keyboard shortcut H). Click and drag the Hand to the area of the other keyframe.

7. Switch to the Selection tool and click and drag upward on the larger of the two purple dots coming from the keyframe. Drag the handle slightly upward to mirror the way you set the other handle.

Your straight motion path is now a graceful arc.

8. Choose Fit to Window in the View Mode pop-up menu. Your straight motion path has turned into an arc.

9. Preview the effect to make sure it's what you want.

10. Save the motion path as a Favorite. When it shows up in the Effects tab's Favorites bin, name it "Small Arc."

11. Save the project.

You've now created some motion paths, and with a little practice you'll get very good at making them.

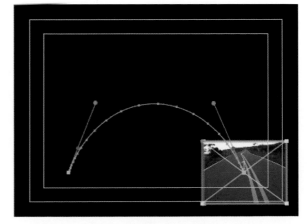

What Do Ease In/Ease Out and Linear Mean?

Ease In/Ease Out and *Linear* are terms related to the velocity of a clip as it moves through keyframes.

When you Control + click on a Center keyframe, you have a few choices in the contextual menu. Both Ease In/Ease Out and Linear keyframes will give you Bézier handles to control not only the curves of the motion path, but also the velocity of the clip as it flies along the path.

You might have trouble understanding what happens when you choose either of these common keyframe behaviors. See if these definitions help:

- **Ease Out** refers to a clip leaving a keyframe position more slowly and softly than linear interpolation. Only the first keyframe in a motion path can be an Ease Out keyframe.

- **Ease In** refers to a clip landing on a keyframe position more slowly and softly than linear interpolation. Only the final keyframe in a motion path can be an Ease In keyframe.

- **Ease In/Ease Out** behavior applies only to a keyframe between the first and last keyframes. This will give the clip a "slingshot" feel as it travels through the keyframe.

- **Linear** means the keyframe velocity of the clip is constant, whether it's the first keyframe, the last keyframe, or one between.

COMPLEX MOTION PATHS

Although most of the time you can get the lion's share of your work done with a simple motion path, sometimes you need a clip to do a few tricks before it exits the video composite. For example, a clip could fly on, present itself for a few seconds, then move to another part of the screen as it faded or scaled down a few seconds later. That's where complex motion paths come in. A complex motion path contains more than two keyframes. It can have three keyframes or a hundred (see Figure 4-19).

Complex motion paths, like simple motion paths, can have Bézier curves, corner points, or both. The shape of the curve you make is controlled by a Bézier handle.

A complex motion path is usually required for a special effect such as a *closed motion path:* a circle, square, or polygonal shape. A closed motion path has its first and last keyframe set at the same X, Y positions at different points in time. (You'll make a closed motion path a little later in the chapter.)

As another example, if you wanted an element in your clip to jitter and shake, you'd need to set many Center keyframes over a short period of time to make an angular complex motion path.

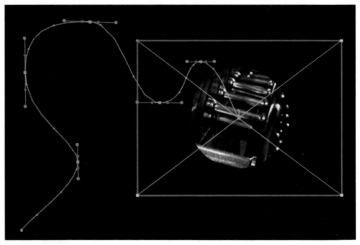

FIGURE 4-19

A complex motion path can have dozens of keyframes.

For me, the easiest way to make a complex motion path is to modify a simple motion path, but you can also create one from scratch if you like. The next section will give you advice on how to approach both of these techniques.

Creating a complex motion path from scratch

You can make a complex motion path from scratch by using one of two techniques: the playhead method or the Pen tool method.

The more intuitive approach is the playhead technique, where you move a wireframe on the Canvas. The Pen tool method is useful for setting keyframes at particular points in time — musical beats, for instance — and then deciding how your motion path should look after the timing is set the way you wish.

Playhead method:

1. Double-click a clip in the Timeline, and then place the playhead where you want the clip to start moving.

2. Set your first keyframe for Center (Control + K).

3. Move the playhead to the next place you want your clip to move.

4. Move the wireframe to a different part of the Canvas. A new keyframe is set.

5. Repeat steps 3 and 4 until you finish your motion path.

Pen tool method:

1. Double-click the clip to reload it into the Viewer.

2. In the Keyframe Graph and in the Center parameter, click with the Pen tool where you want to place the keyframes for your motion path. Use the Timeline Ruler, Viewer Ruler, Markers, or Audio Waveforms to help you find where you wish to place the keyframes.

3. Navigate to the first keyframe in the Viewer or Timeline.

4. Drag the wireframe to the area of the Canvas where you want to place that keyframe.

5. Repeat the steps 3 and 4. Each time you navigate to a new keyframe, move the wireframe.

note

As you're experimenting with motion paths, you might want to scale down your clip and zoom out your Canvas to 50% or so. Also, make sure you're in Image + Wireframe mode.

Making a complex motion path from a simple motion path

You can make a complex motion path by modifying an existing simple motion path. There are a few different ways to do this.

- Playhead method:

    1. Place the playhead in a position other than on the first or last keyframe of the existing simple motion path, and then drag the wireframe to new area of the Canvas. You will make a Corner Point keyframe in this instance.

    2. If you wish to make additional Center keyframes, move the playhead to another place in the Timeline and then drag the wireframe to a new location.

- Pen tool method (Canvas):

    1. With the Pen tool, click directly on the existing motion path to add a keyframe.

    2. Use the Selection tool to move the keyframe to a new location on the Canvas. The motion path will follow as you drag. You'll get a linear keyframe with a Bézier handle.

    3. Once you place your keyframe in its new location, you can drag the Bézier handle to reshape the curve.

    4. To make additional Center keyframes using this technique, click on different sections of the existing motion path with the Pen tool to make each new keyframe.

- Pen tool method (Keyframe Graph):

    1. After you've made a simple motion path, click with the Pen tool between the two existing keyframes for the Center parameter in the Keyframe Graph.

    2. Use the Pen tool or the Selection tool to drag the resulting keyframes in the Canvas to the position you want. Corner-point keyframes will result.

    3. If you want to make additional Center keyframes, just click in the Keyframe Graph with the Pen tool to make each new keyframe. (Make sure you're parked on the keyframe while you drag the wireframe to a new position on the Canvas, or you will make keyframes you don't need.)

Going though the above scenarios will prepare you for creating complex motion paths. To lock in a few of these concepts, let's step through a simple exercise.

EXERCISE 4-4: CREATING A COMPLEX MOTION PATH

In this exercise you'll learn the rudiments of making complex motion paths. You'll first learn how to change linear keyframes to corner-point keyframes, and then you'll see how to use the Pen tool to create additional keyframes.

Return to the Chapter 4 Sequences bin and open the Chapter 4 Exercise sequence. Move to the Exercise 4 marker.

1. Lasso all three clips to select them, and then drag and drop your "Straight Line" motion path from Exercise 4-2 onto any of the clips.

2. Drag the playhead to a position between the two keyframes. The wireframe moves to a different spot on the motion path.

3. Drag the wireframe to a new position on the Canvas. A new keyframe is automatically set. It should be a corner-point keyframe.

4. Preview the effect and then save it as "Corner Point Path."

You'll now make a corner point into a linear keyframe, which will turn it into a smooth curve that you can adjust.

5. Control + click on the newly set corner-point keyframe. Choose Linear from the contextual menu to make the keyframe add a curve to the motion path.

6. Adjust the Bézier handles to your satisfaction.

7. Preview the effect, then save and name it.

You'll now use the Pen tool to add keyframes to an existing motion path on a different clip.

8. Move the playhead to the second clip and select it. With the Pen tool, click anywhere along the preset motion path to make a new keyframe.

9. With the Selection tool, click and drag the new keyframe to another area of the Canvas. This time, the keyframe that's added is a linear keyframe with Bézier handles instead of a corner point. (Recall that you got a corner point by just dragging out the wireframe.)

10. Adjust the Bézier handles to your satisfaction.

11. Preview the effect, then save it as a favorite by pressing Control + F. Name it in your Favorites bin.

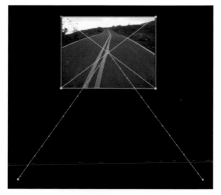

STEP 3

A new keyframe is automatically set when you drag the wireframe to a new position.

You can also set the Center parameter right in the Keyframe Graph:

12. Drag the playhead to a point midway through the third clip, and then double-click the clip to load it into the Viewer. In the Motion tab, enter new values for Center. A new keyframe will be set. (Alternatively, you can make a new keyframe by just clicking between the existing key-frames with the Pen tool.) Your new keyframe will now stand at a new X, Y position in the Canvas, and the motion path will be altered.

13. Preview the effect, and then save it as a Favorite. Save the project.

Making closed motion paths

Before we end this chapter, there's one last skill I want you to have: creating a closed motion path. With a closed motion path you can make a clip travel around a motion path and then return to its starting position. A closed motion path can be a polygon or an ellipse.

A circular motion path is a handy thing to have around. You could use it to make clips orbit around other clips, for example. I'll show you how to use a Circle generator to precisely adjust your circular motion path.

EXERCISE 4-5: MAKING A CIRCULAR CLOSED MOTION PATH

In this exercise you'll be making a circular motion path. Move to the marker for Exercise 5. A clip has been added to the Timeline, as well as a Circle generator on V2, with its visiblity turned off.

1. In Image + Wireframe mode, scale the clip to 25% so you can work with it easily. Place the wireframe at the bottom of the Canvas. After you've done that, load the clip into the Viewer.

2. Put the playhead near the beginning of the clip and set your first Center keyframe in the Motion tab. Clean up the X, Y values as follows:

   Keyframe 1:   X = 0   Y = 80

3. Press Shift + Right Arrow three times to place the playhead 3:00 later, and then click and drag the clip upward in the Canvas. Reset the values to read as follows:

   Keyframe 2:   X = 0   Y = −80

tip

You can return your Center parameter keyframe to a default corner point. Just Control + click the linear keyframe in the Canvas and choose Make Corner Point from the pop-up menu. Alternatively, you could click the keyframe with the Pen Smooth tool to return to a corner point.

4. Place the playhead near the end of the clip and set the keyframe values in the Motion tab to the following:

    Keyframe 3:   X = 0   Y = 75

5. The values of Keyframe 3 are slightly different from those of Keyframe 1 so you can Control + click on it a bit more easily to bring up a Bézier handle. (You may need to zoom into the Canvas a bit to see the Bézier handle.) Once you've Control + clicked on it, choose Linear and drag the Bézier handle to a horizontal position. Repeat the process to add Bézier handles to the first and second keyframes. Clean up those numeric values in the Motion tab:

    Keyframe 3 (reset):   X = 0   Y = 80

6. Adjust the Bézier handle and the two velocity handles until you've created a circular shape.

7. Click on the Shape Generator in the Timeline and press Control + B to turn the clip's visibility back on.

8. Load the Circle generator into the Viewer, and then click the Viewer's Controls tab.

9. Set the Size to 65% and the Softness to 0. Then press Enter.

10. Click on the original clip on V1 and use the circle shape you see on V2 as a guide to make your motion path as perfectly round as possible. (You won't see your clip right now, as the circle is covering it up.)

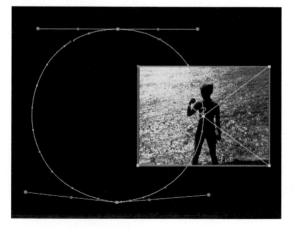

STEP 10
You will use the Shape generator as a guide to adjust the path.

11. After you're satisfied with the shape, select the Circle Shape generator and press Control + B once more to hide it and show your clip.

12. Preview the effect to see your clip travel in a circle. Save your Circular Motion Path as a Favorite. Name it "Circle" and save it. Then save your project.

You've learned a lot in this exercise. By using the Shape generator as your guide in making the circular motion path, you received your first lesson in dealing with more than one video track.

Troubleshooting

Keyframing problems are probably the most vexing issues facing new video compositors. Most keyframing problems can be solved by looking for keyframes you might have added by mistake.

Also, keep in mind that the issue that trips people up most often is not working on the proper copy of a clip. Review the previous chapter if you think you're having problems with that.

A motion effect hiccups or stutters as it plays

You probably changed a parameter when your playhead was not parked on the keyframe you were intending to alter. By merely nudging a wireframe or slider by mistake, you'll add an unwanted keyframe.

To fix this, double-click the clip and carefully examine the keyframes in the area around the "hiccup." Inspect the various Viewer tabs until you locate the parameter that's giving you problems. Zoom in on the Keyframe Graph area and navigate to each keyframe using the keyframe navigation techniques you've learned. Remove the bum keyframe and you should be good to go. You'll need to re-render the effect.

A clip isn't changing parameters over time

Either you're not working on the proper copy of the clip or you didn't keyframe the parameter properly. For example, you may have keyframed a value that was exactly the same as the first keyframe, causing no change in its parameter.

If you aren't positive that you added the effect to the proper copy of the clip, double-click the clip in the Timeline and inspect the appropriate Viewer tab to check it out. If the effect or parameter was not keyframed, then you were not working on the proper copy of the clip. Double-click it and repeat the process of adding and keyframing the effect.

If you're sure that you were working on the proper copy of the clip, then you probably failed to keyframe the parameter properly. Where most people slip up is forgetting to move the playhead, thereby changing the parameter of the original keyframe a second time by mistake. You can fix this by readjusting the original keyframe's value. After that, just move the playhead down the Timeline or Keyframe Graph and add a new keyframe by setting the parameter to a different value.

Your keyframed real-time effects look shaky

If you're doing things like scaling and moving your clip across the screen using keyframes, you should preview your effect in real time. If the movement is a bit shaky and you see an orange or yellow bar above the clip, don't be overly concerned. It's only a preview and doesn't reflect the final quality of a rendered effect. Depending on your processor, you may have varying performance when it comes to the smoothness of your Unlimited RT (orange bar) and Proxy (yellow bar) real-time previews.

Once you're satisfied with the basic movement of the effect, it's a good idea to render it by selecting it and then choosing Sequence → Render Selection → Video. You should also view it on a video monitor to see how it will look for final output.

Wrap-up

Now that you've completed this chapter, you've learned one of the most important elements of video effects creation: animating effects. You understand techniques for changing parameters in the Motion tab to change the shape of the clip over time. And you're now able to keyframe parameters in the tabs of the Viewer and Canvas.

As you continue through this book, you'll see keyframing come up again and again in effects creation.

5

Layer Techniques

In this chapter you'll learn how to work with video layers. You'll experiment with classic motion graphics techniques such as creating picture-in-picture effects, simulating a 3D look in 2D space, and animating graphics using layer sequencing. You'll also learn an advanced technique called layer splitting, which lets you fly an object from behind a layer to in front of it. In addition, you'll practice nesting clips, which is a key technique you'll use throughout this book.

Layer Fundamentals

When you build a layered composition in FCP, imagine building a theatre set on a stage, starting with a backdrop and adding more and more objects, from back to front, until the stage is set with a complete scene (see Figure 5-1).

As soon as you add a clip to the top layer, or video track, in the Timeline, it's placed in the foreground in relation to other layers in the composite, or stack. Clips at the bottom of the stack are obscured by clips that you add to upper tracks. In its simplest form, compositing consists of positioning, moving, and resizing layers so you can combine them into a scene.

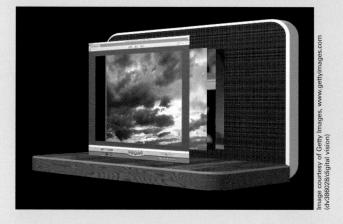

Image courtesy of Getty Images, www.gettyimages.com (dv386028/digital vision)

ADDING TRACKS

Final Cut Pro offers several ways to insert audio and video tracks into the Timeline. The most precise way to insert tracks is by using the Sequence menu. This menu brings up a handy dialog box that allows you to insert audio and video tracks exactly where you want them.

To insert a track quickly, use one of the following methods:

- Drag a clip into the Timeline as an Overwrite Edit (down-facing arrow) in the blank area above an existing track. A new video track will automatically be created. (Audio tracks will also be created if there is audio linked with the video clip.)

- Control + click on the Destination button on the top video track, and choose Add Track from the pop-up menu. (You can do the same for an audio track on the A2 Destination button.)

- Control + click in the blank area just above your highest track, and choose Add Track from the pop-up menu (see Figure 5-2).

- Choose Sequence → Insert Tracks. The Insert Tracks dialog box will launch (see Figure 5-3).

note

In this book I use the terms "layers" and "tracks" interchangeably.

tip

When you drag a clip upward or downward in the Timeline's stack of tracks, press the Shift key to constrain its vertical movement.

FIGURE 5-2

Control + click above the highest track to add more tracks to the Timeline.

FIGURE 5-3

Choose Insert Tracks from the Sequence menu to bring up the Insert Tracks dialog box.

note

Other compositing applications treat layers differently from FCP. In those applications, you can have only one item per video track. In FCP, however, you can line up numerous clips horizontally along any track.

PERFORMING A SUPERIMPOSE EDIT

Superimpose Edit is confusingly named. It does not blend the contents of two or more layers, as you might expect. What Superimpose Edit actually does is insert a selected clip (or clips) from the Browser or Viewer directly above a given clip in the Timeline. If you Superimpose Edit more than one clip into the Timeline, the clips stack vertically in separate tracks. Transparent blending of the images in the stacked clips — what you normally think of when you hear "superimpose" — happens only when you adjust the opacity of a clip on a particular track.

To execute a Superimpose Edit, target the Timeline clip, park the playhead on the clip, and press F12.

tip

In the Insert Tracks dialog, you can insert a track before the base track (V1 is the default base track) or after the last track.

Making a "Super Stack"

If you want to pile up a whole slew of clips in a hurry, you'll like the following technique. I call it a "Super Stack."

1. Create a new sequence. (If you perform this maneuver in an existing sequence, it will push up the other clips to other tracks — something you may not want to do.)

2. Target V1 in the Timeline. (It's your choice whether you want to put a background clip on V1 or not.)

3. Park the playhead where you want to put the stack of clips.

4. Double-click the bin your clips reside in, then change its view to Large Icon by going to View → Browser Items → As Large Icons.

5. Sort the Icons Left to Right and Top to Bottom in the bin, then select them by lassoing them with the Selection tool. The order in which you select the clips — left to right or top to bottom — will be the order in which they are stacked on the Timeline. The first clip you select will be placed in the top-most video track. The last clip you select will be placed in the lowest available video track (track V2 in this example). Other clips will be spread out, in order, in between.

Stacking Order

To make vertical effects in Final Cut Pro, you have to understand the stacking order of the application's video layers. Here's a quick summary:

- The default *base track*, V1, is always in the background.

- A clip added to track V2, occupying the same place in time on the Timeline as the clip on V1, will be in the foreground.

- A third clip, added to V3 at that point in the Timeline, will become the foreground in relation to both the preceding clips.

To move a clip closer to the foreground, click and drag the clip upward in the stack of clips in the Timeline. When the clip is at the top of the stack, you'll see it in the Canvas. To move a clip toward the background, move it downward in the stack. To precisely position clips in the stacking order, you may have to strategically insert tracks with the Sequence → Insert Tracks dialog box.

6. Drag and drop the selected clips onto the purple Superimpose box in the Canvas (see Figure 5-4), or simply press F12. The clips will be stacked in order in the Timeline. You can now overwrite the background of your choice onto V1.

COPY-AND-PASTE BASICS

If you've used Final Cut Pro for awhile, you know how quickly you can put clips into the Timeline with Copy/Paste. To make sure you're working as efficiently as possible, here's a quick review of Copy-and-Paste techniques:

- The shortcut for copying clips is Command + C. The shortcut for pasting clips is Command + V.

- If you'd like to paste as an Insert Edit instead of a regular paste (which will overwrite clips) use Option + V.

- If you'd like to paste clips to a different vertical track, set the Auto Select button for the track you wish to paste to. (Note: As of FCP 4.1, the Destination buttons no longer rule this task.) Setting Auto Select buttons for multiple tracks will allow you to paste to all of those tracks at the same time.

- A clip will be pasted either at a set In point or where the playhead is placed, on the lowest track where an Auto Select button is enabled.

FIGURE 5-4

Drop a clip into the purple area in the Canvas to perform a Superimpose Edit.

---

tip

When I'm stacking up clips using Superimpose Edit, I usually work without In or Out points set and no clip on V1. That way I'm not limited by the set In and Out point duration or the duration of the clip on V1. If I do want the stack to be a set duration, I first check the Browser's Length column to make sure that the clips are long enough.

tip

If you'd like to delete sections of the stack as a Lift Edit, enable the Auto Select buttons and set In and Out points in the tracks from which you'd like to remove material. Press the Delete key, and the selected sections of the stack will be removed.

tip

Because the Super Stack is layered in its own sequence, you can treat it like a nest and then re-edit it into your main sequence as a single layer. Nesting will be discussed later in the chapter.

note

You can drag and drop clips and sequences from one project to another. Position the two Browsers side-by-side, and then drag and drop items from the source project into a bin in the destination project.

note

In the Paste Attributes dialog box, you can also choose to paste "content": the video frames from another video clip, such as a color matte. This will be discussed in Chapter 11.

FIGURE 5-5
Check the attributes you want to paste onto the selected clip.

- Selecting an entire clip and then copying it overrides the Auto Select function, even if it is engaged for that track.

- You can copy and paste right in the Timeline using a contextual menu. Control + click on the clip to access the menu.

- You can copy and paste a sequence (or nested sequence) from one project to another. Select the sequence you want to copy and press Command + C. Click on the Project tab you wish to paste into, and then click in the Name column and press Command + V.

COPY/PASTE ATTRIBUTES

If you did the optional exercises in Chapter 1, you've already seen the Copy/Paste Attributes function. This powerful operation will save you time and promote consistency in your work. You can paste any settings (filter or motion settings, for example) from one clip to several clips in the blink of an eye.

Let's say you've applied several effects to a clip, and now you want to apply the same group of effects to many other clips. Here's how it works:

1. In the Timeline, select the source clip and then press Command + C. All of the settings you've applied to the clip — motion, filters, drop shadows, and so on — will be copied along with the clip.

2. Select the clips you wish to affect and press Option + V. The Paste Attributes dialog box will appear.

3. In the Paste Attributes dialog box, check the attributes you want to copy from the source clip to the selected destination clips (see Figure 5-5).

4. Click OK. The effects will be applied to the selected clips (see Figure 5-6).

Here are a few more things to know about Copy/Paste Attributes:

- If you check the Basic Motion box, all Motion tab settings will be replaced. Unfortunately, there is no way to select Scale or Center.

- If you Copy/Paste Attributes, all Speed, Motion, and Time Remap settings will be replaced as well.

- If you already have filters in place in the destination clip, the newly pasted filters will be added to them, rather than replacing them.

Images courtesy of Thinkstock Footage (V0017553, V0017545, V0017548, V0019964)

FIGURE 5-6

The original stack of clips, with no effects applied, is shown on the left. On the right, the attributes from a different clip (Drop Shadow, Color Corrector filter, and Round Rectangle Mask Shape) have been applied to the comp with Copy/Paste Attributes.

FLYING PICTURE-IN-PICTURE EFFECTS

In a Flying PIP effect, a pattern of clips moves across the screen. This simple technique will come in handy in many motion graphics situations.

EXERCISE 5-1: MAKING A FLYING PIP EFFECT

Now that you know how to stack up clips in different tracks, or layers, it's time to put that skill to good use in a Flying PIP effect. To get started, go to the Chapter 5 bin, open the Chapter 5 Sequences bin, and then double-click the Chapter 5 Exercise sequence. Place the playhead at the beginning of the sequence. A background sequence has been placed on V1. There's a stack of identical clips called "Jet Fighter" in the Timeline as well. You'll learn how to animate these multiple layers.

1. Because the Jet Fighter clips are stacked up on one another, it looks like there's just one plane. To show several planes, you'll need to offset the position of the clips.

    a. Load the V3 clip into the Viewer.

    b. Click the Motion tab. In the Center parameter, enter X = −175 and Y = 0.

Images courtesy of Getty Images, www.gettyimages.com (ev01081/Photodisc, ev01146/Photodisc, dv856024/digital vision)

STEP 1

Because the Jet Fighter clips are stacked up, it looks like there's only one plane.

tip

FCP also offers a Remove Attributes function that's just as handy as its counterpart, especially when you've applied a filter to bunch of clips and then, much later, change your mind. Just press Command + Option + V to fire up the Remove Attributes dialog box.

tip

I usually leave the Scale Attribute Times box unchecked in the Paste Attributes dialog box. This preserves the placement of the keyframes from the source clip to the clip I'm pasting attributes into.

2. As you did with the V3 clip, continue to offset the X value by 175 pixels for the clips on V4 and V5. This places the clips horizontally with perfect spacing. You may want to shrink the Canvas so you can see what is going on. Check each layer to ensure that the values are as follows:

V2 clip: X = 0, Y = 0

V3 clip: X = −175, Y = 0

V4 clip: X = −350, Y = 0

V5 clip: X = −525, Y = 0

3. Zoom the Canvas out to 25% so you can see the offstage area. With all but the V1 layer selected, and working in Image + Wireframe mode, click and drag the V2 wireframe offstage to the right. Note that all the other wireframes remain equidistant and, when selected, move as a unit.

4. Make sure the playhead is at the beginning of the Timeline and then, with the layers still selected, set a keyframe by clicking the Add Motion Keyframe button in the Canvas.

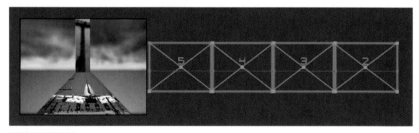

STEP 4

Click the Add Motion Keyframe button to add the first keyframe.

5. Move the playhead forward 2 seconds by holding down the Shift key and tapping the Right Arrow key twice.

6. Shift + drag the V5 wireframe to the left. The other layers should move in unison. Keep going until the V2 layer has gone all the way through the Canvas.

7. Step through the effect to see that your clips are flying through the screen as you'd expect. You can preview the effect in the QuickView window, or render it by selecting the V5 clip and pressing Command + R.

Now you can fly multiple picture-in-picture effects across the screen. The secret lies in spatially offsetting the clips by precise X values. You could also offset clips vertically or diagonally.

Preview the effect. The planes should fly across the screen, one after another.

Advanced Layer Techniques

You can do lots of cool tricks with layers. In this section you'll look at a couple of animation techniques — layer splitting and layer sequencing — that will help you create interesting visual patterns and come up with new ways to present information. Let's look at layer sequencing first.

LAYER SEQUENCING

The idea behind *layer sequencing* is to create an effect in a layer, and then have another layer come in and perform a similar (or identical) stunt at a slightly later time. After doing Exercise 5-1 you're already familiar with offsetting layers in space. In the following exercise you'll be offsetting them in time as well.

Your goal is to do a majority of the work on a single layer, and then perform a Copy/Paste Attributes function on a group of layers. That way, you can cut down on repetitive work. After the job of animating is done, you can then change the timing in each layer, offsetting each one by a given increment. Over time, a pattern will build up, with startling results.

X,Y Coordinates in FCP

To precisely align objects in clips lying on different layers, you need to know about positioning elements on the X,Y axis. If you remember X,Y coordinates from high school geometry, you should be all set, right? Wrong. In Final Cut Pro, the positive and negative numbers aren't in the places you'd expect them to be for a clip's X,Y position. (Note that Title 3D and some third-party applications use their own X,Y coordinate systems as well.)

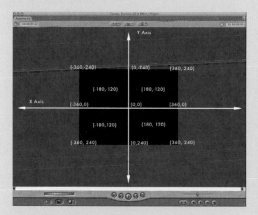

Here's an illustration showing how 2D space is set up in FCP. Don't worry, you'll get used to it.

EXERCISE 5-2: MAKING A STARBURST USING LAYER SEQUENCING

Move to the marker for Exercise 2. I've already stacked up your clips, and they're ready to go.

1. You'll first work on just one clip, turning all of the others off. Solo the V2 clip by selecting it and pressing Control + S.

2. Load the clip into the Viewer and click the Motion tab.

3. Move the playhead to the beginning of the stack. Press Control + K to set a keyframe.

4. Make the following adjustments in the Motion tab:

   Scale: 40

   Center: X = –365, Y = 20

   Anchor Point: X = 220, Y = –120

5. This next move will fly your clip onto the screen and reshape it into a parallelogram. Move the playhead forward 2:00 by pressing Shift + Right Arrow twice, press Control + K, and then type in new values as follows:

   Scale: 20

   Center: X = –220, Y = 120

   Distort:

   Upper Left: X = –120, Y = –120

   Upper Right: X = 220, Y = –120

   Lower Right: X = 120, Y = 120

   Lower Left: X = –220, Y = 120

6. Again, move the playhead forward. This time move it 4:00, and then set another keyframe by pressing Control + K.

7. You'll now perform a Copy/Paste Attributes function.

   a. Copy the V2 layer by selecting it and pressing Command + C.

   b. Lasso all the other layers except V1 (you may want to make your tracks skinnier by toggling track height using Shift + T).

   c. Press Option + V and check the boxes for Basic Motion and Distort in the Paste Attributes dialog box.

note

The clips in Exercise 5-2 are all by Getty Images (www.gettyimages.com). Six of the clips are by digital vision (dv395008, dv856009, dv856024, dv856031, dv856022, and dv808013). The other six clips are by Photodisc (ev00954, ev00655, ev01081, ev01137, ev01146, and ev02039).

8. Click OK. All of the other layers will now have the same keyframe values up to this point.

To see the results, you can turn on all of the layers by selecting V2 and pressing Control + S. Note that because all the layers are stacked on top of one another, you should see just the V13 layer.

9. Now you'll change the rotation values for each layer. Offset each layer by 30 degrees. Here's how it breaks down, beginning with the foreground layer on V13 at the top of the stack.

> V13: 330
>
> V12: 300
>
> V11: 270
>
> V10: 240
>
> V9: 210
>
> V8: 180
>
> V7: 150
>
> V6: 120
>
> V5: 90
>
> V4: 60
>
> V3: 30
>
> V2: 0

STEP 8
All the layers are visible, but because they're stacked up, you can see only V12.

10. You should now see the pattern emerge. You may want to step through the effect or launch Quick-View to preview it.

11. Now comes the layer sequencing, where you'll make each layer appear at a different time. The timing of the pattern varies for an interesting effect.

a. Select all layers except V1 and V2.

b. Type +100 and press Enter. The entire stack will be offset by 1:00, except for V1 and V2.

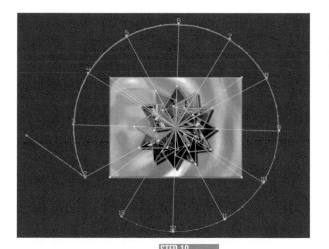

STEP 10
As you rotate each layer, a pattern emerges.

c. Select all layers except V1 and V2. Type + 100 and press Enter (see the pattern here?). The stack will offset once more by another 1:00, except for V1, V2, and V3.

d. Repeat this process until you've got all twelve layers offset by 1:00.

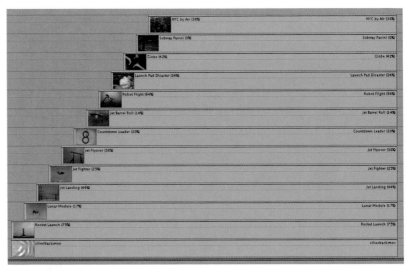

STEP 11

Here's what the Timeline looks like when you offset each layer by the same amount of time and use the Razor Blade All tool to clean up the Out points.

STEP 12

Preview your effect in the Quick-View window. It looks like an origami creation.

12. Good going! Your work is done. Take a look at your handiwork in the Quick-View window. When you're sure you've got the effect right, you can render it.

I hope you can see the power of sequencing layers in motion graphics compositions. By doing all of the hard work in one layer and then using Copy/Paste Attributes, you can save a lot of time.

I hope that you also noticed the power of the anchor point. No position keyframes were needed after the form flew in from offstage. Everything else was performed by key-framing rotation around a strategically placed anchor point, located in the upper right of each parallelogram thanks to Copy/Paste Attributes.

Now that you have layer sequencing down pat, let's move on to layer splitting.

SPLITTING LAYERS

As you know, FCP is a 2D graphics environment, but you can simulate a 3D perspective by adjusting the scale and position of layers. You can get even fancier, however, and make an object fly from behind a layer and then travel in front of it. But how can you make a background object switch layer position as it scales? There's no practical way to keyframe layer position. The answer lies in *splitting layers*. You place an Add Edit (Razor Blade splice) where the object clears the foreground layer, and then place the flying object in a video track above the foreground layer precisely at that point in time. (To pull this off, it's helpful to have all the animation completed before you hack the clip in half.)

If the technique I just described still isn't clear, the best way to understand it is to experience it for yourself. I'll set up the composite for you, since you don't have much experience making mattes yet. You'll be responsible for the animation and the layer splitting. You'll even incorporate what you've learned from the earlier layer-sequencing exercise.

EXERCISE 5-3: CREATING A 3D LOOK BY SPLITTING LAYERS

In this exercise you'll get some practice in the art of layer splitting. In this composite, a pocket watch will fly from behind a building and land in the foreground.

Get started by moving to the marker for Exercise 3 in the Chapter 5 Exercise sequence. The "Clouds at Sunset" and "Kenzo" clips have already been added for you as backgrounds for the "Clocks and Letters" clip.

1. As you can see, the "Clocks and Letters" clip (the pocket watch) on V4 is scaled down in front of the building. That's not what you want. You'll want to have the clip come from behind the building. Hide it behind the building by dragging the layer down to V2.

2. Load the Clocks and Letters clip into the Viewer. Click on the Filters tab and inspect the filters. Note that this clip has two filters on it. Drag out the Video tab so that you can see the clip and the Filters tab at the same time. Note that a Matte → Mask Shape → Oval filter has been added to cut a hole for the watch. Uncheck the Enable Filter checkbox momentarily to see the entire clip. Check the box again to engage the matte. This clip also has Matte → Feather Edges applied to soften the edge a bit. We'll talk more about mattes and feathering in Chapter 8.

Using Auto Select to Add a Filter to Multiple Layers

Auto Select buttons influence editing tasks that take place on multiple tracks. For example, you could add filters to multiple tracks. Try this:

1. Set In and Out points around your stack of clips.

2. Click the Auto Select buttons for the tracks that contain the clips you want to add the filter to.

3. Select a filter from the Effects menu.

4. The filter will be added to each clip between In and Out points on all Auto Selected tracks.

Here are some Auto Select keyboard shortcuts:

- Press the Command key and a number on the numeric keypad to enable the Auto Select button for that video track.

- Press the Option key and a number to enable the Auto Select button for that audio track.

- Command + 0 toggles Auto Select buttons on and off for all video tracks.

- Option + 0 toggles Auto Select buttons on and off for all audio tracks.

- Option + clicking any Auto Select button will "solo" it, making it the only track that's selected.

3. Select the "Kenzo" clip and press Control + S to solo the clip. Change the background to "Checkerboard" and check out the transparent areas of the clip. You'll fly your Clocks and Letters clip through this hole. Unsolo the clip by pressing Control + S once more.

4. You'll now animate the Clocks and Letters clip.

   a. Solo this layer to work on it more easily.

   b. Place the playhead at the beginning of the stack of clips.

   c. Press Control + K to set a keyframe. Set Scale to 36 and Center to X = 65 and Y = −36.

5. Move the playhead forward 1:00 and then drag the wireframe to the open area. Set a keyframe for Center at X = −92 and Y = −90.

6. Move the playhead forward once more, but this time make it 2:00. Click on the wireframe and drag it completely off the Canvas. Make the settings read as follows, and the watch will fall offscreen to the lower right:

   Scale: 70

   Center: X = 120, Y = 145

7. Control + click on the keyframes and choose Linear from the contextual menu.

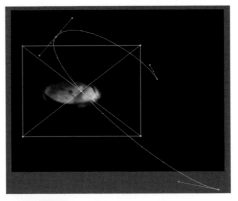

STEP 7

The watch's motion path should look like this.

8. Unsolo the Clocks and Letters clip. Step through the effect and note that the watch still falls behind the building in the latter half of the animation. You'll need to split the position of the layers at the apex of the motion path.

  a. Park the playhead on the second Center keyframe. In the Canvas, note that the clip has cleared the building.

  b. Option + click the Auto Select button for the Clocks and Letters clip on V2. Use the Razor Blade tool to click at the playhead position (or press Control + V).

  c. Using the Selection tool, Shift + drag the latter half of the Clocks and Letters clip to V4. This half of the clip will play in front of the building, since it is now in the foreground.

9. Now that the layers are split, you can use layer sequencing to make more than one pocket watch fly from behind the building.

  a. Move the Kenzo clip and the Clocks and Letters clip to V5 and V6, respectively.

  b. Working from V2, Shift + Option + drag the earlier part of the layer to V3.

  c. Repeat the process for V4.

  d. Now Shift + Option + drag the V6 layer to V7.

  e. Repeat the process for V8.

  f. Move the V3 layer forward 20 frames. Select it, type +20, and press Enter.

  g. Move the V4 layer forward 40 frames. Select it, type +40, and press Enter.

  h. Move the V7 layer forward 20 frames. Select it, type +20, and press Enter.

  i. Move the V8 layer forward 40 frames. Select it, type +40, and press Enter.

Your layers are now sequenced and split. After previewing the effect, go ahead and render it by selecting the layers and pressing Command + R. This technique lends a 3D illusion to the pocket watches, which appear to be in flight.

note

As an option, you can add Motion Blur to the pocket watch effect. Try 65% at 32 Samples. Note that adding Motion Blur will drastically increase render time and slow the rate at which the Canvas updates. It's worth it, though, as the watch's motion looks much more realistic.

Clouds image courtesy of Thinkstock Footage (V0014909)

STEP 9

By combining layer splitting and layer sequencing, you've made a squadron of pocket watches fly from behind a building into the foreground. Very surreal!

Prerendering

Prerendering complex layered sequences will save you time when compositing, as your computer won't have to calculate values on multiple layers, but only the single prerendered layer.

Candidates for prerendered elements are those that are already animated and that you don't plan to alter. In Exercise 5-3, for example, you didn't need to change the "Kenzo" clip's alpha channel, so I prerendered it for you.

Prerendering is not hard to do. You're just exporting video via QuickTime and then re-importing that element back into FCP. Usually you do this with one crucial option engaged: exporting with the alpha channel intact by choosing the proper codec (compression scheme). Here's one way to set up a prerender:

1. Nest the elements you want to export (nesting is discussed later in this chapter). Select the nested sequence and then press Command + 0. The Sequence Settings dialog will open. In the Compressor menu, choose the codec you'd like to use. Choose a lossless codec that will carry the alpha channel, such as Animation or None. Doing so will ensure that renders are pristine and transparency is preserved. Make sure that your color depth is set to Millions of Colors +. Click OK.

2. Set In and Out points to export only the nested effect; otherwise, the entire sequence will be exported.

3. Go to File → Export → QuickTime Movie. Leave the Setting menu at Current Settings, and make sure the box for Make Movie Self-Contained is checked. Click Save.

4. In the Save dialog box, navigate to a good storage place on your media drive and then click Save. Your prerendered element will then be placed on your media drive.

5. Re-import the item into FCP.

Your workflow will be snappier and easier to manage. Alpha channels are already cut, and you won't have to manage a bunch of extra layers. Even if you've got the latest and greatest computer, be smart and prerender items you've already locked down in your composition.

The use of new codecs is changing the workflow for prerendering, so keep your eyes peeled for the latest codecs. For example, as of this writing, there is a new None codec that supports 16-bit color depth. If you're curious about codecs, check out www.onerivermedia.com and see what Marco Solorio has to say about current codecs and quality. He and Adam Wilt (www.adamwilt.com) are the best sources for this type of information.

Whenever I'm exporting for compositing between FCP and another application, I use the Microcosm codec from TheoryLCC. It provides an uncompressed 64-bit RGB + Alpha file that's much smaller than the comparable Animation codec file (at 6:1). There's a try-out version at www.digitalanarchy.com.

Nesting

Nesting — grouping several layers of clips into a single unit — is one of the most powerful things you can do in Final Cut Pro. There are a lot of reasons why you'd want to nest multiple layers into a single layer:

- Neatness counts. Sometimes you just want to keep a group of clips in one neat package (see Figure 5-7). Layered compositions can get unruly, and grouping them helps to prevent unnecessary scrolling in the Timeline. Title elements are a good example of items you'd want to handle as a package.

- You can add one or more filters to a nested sequence to affect many layers at once. For example, you could add a Basic 3D filter as a motion controller, a color correction filter to shade many shots at once, or a distort filter to warp the layers as a unit (see Figure 5-8).

- You can add motion graphics effects to several layers at once with the Motion tab parameters: Distort, Rotate, Scale — you name it (see Figure 5-9).

- Copying and pasting multiple nests in a layer sequence can be a quick way to build up footage in your comp (see Figure 5-10).

Clip courtesy of RobPongi.com

FIGURE 5-7
This 6-layer design is easier to handle as a single, nested unit.

FIGURE 5-8
Here, the Fisheye filter works on all of the nested layers at once.

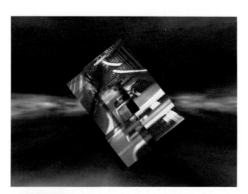

FIGURE 5-9
The nest has been animated to rotate and scale down over time.

FIGURE 5-10
Multiple copies of the nest are flying through the comp with the Basic 3D filter in a layer sequence.

tip

You can create an over-sized "stage." Make your nested sequences larger than the native frame size for panning and scanning a layered Adobe Photoshop file, or moving a larger form with Basic 3D, for example. More on this a bit later.

note

Layered Photoshop files show up as nested sequences the Browser. You can treat them as you would any other nested sequence. You can also step into the nest and affect the layers with filter or motion effects individually. Very cool! More about layered Photoshop files in Chapter 14.

- Nesting can alter FCP's render-processing pipeline. This allows you to add a motion effect and then have the filter work on the clip after the motion effect has been processed. Usually, the motion effect will take precedence. You'll learn more about render order in Chapter 10.

- Once you've nested layers together and rendered the effect, the render files will be preserved. This means that you can copy/paste or duplicate the nest without having to re-render the items.

CREATING A NEST

It's very easy to group items into a nest. Here's how:

1. Select the clip or clips that you'd like to group together in the nest.

2. Go to Sequence → Nest Items or press Option + C. The Nest Items dialog box will launch.

3. Typically, you'll leave the settings at their default values. Name the new nest and then click OK (see Figure 5-11).

4. The layers will then collapse into a single, light purple layer.

   The nest will show up as a sequence in the Browser.

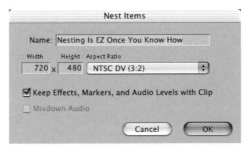

FIGURE 5-11
Name your nest in the Nest Items dialog box.

ADDING EFFECTS TO A NEST

To add effects to a nested sequence in the Timeline, just select the nested sequence as you would any other clip, and then go to Effects → Video Filters and make your choice. You can also drag and drop filters onto nests. But how do you make motion adjustments or do keyframing? As with any other clip, you'll have to load it into the Viewer first. Normally, you double-click on clips to load them into the Viewer, but when you double-click a nest, it opens into its own Timeline instead. If you'd like to load the nest into the Viewer, do one of the following:

- In the Timeline, select the nest and then press the Enter key.

- In the Timeline, Option + double-click on the nest.

- Drag and drop the nest from the Timeline or Browser into the Viewer.

- Engage the Auto Select button for the track where the nested sequence is located, and then choose Open mode from the Playhead Sync pop-up menu in either the Canvas or Viewer.

After the nest is loaded into the Viewer, adjust or keyframe filters or motion effects as you would with any other clip.

tip

To make an instant copy of a nest, select the nest, hold down the Option key, and drag the nest somewhere else in the Timeline.

DUPLICATING NESTS VERSUS COPYING AND PASTING THEM

Duplicating nested sequences is different from copying and pasting them. It's critical that you understand this distinction, so read on.

Once you nest items, you can consider this original nest a "parent." If you make any changes within this nest, the changes will immediately update in every copy of the nest in a sequence or project. These copies are called "children." Individual effects can be applied to a child nest *as a whole*, but the contents of a child nest — including filters and motion effects — are dictated by the parent sequence. This can be frustrating if you want to change an element within a child nest. For example, let's say you've copied and pasted a nested title element into your

Blending Nested Sequences

You can blend multiple nested sequences with opacity. Just stack them up in the Timeline, turn on Clip Overlays, and use the Pen tool to set keyframes to fade back and forth to your multilayered comps. This is a very common blending technique.

By adding the dimension of composite modes, you may start to come up with more interesting blends. Stack up two nested sequences and then apply a composite mode to the upper nest. Select the nest and go to Modify → Composite Modes and try a few on for size. Once the images are blended, you can keyframe the opacity as I described above. This technique will be explained further in Chapter 10.

tip

To move a clip or clips upward (and constrain them vertically) in the Timeline, select them and then press Option + Up Arrow. (If the items have audio, you'll need to either lock the audio or Option + click on the video portion of the clip.) You can select additional clips by Option + Command + clicking them. You can also move layers downward with Option + Down Arrow. Note that there can be no other layers in the way of the clips you're moving.

sequence. Every time you change the name of the person in a title generator, the name changes in all your other titles, which is not what you want to do. You need to break the parent-child relationship.

Instead of copying the nested sequence, you need to *duplicate* it and make your changes to the duplicate. Duplicating a nest essentially creates a new parent sequence, which is very useful indeed. Here's how to do it:

1. In the Browser, Control + click on the nested sequence icon. Choose Duplicate from the contextual menu and a duplicated nest will bear the same name but will be followed by the word "Copy." (This is a little confusing; it would be better if the name were followed by "Duplicate.")

2. Your duplicated copy of the original nest is now ready to be renamed. Make sure you change the name so that you can easily make the distinction between the duplicated nest and the original.

3. Now any changes you make within the nest — like changing a name or choosing a different tint for a color matte — won't disrupt any other nests, as this nest is no longer related to the original.

Now that you know how to put these techniques into play, let's do an exercise where you'll nest a composition that's already made for you.

EXERCISE 5-4: NESTING MULTIPLE LAYERS

In this exercise you'll nest multiple layers and then add effects to that nest. You'll also get experience with copy/pasting and with duplicating sequences. After completing the exercise, you'll have enough confidence to create compound effects.

To get started, move to the marker for Exercise 4 in the Chapter 5 Exercise sequence. I've already made a layered composite for you.

1. As you can see, the ten-layer composite takes up quite a bit of vertical space in the Timeline. Let's group these layers into a nest.

    a. Select just the video layers by lassoing them with the Selection tool.

    b. Press Option + C. The Nest Items dialog box will launch.

    c. Name the layer "Robot_Parent_NEST" and then click OK.

    d. The ten layers will now collapse into one nest.

2. Now you're free to add effects to the nest. At this point, scale down the layer to 25% in the Viewer's Motion tab or in the Canvas.

3. Move the nested comp to the upper-left part of the screen, just inside the Title Safe Overlay (View mode pop-up → Overlays → Title Safe), which is the inner box.

4. Select Robot_Parent_NEST and Shift + Option + drag the entire comp up one track. This will instantly paste a copy of the comp directly above the original one in the Timeline.

5. In the Timeline, select the nest and then, working in the Canvas, Shift + drag it to the inside of the Title Safe area, on the lower left.

6. With the new nest selected, press Command + 9 to open the Item Properties dialog box for the nest. Change its name to "Robot_Child_NEST" and then click OK. This nest has the same layers inside it as the Robot_Parent_NEST.

7. You'll now duplicate the original Robot_Parent_NEST. Go to the Browser and Control + click on the sequence icon for Robot_Parent_NEST. Choose Duplicate from the contextual menu. A duplicate sequence with the word "Copy" added to it will be created. Change its name to "Robot_Duplicate_NEST." Remember, this is no longer related to the original Robot_Parent_NEST, since you duplicated it rather than copying and pasting.

8. Now you'll edit the Robot_Duplicate_NEST back into the Timeline. Working from the Browser, click and drag the sequence icon for the Robot_Duplicate_NEST into the Timeline to V3, directly over the other nested sequences at the Exercise 4 marker.

9. Scale down the duplicate to 25% and position it in the middle of the frame. All the images should look the same at this point.

10. You'll now see how the parent/child relationship works. Any changes you make to the parent will take place in the child as well, and changes you make to the child will update in the parent. Let's try this:

    a. Double-click on the Robot_Parent_NEST to open it in the Timeline.

    b. Double-click on the orange color matte and change its color in the Controls tab.

    c. In the upper-left portion of the Timeline, click on the Chapter 5 Exercise tab to see the changes in the parent and child sequences. Note that the duplicated sequence has not been affected by the color change, but the copied-and-pasted child has.

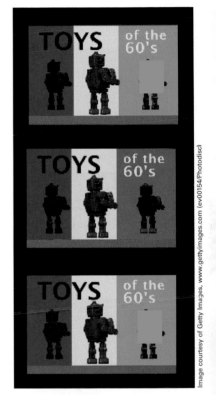

Image courtesy of Getty Images, www.gettyimages.com (ev00154/Photodisc)

STEP 10

The duplicated sequence (center) was not affected when you changed the parent clip.

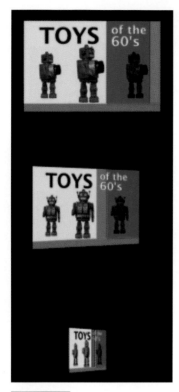

The nests spin and fly up at different times.

tip

If you have any jagged edges when scaling or swiveling graphics with motion effects or the Basic 3D filter, add the Anti-Alias filter to the bottom of the stack with a low setting (1 or 2 is good).

11. As a final step you'll add some effects to the nest. Here's an easy way to control the motion of the nested sequences using the Basic 3D filter.

   a. Select the nest on V3 and then go to Effects → Video Filters → Basic 3D.

   b. Option + double-click on the nest so you can adjust the filter controls.

   c. In the Timeline, move the playhead to the beginning of the stack.

   d. In the Filters tab, make the following adjustments, and then set keyframes for each:

   Scale: 0

   Y-Spin: 90

   e. Move the playhead forward 1:00 and change the values to the following:

   Scale: 90

   Y-Spin: 0

12. Now you'll Copy/Paste Attributes from the V3 Robot_Duplicate_NEST to the V1 and V2 nests.

   a. Select the V3 nest and press Command + C.

   b. Select the other two nests and press Option + V.

   c. In the Paste Attributes dialog box, check Filters and then click OK.

13. Step through the effect in the Timeline. You can see that all three nested sequences are being controlled individually, with their own copies of the Basic 3D filter added.

14. Now you'll offset the nested layers.

   a. Select the V1 nested sequence and move it forward :10.

   b. Select the V2 nested sequence and move it forward :20.

   c. Preview the effect once more and note that the timing is now staggered.

Congratulations! You've mastered the basics of nesting. You can now use nesting to create complex layered compositions.

OVERSIZED LAYERS AND NESTS

The technique of using oversized layers is not a new one. Animators have been "panning and scanning" layers behind cartoon characters for decades, creating the illusion that the characters are walking along in a scene. The characters are actually moving in place while the background pans behind them. Let's talk about how you can do this in FCP.

Panning and scanning oversized images

This effect is often done with oversized Photoshop files or digital photos that are brought into FCP. (See Chapter 14 for information on preparing the Photoshop images.)

1. Import a large graphic into FCP.

2. Once you place it into the Timeline, FCP will auto-scale the image to fit. You don't want that. To prevent auto-scaling, load the image into the Viewer and click the Reset button. You'll then see the true frame size of your graphic.

3. Animate the graphic as you would any other layer. Use Scale to zoom in and out, and Center to accomplish panning.

4. If you see any artifacts, 1 pixel of vertical blur from Telly's H/V Blur (included on the companion DVD) will help. Adding blur is often necessary when you use images scanned from magazines.

5. If you want to ease the start and stop, make sure to engage the Ease In/Ease Out keyframe option in the Canvas by Control + clicking directly on the keyframe and choosing it from the contextual menu. Use QuickView's preview options (see Chapter 4) to dial in the smoothness of the effect.

Using oversized nested sequences

When you nest layers, there's no reason the nest has to be in your native frame size. In fact, it can be smaller or larger than your native frame size. Why? To pan and scan oversized layers.

This "camera and stage" technique creates an effect that's similar to a classic animation stand: the camera is locked down, but the stage itself moves, lending the illusion of a motion-control camera (see Figure 5-12). In FCP the "camera eye" is the standard DV frame and the "stage" is the oversized nested sequence. The DV frame does not move, but the oversized layer within it does.

Here are some ways you could use this technique:

- Create motion graphics in an oversized comp so that you can fully scale, rotate, and change positions of a pattern without unsightly edges showing up in a Standard-Def or DV frame.

- Create a tableau of full-sized clips on an oversized motion graphics background, say from LiveType, and nest them. Scale the nest in and out toward the clips (all the way to 100%) to simulate a motion-control zoom move.

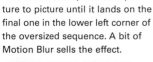
FIGURE 5-12

A virtual camera pans from picture to picture until it lands on the final one in the lower left corner of the oversized sequence. A bit of Motion Blur sells the effect.

Images courtesy of Getty Images, www.gettyimages.com (ev02552/Photodisc, rbrp_0116/rubberball productions)

- Bring an oversized text composition from LiveType into FCP and manipulate this huge graphic with FCP's motion controls and filters. To access the HDTV export settings in LiveType, go to Edit → Project Properties. For the highest quality, be sure to check the box for Render Fields and uncheck the box for Upper First.

Now that this chapter has come to a close, I hope you see how far you can go with video layers. Although there are many more techniques to learn, this core set of skills should put you on a path toward creating your own intricate layered effects.

Troubleshooting

This section will help you deal with problems associated with clips on multiple layers, including nested clips.

When you dropped a clip into the Timeline, it split the stack of video layers in half

You probably dragged in a clip as an Insert Edit, when you meant to do an Overwrite Edit. An Insert Edit pushes all clips down in the Timeline, splitting the video layers.

You have to keep a careful eye on the Selection tool as you drag your clip into the Timeline. You want to drag the clip to the bottom half of the desired video track; when you're there, the Selection tool turns into a downward-facing arrow, indicating an Overwrite Edit. This is what you want to see. If you see an arrow that points to the right, you're set up for an Insert Edit, which you don't usually want when you're working with vertical tracks. Drag the clip past the faint line within the track to force the Selection tool to change into the downward arrow.

You can't see a clip that you vertically edited into the Timeline

It's likely that you don't have the order of your video layers correct, and a fore-ground layer is obscuring your clip. Recall that the higher a clip lies on the Time-line, the further in the foreground it is.

You can either alter a motion parameter of the foreground video layer (by scaling the clip down, for example), or move the clip to a higher video track.

You dragged a wireframe, but nothing moved in the Canvas

You probably dragged the wireframe of the wrong video layer. Make sure you select the correct clip in the Timeline before you drag the wireframe in the Canvas.

A clip in the Canvas is obscured by other layers

You have a few options for viewing a layer while you're working on it. (Note that these options will cause you to lose some portion of your render files.)

- Turn off the other tracks by Option + clicking on the Track Visibility button in the Timeline.
- Solo the clip you want to see by selecting it and pressing Control + S.

An alternative to re-rendering after soloing a clip or track is to choose Open mode from the Playhead Sync menu. After setting In and Out points and clicking the Auto Select button for the proper track, you can solo the affected clip in the Viewer instead. Turn off clips you don't want to see by selecting them and pressing Control + B. Ether way, you do not lose your render files or have to perform an Edit → Undo unless you make a change.

Wrap-up

With the completion of this chapter, you've mastered one of the most important concepts related to effects creation: video layering. You can now keyframe Motion, Filters, and Controls parameters along multiple video tracks to create richer and more complex videographics.

Let's press ahead to the next chapter, where we'll be focusing on Final Cut Pro's video transitions.

WHAT'S IN THIS CHAPTER

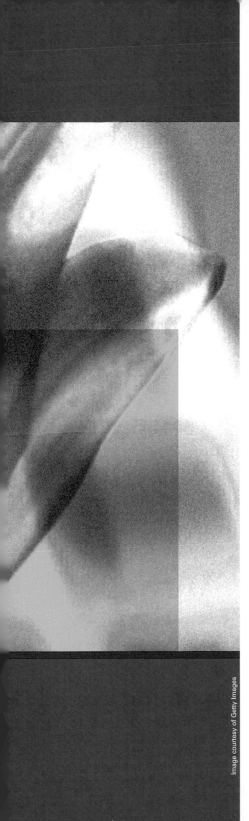

Image courtesy of Getty Images

6
Transitions

Final Cut Pro has a huge assortment of transitions. You can create even more transitions by using motion effects or filters in unconventional ways. In this chapter you'll learn the basics of applying and adjusting transitions. Then you'll learn some novel ways to use them as video composites, creating impressive effects such as making objects appear out of nowhere or wiping an object across a background to reveal a different background. With the techniques you'll learn in this chapter, your compositions will stand out from those made by people who simply use Final Cut Pro's transitions right out of the box.

Transition Basics

A *transition* is a scene change that occurs over time. In a dissolve, for example, one shot blends into the next, with the two shots overlapping as the change occurs. In Final Cut Pro, you can either drag a transition from the Effects tab onto an edit point or select one from the Effects menu. Here's a quick overview of each method.

DRAGGING A TRANSITION FROM THE EFFECTS TAB

The Effects tab method is the most straightforward way to add a transition to an edit point.

To drag a transition from the Effects tab, follow these steps:

1. Click the Effects tab in the Browser.

2. Click the triangle next to the Video Transitions bin. You'll see several groups of transitions, such as Slide and Wipe (see Figure 6-1).

3. Open a bin, and then click a transition to select it.

4. Drag the transition to the Timeline and onto the edit point, and then release the mouse button.

   The transition is automatically centered on the edit point in the Timeline.

To verify that your transition has been applied, make sure the Transition icon stretches across the edit point.

SELECTING A TRANSITION FROM THE EFFECTS MENU

To select a transition from the Effects menu, follow these steps:

1. Select the edit point using the Selection arrow or the Roll tool. (If your playhead is near the cut, you can press the V key to select the edit point.)

   When the transition area turns brown, the edit point has been selected and is ready to receive a transition (see Figure 6-2).

2. Choose Effects → Video Transitions, and then select a transition from the list.

3. Release the mouse button.

   The transition is instantly applied.

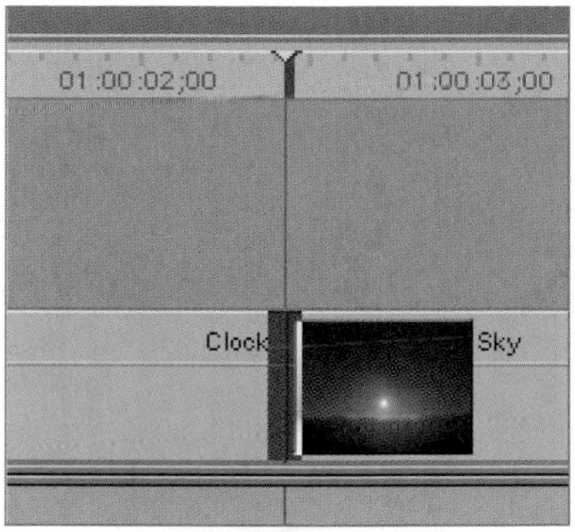

FIGURE 6-2

The edit point turns brown when selected.

THE DEFAULT TRANSITION

FCP's default transition is a standard dissolve. To apply the default transition, select an edit point and go to Effects → Default Transition (or press Command + T).

Changing the default transition

A dissolve is a good general-purpose transition, but you might want to use another transition as your default. Any transition can be your default.

1. In the Browser, click the Effects tab.

2. Click the Video Transitions bin's triangle to open the bin.

3. Click the triangle next to the bin that contains the type of transition you have in mind (Slides or Wipes, for example).

4. Find the transition you'd like to use as the default, and Control + click its icon.

5. Choose Set Default from the contextual menu.

   The newly chosen transition is now your default transition.

> **tip**
>
> *If you need to add several transitions in a row, you can use the Down Arrow key and Command + T to quickly add a default transition to each edit point.*

Image courtesy of Artbeats Bundle Pack (TM102)

FIGURE 6-3

Drag a single clip or a group of clips onto the Canvas overlay to add the default transition to one or more edit points.

Using Insert or Overwrite with Transition

You can add a single clip or a group of clips to the Timeline, with the default transition added to each edit point.

1. Drag a clip or group of clips onto the Canvas overlay (see Figure 6-3).

2. Release the mouse button.

    The default transition is automatically added to the edit point or points.

HOW TRANSITIONS WORK

To make transitions work properly, it helps to understand what goes on under the hood. The main thing you should know is that two clips must overlap for a set number of frames (usually 30 frames) in a transition.

Understanding "handles"

In a transition there are always two clips that overlap for a period of time. Media that lies before and after a clip's In and Out points are used for *handles*. Figure 6-4 will help you understand the concept of handles. As you can see, in a standard center-on-edit transition, you need media both before and after your set edit points for the outgoing and incoming clip.

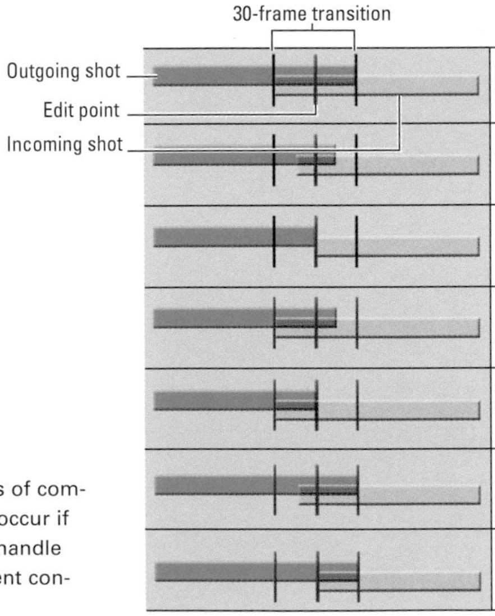

	Description	Result
Outgoing shot — Edit point — Incoming shot — (30-frame transition)	Sufficient outgoing (blue) and incoming handles (pink)	You can add a transition. Here you could add a standard 1:00 transition.
	Insufficient outgoing and incoming handles	You can add a short transition. Here you could add a centered transition with a duration of :15.
	No handles	You cannot add a transition. You'll see an "Insufficient content" error message or an "X" next to the Selection tool. Ripple trim both sides of the edit point to fix this.
	Insufficient outgoing handle	You can add a short transition. Roll the edit point to the left to restore handle.
	No outgoing handle	Your best choice here would be a transition that begins at the cut. For a centered transition, you'd need to ripple trim the outgoing clip.
	Insufficient incoming handle	You can add a short transition. Roll the edit point to the right to restore handle.
	No incoming handle	Your best choice here would be a transition that ends at the cut. For a 1:00, centered transition, roll the edit point to the right.

FIGURE 6-4

Here are some examples of common problems that can occur if you don't have enough handle (FCP calls this "insufficient content for edit").

In most cases, when you add a transition to an edit point, the transition will work. However, if you're having trouble adding a transition, you probably don't have enough frames of handle. Trim off 15 frames on either side of your intended edit point to serve as your handle, close all gaps, then reapply the transition. That should get you back on track.

PREVIEWING A TRANSITION

Once you've applied a transition, you'll want to make sure it looks right. Rather than rendering the transition right away, you can preview it, then make changes if necessary. You use the same techniques for previewing transitions as you would for previewing any effect.

Fine-tuning a transition's timing

In FCP you can tweak the placement, duration, and other parameters of transitions in real time. Here's how:

1. Apply a transition at your edit point.

2. Select the edit point with the Selection tool (A) or the Roll tool (R).

3. Go into Loop Playback mode (Option + L).

4. Press the Play Around Current key (/). You may wish to set your looping for Preview Pre-Roll and Preview Post-Roll to 2:00 (or whatever you choose) in Edit → General Preferences.

tip

Go easy on the cheese! Some of the more specialized transitions should only be brought out for appropriate effects. For example, an Oval Iris transition might be good for a silent movie spoof.

note

In RT Preview mode you'll often see only a "proxy" view of your effect. For example, you probably won't see the modifications such as soft edges or borders that you made in the Transition Editor. Using the QuickView window, you can see these subtleties.

Adding More Transitions to Your System

You can add more transitions to your FCP system by purchasing them from third- party plug-in manufacturers, as described in Chapter 14. With this book, you get two of my own custom transitions. If you followed the directions in Chapter 1, you should see Telly's Directional Blur Dissolve and Telly's H/V Blur Dissolve in the Transitions portion of the Effects menu.

If you are an FCP 3 owner, you may have some interesting transitions from CGM that can still be utilized in FCP 4. To use them, Option + drag them from your original FCP 3 plug-ins folder to your FCP 4 plug-ins folder. This is located in System Library → Application Support → Final Cut Pro System Support → Plug-ins. If you are new to FCP, you can purchase the transitions from CGM at www.cgm-online.com.

5. The real-time transition will begin to loop. Evaluate the transition. If you don't like the timing of it, adjust the transition's placement using the Trim Forward and Trim Backward keyboard shortcuts (Left and Right Bracket keys and Shift + Bracket modifier keys) while you loop. The transition's placement slides forward or backward.

6. Stop looping when you're satisfied with the transition.

RENDERING A TRANSITION

Sometimes previewing isn't enough. To get a really good idea of how your transition is performing, you can render it to disk and then view it in the Canvas, or better still, on your video monitor.

To render a single transition, follow these steps:

1. Make sure that your Scratch Disk Preference is set to send renders to your media drive (Option + Q → Scratch Disks → Set: Media Drive).

2. Select the transition.

3. Choose Sequence → Render Selection (or press Command + R).

4. After the rendering is complete, check out the transition on your video monitor.

To render all transitions in a sequence, follow these steps:

1. Select the Sequence icon in the Browser or click on the Timeline.

2. Choose Sequence → Render All (or press Option + R).

tip

Although you can select the transition's edit point with the Selection or Roll tool, don't double-click on it, because doing so will launch the Trim Edit window instead.

Modifying a Transition

Using a transition right out of the box won't always give you the effect you want. After you've added a transition, you'll probably want to modify it in some way. By sliding sliders and spinning dials in FCP's Transition Editor, you can make your transitions look much more elegant.

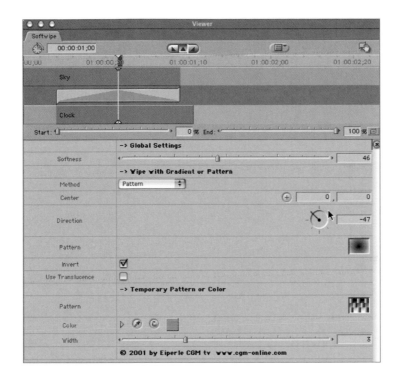

FIGURE 6-5

Here's an example of how a transition (CGM Softwipe) looks in the Transition Editor. The dials, sliders, and other controls will vary, depending on the transition.

With the Selection tool, double-click on the transition icon in the Timeline. The Transition Editor will open in its own tab in the Viewer (see Figure 6-5).

The Adjustment controls are located at the bottom of the Transition Editor. They give you a wide range of control over the look of a transition. Each transition offers a different set of adjustments, so it's important to spend some time here. Unfortunately, none of these adjustments are keyframeable.

As you adjust a transition's parameters, keep a close eye on the Canvas and on your video monitor, where you can see your changes. Sometimes a small adjustment is all it takes to improve a transition. You can also do this with any preview technique, like using the QuickView window.

Now let's take a look at some of the features of the Transition Editor window.

tip

Click on the small adjustment arrows to the left and right of many of the Adjustment controls. Each click implements one positive or negative increment of that effect so you can fine-tune it.

FIGURE 6-6

Whenever I preview a transition and it doesn't look right, I click the Reverse Transition button to see if that will improve it. It often does — and dramatically so.

FIGURE 6-7

Click the Recent Clips button to see a menu of recently selected clips.

FIGURE 6-8

The Transition Alignment buttons let you position a transition at the beginning, center, or end of a cut.

Reverse Transition button

Just above the Reset button (the red "X"), you'll find the Reverse Transition button (see Figure 6-6), which not only reverses movement, but also reverses other parameters, including channel shifts and color values. This button has a small arrow on it; click the button to change directions.

Recent Clips pop-up menu

The Recent Clips pop-up is useful for getting from the Transition Editor to the Viewer (see Figure 6-7). When you choose the clip you want, the Viewer returns to its default mode, with a recently loaded clip ready to use. This button is helpful if you want to quickly get at the Generators menu or other Viewer controls.

Transition Alignment buttons

To align your transition so that it centers on, ends on, or begins from the edit point, you can click one of the three buttons at the top of the Transition Editor (see Figure 6-8). Here are your options.

- **Center on Edit:** In most cases you'll want a transition that's centered on the edit point. It feels more balanced and natural than a transition that begins or ends on the edit point. When a transition is centered on the edit point, an equal amount of each clip is blended midway through its action.

- **End on Edit:** If you want a transition to conclude its action by the time the incoming shot arrives, you'll want the transition to end on the edit point. There are a couple of reasons why you would want to do this. You might not have enough handle on the incoming shot to apply the transition. Or you might make an editorial decision that you want the incoming shot to be brought in on a specified In point.

- **Start on Edit:** If you want a transition to start its action at the point when the outgoing shot has concluded, you'll want the transition to begin on the incoming edit point. This option is also useful if you don't have enough handle on the outgoing shot.

Transition Duration box

You'll often want to change the duration of a transition to fit the pacing of your edit. You can change the duration of the transition in the box located in the upper-left corner of the Transition Editor (see Figure 6-9). Tab to the box and type in a new duration.

You can also drag the edges of a Transition icon left or right to change a transition's duration (see Figure 6-10).

Drag Hand icon

The Drag Hand is easy to spot at the top of the Transition Editor; it looks like a hand holding a transition (see Figure 6-11). When you click the icon, your selection tool turns into a hand, which you can use for dragging and dropping the current transition and all its settings onto another edit point.

Using the Drag Hand is a great way to ensure that your transitions are consistent throughout a sequence. For example, let's say you have a sequence where you want to Dip to Color along several noncontiguous cuts. You want the dip to be 6 frames in duration and you'd like the color to be black. After you've adjusted the first transition so it's what you want, you can use the Drag Hand to drag and drop that custom transition onto each desired edit point.

Unfortunately, you can't use this method to simultaneously add a custom transition over noncontiguous edit points or successive edit points. We'll discuss how you can add a transition to multiple edit points a bit later.

FIGURE 6-9
The Transition Duration box is located in the upper-left corner of the Transition Edit window.

tip

Don't despair when the Transition Editor replaces the previously selected clip in your Viewer. You can always bring the clip you want up again by double-clicking the clip in the Timeline or Browser, or selecting it from the Transition Editor's Recent Clips pop-up menu.

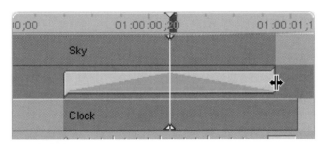

FIGURE 6-10
Drag the Transition icon in the Timeline to change a transition's duration.

FIGURE 6-11
Use the Drag Hand to drag the current transition onto an edit point.

Start and End sliders

Also included in the Transition Editor are the Start and End sliders (see Figure 6-12). They let you control how the transition effect will begin and end.

Transitions work by percentage of completion. These sliders allow you to construct transitions partially started, partially completed, or in both states. I don't often do this myself; it feels abrupt to have incomplete movement in a transition. However, these magic little sliders offer a technique that is essential to making transitions act like multilayer composites.

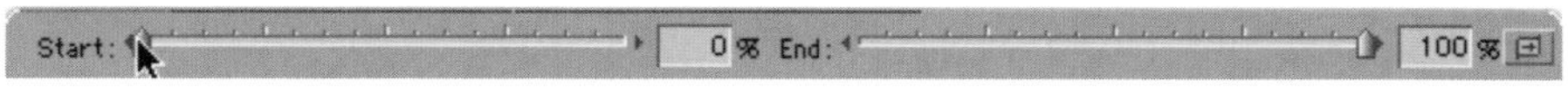

FIGURE 6-12

Use the Start and End sliders to control how a transition will begin and end.

Start: ◄ ▮   ▶ 0 % End: ◄   ▷ 100 % ▣

Trimming Transitions

Ripple and roll trimming typically come into play when your transition isn't working quite right. You'll need to trim a transition if some unwated section of the shot — the slate, for example — shows up in the first few incoming frames or last few outgoing frames. By simply trimming off these frames with the Ripple tool or moving the edit point with the Roll tool, you can save yourself loads of time when tweaking the effect.

If you're well versed in using the Ripple and Roll tools in typical trimming operations, you'll have little trouble understanding how to use them in the Transition Editor. Although you can trim transitions in the Timeline, let's stay in the Transition Editor and see how we can do this a bit more effectively.

RIPPLE TRIMMING IN THE TRANSITION EDITOR

tip

If you'd like to trim more accurately, hold down the Command key as you drag. With Snapping turned off, drag the tool evenly and in a straight line for best results.

To trim frames from only one side of the transition, you can ripple trim in the Transition Editor. Click and drag in the dark blue areas above or below the Transition icon. The Ripple tool will automatically engage, regardless of the tool you previously selected (see Figure 6-13).

As you ripple trim, a new window will replace the Canvas, displaying the last frame of the outgoing shot and its timecode, or the first frame of the incoming shot and its timecode, depending on your operation.

ROLL TRIMMING IN THE TRANSITION EDITOR

A roll trim in the Transition Editor works much like a ripple trim, except that you click and drag the Transition icon rather than dragging in the dark blue areas (see Figure 6-14). Dragging the icon left or right will change the underlying edit point of the transition in the same way a standard roll edit would.

The Roll function engages automatically as you drag, showing you a "two-up" display so you can monitor both the outgoing and incoming shots. Note the timecode moving in both clips in the two-up display. The edit point in the display shows precisely where your transition stands at 50% completion, so engaging the two-up display is instrumental in dialing in your newly chosen edit point. The Transition icon will also update its location in the Timeline as you roll.

> **tip**
>
> *You can change your Sequence Settings → Timeline Options to be in Filmstrip View mode. On the Timeline this is not exactly my cup of tea, but for the Transition Editor it's a great way to see the outgoing and incoming frames in your transition. In fact, it demonstrates very well the handle on both sides of the edit point.*

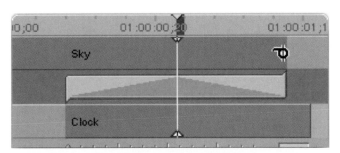

FIGURE 6-13
To ripple trim in the Transition Editor, click and drag in the dark blue area.

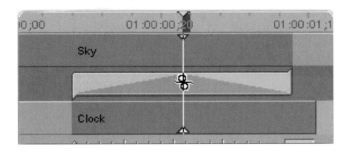

FIGURE 6-14
To roll trim in the Transition Editor, click and drag the Transition icon.

TRIMMING TRANSITIONS IN THE TRIM EDIT WINDOW

To trim your clips more precisely when you already have a transition in place, you can work with them in the Trim Edit window. To open the Trim Edit window, do one of the following:

- Double-click on the center of the Transition icon with the Selection tool, Ripple tool, or Roll tool.

- Select the Transition icon with the Selection tool, Ripple tool, or Roll tool and press Shift +7.

You can ripple or roll trim the edit points in the Trim Edit window. You must first decide whether you're going to ripple the outgoing shot, ripple the incoming shot, or roll trim both sides of the cut simultaneously.

To ripple trim, click on the outgoing or the incoming shot in the Trim Edit window with the Selection tool or Ripple tool. A green bar will light up over the clip on the side of the cut you're about to trim (see Figure 6-15 top).

To roll trim, click on the center of the Trim Edit window with any of the above tools and you should see green lights over both sides of the cut (see Figure 6-15 bottom).

FIGURE 6-15

In the Trim Edit window shown on top, the green bar indicates that you are ready to ripple trim the incoming shot. On the bottom, both green bars are lit up, indicating that you're in Roll mode.

Once you're set up to ripple or roll, you can adjust the edit point in the Trim Edit window using either of the following methods:

- Loop the transition by tapping the Space Bar. In between each loop, tap the Left and Right Bracket keys or the Comma and Period keys to adjust your transition's edit point on the fly. Use Shift + Left/Right Bracket or Shift + Period/Comma to trim multiple frames — a definite power move.

- Use the J-K-L keys to shuttle to your new edit point and then set it. The only place you can't J-K-L is on the outgoing side of a roll edit.

ADJUSTING TRANSITIONS IN THE TIMELINE

When you're under pressure to get things done quickly, it's nice to be able to make adjustments to your transitions directly in the Timeline. Working in the Timeline is often the fastest way to do many tasks, including adjusting a transition's duration.

Adjusting a transition's placement in the Timeline

A good technique for finding the correct placement of your transition is to loop it and evaluate it until the timing feels spot on. This method works especially well for real-time transitions, as you don't have to render between trims.

1. Enable looping by pressing Control + L.

2. In the Timeline, mark an In point approximately 10 frames before the transition and an Out point about 10 frames after it.

3. Select the transition with the Roll tool and play from the In point to the Out point by pressing Shift + \ (backslash) to preview the transition.

4. Roll the transition left or right with the Left or Right Bracket keys or the Comma or Period keys. The Shift key modifier can be used to move the transition multiple frames.

or

1. Select the transition on the edit point with the Roll tool, with the playhead centered on the transition.

2. Engage Play around Current by pressing the \ (backslash) key, and your transition will begin looping.

Aligning a transition in the Timeline

A little earlier you saw that you could make a transition center, end, or begin on the edit point in the Transition Editor. You can do this directly in the Timeline as well.

1. Control + click on the transition you want to align.

2. Select one of the alignment choices from the pop-up menu (see Figure 6-16).

The transition icon snaps to a new alignment.

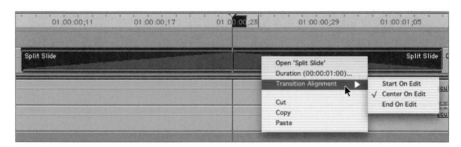

FIGURE 6-16
You can have a transition start, end, or be centered on the edit point.

Adjusting a transition's duration in the Timeline

You can lengthen or shorten the duration of a transition by clicking and dragging it in the Timeline. This is a fast way to adjust the duration without having to open the Transition Editor. You can adjust the transition up to the amount of media available. I loop the transition after I lengthen or shorten the duration.

With the Selection tool, click and drag the edge of the Transition icon to make the duration longer or shorter. The duration pop-up displays a readout showing how much longer or shorter your transition becomes as you drag.

A more precise way to adjust your transition in the Timeline is with the pop-up menu:

1. Control + click on the transition in the Timeline.

   A pop-up menu appears.

2. Choose Duration from the menu.

3. Change the value for duration in the dialog box.

   The duration of the transition changes instantly.

tip

Sometimes you'll want your transition to occur in alignment with an event on your Timeline, most often a musical beat. In FCP, you can time transitions using markers in the Timeline Ruler. Any marker that you've made in your Timeline will also show up in the Transition Editor window. You can then use the Roll function to precisely place the transition at the marker in either window.

Transition Tips

Now that you're getting good at adding and adjusting transitions, it's time to learn some workflow tips, like creating and organizing favorite transitions, duplicating transitions, quickly replacing one transition with another, and adding several transitions simultaneously.

WORKING WITH FAVORITE TRANSITIONS

In Final Cut Pro you can easily make your own custom transitions to meet the needs of a particular project. For example, maybe you'd like to use a quicker dissolve or a modified edge wipe. Once you've created some Favorites, you can organize them in the Favorites bin.

Organizing your favorite transitions

The Favorites bin has practically limitless possibilities when it comes to saving and organizing custom transitions. Keeping track of scads of custom transitions can be confusing, and unfortunately you can't make a new bin in the Effects tab. But there is a clever workaround.

To organize your Favorites, follow these steps:

1. Break off the Effects tab by clicking on it and dragging it out of the Browser.

2. Create a new bin in the Project tab by choosing it from the File menu (or use the shortcut Command + B).

3. Drag the new bin from the Project tab into the Favorites bin, which creates another bin within the Favorites bin. You can drag in new bins as needed to hold different categories of custom transitions.

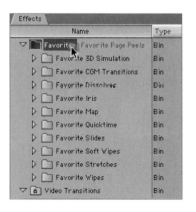

FIGURE 6-17
Bins inside your Favorites bin will help you stay organized.

This way, you can keep all your custom dissolves in one bin, all your custom slides in another bin, and so on, as shown in Figure 6-17.

DUPLICATING TRANSITIONS

Often you'll need to slightly alter the settings of an existing transition, especially when you want to add it to multiple edit points. You can duplicate the
existing transition and then modify its parameters.

1. Select the transition in the Video Transitions bin or the Favorites bin in the
   Effects tab.

2. Choose Edit → Duplicate or press Option + D. A duplicate of the transition
   appears in the Favorites bin.

3. Double-click the transtion to open it in the Transition Editor and make
   changes.

4. Add the newly altered transition to a new edit point (or points) and
   render it.

SWAPPING TRANSITIONS

Sometimes you'll choose a transition, preview it, and realize it isn't at all what
you had in mind. You'll want to quickly replace the dud with a new transition.

Drag and drop a new transition into the Timeline from the Video Transitions bin
or the Favorites bin in the Effects tab, as shown in Figure 6-18.

Alternatively, you can select the transition by clicking on it, and then add your
new choice from the Effects menu.

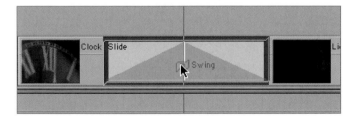

You can replace one transition with
another by dragging and dropping.

ADDING A TRANSITION TO MULTIPLE EDIT POINTS

It's handy to add a transition to many edit points at the same time. You can use
this technique when the clips are not yet added to the sequence, or when they're
already in the Timeline.

Adding multiple transitions horizontally

To add a transition to multiple clips before they're in a sequence, follow these steps:

1. Put the clips into a bin and set the bin to Large Icon view.

2. Arrange the clips in order starting from the top left and ending on the bottom right of the bin, as shown in Figure 6-19.

3. Choose Edit → Select All, and then drag and drop the clips from the bin onto Insert or Overwrite with Transition in the Canvas overlay. Your clips will enter the sequence in order, with the default transition applied to each edit point.

Arrange your clips in storyboard order.

To add a transition to multiple clips in the Timeline, follow these steps:

1. Select the clips.

2. Place the playhead at the beginning of the first clip.

3. Drag and drop the selection back onto the Canvas overlay's Overwrite with Transition area. The default transition will be applied to the edit points you selected (see Figure 6-20).

4. Preview the transition and then render it.

> **tip**
>
> *Before you attempt to add multiple transitions, be sure the default transition of your choice is selected and that each clip has sufficient handle.*

FIGURE 6-20
Here's the result of adding multiple transitions horizontally.

Adding multiple transitions vertically

You can also add the default transition to many layers at once. Here's how:

1. Select an edit point on the first layer.

2. Hold down the Command key and select edit points on additional layers.

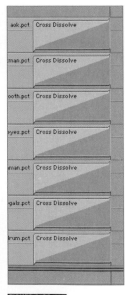

FIGURE 6-21

You can select multiple edit points vertically with the Edit Selection tool.

FIGURE 6-22

Here's the result of adding multiple transitions vertically.

or

1. Use the Edit Selection tool to surround the edit points (see Figure 6-21). (Close the Trim Edit window when it opens; you don't need it for this operation.)

2. Apply the default transition by choosing Effects → Default Transition or pressing Command + T.

   All layers with selected edit points will now have the default transition applied (see Figure 6-22).

3. Render the transition and check it for errors.

Adding multiple transitions in the Timeline

Once you've added a transition, you can add multiple instances of it to any edit point on the Timeline by copying and pasting it or by Option + dragging it to a new place in the Timeline. This is another way to ensure consistency in your transitions.

To duplicate a transition in the Timeline, follow these steps:

1. Copy the Transition you want to use by selecting it and then choosing Edit → Copy or by pressing Command + C.

2. Select the new edit point where you want to add the transition.

3. Choose Edit → Paste or press Command + V to paste in the copied transition at the new edit point.

Here's another great way to duplicate a transition in the Timeline:

1. Select the transition in the Timeline.

2. Hold down the Option key.

3. Drag out a copy of the transition. The cursor should have a "+" to the lower right of the icon.

4. Drop the copy onto the new edit point.

Advanced Transition Techniques

By now you should be very good at creating, applying, modifying, and organizing transitions. In this section you'll learn how to take transitions one step further, using them as tools to create stunning and original effects.

USING TRANSITIONS AS COMPOSITING TOOLS

You can exploit some of the modifications you make in the Transition Editor to trick it into generating new and different effects — effects not found in FCP's Effects menu or Effects tab.

I think of Transitions as "barn doors" that swing open to reveal the incoming shot. The following thought occurred to me one day: "What if the barn doors were permanently propped open so you could see both shots at all times?" By holding those "barn doors" open, you can make a transition act as a vertical effect. If the transition is a real-time transition, then it would be a real-time compositing effect! In fact, there is no other way in FCP to make a real-time compositing effect like this.

To make a transition into a compositing effect, follow these steps:

1. Make sure you have enough "handle" and that In and Out points are set accurately.

2. Apply the transition of your choice to the edit point.

3. Change the duration of the transition to the length of the desired composite by using the Transition Editor or by adjusting the transition's duration in the Timeline.

4. Set the Start and End sliders to the same numbers. Begin with 50% for each. If you'd like to see more options, change the numbers, but keep the values the same for each slider (for example, 30% for Start and 30% for End).

5. To edit cleanly in and out of the composite, use the Razor Blade to trim excess frames from either side of the transition in the Timeline.

After your composite is cleanly bladed, you'll have a solid edit point to transition to and from.

To transition in and out of this composite, you'll have to nest it first and then trim the nest so that it has handles, just like other clips.

---

tip

If you're using a transition as a vertical effect and you're not seeing the portion of the image you want, you can change the X,Y position of the clip in the Canvas in Image + Wireframe mode.

Putting a Clip Beneath Two Transitioning Clips

Every time I see a black background when two clips are transitioning, I want to share the following tip. In almost all cases where you see the Canvas showing beneath two clips as they transition, you can put a clip, title, graphic, or the like there instead to add interest to the transition. You'll need two video tracks and three clips to complete this effect.

To replace the black beneath a transition with a clip or graphic, follow these steps:

1. Choose a transition that shows black underneath it.

2. Move the two clips and the transition by first selecting them, and then dragging them up to V2. As you drag, a new video track will automatically be made.

3. Edit your Background onto V1. This can be any clip, graphic, or piece of text. You can also add motion or filter effects to the background clip if you'd like.

4. Render and enjoy!

ENHANCING THE GRADIENT WIPE

At first glance, FCP's Gradient Wipe looks quite mundane. But as soon as you add a grayscale gradient of some type, you can create transitions that have an organic quality.

1. Create a gradient with FCP's Gradient generator or with Adobe Photoshop.

2. Drag and drop the gradient into the well in the Transition Editor. Drag the Soften slider to the right to make the effect a bit more ethereal or organic.

3. Render and admire your effect.

EXERCISE 6-1: USING TRANSITIONS WITH A CLEAN PLATE

Have you ever wondered how they make someone appear out of thin air in the movies? It all has to do with transitions and something called a *clean plate,* which is a locked-down shot of a scene with no action in it. To do the effect, you'll need both a clean plate and a shot of the actor or object in that same scene. Open the Chapter 6 Exercise sequence.

To make a cable car materialize in a scene, follow these steps:

1. Line up the shots on the Timeline with "Clean Plate" first (with plenty of handle), and then the "Cable Car" shot .

2. Apply a Dissolve.

3. Render and watch the cable car appear.

STEP 2

Apply a Dissolve to make the cable car appear.

EXERCISE 6-2: USING MOTION EFFECTS AS TRANSITIONS

I often think of the *Batman* TV series' innovative technique to wipe from scene to scene: a blurry image rotates while a graphic of a bat scales up to the point where it fills the screen. Another image is revealed as the bat graphic and spinning image recede.

You, too, can use video clips and graphics to transition new footage into the Timeline. What you'll really be doing is revealing a clip on V1 by animating a motion effect applied to a clip on V2. Still another clip on V3 could have a motion effect applied to it in order to mask the "reveal" taking place on the layers below it. You can dream up a lot of different motion effects that could obscure a reveal, like rotation, scale, crop, center, distort, or even a perspective filter like Basic 3D. I'll show you how to mask a reveal by animating the Center property of the clip that's on V3.

In the Chapter 6 Exercise sequence, go to the marker for Exercise 2.

1. Place the outgoing clip ("Thai Boat") on V1.

2. Place the incoming clip ("Grand Palace") on V2.

3. Place the clip that will mask the reveal ("Gold Lady") on V3.

4. Go into Image + Wireframe mode.

5. Scale the Canvas to 50% size.

6. Double-click on the V3 clip in the Timeline to load the clip into the Viewer.

7. Drag the V3 clip's wireframe completely off to the left of the Canvas, at X = −234, Y = 0.

8. Set a keyframe for the clip on V3 by pressing Control + K.

9. Double-click on the clip on V2 to load it into the Viewer.

10. Move the playhead forward 15 frames and then set a keyframe for the Grand Palace clip by pressing Control + K.

11. Move the playhead 1:00 down the Timeline. This is where you want the crop effect to end.

12. Click the Crop tool and drag the Grand Palace wireframe from left to right to reveal the Thai Boat clip. The second keyframe is automatically added.

tip

If you are upgrading from FCP 3, you should still have the CGM Software Patterns on board. These patterns are especially made for the Gradient Wipe.

tip

You can create a gradient using any clip. Just drop the Desaturate filter onto it. A color correction filter will work even better, as it offers not only the ability to desaturate the clip, but also to adjust the levels.

13. Move the playhead forward 15 more frames (2:00 into the effect) and then select the Gold Lady clip. Shift + drag its wireframe to the right until it rests offscreen at X = 316 and Y = 0. This sets that crucial second Center keyframe for the Gold Lady. The Gold Lady clip will look like its flight is "wiping on" the Thai Boat clip as it passes over the Grand Palace clip.

14. Render and enjoy!

STEP 14

When you play the transition, the statue's head sweeps across the screen, revealing a different background as it moves.

You've learned a lot about transitions. Now we'll look ahead and see how we can prevent problems and inconsistencies when applying and modifying transitions.

Troubleshooting

Transitions are lots of fun to use — until you start getting warnings or can't add a transition where you want to on the Timeline.

When you're troubleshooting problems with any transition, the first thing you should do is make sure you have sufficient handle. The most common error, "Insufficient Content," is directly related to handle. In this section I've provided some tests for you to make sure you have sufficient handle, or, as they say in Final Cut Pro lingo, "sufficient content."

"Insufficient Content" problems

Getting the "Insufficient Content" warning is the most common problem people have with transitions. Don't worry. If you get this warning, you can fix it!

There are also a couple of problems related to "Insufficient Content" where you will not receive this warning. We'll first discuss "Insufficient Content" scenarios.

If you see the "Insufficient Content" warning, you probably do not have enough handle, either on the outgoing clip, the incoming clip, or both. (The warning would be more aptly named "Insufficient Handle," because this is what is going on.) This warning occurs most often when you drag and drop clips directly into the Timeline.

If you drag a clip into the Timeline without first setting In and Out points, there will be no handle available for a transition. To remedy this, you'll have to trim enough frames off one or both sides of the transition using the trim tools in the Timeline, the Transition Editor (see the section on "Ripple trimming in the Transition Editor"), or in the Trim Edit window. (If you see the Selection tool with the "X" on it, it means you have no handle at all. In this case, you have to perform a trim edit on at least one side of the cut to create handles.)

To see if you have insufficient handle, follow these steps:

1. Double-click the transition in the Timeline (or press Command + 7) to bring up the Trim Edit window.

2. Note the placement of the outgoing clip's Out point and the incoming clip's In point. If the edit points are at the very limits of their media, you don't have enough handle. You should note whether there is sufficient media after the Out point and before the In point.

A second way to detect handle is to double-click on the outgoing clip (not on the transition) and verify in the Viewer that there is handle after the Out point. Repeat this process for the incoming clip, by noting whether there is handle before the In point.

Select the Slip tool and click on each clip to look for "overlap" in the outline displayed for the clip's media. If there is no overlap, then there is no handle.

A transition's duration is shorter than 1:00

If you've dragged and dropped a 1:00 stock transition and find that the transition's duration in the Transition Editor reads less than 1:00, then you have "Insufficient Content" problems. However, a warning will not pop up if you drag and drop unless you have zero frames of handle. You can remedy this by trimming one or both sides of the transition in the Transition Editor.

A transition cuts into the incoming clip too soon

Even after you've fixed an "Insufficient Content" problem, trouble can occur. For example, you might wish to see the outgoing shot resolve, but the trim you just made on the outgoing shot cuts into the incoming shot too soon during the transition. To fix this problem, you have to recapture the clip with some additional handle. You can avoid this problem next time by logging and capturing liberally before and after your intended In and Out points. You can also capture additional handle in the Log and Capture window.

A transition contains shots from a different place in the tape

This happens when you've captured a whole tape, rather than logged and captured individual clips, and the transition's handle goes into the next take on your clip. You can work around this by making the transition shorter or by selecting a portion of the clip that needs lengthening and applying a slow-motion speed effect to it.

A transition looks terrible when rendered

This is a problem when you're evaluating your transitions and effects without an NTSC or PAL monitor hooked up to your Final Cut Pro system. You may want to revisit Chapter 1 if you need more details on why you need to include a monitor.

You see a jump in the luminance at the center of a transition

If your transitions have a jump in brightness levels or have a milky white appearance after you render them, you may be experiencing some problems with your video processing.

1. You should first check to see if this problem exists by going into your Sequence settings (Command + 0). Click on the Video Processing tab to inspect how your sequence is processing your renders.

2. There's a checkbox that says Always Render in RGB. Leave that box unchecked. Change this to one of the settings for YUV processing instead and click OK.

3. To make sure this won't happen in any new sequences, you'll also want to visit your Audio/Video Settings Preferences and make certain that your Sequence Presets are properly set up for Video Processing. Go to the Video Processing tab in the Sequence Preset Editor to check on this.

Wrap-up

You've learned a lot about transitions and what makes them tick. By now you're adjusting transitions to give them a more polished look, and timing them just so. And you know some amazing advanced tips. Finally, finding out how to trouble-shoot problems should make you feel more confident in dealing with all the issues related to applying, adjusting, and rendering transitions.

Color Correction 7

Color correction is both an art and a science. From an artistic standpoint, you can use certain colors to create moods. For example, a reddish scene might look warm and welcoming, while the same scene with blue tones will have a cooler, more melancholy feeling. On the scientific side, you'll use Final Cut Pro's color correction tools to optimize colors or make an image suitable for broadcast. The techniques you'll learn in this chapter will help you make more intelligent decisions as you work with all aspects of color.

Color Correction Basics

Color correction is often thought of as a way to fix something that's wrong with an image. That's sometimes the case, but to me, color correction is more about enhancing an image by having total control over its brightness, hue, and saturation — the components that comprise color in a digital image (see Figure 7-1). What you do with that control is up to you. Let's look at some of the basics of color correction, and then we'll talk about some of the wilder things you can do with these tools.

WHY PERFORM COLOR CORRECTION?

When you're creating effects, an understanding of color allows you to have precise control over the look of your images, including the effects you've applied to them. First, let's look at some of the reasons for using color correction:

- Maximizing an image's brightness and contrast range
- Color balancing images
- Achieving a particular look or mood
- Matching color and brightness between shots
- Ensuring "broadcast safe" chroma and luma values
- Creating color effects

FIGURE 7-1

Color correction gives you control over the color and brightness of an image. On the left is the original clip. The center clip has been dramatically altered to make the blacks darker and the whites brighter. In the clip on the right, the saturation values have been raised to vividly enrich the colors.

Image courtesy of Thinkstock Footage (V0016028)

FIGURE 7-2

With color correction techniques, you can create a variety of moods for your images, such as a warmer or cooler look. In these shots, the color balance has been adjusted toward red (center) and blue (right).

COLOR CORRECTION WORKFLOW

When I'm doing a standard color correction, I usually perform a number of steps in a particular order: primary color correction, then secondary color correction, adding color effects, and finally "finishing" the piece.

Primary color correction consists of making basic adjustments to the luma and chroma values of your clips, such as:

- Maximizing the brightness and contrast range of your images

- Making initial adjustments to ensure that images are broadcast safe

- Color balancing, which can include white-balancing images to make white look white, and black-balancing to make blacks reflect true black

- Adjusting saturation (often referred to as the color's "strength")

- Altering the color balance of key images, shifting the luminance and chrominance of an image to achieve a specific look or mood (see Figure 7-2)

- Matching all the project's shots to a specified look

tip

Before you read this chapter, read the sections of the FCP manual that cover the tools in your Tool Bench. At the very least you should be familiar with the basic functions of the Waveform Monitor and the Vectorscope.

What Is a Colorist's Role in Post-Production?

In the realm of professional video production, the *colorist* is an artist who can make or break the overall look and feel of a piece. The colorist usually interprets decisions made by others, such as the cinematographer or the director.

When you create projects in Final Cut Pro, chances are that *you'll* be the colorist, and you'll have to rely on your own decisions regarding color. It can take years of experience to become a good colorist, but don't let that stop you from striving to achieve your own goals with FCP's powerful collection of color correction tools.

Start with a Good Video Monitor

To make accurate color adjustments, you need to have a good quality, calibrated video monitor (fed by your video deck). A good monitor, combined with the highest quality signal, will make all the difference for identifying potential problems.

You'll need the video monitor for monitoring precise adjustments dictated by FCP's scopes, and for getting feedback while making judgment calls such as "too hot," "too washed out," or "just right."

Make sure you're monitoring through your video deck at the best possible quality. If you're using a DV deck or camcorder, then monitor Y/C (S-video). If you use component Beta SP, then monitor the component signal. If you're using SDI, then you should monitor the SDI signal.

Secondary color correction uses a color correction filter's Limit Effect function to adjust a single hue, saturation level, or brightness value (or a combination of any of the three) in a scene. A secondary color correction might include the following:

- Fixing problematic areas within an image (for example, one particular color that's oversaturated)

- Making specialty color effects

Finishing the video largely relates to making a final pass to meet broadcast-safe specifications. If you've done this in the primary color correction phase, why do this again? Good question! In the first color correction pass for broadcast safe, you'll maximize exposure for your image within broadcast-safe limits. In the finishing stage, you'll make a final check before delivery of your show. Here are some reasons why you must double-check for broadcast-safe limits:

- You may have introduced illegal luma levels or saturation during the secondary color correction process.

- You added a composite mode to a color corrected clip, driving levels or saturation into illegal territory.

- You introduced a filter after primary color correction, allowing the levels or saturation to slip out of broadcast-safe range.

Now that you have a basic sense of the color correction process, let's look at FCP's color correction filters. Then you'll perform some of the duties of color correction.

Color Correction Filters

This section will introduce you to FCP's two basic color correction filters, which give you the power to fine-tune certain aspects of color. Whether you're balancing color from shot to shot or creating a color effect, you'll want to begin the process by selecting the proper color correction tools for the job. I'm partial to the Color Corrector 3-Way filter because you can influence color in three overlapping brightness ranges. First, I'll provide an overview of the features of these powerful tools. After that, you'll get some experience using them.

THE COLOR CORRECTOR 3-WAY FILTER

The Color Corrector 3-Way filter is the most powerful tool in FCP's suite of color correction tools. You can't go wrong using it for primary color correction — or for any of the more difficult color correction tasks. You can also use its Limit Effect functions for advanced color effects.

What Is Broadcast Safe?

You might be surprised to learn that the definition of *broadcast safe* varies; it depends on the requirements of the outfit that's broadcasting your show.

In general, making your piece broadcast safe means adjusting luma and chroma values to fall into a range that's acceptable to the entity that will broadcast it over the airwaves or duplicate it to videotape or DVD. To change that range, you can use a variety of FCP's color correction filters. To monitor that range, you will use your Video Scopes, located in your Tools menu. The most useful of them are the Waveform Monitor, which you use to check and adjust brightness levels, and the Vectorscope, which you use to check and adjust hue and saturation levels.

How do you know what is required for delivery to a particular broadcast facility? That's your job! Before you deliver your project for broadcast or distribution, ask the engineers at the facility about their specific broadcast-safe requirements. For NTSC, for example, you'll likely deliver a show that has no blacks below 7.5 IRE or whites above 100 IRE, which you check with the Waveform Monitor. Saturation should not venture outside the specific "targets" in the Vectorscope.

If you ignore adjusting for broadcast safe, you may find that the facility's broadcast engineers will refuse to broadcast your show. This can be a devastating blow, particularly if it has a dedicated airdate, and you have not budgeted enough time to go through the time-consuming process of color correction to redeliver the show in time.

There are other sound technical reasons why you must do this, even if you don't have to deliver it to a broadcast entity. For instance, if your colors are too saturated, you'll get distortion in your audio called "ringing." If your whites are too hot, you'll get a line level "hum" in your audio. Your clients won't be happy with that!

As someone who creates effects, you'll often be pushing the limits of broadcast safe, so tread carefully when delivering to high-end broadcast facilities.

In this filter's Visual interface you'll find three color wheels for precise control over hues in an image's blacks, midtones, and whites (see Figure 7-3). Each color wheel has separate sliders to control the levels of a particular brightness range. For example, you could raise the value of the midtones to brighten an image, but leave the colors of the shadows relatively unchanged in the darkest of the blacks.

The Auto Levels buttons—Auto Black, Auto Contrast, and Auto White—are for quickly getting your images close to proper exposure. Auto Color Balance eyedroppers can also bring all your images into the proper color range, and a saturation slider provides control over the entire image's saturation. The Match Hue tools (new to FCP 4) will help you solve problems such as matching your covering shots (or cutaways) to your master shots.

At the bottom of the Visual interface is a set of Limit Effect tools. (These will be discussed later.) With them you can achieve precise control over particular colors in an image. In Final Cut Pro 4, the Limit Effect controls are tucked into a disclosure triangle. Click it to get access to these tools in both the standard Color Corrector and Color Corrector 3-Way filters.

> **tip**
>
> *When you're doing color correction, the Numeric parameters in the Filters tab are sometimes easier to use than the controls in the Visual interface. If you have enough monitor real estate, it's nice to have both windows open while you're working with either of the color correction filters.*

FIGURE 7-3

The Color Corrector 3-Way filter's Visual interface offers controls such as sliders and eyedroppers.

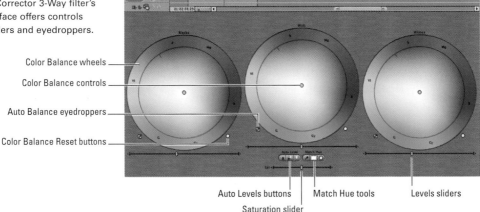

Color Balance wheels

Color Balance controls

Auto Balance eyedroppers

Color Balance Reset buttons

Auto Levels buttons   Match Hue tools   Levels sliders

Saturation slider

Gearing Up and Down

As you're working with a color correction filter, you may want to use the Command key when you're adjusting its controls. If you're in the Visual or Numeric view, holding down this key provides "gear down" behavior for making smooth and precise adjustments. The exception is moving the Color Balance controls in Visual mode. Holding down the Command key in this mode "gears up" control, which means that the Color Balance controls will move more easily across the color wheel.

THE COLOR CORRECTOR FILTER

The standard Color Corrector filter is also a good choice for general color correction duties. Its parameters are a bit different from those of the Color Corrector 3-Way, but are still very useful. The Color Corrector filter may be a better choice for certain video capture cards, as it will run in real time in that realm, while the 3-Way version may not (the opposite is true in DV systems).

The filter's main controls feature a color wheel on the left for color balance, and one on the right for hue (video engineers call this wheel *phase*). There are a couple of tasks you might want to perform with this filter:

- Shifting a clip's colors with the Hue, or phase shift, wheel. You could use this technique to fix footage that was captured with an analog video capture card with improperly calibrated colors.

- Performing certain Limit Effect tasks, such as selective color effects. Once you've created a selection to change, you simply rotate the phase shift wheel to achieve different hues.

Let's move on the to the primary color correction process.

Primary Color Correction

Putting your images through primary color correction will let you adjust the color in poorly lit or improperly exposed footage, establish the look of your master shots, and ensure you're starting the process in broadcast-safe range. In addition, primary color correction will provide a good base to work from if you do additional color correction tasks, such as matching color between two shots or creating secondary color correction effects.

A good color correction plan begins with adjusting your key images, or master shots, to fall into broadcast-legal range for luminance (brightness range) and chrominance (color range). During that process, contrast is maximized. Next, you'll color-balance each image. For primary color correction, the best tool is usually the Color Corrector 3-Way filter.

MAXIMIZING CONTRAST

The first step in primary color correction is maximizing contrast. You can do this quite easily with either of the main color correction filters. Why maximize contrast? Distributing the luma levels across the grayscale spectrum will automatically

note

If you click the Auto Contrast button, you don't need to click the Auto White or the Auto Black buttons. The Auto Contrast button does both tasks.

improve image fidelity from the start. Maximizing contrast often rectifies most of your basic problems regarding exposure, brightness level, and color. To distribute the luma levels:

1. Apply either color corrector filter to an image.

2. Click the Auto Contrast button to set the contrast values.

That's it! After you click Auto Contrast, you should see the levels of your image become more widely distributed on the Waveform Monitor.

OPTIMIZING LUMA LEVELS

After setting the contrast, you'll need to make sure the image is within broadcast-safe limits, which means that you'll have to check the levels of luma and chroma and then perhaps adjust them.

Checking for excess luma

tip

Click the Auto Contrast button only once, or you'll redistribute the pixels, giving you inaccurate results. If you want to click the Auto Contrast button again, you should first reset the filter in the Filters tab by clicking the red "X."

With any luck, the Auto Contrast button took care of excess luma. Enable the Range Check Overlays to see if it did indeed do the job. To see this overlay in action, go to the View Mode pop-up menu in the Canvas and make sure that Show Excess Luma is checked (or use the keyboard shortcut Control + Z).

If you see a check mark in a green circle, you're within broadcast-safe standards. However, if you don't see a small upward-pointing arrow next to the check mark, you're not *quite* in the ideal zone for maximum luminance. You can make adjustments for this. If you see an exclamation point and red "zebra stripes," your image is out of broadcast-safe range and is too bright.

Color Correction Window Arrangements

FCP 4 offers some new window arrangements for color correction, such as Window → Arrange → Color Correction, or Window → Arrange → Multiple Edits, which brings up the Video Scopes in the Tool Bench. The Scopes will tell you exactly how the luma and chroma levels are reading as you make your adjustments with the color correction filters.

Your Viewer, Canvas, and Tool Bench will be arranged along the top of the screen, with the Tool Bench on the right. You can pick the Tool Bench layout, as well as the clip you wish to display within it.

Adjusting luma

If you're not in the ideal zone and your image is a bit too dark, or if you have red zebra stripes and your image is too bright, you'll need to make some adjustments to it. Here are some tips:

- Bring up your video scopes so that you have a more objective view of the signal as you adjust it. Go to Tools → Video Scopes, and then select Waveform from the Video Scopes' Layout menu. Select a view from the Video Scopes' View menu. In this case, you probably want to have it enabled for the current frame.

- If you don't see a small upward-pointing arrow next to the check mark, you'll need to raise the Whites Level slider slightly. Click the small right-facing arrow next to the Whites Level slider (see Figure 7-4). When you see the check mark, you've maximized the brightness.

- Step through the entire clip, noting whether anything bright enters the frame. Make sure you don't see any exclamation points as you step through. If an exclamation point does show up, make small adjustments by clicking the left-facing arrow next to the Whites Level slider until it's replaced by the check mark with the upward-pointing arrow (see Figure 7-5).

- You can also make fine adjustments to the other Level sliders after the image is brought into legal spec. For example, if your midtones are still dark, you can raise the Midtones Level slider to the right, as long as you don't venture back into illegal levels.

The next step in primary color correction is ensuring that there are no areas of excess chroma and that saturation is within an acceptable range.

note

Setting the luminance levels above 100 but below 110 maximizes brightness levels in the primary color correction process. If green zebra stripes appear anywhere on the image, you have luminance values above 100 IRE in your source, which is fine. If you see red stripes, you have levels above 110 IRE, which you must adjust.

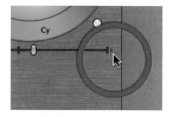

FIGURE 7-4

Click the small arrow to make fine adjustments to the whites.

FIGURE 7-5

If you see an exclamation point and red zebra stripes (left), the clip is out of broadcast-safe range for luma. If you see a check mark and a small upward-pointing arrow (right), luma levels have been optimized.

OPTIMIZING CHROMA LEVELS

After contrast and luma are set, you'll want to bring the image into broadcast-safe range for chroma, which pertains to hue and saturation levels. Like luma, the chroma must not be too "hot" for broadcast-safe specs, so you might need to adjust it. The best tools for this are the Range Check Overlays and the Vectorscope (see Figure 7-6). When you're optimizing chroma levels, you'll need to find out whether you have excess chroma levels.

Checking for excess chroma

To quickly check an image for excess chroma, use the Range Check Overlays. If there are any saturation values that exceed broadcast-safe specs, you'll see both an exclamation point and zebra stripes in the image.

To see the Range Check Overlays for excess chroma, first go to the Canvas's View Mode menu and make sure Show Overlays is checked. Then, go to View → Range Check → Excess Chroma.

If you see a check mark inside a green circle, your saturation levels are within the broadcast-safe realm. If you see an exclamation point, you'll need to reduce excess chroma.

note

Other displays, like the Histogram and the RGB Parade, will also guide you in setting the proper levels for luminance.

note

Be sure to turn off any Range Check Overlays before outputting your video or exporting video or a still frame. If you see a plain white frame after you export your still image or video, that's a sign you left Range Check Overlays on.

tip

Keep your eye on both your video monitor and your scopes as you make fine adjustments, never relying exclusively on one or the other. Although FCP scopes are fine for most situations, a dedicated hardware waveform monitor and vectorscope will be necessary if you deliver a lot of shows for broadcast.

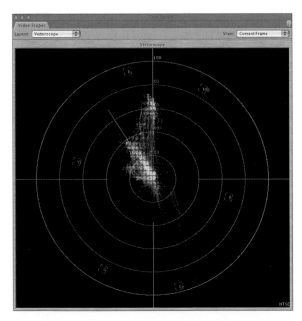

FIGURE 7-6
Check Hue and Saturation values with the Vectorscope. Here, reds and yellows dominate the scope.

Adjusting for excess chroma

If an image is oversaturated, you'll need to adjust the Saturation slider in a color correction filter.

To adjust chroma levels to make them broadcast safe, follow these steps:

1. Bring up the Vectorscope by going to Tools → Video Scopes and choosing Vectorscope from the Layout menu. (This is an optional step, but it's nice to see how your adjustment is working on the image.)

2. Select a view from the Video Scope's View menu. In this case, Current Frame is fine.

3. With the playhead on the clip, click and drag the color correction filter's Saturation slider to the left until the exclamation point is replaced by the Range Check's check mark in the green circle. (Note: There are no + or − signs that show up when monitoring chroma, as there are with luma.)

4. Click the small arrow to the left of the Sat slider a few times to bring the level down another few notches. This is to make sure that your colors remain legal for the length of the clip as it plays.

5. Step through the entire clip and make sure you don't see an exclamation point at any time. If an exclamation point does show up, click a few more times on the small arrow at the left of the Sat slider.

6. You may want to take a look at the Vectorscope to check that the saturation level is not extended beyond its targets, which are displayed with the letters R, Mg, B, C, G, and Y. Each letter represents one of the primary hues for color in broadcast television: red, magenta, blue, cyan, green, and yellow.

7. Check the video monitor and look for excess chroma as well. The Range Check Overlays will tell you that your colors are in the legal range, but your shot may still have colors that look too "hot." Your scopes are valuable tools, but sometimes you'll simply have to trust your own judgment (see Figure 7-7).

After you've adjusted for excess luma and chroma, it's time to perform a basic color balance for the key images.

tip

Although the ranges of influence for the Luminance Levels sliders — Blacks, Mids, and Whites — overlap a bit, you can use them to adjust certain colors without affecting others that are in a different range. For example, move the Mids slider to the right to brighten your midtones without affecting the darker shadows or the brighter highlights. To brighten your highlights, move the Whites slider to the right.

tip

It's your job to check levels throughout the entire length of each clip to ensure you can achieve maximum exposure without exceeding what is too "hot" to be broadcast safe. Video is evaluated only where the playhead rests, so you'll want to step through the image and look for any objects that might cause the image to venture into illegal luma levels.

FIGURE 7-7
Although both of these images are broadcast safe, the one on the right is too saturated. Trust your eyes when adjusting saturation values.

> **tip**
>
> *You can monitor excess luma and excess chroma at the same time with the Range Check Overlays. Choose View → Range Check → Both.*

COLOR BALANCING AN IMAGE

One of the final adjustments in primary color correction involves color balancing shots that were not accurately balanced at the shoot. Color Corrector 3-Way is a good tool for this because you can balance colors using white, black, and gray items in your image. Sometimes performing a white balance is all your image needs.

To color balance an image, follow these steps:

1. Click the Color Corrector 3-Way filter's Visual button to view the color wheels for blacks, midtones, and whites.

2. Click on the Auto Balance Color eyedropper for the Whites wheel, and use it to click on the best-exposed white element in the image in the Canvas (a white T-shirt or wall, for example).

3. If the image still looks as if it has inaccurate color, then you'll need to black-balance the image as well. Click on the Auto Balance Color eyedropper for the Blacks wheel, and then click on the best-exposed black element of the image in the Canvas. To avoid an incorrect reading, make sure that the object is actually black before you click on it.

4. If you still aren't getting a satisfactory color balance, you can use the Mids wheel's Auto Balance Color eyedropper to click on something in the Canvas that's neutral gray, which is rather tough unless you have a decent chip chart. (See "Color Correction Begins at the Shoot.")

> **tip**
>
> *If you need to start over on the color balancing process, hold down the Shift key while you click the Reset button of any color balance wheel. All three color wheels will reset.*

If you're still having trouble with color balance after following the above steps, you'll need to push your Color Balance controls toward or away from certain colors, which we'll do in the next section.

Adjusting color balance

Even after you've color-balanced an image, it may still have certain colors in it that you need to neutralize. For example, if a shot still has too much green, you should gently push the Whites or Mids Balance control indicator towards the opposite color — magenta — on the color wheel.

Note that if you push your values too far, you'll move into the realm of color effects rather than color balance, so show some finesse when you make the adjustments. You'll notice that the Color Balance control indicators are hard to move — that's to constrain you from making wild adjustments. A Whites Balance adjustment is usually slight.

To make color-balance adjustments:

1. Use your eyes to evaluate which color is dominating the image. Then evaluate it in the Vectorscope and on your video monitor to verify which hue is causing the colorcast. You should see vectors of the errant hue pointing towards one of the color targets in the Vectorscope, or a stronger reading for that color's brightness in the RGB Parade scope.

2. Click and drag the Color Balance control indicator away from the color that you want to control, checking the Vectorscope and your video monitor as you work.

3. Keep dragging the Control Indicator until you begin to see the whites in the video monitor turn to the shade you're looking for. Continue to finely tune the color you intend for the image (see Figure 7-8). Although FCP's scopes and readouts will help you, keep in mind that there's a bit of subjectivity involved in creating a final color balance for your key images, so keep your eyes on the calibrated video monitor as well.

note

When white-balancing an image, make sure an object is actually white before you click on the Canvas, or you'll create a colorcast in the image. You should also avoid blown-out images where there are no color values at all. If your white balance came out poorly, you can undo it with Command + Z and try again for a better result.

Image courtesy of Thinkstock Footage (V0014409)

FIGURE 7-8

Use your Vectorscope and your eyes to detect the color that's giving you trouble. In this case, the video was shot with a filter on the lens, lending a yellowish cast to the image (left). To adjust the color balance, move the balance indicators away from yellow and toward blue (right).

Now that you've set the proper exposure, luma, chroma, and color balance, you're done with primary color correction. With any luck, you've cleaned up all the major problems with exposure and color. However, if your image still doesn't look right, you may have to make further adjustments.

tip

You can also use color balancing to establish a basic look for your master shot. If you want to match the rest of your shots to a cooler look, push the appropriate Color Balance indicator(s) toward blue. If you want your master shot to have a warmer look, push them toward red.

EXERCISE 7-1: PRIMARY COLOR CORRECTION

Now that you have a basic idea of how to do a primary color correction, let's do an exercise. Open the Chapter 7 Exercise sequence in the Chapter 7 Exercise Sequences bin, which is in the Chapter 7 bin. You'll be working on the first clip in the sequence: "Teen Pan CU." In this case, the scene was shot with a blue filter on the lens. Your task is to recover the original colors of the image so that it will match shots that were shot without the filter.

1. Park the playhead anywhere on the clip and then engage the Range Check Overlays by going to the View Mode pop-up menu in the Canvas and choosing Show Excess Luma.

2. Bring up the Waveform Monitor to check your results as you work. Go to Tools → Video Scopes and then choose Layout → Waveform and View → Current Frame.

3. Click the Auto Contrast button to maximize the exposure. The Range Check Overlay for excess luma should show the check mark in the green circle, with a small arrow beside the check mark. If there's no arrow, adjust the Whites Level slider until luma is properly maximized.

Images courtesy of Thinkstock Footage (V0014602)

STEP 1
Evaluate the image. You'll see that the skin tones are much too blue.

4. Switch the Range Check Overlays to check for excess chroma by going to View → Range Check → Excess Chroma. There should be a check mark inside the green circle. This shows that you are in broadcast-safe range for chroma.

5. Evaluate the image by eye on the video monitor. You'll see that you need to move the Sat slider a bit to the right.

6. Perform a color balance adjustment. Click the Select Auto Balance Color eyedropper to the left of the Whites color wheel, and then click on the white of one of the teen's eyeballs (zoom in if you need to) — this is the only white available in the shot. The shot will be less blue now.

7. To improve the blacks, click on the Select Auto Balance Color eyedropper next to the Blacks color wheel, and then click in the iris of the same eyeball. The blacks will be shifted from blue as well.

8. Check the Vectorscope to take a look at chroma values. You'll see that the shot still has a lot of blue in it.

9. Because the shot is still too blue, you'll need to perform a basic color balance. Note that the Blacks and Whites Color Balance indicators are pointing between red and yellow. To get the skin tone looking more realistic, push the Mids Color Balance indicator toward red.

The blue colorcast has been neutralized, making the image much more pleasing to look at.

As a final step, push the Mids indicator toward red. The skin tone now looks more realistic.

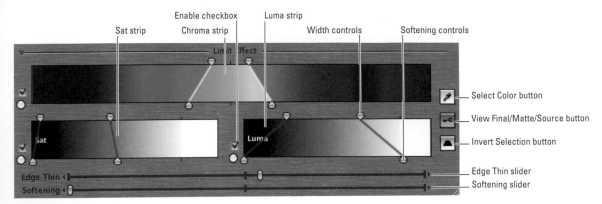

Sat strip — Enable checkbox — Luma strip — Width controls — Softening controls

Chroma strip

Limit Effect

Select Color button

View Final/Matte/Source button

Invert Selection button

Edge Thin slider

Softening slider

The Limit Effect area of the color correction filters lets you adjust one particular hue, luma, and/or chroma range.

Secondary Color Correction

Secondary color correction involves fine-tuning a single color in an image. Isolating a color and then adjusting its hue, luma, or saturation range — or a combination of these three color attributes — is the goal. For this kind of control, you'll be using the Limit Effect features (see Figure 7-9).

There are two main reasons to employ secondary correction:

- To fix problems that couldn't be rectified using other methods of color correction. This situation occurs when the majority of an image looks great after primary color correction, but has an area that is distracting or causes the values to travel out of broadcast-safe range.

- To make stylized color effects where hues, brightness, or saturation are significantly altered (see Figure 7-10). With secondary color correction effects, you can choose a single color — a blue sky, for example — and oversaturate it, change its color, or even make it change color over time.

Using secondary color correction, you can make some radical color changes if you like. Here, the blouse's original magenta (see Figure 7-7) has been changed to blue.

Secondary color correction requires making a special kind of matte (similar to one you'd make with the Chroma Keyer) that will limit a specific range of luminance, hue, and/or saturation. Mattes are discussed in detail in the next chapter, so if you have any trouble with the following exercise, read Chapter 8 and then come back to the exercise.

Color Correction Begins at the Shoot

When you're shooting video, choosing a color palette and using its key color tones will save you loads of time in the color correction process. Keep that color palette in mind when designing the set, lighting, and costumes. If you can, have the director of photography (DP) shoot some test footage for you. By doing some work up front, during the color correction process you'll merely be enhancing colors, not changing them.

The DP should shoot a wide contrast range, providing some visible shadow in the blacks and readable detail in the highlights. If details are lost at the shoot — by crushing the blacks or blowing out the highlights within the camera — you won't be able to recover them during the color correction process.

If you have a chip chart, waveform monitor, and vectorscope on the set, you can accurately set the brightness and color values in your camera. (A *chip chart* is a piece of cardboard that shows black, white, a series of standard colors, and a swatch with an 18% grayscale for balancing mid-tones; see the figure below.) A PowerBook running FCP hooked up to your camera can provide a cheap alternative to hardware scopes on the set.

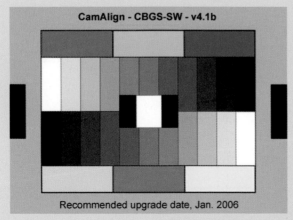

CamAlign - CBGS-SW - v4.1b

Recommended upgrade date, Jan. 2006

Some cameras — notably the newer Panasonic cameras like the DVX-100, SDX-900 and Varicam HD — have adjustable gamma ratios that extend the contrast range quite a bit.

I prefer to use no filters on the camera, which gives me more choices in post-production. Many DPs might argue this point, particularly if they're not aware of recent advances in color correction. You don't want to degrade your beautiful HD footage with a lens diffuser or filter before it hits tape, do you? Trust me, you don't.

Here's a chip chart from DSC Labs (www.dsclabs.com).

This pattern is reproduced with the permission of DSC Labs. Further reproduction or use in camera alignment, or as an on-the-set-reference, is prohibited. Also, such use could result in seriously degraded image quality.

EXERCISE 7-2: CONTROLLING A SINGLE COLOR

In this exercise, the basketball player's shirt is very saturated, but the background is not. If you raise the overall saturation to balance it out, then the red shirt will send the image out of broadcast-safe range. To fix this problem, you can either desaturate the red shirt or bring up the saturation of the foliage. You'll do the latter.

Open the Chapter 7 Exercise sequence. Navigate to the Exercise 2 marker in the Timeline to get started.

1. Park the playhead on the clip. Go to Effects → Video Filters → Color Correction → Color Corrector and then double-click the clip to load it into the Viewer. In the Color Corrector tab, raise the saturation slider with Range Check Overlays engaged and watch the color of the trees intensify to a vibrant, oversaturated look that is still broadcast safe. Click the Reset button in the Filters tab.

2. In the Filters tab, click on the Color Corrector tab and choose Visual mode. Then turn down the disclosure triangle to use the Limit Effect tools.

3. Using the Select Color eyedropper, go to the image in the Canvas, and click some green foliage.

4. Click the View Final/Matte/Source button (the one with the key on it). You'll see a grayscale matte.

Image courtesy of Thinkstock Footage (V0020037)

STEP 1
If you increase saturation to boost the greens, the overly saturated red will push the image out of broadcast-safe range.

STEP 4
Click the View Final/Matte/Source button to see a matte that will allow you to isolate and work on a single color.

5. The matte needs some improvement.

    a. Click twice on the View Final/Matte/Source button, and then Shift + click the Select Color eyedropper and click once more on a lighter or darker green area. Continue Shift + clicking if necessary.

    b. Click again on the View Final/Matte/Source button to see the matte, which should now include more white.

6. Near the bottom of the Limit Effect area you'll see two sliders: Edge Thin and Softening. These controls let you adjust the edges of the matte.

    a. Move the Edge Thin slider to the right.

    b. Click the small arrow two or three times to move the Softening slider to the right.

7. Click twice on the View Final/Matte/Source button and raise the saturation slider with Range Check Overlays for Excess Chroma engaged. That way, you can raise the saturation to match the intensity of the player's shirt without going out of broadcast-safe range.

8. Experiment with the Sat and Levels sliders for varying results. You've now completed a secondary color correction.

9. Now comes the fun part. Find a new color for the foliage by spinning the Hue wheel. A blue or purple color for the trees creates a different world!

> **note**
>
> *You can shift the Hue wheel to your chosen color before you make your matte. That way, you can Shift + click areas that are still the original color with the Select Color eyedropper as you make your matte.*

> **tip**
>
> *If you want to limit only the hue, luma, or saturation for a secondary color correction, you must uncheck the other items in the Limit Effect area of either color corrector filter.*

> **note**
>
> *You can also use the Color Corrector 3-Way filter for a Limit Effect task.*

STEP 9

Have some fun by trying out different colors for the foliage.

Solving Common Color Problems

You may need to use additional techniques to obtain the best possible color correction. For example, if the colors in a wide shot don't match the close-up, you'll need to use FCP's Match Hue tools in either of the color corrector filters. Let's look at Match Hue and other color correction techniques.

tip

When you select Open mode in the Playhead Sync pop-up menu, the clip the playhead is parked on will automatically open in the Viewer when that track is also Auto Selected. This is helpful when adjusting color correction filters in the Filters tab.

COLOR MATCHING

With the proliferation of low-cost DV camcorders, a lot more multi-cam shoots are taking place. If more than one camera was used, you'll need to pay more attention to color matching. Even if you use a single camera, shooting over a series of days with altered lighting and changing technical situations can cause shifts in luminance and chrominance. Having unmatched colors between a master shot and covering shots looks unprofessional. The goal here is to create tonal continuity from one scene to another. If the shots do not match well, you can try copying and pasting a color correction filter or using Match Hue.

Simple color matching using copy and paste

The simplest way to make shots match is to copy and paste the same color correction filters to shots that were taken at the same place and time. Here are a few ideas:

- Copy a master shot's color correction filter and then paste it into the covering shot's Filters tab.
- If you have many clips you want to apply the color correction filter to, you can use Copy/Paste Attributes.
- Use the color corrector's Drag Filter icon to drag a color correction filter to selected clips on the Timeline (see Figure 7-11).
- Go to Modify → Copy Filters and choose where you wish to copy from or to. (Note that the current clip defines copying functions. For example, if you are copying *from,* you're copying color correction settings from a previous clip in the Timeline *to* your current clip. If you're copying *to,* you're copying from your current clip *to* a clip forward in the Timeline.)

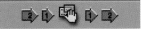

FIGURE 7-11
You can use the color corrector filters' Drag Filter icon to apply a filter to a particular clip in the Timeline.

Match Hue

If you've copied the color correction filters from your master shots and find that your covering shots are still not matching, you can turn to the filter's Match Hue tools. The Match Hue controls consist of an eyedropper, a Match Color swatch, and a Reset button (see Figure 7-12).

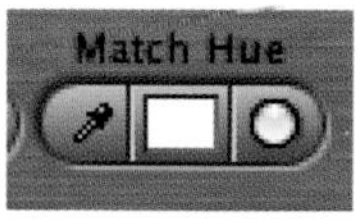

FIGURE 7-12

Each color corrector filter includes Match Hue tools.

Here's how to work with the Match Hue tools:

1. Press Option + 7 to bring up both clips in the Frame Viewer so you can compare them side by side.

2. Be sure that you've pasted the color correction filter(s) from the clip you want to match into the clip that does not yet match. Check to see if this simple technique has matched the hues properly. If not, move to the next step.

3. With the Select Auto Color Balance eyedropper tool, go to the clip that contains the correct colors and click on a color that is found in both clips. When the selected color comes within range, one of the Select Auto Color Balance eyedroppers will turn green.

4. Load the non-matching clip into the Viewer, and then click on the Color Corrector filter tab for that clip. The same green eyedropper will be lit.

5. With the eyedropper, click on the color that you selected in the previous clip. The colors should now match better.

tip

After you find the correct hue in the Color Balance wheel, you can constrain the saturation strength (Magnitude) parameter by holding down the Shift and Command keys as you drag the Color Balance indicators.

Match Hue can get you in the ballpark for luma and chroma values, but is not a magic way to find a precise match for an entire shot. If the clips still don't match, you'll need to compare luma values first and make small adjustments as you look at the clips in the Frame Viewer and Waveform Monitor.

If the clips *still* do not match, you'll need to compare and adjust chroma values. For this, you'll be adjusting the Saturation slider and dragging the Color Balance indicators away from the problematic colors. Compare the clips in the Frame Viewer and Vectorscope.

If you're having trouble matching shots even after making fine adjustments, you might need to alter one or two colors rather than trying to do a Match Hue for the entire image. For this, you must do a secondary color correction on specific colors using the Limit Effect function, as described in Exercise 7-2.

The best way to understand the Match Hue function is to perform one. We'll do that in the following exercise.

Comparing Images for a Match Hue

Before you do a Match Hue, you should know how to quickly compare the images you want to match.

Use the Frame Viewer for a side-by-side view of the images you wish to compare. Here's how:

1. Park the playhead on the clip you want to use for comparison.

2. Click the Auto Select button on the proper video track for the clip.

3. Go to Tools → Frame Viewer (or press Option + 7).

4. From the menu in the lower-left corner of the Frame Viewer, choose Current Frame. The frame under the playhead appears on the left side of the Frame Viewer.

5. From the menu on the right, choose the proper setting to see the other frame (for example, Next Edit).

6. Make adjustments to the window or click the Swap or Split button to best see the areas of the clips you want to compare.

EXERCISE 7-3: PERFORMING A MATCH HUE

Open the Chapter 7 Exercise sequence, and then move to the marker for Exercise 3. There are two clips in the Timeline: "All Smiles Gal" and "Black Tank Woman."

1. Evaluate the two clips in the Frame Viewer.

    a. Choose Current Frame from the menu on the left.

    b. Choose Next Edit from the menu on the right.

    You'll see that the skin tone does not match between the two clips.

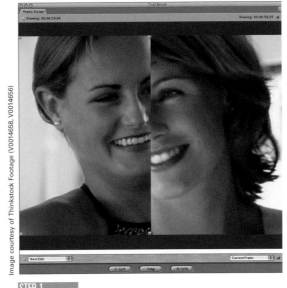

Image courtesy of Thinkstock Footage (V0014658, V0014656)

STEP 1

Place the two images in the Frame Viewer and evaluate the skin tones.

2. Select the All Smiles Gal clip and go to Effects → Color Correction → Color Corrector 3-Way to do a primary color correction.

    a. Click the Auto Contrast button.

    b. Engage the Range Check Overlays and then optimize luma and chroma. (Make sure you don't oversaturate the clip by raising the Sat slider too high.)

c. Perform a white balance by clicking on the woman's teeth with the Auto Balance Select eyedropper for Whites.

3. Copy and paste the Color Corrector 3-Way filter into the other clip's Filters tab and then evaluate the clips in the Frame Viewer once more. Although the same color correction has been applied to both clips, they don't quite match yet, so you'll need to do a Match Hue for skin tone.

4. Load the All Smiles Gal clip into the Viewer, and then go to the Color Corrector 3-Way tab and click the Select Auto Balance Color eyedropper in the Match Hue tool area. With the eyedropper, click between the eyes of All Smiles Gal. You should note that the Match Hue color swatch has turned the same shade for skin tone and that the eyedropper beside the Mids Color Balance wheel has turned green.

5. Open the Black Tank Woman clip in the Viewer, and then click on the Color Corrector 3-Way tab. Note that the eyedropper is also green here. Click the green eyedropper and then click once more between the eyes of Black Tank Woman. After you click on the skin tones of the Black Tank Woman, the luminance and chrominance will be more closely balanced between the two shots.

6. If the colors are not balanced enough to suit you, a finer adjustment of luma and chroma is in order.

a. Park the playhead between the two clips and bring up the Waveform Monitor and Vectorscope.

b. Keep your eye on the scopes as you continue to tweak the image with the Color Balance indicators and Levels sliders. The purple line between red and yellow in the Vectorscope represents skin tones, so focus your efforts in bringing the color values as close as possible to this line.

c. Using the Left and Right Arrow keys, move one frame to the left and then check the scopes and evaluate the All Smiles Gal clip's vector for flesh tone — but don't make any adjustments. Move one frame to the right and evaluate the Black Tank Woman clip for skin tone. Attempt to match the color by slightly tweaking the controls of the color corrector, using the skin-tone vector as a guide.

tip

To compare many shots quickly, you can line up multiple Frame Viewers of the shots you wish to match across the top of your display. Peel off each Frame Viewer's tab in the Tool Bench to view that Frame Viewer separately.

note

In Match Hue, you pick a single color to try to match. Do not attempt to match colors that are not alike.

Vector for skin tones

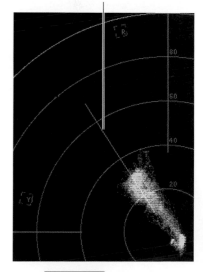

STEP 6b

Use the Vectorscope to help match skin tones.

tip

You can also save custom color correction filters or filter combinations as Favorites.

tip

The Copy Filters function is not limited to color correction filters. You can use its menu commands or keyboard shortcuts to apply other filters to adjacent clips. You can think of this a speedy alternative to Copy/Paste Attributes.

note

Besides the excellent explanations of color correction in the FCP manual, other color correction resources are available. One is Color Correction for Digital Video *by Steve Hullfish and Jaime Fowler (CMP Books). A nice primer for the book is the instructional DVD produced by Digital Film Tree called "Color Correction for Final Cut Pro." For more information, visit www.dig-italfilmtree.com. Digital Film Tree also offers the* Apple Pro Training Series: Advanced Editing and Finishing Techniques in Final Cut Pro 4 *(Peachpit Press).*

7. Evaluate the whites between the shots, and do your best to match the whites by making small adjustments in the Whites wheel of the Black Tank Woman clip, pushing the Color Balance indicator toward blue.

Your shots should now be closely matched in color. It's OK if they're not perfectly matched. The women have different complexions, so if the flesh tones are fairly close, you're doing fine.

You'll get better at this over time as you develop your skills in reading the scopes and your eyes begin to become more sensitive to the properties of color.

APPLYING MULTIPLE COLOR CORRECTION FILTERS

Another technique that can help you solve color correction problems involves applying multiple color correction filters to a clip. For example, you might use an additional color correction filter at the bottom of the filter stack to further control the overall levels and saturation of a clip after a primary or secondary color correction. Or you might want to bring a clip into broadcast-safe limits after using a color correction filter to create a look that goes out of broadcast-safe range. You could make an additional secondary color correction, such as choosing another color to selectively change. For example, you could shift red to blue with one copy of a filter, and then add another filter to change magenta to green — all within the same clip.

ADDITIONAL COLOR CORRECTION FILTERS

Let's look at FCP's other color correction filters.

- **Desaturate Highlights:** I find this filter handy when I've done a primary color correction and the image is saturated perfectly, save for one small area that knocks the image out of broadcast-safe range. Applying this filter will retain the fidelity of the image and will limit the saturation only in the brightest highlights. The result will bring your image back into broadcast-safe range.

- **Desaturate Lows:** Desaturate Highlights and Desaturate Lows are actually the same filter with different default settings. Use the Desaturate Lows filter to get rid of unwanted color lurking in your shadows as a result of a color correction process.

- **RGB Balance:** From time to time, you may experience a particularly difficult color balance issue that can't be resolved in the primary color correction process. The RGB Balance filter offers great control for balancing the luminance in individual color channels. A slight adjustment in the luma range for the proper color channel may help you solve this conundrum. (See Chapter 11 for information on color channels.)

- **Broadcast Safe:** This filter takes care of excess luma or saturation levels that may have cropped up as a result of a color correction job, such as an effect derived from adding multiple color correction filters. Ideally, it should be applied to a nested sequence rather than an individual clip. This way, the filter acts as a fail-safe for color correction adjustments you've already made.

Color Effects

This section will show you how to use the color correction filters to do more than simply fix color problems. You can create some pretty wild color effects with these filters. Set aside some time to experiment.

COLOR TINTING AND TONING

By altering both luma and chroma values with the Color Corrector 3-Way filter, you can easily create looks with varied contrast and color. You can produce some dramatic looks by simply adjusting Levels and Saturation.

Three-way tint

You can make interesting tints with the Color Corrector 3-Way filter. Just adjust the color balance of the three Color Balance wheels. You'll be pushing your controls a bit further than you were in primary color correction.

Crushing the blacks

"Crushing the blacks" is an expression colorists use to describe making shadows flatter and blacker. There will be fewer details in the shadows, but the tradeoff is blacker blacks and an image that has more contrast. I often crush the blacks when footage has weak lower-end midtones.

To crush the blacks, apply the Color Corrector 3-Way filter and move the Blacks Level slider to the left until you're satisfied with contrast and depth of the black elements in the frame. Touch up the look by nudging the Mids Level slider to the right just a bit.

tip

You can adjust both highlights and shadows at the same time by applying either the Desaturate Highlights or Desaturate Lows filter and checking the Enable checkbox for both Highlights and Lows Desaturation.

tip

Monitor your adjustments with the RGB Balance filter with the RGB Parade scope for balancing luma in particular color channels.

note

Unchecking the boxes for the Broadcast Safe filter's Luminance Limiting and Saturation Limiting will not prevent the sliders from moving, but it does disable the effect.

Overdriving the highlights

Moving the Whites Level slider slightly to the right will overdrive (or "blow out") the highlights, making them much brighter. The tradeoff here is a reduction of detail in the brightest regions of the image.

A better black-and-white

To lend a more interesting look to your black-and-white image, try crushing the blacks by lowering the Blacks slider, blowing out the highlights by raising the Whites slider, or experimenting with midtone values (see Figure 7-13).

FIGURE 7-13

The image on the left was treated with the Desaturation filter to create a black-and-white look. Its levels could use some adjustment. The Color Corrector 3-Way filter was applied to the image on the right. All three ranges were adjusted to achieve a better looking image.

Image courtesy of Thinkstock Footage (V0014649)

SELECTIVE COLOR EFFECTS

Now that you've spent time doing secondary color corrections, you should be aware that you can make other color effects by using the Limit Effect tools. Try out some of these effects.

- **Selective tint:** You can achieve an instant color effect by reversing the matte of a Limit Effect operation. Just click the Invert Selection button. The difference this time is that the colored object you earlier isolated is untouched, and everything except the object will now become the tinted color you chose from the Hue control wheel. You'll probably need to adjust levels and saturation for the rest of the scene. You can shift the Hue control wheel to select a new tint for the scene as well.

- **Isolating a color using desaturation:** Perhaps you recall the scene in the movie *Schindler's List* where you see a shot of a girl in a red coat on a background of black and white. This is an effect you can do now that you know how to isolate a color and reverse the matte in a Limit Effect operation. Click the Invert Selection button to reverse the matte, and then all that's necessary to complete this effect is to take the Sat slider all the way down to zero. Your image will be black-and-white except for the isolated color (see Figure 7-14).

- **Applying Limit Effect to more than one color:** You can adjust more than one color in an image by using the Limit Effect function with multiple color correctors. This works particularly well if the image has a limited number of colors. Solo each filter as you work, so you're not distracted by the other colors and can work on the mattes more easily.

- **Making colors change over time:** Once you've created a Limit Effect selection, you can use the standard Color Corrector and keyframe the Phase Shift parameter to make colors change over time.

tip

You can change the order of the color correction filters in the stack for new possibilities with Limit Effect, as new colors will dominate the image.

FIGURE 7-14
I selected the red shirt and applied the Limit Effect controls, reversed the matte, and moved the Saturation slider to zero.

Adjusting Overall Levels

When you've done a color correction (or added any effect, for that matter), in many cases you'll need to adjust the overall levels in an image. Perhaps you want to brighten the entire picture after performing a Limit Effect function, or maybe you want to bring an image with blown-out highlights into broadcast-safe range. This overall adjustment is sometimes referred to as a levels call, and is performed with a Color Corrector, Color Corrector 3-Way, Levels, or Proc Amp filter.

To use any of these filters to adjust an image's overall levels, make sure that you place the filter at the bottom of the stack before you start making adjustments. I like to use the Color Corrector 3-Way filter because you can adjust the levels in three different brightness ranges, allowing for maximum control over your levels. In addition, you can control hue and saturation for the overall image.

Troubleshooting

Problems related to color usually stem from misunderstanding what is actually going on with your image's luma and chroma settings. Beyond that, problems can arise as you perform color corrections.

Colors are wrong even after primary color correction

Most basic color balance issues are resolved in the primary color correction process. If your colors still appear to be off, you should look into one of these primary causes:

- Your video monitor is incorrectly calibrated. When experiencing color shifts, even after doing a basic color correction, check to see whether your video monitor is correctly calibrated.

- The white balance is off. It's common for blue, green, or orange tones to dominate the whites. This happens primarily when you perform a white balance and choose a color that appears to be white but is not actually white. Try clicking again on a different white object. Use the Zoom tool to get a bit closer to the color you need to pick. I recommend checking your Vectorscope when adjusting for white, so you can see objectively what is going on with the hue and saturation of the image.

No effect occurs when you adjust a filter

It can be frustrating when you attempt to adjust a parameter and nothing happens to your image. If you're experiencing this problem, check out these possibilities:

- You forgot to reload the clip. When you're concentrating on color correction, it's easy to get sidetracked and forget to load the clip back into the Viewer. I know I've said this many times, but it *is* the most common mistake you can make. Choosing Open mode from the Playhead Sync pop-up menu with the proper track Auto Selected will greatly reduce this common error.

- Another common "gotcha" is forgetting to park the playhead on the image you're color correcting.

- You're working on the wrong copy of a filter. If you're working on an image that has multiple copies of the Color Corrector applied for a special color effect, it's easy to get confused about which color correction filter you're working in. Press Control + 1 to turn the filter on or off so that you can quickly identify which copy of a filter you're working on.

A clip is not broadcast safe

Sometimes you'll make a color correction setting that looks great to the eye but is not broadcast safe. This typically happens when you're going for extreme color effects like oversaturation or blown-out highlights. Try one of these solutions:

- Apply the Broadcast Safe filter. Get the look you want visually, nest the sequence, and then apply the filter to bring everything into proper range.

- Perform a levels call to gain finer control over luma and chroma than the Broadcast Safe filter can provide. You'll have to use the Scopes and Range Check Overlays to assist you.

Limit Effect problems

Problems may crop up when there are objects of a similar color in the frame. These objects will make it difficult to isolate the object you want to affect. For example, in the basketball player shot in Exercise 7-2, the color of the skin tone and the color of the basketball are similar, making it tough to create the matte. To make the shot work, I duplicated the image on V2 and cropped only the target-colored object. (You can keyframe the crop if the camera or subject is moving.)

Wrap-up

You've learned the basics of how color works in a digital environment. You've also gotten some practice with the primary and secondary color correction processes. Finally, you were introduced to some phenomenal new selective color correction effects used in popular movies, television shows, and commercials. Continue your study of color, and the quality of your projects will improve throughout your career.

As we move forward in the book, you'll find yourself looking back repeatedly to this chapter to find new ways to use color correction tools.

The next chapter looks at the alpha channel and at using matte and key effects.

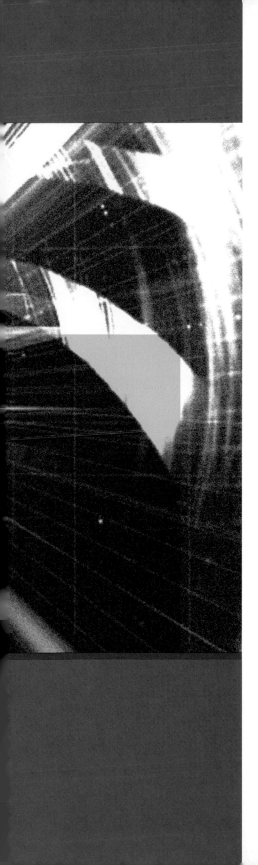

8

Alpha Channels, Mattes, and Keys

Understanding how the alpha channel works will put you far ahead in the game of designing effects. You manipulate the alpha channel to blend overlapping layers so that many images appear at the same time — the very essence of video compositing. Final Cut Pro does not automatically assign an alpha channel, so you must make one, usually by adding a filter or creating a travel matte. By the end of this chapter you'll know quite a bit about mattes, as well as chroma keying, luma keying, and other aspects of using the alpha channel to create effects.

Alpha Channel Basics

In a video image, each pixel is made up of a combination of the colors red, green, and blue. Out of a total of 32 bits, 8 bits of information are set aside for each of the three *color channels*, for a total of 24 bits. Every image has the potential to display an additional 8 bits of information to define areas of transparency. This fourth, transparent channel is called the *alpha channel*. It carries no color information; instead it carries a grayscale value in which the colors black, white, and gray represent the relative opacity of an image.

You can think of an alpha channel as a "mask" that lies between an image and a background. Areas defined in the mask will cause the corresponding parts of the background to be completely revealed, partially revealed, or completely invisible.

The three colors in Final Cut Pro's alpha channel are defined as follows:

- Black indicates areas of 100% transparency
- White indicates areas of 100% opacity
- Gray indicates partial transparency

Figure 8-1 shows how the alpha channel works.

VIEWING THE ALPHA CHANNEL

It's often helpful to view an alpha channel independently of an image. You can easily see the alpha channel by loading a clip into the Viewer, clicking the View Mode pop-up menu, and selecting Alpha+RGB. The alpha channel's grayscale values are represented by shades of red so you can see them more clearly (see Figure 8-2). If you select Alpha, just the alpha channel's grayscale values are displayed (see Figure 8-3).

When you're working with alpha channels, you may find it useful to see the image in the Viewer and Canvas at the same time. With the Playhead Sync menu set to either Gang mode or Follow mode, the playheads will sync up between the two windows so you can monitor both images. In the Canvas, note how your image is playing against other layers. In the Viewer, you can evaluate your image's alpha channel is on its own. I like to work with either a white or a checkerboard background in the Viewer.

Image courtesy of Getty Images, www.gettyimages.com (dv386015/ digital vision)

FIGURE 8-1

An image is made up of three color channels (RGB) and an alpha channel, which affects transparency.

Creating Alpha Channels

You have several options for making an alpha channel. You can add an FCP filter, such as a matte or key filter, to an image. You can create a matte in a separate application such as Boris RED or Adobe After Effects, and then import it into FCP for use as a travel matte (more on this later). Or you can create an alpha channel in another motion graphics application and import it into FCP.

You may not realize you've already made alpha channels by adjusting certain parameters in the Motion tab. Let's look into this phenomenon.

ALTERING THE ALPHA CHANNEL IN THE MOTION TAB

You can alter an image's alpha channel by adjusting opacity or cropping the image. Look at the comp on the left in Figure 8-4. Note that both images have been cropped and that the opacity for the clip on the right has been adjusted to make the clip semi-opaque. If opacity is faded, it follows that the alpha channel should be gray. You can see this by choosing Alpha from the View Mode menu.

FIGURE 8-2

Select Alpha+RGB from the View Mode menu to see the RGB channels' information, together with the alpha channel's grayscale shades in shades of red.

FIGURE 8-3

Select Alpha from the View Mode menu to see the alpha channel on its own.

Image courtesy of Thinkstock Footage (V0021086)

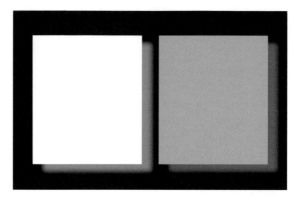

FIGURE 8-4

The illustration on the right shows how the image's Crop, Opacity, and Drop Shadow settings affect the alpha channel.

Adding a drop shadow to a clip also alters the alpha channel. In essence, a drop shadow is nothing more than an offset of the original alpha channel that has been set automatically. By looking at the grayscale image in Alpha view mode, you can see the soft gray edges that define the area and opacity of the drop shadow.

MAKING ALPHA CHANNELS WITH MATTE FILTERS

A common way to add an alpha channel to an image is to add a matte filter. *Matte filters* allow you to knock out, or exclude, selected portions of the image to reveal a layer below it.

Matte filters at a glance

All of the filters in the Matte category will make some portion of an image transparent. Shape matte filters offer geometric shapes such as circles, ovals, or squares (see Figure 8-5), while garbage matte filters let you create irregular shapes. The Extract Matte filter makes a matte from the luma values of an image, while the Image Mask filter makes a matte from luma values in another clip. The Soft Edges filter makes a blended matte, perfect for a vignette effect with edges that fade to the border of the frame.

Let's look at these filters in a bit more detail:

- **Garbage Matte:** Garbage mattes let you draw shapes by manipulating point controls. These filters come in 4-point and 8-point varieties (see Figure 8-6).

tip

If you need more than eight points in a Garbage matte, add a copy of the clip to an upper layer, add an Eight-Point Garbage matte to each layer, and create a more complex shape using the two mattes. Note that you may have to invert one of the mattes to get the desired result.

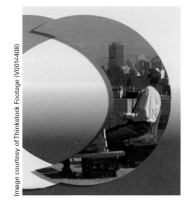

Image courtesy of Thinkstock Footage (V0014408)

Image courtesy of Thinkstock Footage (V0014432)

FIGURE 8-5

Combining matte filters in a single clip provides new ways to shape the matte. Here, two Oval filters are offset to form a crescent shape.

FIGURE 8-6

Garbage mattes let you create a variety of shapes, including irregular shapes. Here, an Eight-Point Garbage Matte has been used to create an octagon.

- **Extract:** This filter takes the luminance information in a clip and allows you to use it as a travel matte (see Figure 8-7). (Travel mattes will be discussed later in the chapter.) Choose To Alpha from the filter's Copy Result menu to use the clip as a Travel Matte Alpha effect. Copying the result to RGB will leave you with a black-and-white image that's suitable for a Travel Matte Luma effect. (You'll learn to make an advanced Extract filter effect in Chapter 12.)

- **Image Mask:** This filter is similar to a travel matte. You can drag and drop clips into a Clip Control well, but the well will not play back travel mattes.

FIGURE 8-7

The "Overpass" clip (left) has a good deal of contrast, making it a good candidate for an Extract Matte effect. The "Whirlpool" clip (center) provides an interesting graphic fill. The effect on the right is produced by selecting Copy to Alpha.

Images courtesy of Getty Images, www.getty-images.com (overpass clip: ev01582/Photodisc; whirlpool clip: WEL_014/Photodisc)

tip

In many matte and key filters, including Extract, the default settings are a bit unwieldy for creating a good matte. It helps to take Softness down to zero before adjusting the Tolerance and Threshold sliders. After you've optimized the matte, you can then increase Softness to take away any jagged "fringe." An effective matte should require no more than a few pixels of softness, so don't overdo it.

■ **Mask Shape:** This filter provides the following forms to help you shape your alpha channel: Diamond, Oval, Rectangle, and Round Rectangle (see Figure 8-8). The position, scale, and shape of each option can be controlled in the Filters tab. An oversized mask shape that's offset partially offscreen can provide a nice vignette effect. You'll work on a Mask Shape filter in an upcoming exercise.

Image courtesy of Getty Images, www.gettyimages.com (ev02326/Photodisc)

FIGURE 8-8

To create this effect, two Oval Mask Shapes were applied to a color matte on an upper track and then inverted.

■ **Widescreen:** This filter cuts off the bottom and top of an image to simulate a widescreen effect. You can adjust the transparent areas as defined by coordinates and crosshairs in the Filters tab.

■ **Soft Edges:** This filter applies a soft edge to any or all sides of your clip (see Figure 8-9). Use the Invert checkbox to punch a hole in the image so you can place another image on a layer below.

FIGURE 8-9

The clip on the left serves as the background. The clip in the center has been soloed to show the transparency of the edges when you adjust the Soft Edges filter's parameters. The blended result is shown on the right.

brick wall image courtesy of Getty images, www.gettyimages.com (ev01575/Photodisc)

Image courtesy of Thinkstock Footage (V0014650)

- **Mask Feather:** This filter blurs the edges in the alpha channel, giving your matte a soft, feathered look.

- **Matte Choker:** The Matte Choker is used primarily in conjunction with a key filter to adjust the alpha channel. You'll learn more about using the Matte Choker when we discuss keying later in the chapter.

Now that you've been introduced to the matte filters, it's time to apply a matte to a clip in a multilayered composite.

tip

Be sure to add a Mask Feather filter after your matte filter is in the stack, or the Mask Feather filter will have no effect.

EXERCISE 8-1: APPLYING A SHAPE MATTE

In this exercise you'll be working with a simple Shape matte. As you follow the steps, you'll see how the alpha channel alters the clip. You'll be able to see the results by flipping between Alpha and Alpha+RGB view mode.

Start by opening the Chapter 8 Exercise bin and locating the Chapter 8 Exercise sequence in the Chapter 8 Sequences bin. Open the sequence and start at the beginning of the Timeline.

1. You'll first add a mask to the "Thai Lady" clip on V2.

   a. Select the clips and go to Effects → Video Filters → Matte → Mask Shape. The matte effect introduces the alpha channel to the clip. Your clip should now have a rectangular matte shape applied to it.

   b. An oval would look better, so choose Shape → Oval from the Shape menu.

   c. Change the settings as follows to center the mask on the woman's face:

   Horizontal: 55

   Vertical: 95

   Position controls: X = −10, Y = 0

2. The scene would look more attractive with the ocean flowing toward the subject, so you'll flop the image. With the clip still selected, go to Effects → Perspective → Flop.

STEP 1c
Center the mask on the woman's face.

STEP 2
Flop the image.

Images courtesy of Thinkstock Footage (Waterside Sunset V0016152; Thai Lady V0017598)

3. You'll now soften the edges of the clip.

    a. With the Thai Lady clip still selected, go to Effects → Video Filters → Matte → Mask Feather.

    b. In the Filters tab, set the matte's Softness to 40.

4. Take a look at the alpha channel you've just created.

    a. Press Control + S to solo the Thai Lady clip and see the alpha channel in the Canvas.

    b. In the Canvas, choose Alpha from the View Mode menu. Check out the matte by inspecting the white, black, and gray oval.

    c. After you've checked the alpha channel, switch to RGB mode in the View Mode menu. While you're in the menu, ensure that you're in Image + Wireframe mode.

5. Press Control + S to unsolo the clip. Click and drag the entire frame to the left to offset it. X = 40 and Y = 0 should work fine.

6. The blue area surrounding the Thai Lady clip is a bit distracting, so you'll tint the clip with a Sepia filter.

    a. With the clip selected, go to Effects → Video Filters → Image Control → Sepia.

    b. Load the clip into the Viewer.

    c. Click on the Filters tab. Use the Eyedropper to tint the clip the same color as the sky. Set Amount to 60 and Highlight to 40.

> **tip**
>
> Mask Feather filters are effective only if they lay at the bottom of the filters stack.

> **tip**
>
> Control + click on a clip's opacity keyframes to smooth them directly in the Timeline.

STEP 3
Use Mask Feather to soften the clip's edges.

STEP 4b
Choose Alpha from the View Mode menu to inspect your matte.

7. Fade up the matted clip at the beginning.

    a. Place the playhead at the beginning of the Thai Lady clip, and then press Shift + Right Arrow to move the playhead 1:00 into the clip.

    b. With Clip Overlays on (Option + W) use the Pen tool (P) to add an opacity keyframe in the Timeline.

    c. Move the Pen tool back to the beginning of the clip, and then click and drag downward to ramp up the opacity.

8. Preview the effect in the QuickView window (Option + 8). When you're satisfied with the results, render the composite by pressing Command + R.

Garbage mattes

Garbage mattes are usually used to cut holes in a section of an image. Garbage mattes provide point controls that you can use to define an area that's an irregular shape. Let's take a look at some situations where you'd use garbage mattes:

- You can cut around objects for use in multilayered effects.

- You can use garbage mattes as "hold out" mattes for an identical image on a higher video track to fix problematic areas of a chroma key.

- You can cut off a horizon and put in your own background (see Figure 8-10).

- You can constrain filter effects to a specific area of a clip by stacking identical clips and then applying a filter and a garbage matte to the clip on the upper track.

- You can use a garbage matte to cut a rough matte around a talking head so you can feather the image.

tip

When you're switching between the Canvas and Viewer to check a matte, it can be inconvenient to use the View Mode menu. Try making a custom keyboard shortcut to select items from the View Mode menu. In my own keyboard layout, I use Command + Option + A for monitoring Alpha+RGB, and Shift + Option + A for monitoring Alpha. Alternatively, you could assign these modes to buttons in your Button Bar.

FIGURE 8-10

You can use a garbage matte to replace a background. The original clip is shown on the left. A couple of Eight-Point Garbage Mattes have been used to cut out the sky (center), and a new sky has been added on a lower track (right).

Images courtesy of Thinkstock Footage (Waterside Boat V0016058; Sunset V0021347)

Controlling your garbage mattes

There are a few things you should know about point controls before you begin using garbage matte filters. Each Point Control is numbered and corresponds to a particular X,Y coordinate on the Canvas. When you want to enable a point, you click on the Point Control, and then click and drag on the corresponding crosshairs in the Canvas. Once you let go of the mouse button, you'll have to click on the Point Control again to adjust a matte point.

EXERCISE 8-2: ADDING A GARBAGE MATTE

In this exercise you'll create an effect using two Four-Point Garbage Matte filters. That effect simulates a fire taking place inside a train. We'll be cutting two holes into the windows of a train and then filling those holes with some flames from another clip. Finally, we'll reapply the windows with a composite mode to blend the images on the highest video track.

Open up the Chapter 8 Exercise sequence and park the playhead on the marker for Exercise 2. You'll see four layers stacked up in the Timeline. Three of them are actually nested sequences, but each nest is made up of a single clip. (See "Nesting a Clip for use in a Garbage Matte.") Three of the images are duplicated, locked-down shots of a train, called "Express Train." Another clip, called "Flames," lies on V2.

1. You'll begin by applying a 4-Point Garbage Matte to the nested clip on V4. Select it and then go to Effects → Video Filters → Matte → 4-Point Garbage Matte.

2. Set the Canvas background to Checkerboard. Select the V4 nested clip and press Control + S to solo it. That way, you can cut out the train windows without being confused by the other layers. Work on the right window first.

   a. Zoom in on the Canvas so you can work more precisely.

   b. Click on the Point Control for Point 1.

   c. In the Canvas, click on the upper-left corner of the train's window.

   d. Repeat this process for the other three corners of the window.

   e. Turn View Mode to Final in the Filters tab. You don't need to see these numbers now that you know how to click the Point Controls and move the crosshairs in the Canvas.

3. You'll now make a garbage matte for the train window on the left. You'll first need to copy and paste the garbage matte filter within the Filters tab.

   a. Working in the Filters tab, click on the garbage matte filter's name to select it.

   b. Press Command + C and then Command + V. A second 4-Point Garbage Matte will be added to the top of the stack; it will have a "2" next to the name.

   c. In the Options area of both filters, click the Invert button.

   d. Repeat the process of clicking on the point controls in the Filters tab, and then move the crosshairs in the Canvas to the corners of the window to cut a hole.

   e. Add an Invert filter to the bottom of the stack. Choose Alpha from the Channel menu. The train's front windows should now be isolated from the rest of the nested clip.

4. After you cut the mattes for both windows, you'll need to stylize them just a bit.

   a. Note that the train windows are rounded at the corners. Adjust the Smooth parameters to taste for both filters. I've got my slider set to 12.

   b. The edges are ragged, so raise the Feather slider to 3.

   c. Because feathering works from the center of an edge, your matte has a softer edge, but it is now a bit too small due to the feathering. That's what Choke is for. Raise the slider to about 8 to get the edge back.

When you're satisfied with your work, unsolo the V4 nested clip by selecting it and then pressing Control + S.

STEP 4

Once you've cut out the train windows, feather the edges a bit.

Nesting a Clip for Use in a Garbage Matte

A garbage matte's control points conform to X,Y coordinates in the Canvas, not to positions in your image. If you scale, move, rotate, or distort an image and then attempt to add a garbage matte to a portion of the image, the control points will not match where you're clicking and dragging. If you're using mattes in OfflineRT, you'll also have this problem.

If this behavior is causing you trouble, you can first alter the clip (by scaling it, for example) and then press Option + C to nest the image. Then add a garbage matte filter to the nested clip. This extra step will make it easier to control the shape of the matte.

STEP 6

The train now has holes where
the windows were.

STEP 7b

Drag the Flames clip into place in
the windows.

5. You'll now apply the same filters to the V3 copy of the Express Train
   nested clip. Before you get started, solo the clip by selecting it and pressing
   Control + S.

   a. In the Filters tab, Command + click to select both of the Garbage Matte
      filters in the V4 copy of the nested clip.

   b. Press Command + C to copy the filters.

   c. Load the V3 copy of the nested clip into the Viewer. Then, click on the
      Filters tab and press Command + V to paste in the two Garbage Matte
      filters.

6. These filters are working in the opposite way you want them to, so you'll
   have to add an Invert filter to the bottom of the stack to invert the alpha
   channel (blacks and whites will swap). Take the Feather slider down to 1 and
   the Choke slider to 3 for each filter. The holes will now be a bit smaller and
   have harder edges.

7. Now that you've got the holes punched out, you can position the Flames
   clip in place.

   a. Select the clip and press Control + B to turn on its visibility.

   b. In Image + Wireframe mode, click and drag the Flames clip into place
      behind the window holes.

   This effect should already be looking impressive, but there are a couple
   more steps you can do to make it even better.

8. To make the effect more believable, you'll apply a composite mode to the
   Flames clip and turn on the background's visibility for the flames to play
   against.

   a. Turn on visibility for the V1 copy.

   b. Control + click on the Flames clip and choose Composite Modes →
      Screen from the contextual menu.

   c. Before you move on, note that you have options to reposition, scale,
      rotate, or distort the Flames clip. Base your decision on whether it will
      improve the realism of the effect. As you can see, I've left my flames
      at full size, but raised them a bit so the sweet spot is playing inside the
      window.

9. As a final touch, you'll layer the windows that you originally cut out in the first few steps of this exercise.

   a. Restore visibility for the Express Train nested clip on V4 by selecting it and pressing Control + B.

   b. Control + click on the V4 clip and choose Composite Modes → Screen to get the window highlights back.

10. Preview the effect in the QuickView window and make any adjustments that you think are necessary. After it's looking good, render the effect.

For an extra touch of realism, restore the window highlights by applying a composite mode.

Having successfully completed this exercise, you probably have your own creative ideas for using garbage mattes. In the following chapter, you'll learn even more tricks for using mattes and composite modes. For now, let's turn to making key effects.

KEY FILTERS

Key filters, such as Chroma Keyer and Luma Key, help introduce an alpha channel around the subject of your clip, so you can composite a different background beneath the subject. This is often done because your subject is moving, making it difficult to cut an alpha channel around it. A good example of a chroma key effect is the nightly TV weather report. To make this effect, the weathercaster stands in front of a blue screen while a map is keyed into the blue areas.

You control a chroma key's alpha channel by assigning a particular color to indicate what is opaque and what is transparent. In a luma key, the alpha channel derives from brightness levels of a clip. To get a clean chroma key effect, you often need a variety of techniques, including multiple filters.

The Chroma Keyer filter

The Chroma Keyer filter (see Figure 8-11) has an arsenal of controls to assist you in making a particular kind of matte. Chroma key mattes are formed by isolating a particular color in the clip (like blue or green) and then shifting the single color into the alpha channel, which creates transparency where the color once was.

Global Keyframe button
Numeric button
Drag Filter icon
Copy Filter controls
Enable Filter checkbox

Saturation Control strip

FIGURE 8-11

The Chroma Keyer offers numerous controls to help you create mattes.

Color Control strip

Select Color eyedropper
View Final/Matte/Source button
Invert Selection button

Luma Control strip

Edge Thin slider
Softening slider
Enhance slider

Here's a look at the Chroma Keyer's controls:

- **Copy Filter controls:** These controls duplicate your current chroma key effect to other clips.

- **Numeric button:** This button gives you the numeric equivalent of the controls found in the visual interface.

- **Enable Filter checkbox:** Use this checkbox to solo the effect. Press Control + 1 to toggle the filter on and off.

- **Global Keyframe button:** Click this keyframe button to add a keyframe for all parameters.

- **Drag Filter icon:** Drag and drop the same parameters onto one or more clips in the Timeline.

- **Color Control strip:** This gradient strip displays the color chosen with the Select Color Eyedropper. You can adjust the upper handles for the range of color that's selected as the key. The lower handles control softness (sometimes called "tolerance"), which helps eliminate "fringe" from the edges of the matte.

- **Saturation Control strip:** This controls the amount of saturation in the selected color for your key. The top and bottom sliders work the same way as in the Color Control strip. You can move the handles simultaneously by clicking and dragging within the strip, or you can adjust the equivalent, called "minimum," in the numeric interface.

- **Luma Control strip:** The controls found in this black-and-white gradient adjust both the range and tolerance of the luminance used to shape the matte. You can move all handles at once by clicking and dragging within the strip, or you can adjust the minimum in the numeric interface.

- **Select Color eyedropper:** This control chooses the color to key in your image.

- **View Final/Matte/Source button:** This button toggles to display three scenarios: the matte as it works on the image, the matte independent of the image, and the image source with no effect.

- **Invert Selection button:** This button inverts the alpha channel of the matte.

- **Edge Thin slider:** This slider makes the matte thinner or thicker around the keyed subject.

- **Softening slider:** This control softens, or feathers, the edge of the matte.

- **Enhance slider:** Use this slider to control any "spill" from excess chroma.

Creating a chroma key

To make a chroma key, follow these basic steps. (Details will follow in Exercise 8-3.) Make sure that you follow the steps in order.

1. Evaluate your raw footage. Before attempting any chroma key effect, scrutinize the image for any defects that were introduced at the shoots, such as a tape defect, a lighting problem, or extraneous items that need to be matted out.

2. Crop or garbage-matte out any unwanted items, such as boom poles, light stands, cables, or hung lights. Cropping also rids the image of black "blanking lines," a necessary step for repositioning a keyed shot. An added bonus of cropping is that with less area to key, you won't need to tweak the controls quite so much.

3. Blur the chroma channels. To smooth the alpha channel created by the key, "pre-blur" the Cr and Cb channels before adding the Chroma Keyer filter. Final Cut Pro 4 has two filters to attack this issue: Color Smoothing 4:1:1 and Color Smoothing 4:2:2. It's very important to add the Color Smoothing filters *before* applying the Chroma Keyer.

tip

Why would you need an identical garbage matted image layered on top of a keyed image? Sometimes a small portion of an identical layer is necessary to patch "holes" or cover up an area of the shot that could not be easily keyed. This additional matte is referred to as a "hold out" matte.

tip

When adjusting tolerances for Chroma, Luma, and Saturation, it's often best to be less scientific and more intuitive as you figure out what works best for a matte. Use your eyes as well as your video scopes.

4. Add the Chroma Keyer filter and then select the color to key. Select the background color using the Select Color eyedropper. Choose a place on the backdrop that appears evenly lit. You should see a good chunk of the color fall away. You can Shift + click on additional areas of the color to knock out more of the matte.

5. Adjust the width and softness of Chroma, Luma, and Sat. Click the View Final/Matte/Source button to monitor the matte independently of the image as you adjust these controls. A good matte will be completely white inside and completely black outside.

6. Adjust Edge Thinning. The Edge Thinning slider controls the edge of the matte. The goal here is to take out the majority of the keyed color's fringe without harming the subtle detail of items that should remain in the image, such as chin line, hair, and fingers.

7. Feather the matte. A bit of softening will smooth the rough edges of the keyed image and fix "stair-stepped" edges. Too much softening can be a problem, however. If the edges of the matte are too soft, color from the backdrop will seep back into the edges of the matte.

tip

A scroll-wheel mouse comes in handy for moving all four handles at once for Luma and Saturation controls. The mouse will also move the Color Control strip.

8. Adjust for spill using the Enhance slider. Moving the Enhance slider just a bit will desaturate any excess blue or green color, or spill, at the edges of the key. (There are Spill Suppressor filters for blue and green screen in the Key filter group, but you should use them with care, as they will affect the color of the overall image rather than just the edge of the matte. A color-correction pass is often necessary when you use these filters.)

9. Choke the matte. A Matte Choker filter will remove any fringe from the edges of your matte. Although the Chroma Keyer offers Edge Thin and Softening parameters, adding a Matte Choker can offer additional firepower for controlling that edge. You'll need to add the Matte Choker below any chroma key filter to have the filter act as a master control for matte edges. From time to time, you'll need to add a second Matte Choker for additional control over the matte's edge.

tip

To make precise adjustments while fine-tuning matte controls, "gear down" by holding down the Command key.

10. Readjust parameters and apply final adjustments after the keying is complete. Here are a few suggestions:

   - You can apply color correction to make the foreground image match the background more believably. For example, you may need to warm up an image that is keyed over a background with warm tones in it. You might also need to correct color problems that were introduced when creating the key. Note that you may want to nest items before color correcting key images, as color correctors applied to the same clip can compromise edges.

- Adding a bit of Gaussian Blur to the background will generally improve the believability of a composite, as it will simulate shallower depth of field, like a telephoto lens might produce.

Now let's follow these steps in an exercise.

EXERCISE 8-3: CHROMA KEYING A SUBJECT OFF A BACKGROUND

In this exercise we'll be keying our subject off the background to make a whole new composite. We'll be keying a woman who was shot against a blue sky and we'll add her to another shot of the same woman.

Double-click the Chapter 8 Exercise sequence and go to the marker for Exercise 3. You should see a stack of five clips already set up for you to work on.

1. Start by evaluating the raw footage. Note that the woman was shot against a clear, blue sky. Scrub through the clip and see if there are any problems, such as uneven lighting or items that come into frame. This is a clip that will key without too much difficulty, since the woman is well lit and the sky is very evenly lit and saturated.

2. Select the clip and press Control + S to solo it.

3. Crop just a few pixels from either side of the clip. Then, crop the top of the clip until it nearly reaches the top of the subject's head.

Image courtesy of Thinkstock Footage (V0020029)

STEP 3
Crop the image.

Shooting Tips for a Successful Chroma Key

With chroma keying, garbage in = garbage out. What this means is that you should begin with the best possible footage. If you are shooting your own projects, you'll want to keep a few things in mind prior to the shoot:

- Light the backdrop evenly. To get absolutely even lighting, you can use a spot meter on the backdrop. A 1:1 ratio from subject to background gives you better results in the final key than lighting that has a backdrop that's brighter than the subject.

- Use on-set video monitors and hardware scopes to double-check the evenness of your lighting setup. FCP's video scopes can substitute as hardware scopes if you hook up a camera to a Mac on the set.

- Make sure the talent casts no shadows on the backdrop, or there will be too great a luma difference to pull a decent key. You'll also need to keep talent from wearing green colors for a green-screen shoot, or blues for a blue-screen shoot.

- A blue or green backdrop is usually used for shots that contain humans because skin tone has very little blue or green in it. For shots with no people in them, you can actually use any color to define the matte shape.

tip

Clicking and dragging left or right between the drag handles in the Color, Saturation, or Luma Control strip adjusts softness for that parameter. In some cases, this improves the matte.

4. Apply the appropriate Color Smoothing filter: Color Smoothing 4:2:2 or 4:1:1.

5. With the clip still selected, go to Effects → Video Filters → Key → Chroma Keyer to add the Chroma Keyer filter.

6. Load the clip into the Viewer and then click on the Chroma Keyer tab.

7. Choose White from the View Mode pop-up menu to set the Canvas to white.

8. Use the Select Color Eyedropper to click on the blue sky. Most of the blue should be removed from the background.

9. After you've picked your initial color, click on the Eyedropper again and hold down the Shift key. Click on a new area of the sky that has not been affected. Continue Shift + clicking until most of the blue has been removed from the image.

10. To adjust the key as it relates to chroma, you can widen the chroma range (the top drag handles in the Color Control strip) just a bit to include more shades of blue. Increase chroma softness by widening the bottom drag handles as well.

11. You'll now adjust the luma tolerance of the matte in the Luma Control strip.

    a. Click the View Final/Matte/Source button and change the Canvas color to black.

    b. Click and drag the top drag handles to widen the range of luma that is affecting the matte. After you see the range that works on the matte most effectively, widen out the bottom handles of the Luma Control strip.

The matte should be taking shape, but if it's still a bit rough you can address that by adjusting the saturation controls.

STEP 8
Use the Select Color Eyedropper to remove most of the blue from the background.

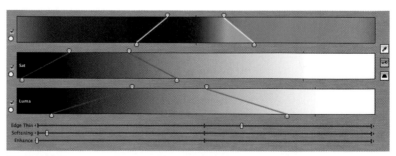

STEP 10
Widen the chroma range. The Chroma Keyer should look similar to this.

12. To adjust the range of saturation, start by finding a range that is most effective with the top drag handles of the Saturation Control strip, and then begin dragging out the bottom handles to find the proper tolerance, or softness, for the matte. Click the View Final/Matte/Source button twice to see the clip in View Final mode; most of the blue "fringe" should be gone. If a small, blue edge line still surrounds the image, you can adjust edge thinning or softness.

13. The Edge Thin slider will "choke" (increase or decrease) the edge of your matte. Slide the slider to the right until more of the fringe falls away. I've choked the edge to 20.

14. The image's edges are still rough, and a bit of blue fringe remains. You'll need to do some edge softening. Use the Softening slider to slightly feather the edges of the matte of the woman. Just a few clicks should do it.

15. You can now make some final adjustments to the composite.

    a. Press Control + S to unsolo the image.

    b. In Image + Wireframe mode, click and drag the V4 clip, "Weightlifter WS," upward and to the left. This will reveal some cropped color mattes.

    c. Blur the background to add some perspective. With the V4 clip selected, go to Effects → Video Filters → Blur → Gaussian Blur. The default setting will do.

As a final step, you can make the woman on V5 fade up with opacity keyframes. A 2:00 duration should do it. Don't forget to smooth those keyframes!

16. Preview the effect, and then select the V5 clip and press Command + R to render it. Your foreground element should be seamlessly integrated with the background.

> **tip**
>
> *The most effective range for deeply saturated colors in the backdrop — like the blue sky in the example clip — is toward the darker side of the Sat Control strip.*

Second weightlifter image courtesy of Thinkstock Footage (V0020028)

STEP 15a
Unsolo the image to see the composite.

STEP 15b
Drag the V4 clip up and to the left to reveal the color mattes.

LUMA KEYS

Luma keys are handy for keying out elements that appear against backgrounds that are brighter or darker than the subject. You create the matte by changing the tolerance (luma width) and threshold (luma softness). Using Luma Key is similar to using the Extract Matte, in that you can copy the result to the alpha channel to create transparency.

Luma keying is not as common as chroma keying, since it's a bit harder to pull a good key without the aid of chroma information. However, this does not mean that you should shy away from this filter. Any subject passing in front of a white wall could be a candidate for a Luma Key, as could an object shot against a piece of black cloth.

Let's look at the Luma Key controls:

- **View:** This menu allows you to see your source image, background image, matte, final image, or all of these in a four-up display.

- **Key Mode:** This menu is for keying a brighter or darker background. There are also choices for keying out similar or dissimilar objects that have similar luminance values.

- **Matte:** This menu places the key either in an alpha channel, which is typical for a luma key, or into the RGB channels to make the clip act as a travel matte.

- **Threshold:** This slider sets the width for the luma range you wish to key out.

- **Tolerance:** This parameter softens the luma values chosen by the Threshold slider.

Figure 8-12 shows the Luma Key controls in the Filters tab.

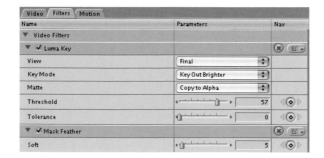

The Luma Key filter's controls.

Now let's look at the steps involved in creating a proper luma key:

1. Evaluate the raw footage. As with chroma keying, you should start by checking the footage from start to finish to see if it has problems related to luma values. Harsh shadows on a subject that is keyed against a dark background will be problematic, as will highlights on a subject that is keyed against a bright background. Add the Luma Key filter and then use the filter's Key Mode menu to key out brighter or darker elements for the matte.

2. Crop or matte out unnecessary areas of the frame. Cropping out unnecessary items from the frame, as well as cropping off the blanking lines (thin black lines at the edges of the frame) will make the next step easier. If there are any irregular or traveling elements, you may need a Four-Point or Eight-Point Garbage Matte.

3. Adjust Threshold. The Threshold slider is where most of the matte is created. Before adjusting it you should take the Threshold slider down to zero so you can see the controls working on the matte. Be sure to switch the View Mode to Alpha or Alpha+RGB as you work to see how your alpha channel looks.

4. Adjust Tolerance. Tolerance is akin to luma softness in the Chroma Keyer filter. Monitor the alpha channel while raising the slider from zero, and adjust it until you see a bit of grayscale in the matte. When you see this, back it off until the matte is once again pure white.

5. Add a Matte Choker. You don't have much control over the edges of a luma key. That's why a Matte Choker is generally a good addition to a luma key effect. Take the Edge Feather slider to zero before you begin working on edge thinning. Find your edge by working the slider while going back and forth from the alpha channel to the Final View. After you're satisfied with the edge, soften it with the Edge Feather slider.

6. Add and adjust Matte Feather. If a matte's edges are still a bit jagged, you can add a Mask Feather filter. Be careful — too much feathering will produce a halo effect.

7. Make final adjustments. You can add filters to alter the look of the keyed element. Color correction or color tinting can add interest to the subject. You can also apply a motion effect or use multiple copies of the keyed element within the composite.

Let's now go into these steps a bit more thoroughly in an exercise.

EXERCISE 8-4: CREATING A LUMA KEY EFFECT

In this exercise you'll create an alpha channel by keying a subject with good contrast against a bright background — in this case a bright, blown-out sky. You'll be keying a roller blader's head and helmet that pokes into the frame. You'll need to have Telly's FX (located in the DVD's Goodies folder) loaded into your Library → Application Support → Final Cut Pro System Support → Plug-ins.

Open the Chapter 8 Exercise sequence, and move the playhead to the marker for Exercise 4 in the Timeline. You should see two clips stacked up.

1. Solo the "Roller Blader CU" clip on the V2 track. Use the Crop tool in Image + Wireframe mode to crop pixels from the left side of the clip, without cutting into the subject's face.

2. With the clip still selected, add the Luma Key filter.

   a. Go to Effects → Video Filters → Key → Luma Key.

   b. Load the clip into the Viewer.

   c. Choose Key Out Brighter from the filter's Key Mode menu. You're doing this because our subject was shot against a bright background.

   d. Choose Final from the filter's View menu.

   e. Move the Tolerance slider to 0.

3. Adjust the Threshold slider to set the luma width of the matte. For this shot, I've chosen a setting of 80. Make sure that most of the black is out of the area you wish to key out. Check this by switching the View Mode to Alpha. Then switch back to RGB mode.

4. Adjust the Tolerance to about 8 to knock out any residual black in the matte.

5. You'll now soften the hard edges of the roller blader's helmet.

   a. With the clip still selected, go to Effects → Video Filters → Matte → Mask Feather.

   b. The Mask Feather filter should now lie at the bottom of the stack. Raise the slider slightly. I've set my slider to 3 to make the edge soft.

Image courtesy of Thinkstock Footage (V0014488)

STEP 4

Adjust the Tolerance to get rid of residual black in the matte.

STEP 6f

The background behind the roller blader is now blurred as she enters the frame.

6. You'll now stylize the background clip with a blur filter.

   a. Place the playhead at the beginning of the Roller Blader WS clip and select the clip. Press Control + B.

   b. Go to Effects → Video Filters → Telly's FX → H & V Blur.

   c. Load the clip into the Viewer.

   d. Move the playhead forward 1:00.

   e. Set a keyframe for Horizontal blur.

   f. Move the playhead forward 1:00 and raise the slider to 100. The background clip will now blur horizontally as the overlying keyed clip enters the frame.

7. Preview the effect, then select the V2 layer and render it to disk.

You've made an attractive composite. Now we'll move on to travel mattes.

Creating Alpha Channels Using Travel Mattes

Travel mattes are the hidden gems of effects creation. The two varieties, Travel Matte Luma and Travel Matte Alpha, provide a stencil that cuts out a place for an image to show through. In addition, you'll usually want a background layer for the stenciled image to play on. Let's look at how to construct a simple travel matte.

CONSTRUCTING A TRAVEL MATTE EFFECT

When you create a typical travel matte effect, you will probably use three layers to construct it. The most important thing in creating a travel matte effect is to have your tracks in the proper order. The other important step is to apply the correct composite mode to the right layer. Let's go through the process now.

Layer order

The first step in creating a travel matte is to prepare the layer order. I think of this construction as a three-part sandwich of layers:

- **Graphic fill.** The image that is cut by the stencil will reside on the upper layer (for instance, V3).

- **Matte.** The image that makes the stencil must lie directly below the clip acting as graphic fill. This image would typically be on V2.

- **Background.** The background lies below the other tracks, usually on V1.

So, how do you make these mattes? Here's the easiest way to create a travel matte luma or alpha effect:

1. Control + click on the clip on V3, which is the one destined for the graphic fill layer.

2. Choose a travel matte from the Composite Mode submenu. If the matte layer situated below on V2 has an alpha channel (text, for example), choose Travel Matte - Alpha. If the layer does not have an alpha channel and is an RGB graphic (usually colored black-and-white for best results), choose Travel Matte - Luma.

You should now see your travel matte effect with the graphic fill inside the area defined by the matte. It should be superimposed over the background clip that lies on V1. The following exercise will give you more experience with travel mattes, so let's get started.

<table>
<tr><td>tip</td></tr>
</table>

I'm often asked if there's an advantage to working with one travel matte over the other. Travel Matte Alpha has one noteworthy benefit: you can use the Matte Utility filters on the clip that has the alpha matte. For example, you can feather the alpha matte clip with the Mask Feather filter. I've found that Travel Matte Alpha provides much cleaner edges than Travel Matte Luma.

EXERCISE 8-5: USING TRAVEL MATTE LUMA

The first travel matte exercise will be a simple one, but the magic is in the technique. You'll use the same clip on V1 and V3, but the clip on V1 will have a good deal of blur attached to it to differentiate it from the V3 clip. The luma matte on V2 (the Highlight Generator) will mask out what is blurry and what is not, according to the generator's width, direction, and softness. You'll finish off this exercise with a couple of variations on the original effect.

Open the Chapter 8 Exercise sequence and move the playhead to the marker for Exercise 5. I've already stacked up the clips in the correct order for you.

1. Control + click the clip on V3 and apply a Travel Matte Luma.

2. You won't see an effect just yet, because you need to make the "Call Center Pan" clip on V1 different from the V3 clip by adding a blur filter.

   a. Select the V1 clip and go to Effects → Video Filters → Telly's FX → Telly's Directional Blur.

   b. Load the clip into the Viewer.

   c. Solo the V1 clip (Control + S).

   d. At the beginning of the clip, set keyframes as follows:

   Amount : 34

   Blur angle: −60

3. Now you'll animate the blur filter. Move the playhead to the end of the clip and then change the blur filter's settings as follows:

   Amount : 100

   Blur Angle: 60

4. Unsolo the V1 clip and step through the effect in the Canvas. You should see that the Highlight Generator is providing a gradual melding of the two images. Areas of black and white in the matte provide different luminance values, which shape the matte.

Image courtesy of Thinkstock Footage (V0020007)

STEP 1

Apply the Travel Matte Luma mode to the clip. You won't see any changes yet.

STEP 3c

Solo the V1 layer to monitor the image as you keyframe the effect.

5. The next task is to make this matte a little wider and softer. To do this, load the Highlight Generator into the Viewer, click on the Controls tab, and make the following changes to the stock generator:

> Highlight Width: 16
>
> Highlight Soft: 14

You should see that the matte has constrained the effect to the boundaries of the newly shaped travel matte (the Highlight Generator).

6. Preview and then render the effect.

tip

The Character Palette is a great source for mattes used in Travel Matte Alpha effects. (See Chapter 12 for information on displaying the Character Palette.)

STEP 5

The Blur effect is constrained to the boundaries of the travel matte.

tip

When you're using another application to produce an image for a matte, make sure that the file is rendered in the external application with "Millions of Colors +" engaged in the output render settings. If it isn't set properly (don't forget the "+"), no alpha channel will occur.

SOURCES FOR TRAVEL MATTES

You don't have to look very far to locate a variety of sources for travel mattes. You can use items within Final Cut Pro, or you can import a matte from another application.

From within FCP, you can separate travel matte sources into those best used for Travel Matte Alpha and those best suited for Travel Matte Luma. The most obvious subdivision between the two is whether or not the source has an alpha channel.

Items without alpha channels are fodder for Travel Matte Luma. Generators, clips, and graphics will work fine for this purpose. Although it's not mandatory, I find it helpful to use black-and-white footage for more predictable results. For other source material, look into some of the textures from LiveType, as well as imports from third-party applications. (LiveType is described in Chapter 12, and third-party applications in Chapter 14.)

Anything that carries the alpha channel can be used as a matte in a Travel Matte Alpha effect. These items include text generators such as Title 3D, as well as LiveType's text generators, objects, and textures. You can also use source footage you've already affected with the Chroma Keyer, garbage matte, or Luma Key (with Copy to Alpha selected in the Matte menu).

EXERCISE 8-6: VIDEO IN TEXT USING TRAVEL MATTE ALPHA

Travel matte effects aren't difficult to create now that you know which layer the matte is supposed to reside on (commonly, V2) and which layer to apply the Travel Matte Alpha composite mode to (V3). In this exercise your layers have already been set up in the proper order. However, it is up to you to apply the composite mode and to tweak the graphic fill a bit.

Open the Chapter 8 Exercise sequence. Move the playhead to the Exercise 6 marker. The playhead should be parked at the beginning of the stack before you begin. The clip on V3 (the "Waterside Sunset") will play as the video within the text. A plain Text generator from the Generators pop-up menu will serve as the alpha matte on V2 (all text generators automatically have an alpha channel). The background track will be the "Clouds Above" shot.

1. So you can see the effect clearly, turn off the visibility for the "Clouds Above" clip on V1.

2. Create a Travel Matte Alpha effect by selecting all the clips on V3, Control + clicking the Waterside Sunset clip, and choosing Composite Mode → Travel Matte-Alpha from the menu. You should now see your video within the text.

LiveType: The Ultimate Travel Matte Creation Tool

LiveType offers loads of source material for Travel Matte Luma and Travel Matte Alpha effects.

- Letters and glyphs. Elements from the Character Palette — like Greek characters, geometric shapes, and dingbats — can be brought into LiveType and used as stencils for travel mattes. Certain LiveFonts also provide some interesting travel matte possibilities.

- Objects. In the Media Browser's Objects tab you'll find a gaggle of elements that can be used as travel mattes. Spend some time experimenting with the various shapes.

- Textures. The Textures tab includes some elements that could work well for graphic fills. Choosing Noise from the Textures menu brings up some great textures that carry an alpha channel. These are great sources for mattes.

Image courtesy of Thinkstock Footage (V0019883)

You can use LiveType to generate Travel Matte Alpha sources like text, glyphs, and objects. Shown here is LiveType's Frost texture, with a Mask Feather filter added in FCP.

Image courtesy of Thinkstock Footage (VU0016153 and V0026819)

tip

You can also select composite modes from the Modify menu.

tip

Clips that have an alpha channel made from a chroma key can provide a matte for Travel Matte Alpha effects.

3. Click on the "Waterside Sunset" clip in Image + Wireframe mode and reposition the clip's X,Y position by clicking and dragging downward just a bit. Note that you can alter what plays inside the text by merely repositioning the clip on V3.

4. Turn on the visibility for the Clouds Above clip.

5. Now you'll add a tint.

   a. With the "Waterside Sunset" clip selected, go to Effects → Video Filters → Image Control → Sepia to add a Sepia filter.

   b. Load the clip into the Viewer and then adjust these settings:

      Amount: 50

      Highlight: 75

   c. Click on the Color Control swatch to launch the Color Picker. Choose a shade of green.

6. Now you'll tint the rest of the clips on V3 using the Copy/Paste Attributes function.

   a. Select the Waterside Sunset clip and then copy it by pressing Command + C.

   b. Lasso the other clips on V3 by to select them.

   c. Press Option + V and then check the Filters box in the Paste Attributes dialog box. Click OK.

STEP 2

Choose Travel Matte-Alpha from the Composite Mode submenu. You'll see the video playing in the text.

STEP 3

Move the clip in the Canvas to change the position of the video that's playing in the text.

STEP 4

Your clip looks radically different when you turn on the "Clouds Above" layer.

d. Load each clip and change the color to complement the blue background. I've chosen rust, rose, and royal blue.

7. Now you're going to add a drop shadow to the travel matte effect.

a. Lasso all of the clips on V2 and V3 to select them.

b. Press Option + C to nest the clips. Name it "Drop Shadow_NEST" and then click OK. Your two tracks will collapse into a nested sequence.

c. Click on this nested sequence in the Timeline to select it, and then press Enter.

d. Click on the Motion tab and then click on the Enable checkbox for Drop Shadow.

e. Click the disclosure triangle and make the following adjustments to the Drop Shadow:

Offset: 6

Softness: 40

8. Preview the effect and then render it when you like what you see.

Nice work! On completing this exercise, you should start to see how you can make stunning composites using both Travel Matte Luma and Travel Matte Alpha effects.

STEP 7

Add a drop shadow to make the text stand out.

Using Other Applications as Travel Matte Sources

Other applications, like Boris RED and Adobe After Effects, offer tools that can make custom mattes. You can add motion to these custom mattes by keyframing them in their native application. Adobe Photoshop has the ability to create alpha channels, so you can import stills with their alpha channels, and then keyframe them in FCP.

When you import a matte that has keyframed motion, you must render it first in the application where it was created, since you can't digitize or capture video with the alpha channel predefined. Boris RED is the exception; you can render out a matte from an FCP Timeline generated from within Boris RED. By default, LiveType will render out an alpha channel.

After the clip is imported into FCP, the areas of transparency will be defined when you overwrite the travel matte above an image. You can either use the element on its own, or as source for a Travel Matte Alpha effect. You'll have to re-render the effect in the sequence's codec before recording to tape or exporting, but you needn't worry about quality problems, as the codecs that carry an alpha channel are of extremely high quality.

You can also create source images for luma mattes in third-party applications. For the sake of convenience, make them pure black, pure white, or shades of gray.

Interpreting Alpha Channels

Final Cut Pro can detect three kinds of alpha channels: straight, black, and white. It's important for you to know how your images were originally created, and with which alpha channels they were rendered. You may need to change the alpha channel's state in a given clip for a couple of reasons: if improper reading of an alpha channel causes fringe (also called "haloing"), or if the alpha channel is reversed from the way you want to use it.

TYPES OF ALPHA CHANNELS

Let's look at the various kinds of alpha channels. I'll also offer some tips on how to correct mistakenly interpreted alpha channels.

- **Straight:** Most third-party applications generate a straight alpha channel. When rendered with a straight alpha channel, images carry only the requisite pixels, even though the backdrop looks black. Your rendered image may not look right until you blend it with other layers and inspect it on your video monitor.

- **Black:** When importing images with alpha channels, you'll come across some that are "premultiplied" onto a black layer. For example, you'll often see this when you get a PICT file from Adobe Photoshop that has been flattened with an alpha channel. In this case, the image is cut out of its background and composited against a solid black layer. Images that are rendered as premultiplied with a black alpha channel and are mistakenly interpreted as straight may serve up a nasty fringe. Changing the alpha channel back to black will fix this.

- **White**: FCP can also interpret alpha channels that are premultiplied with white. This can also happen with flattened PICT files from Photoshop. You can get fringe when images rendered with a white alpha channel are mistakenly interpreted as straight. Fix this problem by reinterpreting the alpha channel as white. (This process is described in more detail below.)

- **None:** You can also disable an alpha channel in any clip. To do so, choose Modify → Alpha Type → None/Ignore. You might do this when you want to preserve the original background of the clip or graphic.

> **tip**
>
> *If you experience fringe around a graphic, reinterpreting the alpha channel should fix it for you. If you want more control over the edge, add a Mask Feather filter to soften the edge or a Matte Choker to knock out any excess fringe.*

CHANGING ALPHA CHANNEL INTERPRETATION

If a clip was improperly imported into FCP, you can change the interpretation of its alpha channel.

- To modify a single clip, select it and then go to Modify → Alpha Type and choose a new alpha channel type from the menu: None/Ignore, Straight, Black, or White.

- To modify a group of clips, first select them in the Browser. In the Alpha column, Control + click on one of the selected items and choose a new alpha channel type from the contextual menu.

Reversing the alpha channel

You might need to reverse the alpha channel for a single graphic or a group of images. This is usually necessary when images were originally prepared for a different editing system, such as Avid Media Composer.

If you need to reverse a single image in your sequence, select it and then go to Modify → Reverse Alpha.

If you have multiple clips that need to have their alpha channels reversed, go to the Browser and select all the clips or graphics you want to modify. Go to the Reverse Alpha column, Control + click on one of the selected items, and choose yes from the contextual menu.

Troubleshooting

Here are solutions to some of the problems you might experience when dealing with mattes, keys, travel mattes, or the alpha channel.

A matte reveals an image instead of hiding it

This is a common problem that, fortunately, has an easy fix. When a matte is behaving in the opposite way from what you want, check the Invert checkbox in the Filters tab. An inverted matte is often needed to counter the addition of multiple mattes, or source material that carries an alpha channel.

Can I make a matte that will cut out my subject from the background over time?

Yes. The best way would be to shoot the scene against a well-lit blue or green screen and then use the Chroma Keyer filter to make the matte. After that, you can put any background behind your subject.

A subject wasn't filmed against a chroma key background

If the person is a "talking head" and isn't moving around much, you can place a garbage matte around the person's head. You can get away with quite a bit of feathering in this case. Be sure to preview your keyframing here, as the person may move out of the matte.

If you don't have a blue or green screen at a video shoot, at least put the subject against a white wall and make sure there are no other objects, such as plants or furniture, in the frame. You can later use a Luma Key to make a matte.

Removing a background that's behind a subject who is walking around is a bit too difficult for FCP to handle. The solution lies in using a third-party application that has advanced masking and rotoscoping capabilities (see Chapter 14 for examples).

There's a blue ring around a subject after the Chroma Keyer filter is applied

Reduce Softening, increase Edge Thinning, or add another Matte Choker. You can also do what I often do: start over.

A Luma Key doesn't seem to be working

If a Luma Key filter is not behaving the way you'd expect, make sure you've selected the proper mode to key out brighter or darker elements. In addition, drop the tolerance to zero before you begin adjusting the Threshold slider. Also, be sure to periodically change the View Mode to Matte as you clean up and adjust the key. Another possibility is that you're working on the wrong copy of the clip. Or perhaps you don't have the keyed-out element on the uppermost video track, and therefore another clip is obscuring it.

A matte effect doesn't show up

This common problem is usually related to working on the wrong copy of a clip or not having the clip on the foreground layer. If you're matting out any identical layers (for selectively filtering certain areas of a clip, for example), it helps to turn off visibility for the underlying layers so that you can work on the edges of the foreground image first.

Wrap-up

Now that you've completed this chapter, you have even more skills to use in building multilayered composites. Whether you want make a mind-blowing visual effect or just need to spice up a presentation, you can use mattes and keys to make your work really stand out.

Now we're going to push ahead into new territory: composite modes. Composite modes will add a new way of blending imagery, giving you even more tools to add dimension and style to your creations.

WHAT'S IN THIS CHAPTER

- Understanding composite modes
- Experimenting with composite modes
- Using mattes and composite modes
- Using key effects with composite modes
- Using color corrector filters with composite modes
- Constructing mode-affected looks
- Creating "film look" effects

9
Composite Modes

Composite modes (sometimes referred to as blending modes or transfer modes) blend multiple images into a single image. We've been blending images throughout the book, but so far we've been doing it by controlling opacity. In this chapter you'll learn new ways to blend images, using Final Cut Pro's composite modes. By practicing just a few simple compositing techniques, you'll greatly expand your video effects toolset. Let's get started.

Composite Mode Basics

You've already seen two composite modes in action in Chapter 8: Travel Matte Luma and Travel Matte Alpha. Those modes are used for constructing mattes, however, which differs from the main focus of this chapter: finding new ways to blend imagery. This section provides a quick overview of composite modes.

HOW COMPOSITE MODES WORK

Composite modes blend images using mathematical formulas. But don't worry; you don't have to memorize any equations or crack any books to understand and use these modes. Thankfully, the Mac does all the hard work. For most effects, you merely apply them, then see if you like them, and you're done!

Applying a composite mode

It's easy to make magic with composite modes. Just stack up two clips in the Timeline, apply the mode to the clip on the upper track, and bingo! — a composite (see Figure 9-1).

There are a couple of ways to apply a composite mode to a clip:

1. Control + click on the foreground clip in the Timeline (V2, for example, in a two-layer effect).

2. In the pop-up menu that appears, choose Composite Mode and select a mode from the submenu.

or

1. Select a clip.

2. Go to Modify → Composite Mode and choose a mode.

FIGURE 9-1
This...

...plus this, using Hard Light mode...

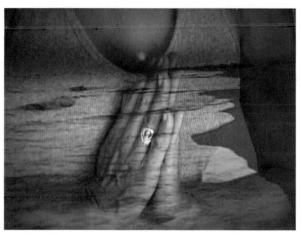

...makes this.

> **tip**
>
> *If you don't like the composite mode you just tried, just select a new one and it will be applied instead.*

If you're new to composite modes, the best way to understand them is to try them out and see how they behave. The following exercise will help you cycle quickly through the composite modes to see what they do.

EXERCISE 9-1: EXPERIMENTING WITH COMPOSITE MODES

If you haven't yet set up a custom keyboard for composite modes, go to Chapter 2 and follow the instructions in Exercise 2-3. After you've set up your custom keyboard, return to this exercise.

Open the Chapter 9 Exercise sequence. I've already included four pairs of clips for you to work on. Just move to the marker for Exercise 1 and you'll be set up to try out the different modes.

tip

You can change several clips to the same composite mode at the same time. First, select the clips you want to change. Then, Control + click on one of the selected clips and choose the new mode from the contextual menu (or call up the mode from your custom keyboard). All the selected clips will have the mode changed instantly.

1. Park the playhead over the first stack of clips. The "Orange Grid" clip should be on track V2, and the "Martial Artist" clip on V1.

2. Select the Martial Artist clip and toggle through the various composite modes by pressing the composite mode keys that you've added to the numeric keypad. Now, select Overlay mode and see how it affects the blend.

3. Move the playhead to the next set of clips. Martial Artist is now on V2, and Orange Grid is on V1. Once again, try Overlay mode on the V2 clip. Note how the clip order makes a difference in how the composite looks.

4. Enable the Clip Overlays button (Option + W) to see the Opacity Control Line overlay. Toggle through the modes again, but this time, reduce the opacity to see how you can control the relative strength of the modes.

5. As you try each mode, take note of any modes you particularly like (or don't like), or any common behaviors that you notice.

6. Try the other clips in the Timeline and see how the various composite modes affect them. Note that the modes act differently, depending on whether the clips are light, dark, or grayscale.

STEP 2
Overlay mode looks like this when the Martial Artist clip is on V1.

STEP 3
When the Martial Artist clip is on V2, Overlay mode looks like this.

Which modes did you like best? Add, Screen, Overlay, Soft Light, and Hard Light are the ones I use most often (not counting travel mattes). Now that you have an idea how the modes work, let's look more closely at the behavior of each composite mode.

A Look at Composite Modes

In this section we'll look at FCP's composite modes and see how each one blends images. As you start to experiment with these modes, you'll develop a feel for how each one reacts in common situations. For example, when you apply Add mode the blend will often look "blown out," with bright highlights. You can count on consistent behaviors with each of these modes because of the math behind each one. Having a general sense of the how the math works will help you pick the right composite mode for a particular situation. It may take a while to develop this sense, but keep at it and you'll soon get better at picking modes.

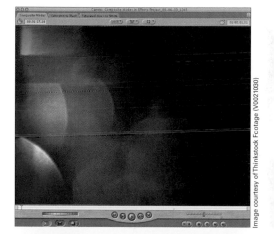

Although it's easier to think of modes as blending only two clips together, the reality is that Final Cut Pro will attempt to blend all clips in a stack according to the mode that's applied to each clip. If you have more than two clips in a stack, as you would in a simulated film look, you can continue to apply modes to each clip and FCP will make an image based on the modes chosen.

The best way to learn about composite modes is to take some images, apply composite modes to them, and compare the results for each mode. In the following section we're going to do just that. I've used four examples to demonstrate each mode.

The first set of images blends a foreground clip with saturated colors going to black (V2), and a clip with a standard palette of RGB colors (V1). (See Figure 9-2.)

FIGURE 9-2

The first blended image combines a foreground clip with saturated colors going to black (top) with an RGB clip (bottom).

The second set of images blends a foreground clip with saturated colors going to white (V2), and a clip with a standard palette of RGB colors (V1). (The RGB clip is the same one used in the first set of images.) (See Figure 9-3.)

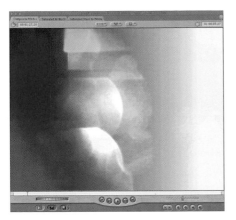 

tritrb05015 Getty Images, www.gettyimages.com

FIGURE 9-3

The second blended image combines a foreground clip with saturated colors going to white (left) with an RGB clip (right).

The third set of images blends an RGB monochromatic clip in the foreground (V2) and a grayscale clip on V1. (See Figure 9-4.)

FIGURE 9-4

The third blended image combines a monochromatic clip (left) with a grayscale clip (right).

tip

You can use Normal as your composite mode reset function. I've mapped Normal to my custom keyboard to do this quickly.

The fourth set of images blends a linear gradient (V2), and a standard-palette RGB clip (V1). (See Figure 9-5.)

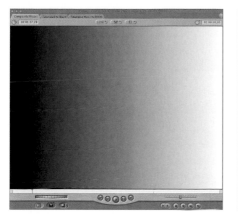 

Image courtesy of Thinkstock Footage (V0017575)

Image courtesy of Thinkstock Footage (V0017575)

FIGURE 9-5
The fourth blended image combines a foreground gradient (left) with an RGB clip (right).

Now let's look at each of the composite modes and see how each one affects these images.

NORMAL

All clips have a composite mode attached to them. By default, this mode is Normal. As you'd expect, no blending takes place with underlying clips.

ADD

Add takes the brightness values of two vertically stacked clips and adds them together, tending to push the combined colors towards white. The end result is a "blown out" look for the blended images (see Figure 9-6). You see a lot of whites in images blended with Add mode because when the two brightness values are added together, they often exceed the value of absolute white. When this happens, brightness values are "clipped" at pure white (at a luminance value of 255).

> **tip**
>
> *You can make the strength of Add more intense by duplicating the mode-affected layers. Building up lighter areas makes it possible to use them as travel matte effects after the layers are nested.*

FIGURE 9-6
Here's how Add mode affects the sample images.

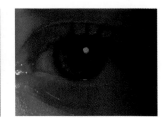

FIGURE 9-7

Here's how Subtract mode affects the sample images.

SUBTRACT

At the risk of stating the obvious, Subtract mode is just the opposite of Add mode. This mode takes the color channel values and subtracts them from each other, pushing the blended colors towards black (see Figure 9-7). There are a lot of blacks in Subtract-mode blends, because when the brightness values are subtracted from one another, they will often exceed absolute black. When the subtracted brightness values are below zero, the image displays black.

DIFFERENCE

 note

In Subtract mode, whether the overlaying image is brighter or darker than the layer below is significant. Try switching the layer order and see what happens.

In Difference mode, the blended image is the result of the difference between the pixel values of the two images. Difference is similar to Subtract, but if the subtracted values exceed zero (for black), the result will not be black, but rather the absolute value, or "spread," between pixel values. The greater the spread between pixels, the brighter the image will be. If the overlapping images are identical, the result is a pure black image.

With the vivid colors that often result, Difference tends to create a rather psychedelic look (see Figure 9-8).

FIGURE 9-8

Here's how Difference mode affects the sample images.

FIGURE 9-9

Here's how Multiply mode affects the sample images.

MULTIPLY

Multiply is another mode that tends to create a rather dark blend of imagery (see Figure 9-9). Pixel values are determined by multiplying them together and then dividing by the maximum-luminance value of 255. Similar to a Luma Key, Multiply mode works well for stripping away white values while keeping all other colors intact. If you've got a graphic on a flattened white background, use Multiply to knock out the white. Multiply is also good for restoring blacks in overexposed footage. The layer order does not matter in this case.

SCREEN

Screen mode blends the pixel values from both layers. This makes the blended image brighter overall, but will clip luma values at 100% white. In this blend, the inverse of the pixel values from each layer are multiplied together and the final result of that is inverted (see Figure 9-10). Layer order is not important. Just remember that if an underlying image is lighter than the overlaying image, there is no change in the blend. If the underlying image is darker, Screen mode will make it lighter. Screen mode acts like a Luma Key, except it strips away black instead of white, keeping the other colors of the image intact.

If you've got a graphic on a flattened black background, Screen would be an excellent choice to knock out the black. It's also good for restoring highlights in underexposed footage.

> **note**
>
> *It's possible to produce broadcast-illegal whites and blacks with Add and Subtract modes. If this is an issue, be sure to check your work on the Video Scopes and make any necessary adjustments with a Levels filter or a color correction filter.*

FIGURE 9-10

Here's how Screen mode affects the sample images.

FIGURE 9-11

Here's how Overlay mode affects the sample images.

OVERLAY

Overlay is a combination of the Multiply and Screen modes. When applied to a clip on an upper layer, dark areas above 50% luminance are multiplied, while light areas below 50% luminance are screened with the underlying layer. Mid-tone values have no effect in this mode. In the affected image, lighter areas of the clip will project their brightness to the underlying clip. Darker values of the affected clip affect darker areas in the same fashion (see Figure 9-11).

Stacking order does matter here, as the underlying image tends to be a bit stronger in the blend. The result is a blended image with lots of contrast, carrying more saturation and a unique blend of colors in the highlights and shadows.

tip

If you like contrasty looks, this mode is for you. Don't like over-saturation? Then check this out: oversaturated tones can be tamed by merely taking down the Opacity slider a few notches.

HARD LIGHT

For a dark and oversaturated composite, I usually reach for Hard Light (see Figure 9-12). This mode functions like a more intense version of Overlay, except that dark foreground tones tend to dominate the lighter background colors in the mode-affected clip. The Hard Light clip is usually the dominant image in the blend. Like Overlay, Hard Light ignores midtone values.

FIGURE 9-12

Here's how Hard Light mode affects the sample images.

FIGURE 9-13
Here's how Soft Light mode affects the sample images.

SOFT LIGHT

Soft Light is similar to Overlay, but less intense (see Figure 9-13). This mode either darkens or lightens a clip's colors, depending on its color values. If the mode-affected clip is lighter, the overall composite will be lighter. If the mode-affected image has darker tones, the image will be blended toward the darker side. As with Hard Light, midtone values seem to be ignored.

If you're looking for an understated lighting effect with a minimum of contrast, Soft Light is the way to go.

DARKEN

In Darken mode, the color values on the upper track are compared on a per-channel basis with the values on the lower track. This mode selects the darker of the two to display (see Figure 9-14). You'll probably have new colors in the blend as a result because of the per-channel aspect of the mode. The order in which you stack the clips doesn't matter.

FIGURE 9-14
Here's how Darken mode affects the sample images.

FIGURE 9-15

Here's how Lighten mode affects the sample images.

LIGHTEN

An even lighter treatment than Soft Light is Lighten mode, which is the inverse of Darken. Lighten compares pixel values on a per-channel basis and chooses the lighter of the two (see Figure 9-15). As with Darken, you're likely to get different colors than those in the original images (unless the image is grayscale).

Now that you know a little bit about the math behind each composite mode, you can better understand what's going on when you apply a mode. Of course, you can continue cycling through the modes to find the ideal one, but by keeping the information above in mind, you'll be able to pick the right one more quickly.

Grayscale Blends

Now that you've seen what composite modes can do with multicolored images, consider what they do to grayscale images. Once you start experimenting, you'll realize that you could use the blend as a travel matte. But how? You've got two layers, but the effect won't work unless the matte is on a single layer. The devil is always in the details. You could first nest the images and then set them up as a matte.

Here are some examples of composite modes applied to a grayscale blend that's made up of a linear gradient and a solid image.

Multiply mode   Hard Light mode   Darken mode   Overlay mode

Composite Mode Effects

Now that you know how composite modes blend two images together, what else can you do with them in the world of video effects? I'd like to share a number of techniques that I think you'll find valuable when you're creating effects. Let's look at some of them now.

ADDING COMPOSITE MODES TO DUPLICATED FOOTAGE

Using a composite mode, you can vastly improve the contrast and saturation of a rather bland clip in an instant. Simply duplicate the footage on different tracks and add a mode to the overlaid clip (see Figure 9-16). I'll provide step-by-step instructions for creating this effect in the next exercise.

FIGURE 9-16

The original clip (left) is duplicated, and Hard Light mode is applied (center). In another example, Multiply mode is applied to the duplicated clip (right).

Image courtesy of Thinkstock Footage (V0014412)

EXERCISE 9-2: CREATING A SOFT-FOCUS LOOK

In this exercise you'll learn how to convert a lifeless, flatly lit shot into a dreamy, soft looking image — a look you can't achieve with filters. Open the Chapter 9 Exercise sequence. There's already a clip waiting for you; just move to the marker for Exercise 2 to start.

1. Duplicate the clip onto V2 by Shift + Option + dragging it above the V1 clip.

2. Now we're going to texturize the overlaid clip by adding some Gaussian blur.

    a. With the clip on V2 still selected, go to Effects → Video Filters → Blur → Gaussian Blur.

    b. Double-click on the clip and then go to the Filters tab, where you'll have access to the Blur parameters.

tip

You can also use composite modes to instantly blend duplicated graphic backgrounds together for a more complex look. The Textures from LiveType can be easily imported into FCP to do this trick.

Image courtesy of Thinkstock Footage (V0016012)

Duplicate the original clip onto V2.

STEP 2b
Add a Blur filter to create a soft-focus look.

STEP 4
Set Opacity to 65%.

In the sample clip I've cranked up the Blur to 18 to illustrate the effect, but often a much lighter touch is needed. Try a radius of 8.

3. Apply a composite mode to the clip on the upper video track by choosing it from the contextual menu, or by using one of your custom keyboard short-cuts. (I usually go for Screen, Overlay, Soft Light, or Hard Light.)

4. Because each mode has different needs for opacity strength, you'll want to be able to adjust this at will. With Clip Overlays enabled, click and drag the Opacity overlay line downward to 65%. For this technique, I usually play in the 30-65% Opacity range. (Be sure to check your video monitor while you do this, as looks can be deceiving on a computer monitor.)

With the recipe for these looks in hand, you can now explore other some of the effects that this technique can provide.

BLENDING FROM ONE COMPOSITE MODE TO ANOTHER

The main drawback to using composite modes in FCP is that you can't keyframe them. Modes are either on or off. So how can you keyframe a composite mode's intensity or keyframe from one mode to another? The answer is that, technically, you can't (at least with stock Final Cut Pro filters, you can't). But take heart! I can provide a workaround that does something very similar. The secret lies in shifting the opacity of duplicated clips that have different composite modes applied. Let's try this in an exercise right now.

In the following exercise you'll blend two images to simulate a look in which one composite mode blends into another.

EXERCISE 9-3: BLENDING COMPOSITE MODES

Open the bin for Chapter 9 and locate the Chapter 9 Exercise sequence in the Chapter 9 Sequences bin. There's a clip already in the Timeline: an aerial shot of New York City, and a clip in the bin called "Jet Flyover." Just move to the marker for Exercise 3 and you'll be ready to go.

1. Option + click the Auto Select button for V1, and then move the playhead to the beginning of the clip in the Timeline. Click the Mark Clip button or press X to mark In and Out points.

2. Click the Destination Control button for V2 to target the track. Load the Jet Flyover clip into the Viewer. Mark an In point 1:00 into the clip. Overwrite the clip onto V2.

3. Shift + Option + drag the Jet Flyover clip from V2 to V3. This sets a duplicate of the clip onto V3.

4. Shift + Option + drag the Jet Flyover clip once more, this time from V3 to V4. In a bit you'll crop this video layer and use it as a background for some text.

5. Now that your clips are in place, it's time to set their composite modes.

   a. Select the clips on V3 and V4, and then Control + click on one of them and choose Composite Mode → Screen from the contextual menu. (Or you can use your custom-made keyboard shortcut if you wish.) This will put both of these layers into Screen mode.

   b. Control + click on the clip on V2 and choose Composite Mode → Overlay from the contextual menu.

6. You'll now add the title elements. Go to the Chapter 9 bin and locate the Chapter 9 Titles bin.

   a. Drag and drop both the "NYC Big" and "Cities of Power" titles into V5 and V6 as Overwrite edits. The order does not matter in this case.

   b. Trim them to the length of the other clips if necessary.

7. To finish preparing the titles, you'll crop and blur the Jet Flyover clip on V4 to have something for the titles to play against.

   a. Turn off the clip visibility for the clips on V1, V2, and V3 by selecting them and pressing Control + B. Now you should see the V4 layer underneath the titles.

Crop the Jet Flyover clip.

b. Click on the Jet Flyover clip on V4 to select it. Select the Crop tool by pressing the C key.

c. Crop out the areas around the text as shown.

d. With the Jet Flyover clip still selected, choose Effects → Video Filters → Blur → Gaussian Blur. The blur will be applied.

e. Double-click on the clip to load it into the Viewer. Click on the Filters tab and set the Radius parameter to 20 for the Gaussian Blur filter.

8. Nest the title elements, which include the Jet Flyover clip on V4 and the two title elements.

a. Select the items on V4, V5, and V6. I like to lasso items that are vertically stacked with the Selection tool.

b. Press Option + C. The Nest Items dialog will appear. Name the nested sequence "NYC Title_NEST" and click OK. The clips will collapse into a nest on V4.

9. Put a layer of "slug" on V5. You'll use this to fade the composite from and to black.

a. Go the Viewer's Generators menu to select the Slug generator. Click on the Duration Timecode field in the upper-left part of the Viewer.

b. Enter 8:15 in the numeric field.

c. Lock the A1 and A2 audio tracks.

d. Drag and drop the slug onto V7, aligning it with the beginning of the other tracks.

10. Option + click the V5 Auto Select button to make certain the button is "soloed." This will ensure that you'll put a splice, or Add Edit, only on the slug track.

11. You'll now make the requisite edits for the slug track.

a. Tap the Up Arrow key to place the playhead at the beginning of the stack of clips. Then move the playhead forward once more by typing +100 and pressing Enter.

b. Press Control + V to make an add edit at this point on the slug.

    c. After you've done that, type +615 to move the playhead forward once more.

    d. Press Control + V to make another add edit.

After that, click on the slug between the two add edits and press the Delete key.

The slugs at either end of the composite are now ready to be keyframed to fade the effect from and to black. Don't worry if the Canvas remains black for the next few steps.

12. Let's get started by keyframing the first slug's opacity. At this stage, be sure to turn on Clip Overlays with the shortcut Option + W, if you haven't already toggled them on.

    a. Tap the Up Arrow key to go to the beginning of the stack.

    b. Set an Opacity keyframe for the slug on V5 by first selecting the Pen tool and then clicking on the Opacity clip overlay at the beginning of the stack.

    c. Set another keyframe for opacity at the end of the V5 slug layer. Here, click on the opacity line of the slug once more and drag it downward to fade it to zero opacity. The composite will now be fully faded up.

    d. Repeat this process for the second slug, but reverse the order of the keyframes. The effect will now fade to black.

13. You'll now work on keyframing the other layers.

    a. With the playhead at the beginning of the stack of clips, and all clips deselected, type +300 and press Enter. You're now 3:00 into the composite. If you haven't yet done so, select the clips on V1, V2, and V3 and turn on their clip visibility by pressing Control + B.

    b. With the Pen tool, click on the Opacity overlay (the black line) for the NYC Title_NEST on V4. Drag it all the way down to set a keyframe for zero opacity.

    c. You'll also want to set a scale keyframe for the nest so the title can zoom up on the fade-in. Just select the nest with the Selection tool and tap the Enter key to load the nest into the Viewer. In the Motion tab, set a scale keyframe and change the value to 45.

    d. Click on the Timeline to select it. For the Jet Flyover clip on V3, click once on the Opacity overlay with the Pen tool. This sets a keyframe for 100% opacity at this point in time.

e. For the Jet Flyover clip on V2, click on the Opacity overlay and drag it all the way down to set a keyframe for zero opacity.

14. You'll now add keyframes to simulate shifting the modes with opacity keyframes. You'll also scale up the title.

   a. With all clips deselected (Shift + Command + A), type +200 to move the playhead forward 2:00.

   b. With the Pen tool, click on the overlay for the NYC Title_NEST and drag upward to add an opacity keyframe to fade the titles up. Press A to switch back to the Selection tool.

   c. While still working in the Timeline, select the nest on V4. Go into Image + Wireframe view mode to see the wireframe of the NYC Title_NEST in the Canvas. Scale the nest up by clicking and dragging one of the corners of the wireframe outward until the wireframe fills the Canvas. The titles should now be full-screen.

   d. At the same playhead position, use the Pen tool to drag the Opacity overlay for the Jet Flyover clip on V3 to fade opacity down to zero. For the Jet Flyover clip on V2, use the Pen tool to fade up opacity to 100% by dragging the Opacity overlay upward. At the same playhead position, use the Pen tool to drag the Opacity overlay for the Jet Flyover clip on V3 to fade opacity down to zero.

   e. For the Jet Flyover clip on V2, use the Pen tool to fade up opacity to 100% by dragging the Opacity overlay upward.

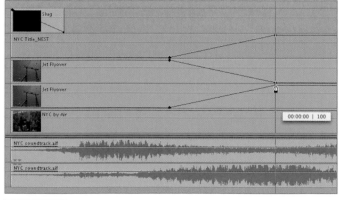

STEP 14d

Use the Pen tool to drag the Opacity overlay in the Timeline.

15. In this step, you'll smooth each keyframe to elegantly fade your clips in and out of their modes. Do this for your scale keyframes for the NYC Title_NEST as well.

   a. Control + click on each opacity keyframe in the Timeline to choose Smooth from a contextual menu.

   b. To smooth the scale keyframes for NYC Title_NEST, just select the nest and tap the Enter key to load it into the Viewer. Control + click on each of the two scale keyframes and choose Smooth from the contextual menu.

16. Adjust the opacity of the final blend to taste.

17. Preview the effect and then render it.

Now you know how to create the illusion of switching composite modes in a piece of footage. Although we faded opacity from Screen to Overlay mode, you can try different modes for dramatically different results. Footage behaves differently with each mode, so it's up to you to make good creative decisions. It's a happy problem, because you can now move forward with the knowledge that you can use more than one mode in any composite.

STEP 17

Render the effect to see the results of your work.

USING COLOR CORRECTION WITH COMPOSITE MODES

You can use a color correction filter to create color effects, which are further enhanced by adding composite modes. Did the light bulb in your head just go on? That's right, you already know how to do both of these things, but perhaps you've never tried them in tandem. Here's how:

1. Stack two clips as you normally would for a composite mode effect, and then apply a composite mode to the clip you want to affect.

2. Apply a color correction filter to either clip, or both clips, depending on the mode you want to affect and the look you're going for.

3. Move the Color Balance controls or Levels sliders to alter the color in the affected clip. Make sure you can monitor the results as you work.

4. Preview the effect and then render it when you're satisfied with the results (see Figure 9-17).

ev01891, ev01889, ev01081/Photodisc by Getty Images, www.gettyimages.com

FIGURE 9-17
Here the Microphone clip (left) was blended with the Blues Man clip (right). The Add-mode-affected clip (Blues Man) was then color corrected to match the background clip (right).

You can also use the Limit Effect portion of a color correction filter to choose a particular color to enrich using composite modes. (See Chapter 7 for more information on color correction.)

1. Stack clips as you did in the previous example, but don't apply your modes yet.

2. Apply a color correction filter to either clip, or both clips, depending on the mode you want to affect and the look you're going for.

3. Perform a secondary color correction using the Limit Effect controls in either color correction filter.

4. Apply the mode of your choice to the foreground clip (see Figure 9-18).

5. Preview the effect and then render it when you've got it right.

Using this technique, you can keep stacking layers and apply new modes, adding
as many color correction filters as the job requires.

USING MATTES WITH COMPOSITE MODES

You can use composite modes in conjunction with cropping, matte filters, and
travel mattes to isolate particular areas in an image and apply effects to just
those areas (see Figure 9-19).

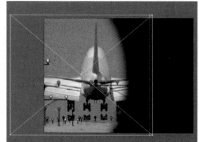

EXERCISE 9-4: MATTES, POPS, AND MODES

In this exercise we'll make an effect using mattes and composite modes. The matte will track the action, and you'll add some video *pops* (single frames of unrelated footage treated with modes) to add even more texture and excitement to an action-filled clip.

I've edited a clip — a shot of a snowboarder leaping off a cliff — into the Timeline for you. Go to the marker for Exercise 4 to get started.

1. Using the technique from the last exercise, Shift + Option + drag the snowboarding clip above V1 to place a copy onto V2.

2. Control + click on the clip on V2 and choose Composite Mode → Add from the contextual menu (or use your custom keyboard shortcut for Add).

3. You'll now set up the composite.

   a. With the clip still selected, go to Effects → Video Filters → Matte → Mask Shape. Step through the clip and check out the effect. The snowboarder will be isolated by the matte.

   b. Double-click the clip to load it back into the Viewer. You'll need to adjust some parameters.

   c. In the Filters tab, set the shape to Round Rectangle in the Shape parameter menu.

   d. Set the Horizontal Scale to 40 and leave the Vertical Scale set at 50.

   e. If necessary, tap the Up Arrow key to move the playhead to the beginning of the clip.

   f. Still working in the Filters tab, click the Point Control button (the crosshairs) in the Center parameter, and then locate the crosshairs in the Canvas. Drag the crosshairs to a new position to center the snowboarder in the matte. (Hold down the mouse button to view the position of the crosshairs as you move around the Canvas. Let go of the mouse button when you reach the center point you want.)

   g. Click the keyframe button for the Center parameter.

4. Deselect the clip, and then type +600 and press Enter. This will take you to the portion of the clip where the snowboarder is in midair. Note that the matte is not centered on the snowboarder at this point.

STEP 3a

The snowboarder is isolated by the matte.

STEP 3f

Center the snowboarder in the matte.

STEP 4

Note that the snowboarder is off-center.

You'll need to re-center the matte and add a keyframe for the position of the matte.

   a. With the clip still loaded in the Viewer, go to the Filters tab and click the Point Control button in the Center parameter of the Mask Shape filter.

   b. Click and drag the point controls in the Canvas to re-center the subject within the matte.

   c. A keyframe for Center will be set when you let go of the mouse button.

STEP 4b

Center the snowboarder in the matte.

5. The goal now is to keyframe the matte so that it will move gracefully with the snowboarder.

   a. Type –300 and press Enter. The playhead moves to an earlier segment of the clip where the snowboarder is about to disappear into some snow kicked up by the board.

At this point, use the Point Control crosshairs to center the snowboarder in the matte. You know the drill.

   b. Type –115 and press Enter to move the playhead once more. Here, between the beginning and the middle of the clip, you'll be re-centering the matte and adding a keyframe.

   c. Click on the Point Control button and then click and drag the crosshairs in the Canvas to center the matte on the snowboarder once more.

ev02119/Photodisc by Getty Images, www.gettyimages.com

6. You'll now repeat this process until the snowboarder remains centered throughout the whole clip. This may take a number of keyframes. Your goal is to use only as many as you need, or the matte will jump around too much.

   a. Park the playhead in between any set keyframes and evaluate the centering of the subject within the matte. A good place to start this process is when the snowboarder comes from behind the snow he kicked up and back into the shot.

   b. Scrub the playhead forward until you see the snowboarder emerge from behind the snow.

   c. Click on the Point Control button in the Filters tab, and then click and drag the crosshairs in the Canvas to center the matte on the snowboarder once more. New keyframes will be set after you let go of the mouse button.

   d. Continue to place the playhead at intervals between set keyframes. At each playhead location, evaluate the matte's position. If the image is centered in the matte, leave it alone. If not, you'll have to reposition the matte.

tip

If you're wondering if there's an automated process to have the matte follow the snowboarder, there is: it's called motion tracking. FCP doesn't have a motion-tracking function, but certain third-party applications do. More on this in Chapter 14.

You could continue this process until every frame is keyframed, but you don't want to go that far. Preview the effect to make sure the snowboarder remains centered inside the matte from the first keyframe to the last. It might take a number of keyframes to get the job done.

7. The next step is to make the matte fly offscreen along with the snowboarder. It's a bit tricky, but it looks really cool when you've nailed it. You'll first set a few keyframes to control the matte before it flies off the screen, and then set up the QuickView window. We'll tweak the keyframes in the next step.

   a. Since you already have a keyframe set when the snowboarder is in midair, move the playhead to the last frame where you can see the snowboarder in the frame.

   b. Reposition the point controls to set another keyframe here as you did in previous steps. The matte should be partially offscreen here.

   c. You'll need to set a keyframe between the mid-air keyframe and the last keyframe you set. Move the playhead between the keyframes and then adjust the point controls in the Filters tab to center the image in the matte once more. A keyframe will be set here.

   d. You'll need to see the offstage area in the Canvas to adjust the final keyframe. Set the magnification to 50% in the Zoom pop-up menu in the Canvas.

   e. Set In and Out points around the last 2:00 of the composite.

   f. Open the QuickView window with the shortcut Option + 8. You need QuickView to preview this non-real-time effect.

   g. Set the Resolution to Half in the QuickView window's pop-up menu.

STEP 7b
The matte is now partially offscreen.

8. You'll now be fine-tuning the positioning of the matte with the point controls as QuickView loops.

   a. With the clip still loaded in the Viewer, place the playhead 5 frames after the Out point. (Your Canvas will now be black. Don't worry. That's because you're setting a keyframe at a point after the clip ends.)

   b. In the Filters tab, set a keyframe for Mask Shape → Center by clicking the Insert/Delete Keyframe button for the parameter. The values do not matter at this point.

   c. Click the Play button in the QuickView window to begin to loop this part of the effect. It may take a few moments while the frames load into RAM.

   d. In the Filters tab, click the Point Control button for the matte's position.

   e. Drag the corresponding crosshairs in the Canvas downward and offstage and slightly to the right as you note the position of the snowboarder falling in the matte in the QuickView window.

   f. With the mouse button still held down, you may need to make very slight adjustments to the crosshairs' offstage position as the clip loops.

9. After you have the positioning roughed in, you can adjust how fast the matte falls. Your goal is to keep the snowboarder centered in the matte as it moves out of the frame. The best way to do this is by adjusting the Out point in the Filters tab.

   a. As the clip loops in the QuickView window, move the keyframe left a frame or two. You should see the matte moving more quickly as you nudge the keyframe to the left one frame at a time. Your goal is to make the matte coincide with the snowboarder falling as naturally as possible.

b. Click the Play button in the QuickView window to stop the looping at any time. Close the window when you're satisfied with the speed and position of the matte as it moves offscreen.

10. Now that your snowboarder is moving with the matte from beginning to end, it's time to put some flavor into this composite. You'll do so by adding some pops to create a grungy look.

a. Load the "Film Countdown Leader" clip into the Viewer from the Chapter 9 Clips bin.

b. Click the Destination button for V3 to target the track. Press Option + X to remove any In or Out points.

c. In the Film Leader clip, find an interesting frame and then mark In and Out points by pressing I and O simultaneously without moving the playhead. This marks just one frame of the clip.

d. Overwrite the frame onto V3 anywhere you like (perhaps on a downbeat of the music) by placing the playhead where you want the edit, clicking the Destination button for V3, and then pressing F10.

e. Continue to find interesting pieces of the Film Leader to pop on over the composite at random places. Use other clips if you like.

f. For each pop, change the composite mode to Add, Screen, Overlay, Hard Light, or any of the other modes you'd like to try. You may have to zoom in on the Timeline a bit to do this (press Command and the + key with the Timeline selected). Render the comp when you're done.

This exercise demonstrates combining composite modes with mattes to find new ways for blending footage. You can find additional uses for video pops and textures that are highlighted by blending modes.

tip

You can overlay footage of different durations to add to the random feel of high-energy composites. I tend to keep my pops between one and eight frames. There are no rules here, though — experiment as much as you like.

STEP 10f

Play with some composite modes until you like the look.

USING KEY EFFECTS WITH COMPOSITE MODES

You can use Chroma and Luma Keys to define areas where you can apply a composite mode. (See Figure 9-20.) You can use this technique to apply a composite mode in a couple of different situations:

- When you want a Luma Key or Chroma Key to define an individual area of control where you'll apply new effects. Call up this area by sampling either color or luminance values within the clip in the Filters tab. This is generally what you'd do for footage that is not shot against a blue or green screen.

Image courtesy of Thinkstock Footage (V0020007)

FIGURE 9-20

The original image is on the left. A Chroma Keyer filter has been added to knock out the blue background (center). The clip was then blended with another clip using a composite mode (right).

■ When you want a Luma Key or Chroma Key to cut out an entire object that you can apply a composite mode to. You'll generally use this technique with people and objects that were shot against a blue or green screen.

FILM LOOKS

If renting a film camera is not in your budget and you still want to achieve a rich, saturated, and stuttery film-style look for your video piece, you can do it with a combination of FCP filters and composite modes. You already know the basic recipe: add a mode to a duplicated clip on an upper track. Add a bit of blur and you're nearly there. However, you can add a few more subtle touches to get a wider variety of film looks. We'll play with some of these in the following exercise.

Film Look Ideas

If you really want a film look, think about shooting your piece on film. I'm being serious here: it's possible to have your film transferred to tape and then edit it using Final Cut Pro. If you have a small budget this may not be an option, but there's no easy way to precisely duplicate the look of film. However, there are new cameras that simulate the look, including certain HDTV cameras and the amazing Panasonic DVX100 that I mentioned back in Chapter 1. If you can't buy a camera like these, keep in mind that you can rent one. (Remember, you'll need production insurance to qualify for rentals.) The cost to shoot and edit in HDTV is coming down radically, and the worldwide trend is toward widescreen, so you may want to seriously consider it.

Another technique you might try is shooting from the hip with a cheap Super 8 camera (available at a garage sale near you), and then transferring the film to videotape. You can probably find a film-to-tape transfer facility in a city near you, but you can also do the job yourself by projecting the film onto a white wall (a screen might be too shiny) and re-shooting it with a 3 CCD camcorder.

note

In addition to the techniques you'll learn in this chapter, there are numerous third-party options for film-look effects. We'll discuss some of these options in Chapter 14.

EXERCISE 9-5: CREATING A FILM LOOK

We'll start with the premise that film looks are based on duplicating footage and applying a mode to the overlaid clip. But in this exercise we'll go further, exploring new techniques for altering the look of your video.

Go to the marker for Exercise 5. There's a sequence already edited into the Timeline for you to work on. (If you'd prefer to work on your own cut instead of the prefab sequence, construct it at the end of the Exercise sequence.) Use the clips in the Chapter 9 Clips bin.

1. Nest the clips by selecting them and then pressing Option + C. Name the nest "Original Sequence_NEST."

2. Select the nest in the Timeline and press the Return key to load it into the Viewer.

3. Now it's time to do your color correction.

   a. Go to Effects → Video Filters → Color Correction → Color Corrector 3-Way to apply the filter.

   b. Click on the Color Corrector 3-Way tab to access the visual interface of the color-correction filter.

   c. Perform any necessary color-correction and color-level modifications on the nested sequence. The idea here is to make the color correction match the look you're ultimately going for. (If you like, you can try a number of different color corrections on copies of the original nest. To do so, copy the "Original Sequence_NEST" and paste copies of it a bit further down the Timeline.)

STEP 3c

The original image is shown on the left. The color-corrected version is on the right.

4. Shift + Option + drag the "Original Sequence_NEST" above the V1 clip to V2.

5. Apply a mode, such as Overlay, to the clip on the upper video track by choosing it from the contextual menu, or by typing one of your custom keyboard shortcuts.

6. Take the clip overlay for Opacity down to 50%.

7. Next, you'll de-interlace your nested sequences.

    a. Select both nested sequences and go to Effects → Video Filters → Video → De-interlace. This will reduce the interlaced look of video frames, mimicking the flickery look of film motion.

    b. Load the nested sequences into the Viewer and then inspect the Filters tab to make sure the Field parameter for each filter is set to Lower Field First.

8. Add a bit of blur to the clip on V2. This will help hide the field-based artifacts, with an added bonus of lending an overall soft and misty look.

    a. With the nest on V2 still selected, go to Effects → Video Filters → Blur → Gaussian Blur. The default of 2 pixels is fine, but you may try another setting if you wish.

    b. With the Auto Select button enabled for V2, mark In and Out points around a small section and do a test render for the composite. A 1:00 duration will do.

    c. Render the section with Command + R. (Note: Since de-interlacing is a rather complex operation, rendering may take a few minutes.)

    d. You'll definitely need to preview this aspect of the effect on a video monitor, as the change is not as noticeable on a computer monitor.

    e. On V3 we'll add simulated film grain. To do this, we'll use a generator called Noise. Go to the Generators pop-up menu on the Video tab of the Viewer and choose Render → Noise. (You can also find it in the Browser's Effects tab → Video Generators bin → Render bin → Noise.)

    f. Edit the Noise generator onto V3 and add the composite mode of your choice. I usually go for Screen mode.

g. Drag the Opacity Adjust line down to between 4 and 20.

h. You can take this effect even further by loading the noise into the Viewer and then checking the checkbox for Color in the Controls tab. Your noise then takes on colors. Try out some different colors and see how they look.

i. You can scale and distort the Noise clip's wireframe to change the size and shape of the grain if you wish.

9. You may remember using film scratches from the exercise in Chapter 1. You can add scratches and other electronic "clutter" to your composite by making your own "Dust and Scratches" clip.

a. Go to the Generators menu and choose Slug. Mark off a 15:00 duration by clicking in the duration field and entering 15 and pressing the decimal key on the numeric keypad ("15."). Then press Return or Enter.

b. With the Viewer still selected, go to File → Export → Using QuickTime Conversion.

c. Click the Options button in the Save dialog box. In the Movie Settings dialog box, click the Settings button to set the proper compressor for your sequence (Photo - JPEG in this case). Set the Frame Rate to 29.97. Click OK.

d. In the Movie Settings dialog box, click the Size button and make sure Use Current Size is selected. Uncheck the options for Sound and Internet Streaming.

e. Click the Filter button and find Special Effects in the menu that appears. Turn down the Special Effects triangle and select the Film Noise filter. A menu (Hairs, Scratches, and Dust options) and sliders will appear, as well as an animated sample of the filter. Experiment with these controls, and click OK when you're done. Then click OK in the Movie Settings dialog box.

f. Name your clip "Film Scratches" and save it to your media drive.

g. Click the Save button.

STEP 8i
Scale the Noise clip's wireframe to change the size and shape of the "noise" grain.

h. After the slug has been processed, import it back into FCP and place it on an upper track, say V4. Then enable the composite mode of your choice. I usually go with Screen, Overlay, or Hard Light.

STEP 9e
Add some dust and scratches to your clip.

STEP 10
Apply a Soft Edges Filter to the V1 layer and Add mode to the V2 copy.

10. Experiment with the following options if you like.

- Use the Blink filter to flash the upper video track on and off. This option lends a stuttery look to the clip, like film flickering through a projector. To achieve this look, select the overlaid clip and go to Effects → Video Filters → Video → Blink. Adjust opacity the way you see fit; I've had good luck by blinking one frame on and one frame off.

- Stop Motion Blur can also provide some interesting effects. Working on the V2 clip, with the filter set at its default, and with a Gaussian Blur added, you can get a nice smeared look. Once you tweak beyond the conservative default settings, things can get a bit out of hand, showing you too many frames before and after the current one — but hey, it's yet another look you can add to your collection.

- You can also add a "vignette" look by adding one of the filters found in Effects → Video Filters → Matte to the V2 clip. Play around with the locations of the respective matte points and toggle through the modes to find the right look. Add a Soft Edges filter to the clip on V1, and then switch the V2 layer to Add mode.

11. You may also want a "letterbox" look for your clip. Try some of the following options. Before you attempt the widescreen look, you should first nest the layers that make up your film look. Select all the items and press Option + C. Name the nested elements "Widescreen Look_NEST."

    - With the nest selected, go to Effects → Video Filters → Matte Widescreen.

    - Since a crop may render faster than a Widescreen filter, just use the Crop tool on the new nest if you wish.

    - Use cropped slug layers on upper tracks to serve as mattes for your widescreen look.

12. You might want to try jittering the frame (or nested clips, in this case) by nudging it in a random direction. It's a fairly time-consuming process to make the sequence jitter like a frame would in a projector, but you can pull it off. If this sounds like something you'd like do, try the following steps on a copy of the nested effect.

    a. Paste a copy of "Widescreen Look_NEST" a bit further down in the exercise sequence Timeline.

    b. Click on the nest to select it.

    c. Change the Field Dominance for the nest to prevent artifacting. Press Command + 0. Choose Field Dominance → None. Click OK.

    d. Place the playhead at the beginning of the sequence.

    e. With the nest still selected, set a global keyframe by pressing Control + K. Move the playhead forward a random number of frames (try 8 frames for this example) by tapping the Right Arrow key.

    f. After you've advanced the playhead, set another global keyframe by pressing Control + K.

    g. Go forward one more frame by tapping the Right Arrow key.

    h. Nudge the wireframe up or over one or two pixels. To avoid blurriness during the vertical displacements, enter the numbers by hand in the Motion tab.

    i. Move the playhead forward a few more frames, and then nudge the wireframe once more.

    j. Repeat this process for as many "jumps" as you need.

note

There are a number of third-party plug-ins that will automate the jittering process. LiveType will do so as well. See Chapter 14 for details.

tip

Before outputting your composite mode piece, make sure to monitor the finished output in case something has gone out of range (which tends to happen when you start messing around with modes). Refer to the information in Chapter 7 if you need more direction.

13. A stylistic camera POV shot sometimes calls for a view from the camera's viewfinder. You could create a viewfinder graphic in another application, or use FCP's Viewfinder effect. Select the nest and then go to Effects → Video Filters → Video → Viewfinder. If the REC icon bothers you, drag its point controls for location somewhere off the Canvas.

After you've previewed a number of combinations of these effects, render your favorite combination and play it back. A reminder: Rendering long sections of de-interlaced footage is fairly time consuming, so you may want to do this when you're away from your Mac.

Edge-Defocused Viewfinder Look

You can make a variation of a vignette effect that reflects the look of a 16mm film camera's viewfinder using Multiply mode and the Oval generator.

1. Choose the Oval generator from the Shapes category in the Generators menu in the lower-right corner of the Viewer, or in the Effects tab → Generators bin → Shapes bin → Oval.

2. Overwrite the Oval Generator above the rest of the nested effect. Double-click the Oval generator to load it into into the Viewer.

3. Set the parameters to Size: 107; Softness: 55; Aspect: 1.33. Leave the color at white. Set the mode to Multiply using the method of your choice.

The underlying clips will now simulate the "edge defocusing" you might see in a film camera. If you'd like to add a Viewfinder filter to the mix, you'll have to nest the elements first, and then add the filter to the nest.

(Thanks to Adam Wilt for this flavorful recipe.)

Troubleshooting

Fortunately, there aren't too many problems with composite modes that can't be solved by switching layers, adjusting opacity, or trying a different mode. Try these things first if you're having trouble.

There's a black frame on duplicated footage

If you're wondering why a Subtract or Difference mode results in a black frame, it's because of the math. The mathematical values of the clips' pixels were subtracted from each other and had a result of zero (or lower). This is why you do not use these modes when you are duplicating footage. Modes like Subtract or Difference work best when the images you are blending are different.

Your "film look" is not convincing

Will a film look created by composite modes and filters look exactly like actual film? Unfortunately, it won't. It will, however, create a "look" quite unlike standard video, which you can add to your bag of tricks. Film looks the way it does because it is chemically processed, and video derives its look via an electronic process. The other factor is that film and video move at different frame rates (speeds), lending film that "dreamy" quality and video that overly sharp look. Fear not! There are new video camera techniques and filters coming out all the time that will help you create film looks.

Make sure you check the film look you created on a video monitor to see how it looks there. The Canvas will not display rendered graphics very well.

Wrap-up

Now you have some crucial information about making composite modes work for you. I emphasized some techniques for making unique blends, such as using mattes and duplicating clips, to create mode-affected looks. In the next chapter we'll continue to see composite modes in action when they're combined with Final Cut Pro's selection of generators.

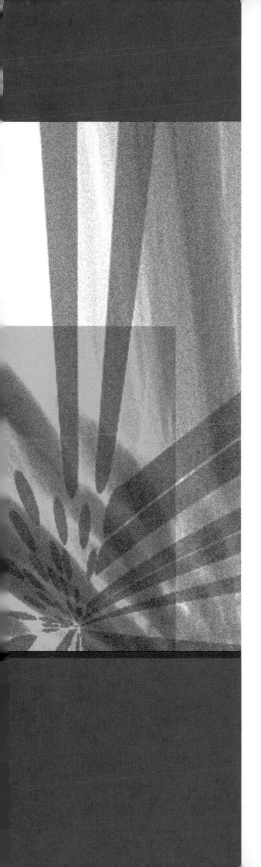

Video Generators 10

Final Cut Pro comes with the ability to create its own source footage. These video elements are called *generators*. FCP's generators consist of test patterns, gradients, color layers, video noise, and text. The key to understanding generators is to treat them like other footage you've captured or imported; add filters to them, blend them with existing clips, use them as travel mattes, or use many of the other techniques described in the book. Generators can do more than you'd think at first glance; they're another set of tools you can use for effects compositing. Beyond obvious uses as backgrounds, you can also use generators to create displacement maps, matte elements, and other items for advanced effects.

Generator Basics

Let's start with a quick overview of some practical uses for generators. Then I'll briefly describe some common generators. I'll skip text generators here, because they'll be covered in Chapter 12. In this chapter you will, however, learn how to do some text effects related to generators.

Generators are located in a couple of places. In the Browser, go to the Effects tab's Video Generators bin. You'll also find a Generators pop-up menu in the bottom-right corner of the Viewer's Video tab. (Access the menu by clicking the button with an "A" inside a strip of film; see Figure 10-1.)

USES FOR GENERATORS

With all of the wonderful backgrounds you can import from LiveType — gradients in particular — generators are used less frequently nowadays to make general-purpose backgrounds. Still, it's important to know how to use generators as source material for backgrounds, and for other purposes as well, such controlling opacity in a travel matte luma effect.

An important thing to keep in mind when using generators is that they're in a raw and fairly unusable state when you first open them. Put simply, you can use generators as source material for a multitude of purposes in effects creation. But to get the most out of them, you've got to know how to enhance them.

Need some ideas? Let's first dish up the obvious:

- You can use any generator as a simple background for a composite.

- You can make a generator take on basic motion properties, like crop or scale, which can then be keyframed. This might make a cool pattern.

- It's possible to blend generators with each other or with other clips using composite modes or opacity.

- You can add a filter to a generator to alter its look subtly or drastically, creating a more interesting background for an effect or lower third.

■ You can make a swirling gradient effect by using some of the techniques you learn in this book. Export the movie as QuickTime and then re-import it into FCP for use as a dynamic displacement map or a bump map. Drag and drop a movie into the Clip Control well of one of my custom filters, such as Telly's Bumpmap or Telly's Displace.

GENERATORS AT A GLANCE

You'll get plenty of practice using generators soon, but let's take a look at some common generators first.

■ **Bars and Tone:** Although this generator is used for calibrating video, why not use these test signals for design elements? Crop, rotate, or distort them. Add filters to Bars and Tone, such as color correctors, distortion, or blurs — you get the idea (see Figure 10-2).

■ **Matte → Color:** Although this generator might seem like a "plain Jane" at first glance, it has a number of uses in addition to providing a single-color backdrop. You could make a color backing for a picture-in-picture effect or title. Just put the color on V1 and the clip on V2, and then change a motion effect (or add a matte filter) for each layer. I like to use cropped color mattes as lines or bars to separate areas in a composition (these lines can also help you align text or other elements in a composition; see Figure 10-3). You can use them as color washes by blending them with other clips, using opacity or a composite mode. Just put a color matte or colored gradient on V2, and a clip on V1. Change the composite mode for the V2 generator. This creates an instant party gel or day-for-night tint!

■ **Render → Gradient and Custom Gradient:** There are a number of uses for these generators. Gradients can be used for some of the tasks I've already mentioned for color mattes. And as you may recall from other chapters, you can also use gradients to control travel matte effects. (The Custom Gradient has a few more options if you'd like to keyframe the position of the gradient.)

■ **Render → Highlight:** The Highlight generator can be used as a simulated light source within a piece of text, or as fill for travel matte effects. You can also use it to control the opacity of a travel matte effect, such as a Z-depth matte, which will be explained later in this chapter.

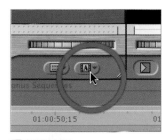

FIGURE 10-1
The Generators pop-up menu button is located at the bottom of the Viewer's Video tab window.

tip

Stack up two color mattes, then crop each one — one horizontally and one vertically. You can then use them as a quick alignment grid.

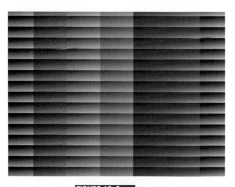

FIGURE 10-2
These cropped and distorted color bars have a Color Corrector 3-Way filter applied to them. A custom gradient with Hard Light enabled is stacked over it on V2. A Replicate filter has also been added to the gradient to create a Venetian blinds look.

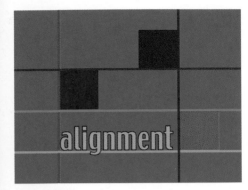

FIGURE 10-3
Color mattes are useful for both design and utilitarian purposes.

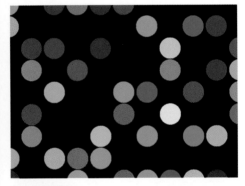

FIGURE 10-4
You can alter the color of the Particle Noise generators in the Controls tab.

FIGURE 10-5
Combine the Noise generator with composite modes or filters to overlay clips with interesting textures.

■ **Render → Particle Noise:** This generator offers up randomly generated circles, squares, diamonds, or a combination of all three. You can use a random color generator, or have the shapes play in black-and-white. You know what that means, right? It's a great source for travel mattes. Add a filter or two, such as a blur or distort, and you could use this generator to create interesting fractal noise for an organic-looking travel matte. I also like to use particle noise generators as a motion graphics backdrop, or blend them with clips using composite modes (see Figure 10-4).

■ **Render → Noise:** Noise has a number of uses, but I chiefly use it, along with composite modes or opacity, to add a bit of simulated film grain to clips. You can add color for some attractive effects (see Figure 10-5).

■ **Shapes → Circle, Oval, Rectangle, and Square:** These shapes are very handy as simple graphic elements, as backing for matted clips, and as sources for travel matte luma effects, such as a vignette. Generator shapes do not have an alpha channel, so usually I have to use a duplicate as a travel matte to get one. You'll practice this in an upcoming exercise.

Think of generators as source material that's always close at hand. Being inventive with generators gives the FCP effects designer a distinct advantage over an average effects operator.

Filter and Mode Effects with Generators

To take advantage of the full potential of generators, you'll need to use your knowledge of composite modes, filters, and motion effects. Many more uses for generators will surface once you've tried one or more of the following:

■ Nest a single generator or group of generators prior to adding a filter effect. This will change the render order of the effect (more on this a bit later in the chapter).

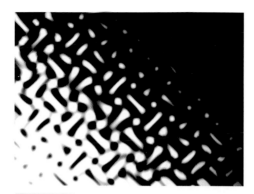

FIGURE 10-6

Two Ripple filters have been added to a linear gradient to make a luma matte. The settings in each filter were altered to provide the pattern. Experiment with your own settings to find similar looks.

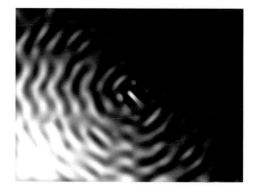

FIGURE 10-7

A color corrector filter and Telly's Radial Blur have been added to the same generator.

- Add more than one copy of the same filter to a generator (or nested generators), and then change the setting of the newly added filter (see Figure 10-6).

- Add more than one kind of filter to the generator (see Figure 10-7).

- Keyframe any of the controls in the Generator, Filters, or Motion tabs.

- Blend generators using composite modes.

When any or all of these techniques are put into play, you'll get radically different effects from these FCP staples.

ADDING EFFECTS TO GENERATORS

You can create some stunning results by adding effects to generators (see Figure 10-8).

Generators generally behave as you'd expect when you add filters and motion effects. However, if a filter doesn't take effect when you apply it, you might have to nest the generator and apply the filter to that. More on this technique later.

Let's get into an exercise that features adding effects to a Particle Noise generator. You'll be adding some blur and changing the composite mode to alter the appearance of the generator.

FIGURE 10-8

Here, a Zoom Blur filter was added to a Particle Noise generator, then duplicated onto V2 with different settings. A composite mode was used to blend the clips.

STEP 3

Change the Time Lapse to alter the randomness of the effect.

STEP 4b

You'll get a completely different effect by adding some blur.

STEP 5

Blend the blurred Particle Noise with another layer using a composite mode.

EXERCISE 10-1: GENERATORS, FILTERS, AND MODES

In the last chapter I touched on using the Noise generator for creating a simulated film grain. I'd like to continue down that path and show you how to create other kinds of textures using a combination of blur filters and particle noise generators. Get started on this exercise by opening the Chapter 10 Exercise sequence and moving to the marker for Exercise 1. A video clip and some music have already been added for you.

1. Park the playhead on the clip and press the X key to mark the clip.

2. Go to the Generators pop-up menu and choose Render → Particle Noise. Overwrite the generator onto V2.

3. Load the generator into the Viewer and then click on the Controls tab. You have some choices here:

    a. Choose the Size of particle. I've chosen 17.

    b. Choose the Shape of particle you want. There are some basic geometric shapes available. I've chosen Random to vary the shapes randomly.

    c. Choose 0 for softness. You'll add a blur filter in a minute to add softness.

    d. Density should be cranked all the way to 5. This crowds the screen with more shapes.

    e. Check the box for Random Color. This will generate a rainbow of colors for the composite.

    f. Change the Time Lapse to 15. This will change the randomness of the shapes several times over the course of the effect.

4. Select the Particle Noise clip and go Effects → Telly's FX → Telly's Directional Blur. (Make sure you've installed the filters that came with this book.)

    a. For Amount, choose 50.

    b. For Blur Angle, choose −30.

5. To blend it with the layer below, apply a composite mode to the generator. I've chosen Add.

6. Continue to experiment with the various settings of the blur filter and the controls of the Particle Noise generator. You may even want to add a color corrector filter to either the clip or the generator to adjust color or levels.

7. After previewing the effect, feel free to render it.

Experiment with filters, motion effects, and modes to alter the stock generators so you can use them in your own effects.

Let's look at the processing order of effects, one of the more important concepts in creating effects with generators.

TRICKING THE RENDER ORDER PIPELINE

To get more mileage out of your generators, particularly when you add filters to them, you'll need to know the order in which FCP processes effects. Changing this order is sometimes referred to as *tricking the render order pipeline.*

The order in which FCP processes categories of effects within a sequence is as follows:

1. Speed effects

2. Filter effects

3. Motion effects

4. Motion blur

5. Opacity

6. Transitions

Why change the render order for effects?

If a filter effect does not behave as you'd expect on a generator, you can often fix the problem by changing the render order of filter and motion effects. Most of the time you'll want to process the motion effects before the filter effects. That way, the filter

Custom Gradient Controls

The Custom gradient has more keyframable parameters then the Standard gradient, and hence more control. That's why I usually reach for it first. The default Custom gradient is a black-and-white linear gradient that offers a gradual change from pure white to pure black, moving from left to right. For making backgrounds (or graphic fill for travel matte effects), change the color to meet the design requirements of your video composite. For travel matte luma effects, leave the gradient black-and-white.

The controls should be considered, as they're useful for making gradients do even more interesting tricks. Gradient Direction has an angle control that will change the angle of the gradient. Gradient Width determines how much of the Start or End color will be displayed. There are other familiar controls here, including controls for Start and End "color stops." Keyframe any of these parameters to make the gradient undulate.

But wait, there's more! Pull down the Shape menu and choose Radial. The gradient becomes circular. Point controls can move the shape, and Gradient Width changes the size of the shape and the amounts of Start or End color making up the radial gradient.

You'll come back to the Custom gradient again and again for ordinary backgrounds, filling travel matte objects, and providing mattes for travel matte luma effects.

effects will affect the clip or generator that has already been processed by the motion effects, rather than the other way around. This can cause a pretty drastic change in how a filter affects a generator — or whether it will take effect at all (see Figure 10-9).

On the left, a Basic 3D filter was added to a cropped gradient with the Y Spin parameter set to –45 degrees. This is not the way you wanted the gradient strip to look. On the right, the cropped generator has been nested and the same filter added. Now the filter can control the cropped gradient in simulated 3D space!

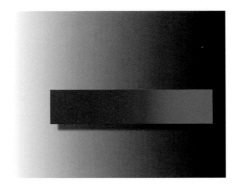 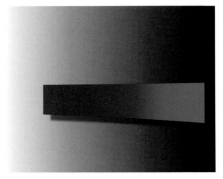

Nesting to change the render order

One of the primary advantages of nesting is that you can switch the order in which effects are rendered. Simply by reordering of the pipeline, you can make some really cool patterns and designs for use in any effects-related project.

It's easy to change the render order of filter and motion effects:

1. First, apply a motion effect to any clip or generator. Something as simple as changing a crop value will do the trick.

2. Then, just select the clip or generator and nest it. With the nest selected, add a filter to the nest. The normal order of processing will be reversed; you've applied a motion effect before a filter effect.

As an example, think back to Chapter 2 when you were "deconstructing" the effect in the first exercise. There was a step in which a Replicate filter was added to a nest ("Accent White Stripes") that contained a single white stripe made from a cropped color matte. If the Replicate filter had been added to the white stripe, nothing would have happened. However, since I nested the clip and then added the filter to that nest, there were as many white stripes as the filter allowed. This worked because the processing order for the effects was switched. If this concept is still not totally clear to you, the following exercise should help.

EXERCISE 10-2: SINE WAVE EFFECT

Here's an effect that will spring to life once you've changed the processing order. In this case you'll make some straight lines turn into a series of sine waves. Although it's true that you can affect the color matte with the Wave filter to make the effect, you can't control the wave to the point where you can see the top or bottom of the shape. To do this, you must swap the render order of the motion effect so that the filter affects just the cropped line, not the entire color matte.

Open the Chapter 10 bin, and then the Chapter 10 Sequences bin. Open the Chapter 10 Exercise sequence and move to the Exercise 2 marker. The seven color mattes and an audio track have already been added to the Timeline for you. The color matte on V1 is meant to be the background color.

1. Working in Image + Wireframe mode, use the Crop tool to make each of the color mattes into lines. Do not crop the matte on V1.

   a. Load the generator on V7 into the Viewer by double-clicking on it.

   b. Click on the Motion tab and turn down the triangle for Crop.

   c. Use the Crop tool in the Canvas to make your line. When you crop, make the line lie in the lower third of the Canvas. I like the settings 78 for Top and 18 for the Bottom.

2. Now that the first line is in place, you can use the Copy/Paste Attributes function to make the rest of the lines exactly the same width.

   a. With the generator on V7 still selected, copy the clip's attributes by pressing Command + C.

   b. Select the rest of the generators on V2 through V6. Press Option + V to launch the Paste Attributes dialog box. Check the box for Crop and then click OK. All of the color mattes will be cropped into lines.

3. Nest each generator individually and name them something appropriate, like "V7 Wave_NEST" and so on.

4. Select the stack of nests by lassoing them. Go to Effects → Video Filters → Distort → Wave. The Wave filter will be added to each cropped line.

5. Option + double-click on each "Wave_NEST" to load them into the Viewer, where you can individually adjust and keyframe each wave. Click the checkbox for Vertical as well.

Forge the waves into a pattern. You can achieve this by using consistent offset numbers for Amplitude (wave height) and Wave length. Experiment and find your own settings if you like. Or use my settings for start and end keyframes, as follows:

a. V7: Amplitude Begin: 20   Amplitude End: 10

   Wave Length: 50   Wave Length End: 40

   Speed: 85   Speed End: −150

b. V6: Amplitude Begin: 30   Amplitude End: 10

   Wave Length: 60   Wave Length End: 50

   Speed: 95   Speed End: −160

c. V5: Amplitude Begin: 40   Amplitude End: 10

   Wave Length: 70   Wave Length End: 60

   Speed: 105   Speed End: −170

d. V4: Amplitude Begin: 50   Amplitude End: 10

   Wave Length: 80   Wave Length End: 70

   Speed: 115   Speed End: −180

e. V3: Amplitude Begin: 60   Amplitude End: 10

   Wave Length: 90   Wave Length End: 80

   Speed: 125   Speed End: −190

f. V2: Amplitude Begin: 70   Amplitude End: 10

   Wave Length: 100   Wave Length End: 90

   Speed: 135   Speed End: −200

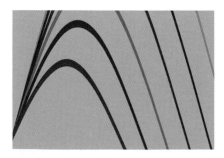 

At first, the tops of the sine waves are cut off. When the filter order is changed, the waves look much better.

6. As an optional step, you can try out composite modes for the lines.

7. Preview the effect in the QuickView window and then render it by selecting the stacked nests and pressing Command + R.

You should now have six lines undulating in a sine wave pattern. You've made a cool new effect and practiced using nesting to reorder the processing of effects. Of course, you could add clips and titles to a comp like this. Use your imagination and keep going with this exercise if you wish. The remainder of the chapter will focus on using generators with travel matte effects.

Generators and Travel Matte Effects

After reading Chapters 8 and 9, you should already realize that the function of many generators is to provide geometric forms for constructing travel matte effects, and to serve as graphic fill for the mattes. Let's first look at how you can make more interesting fill for your travel matte effects.

CREATING GRAPHIC FILL WITH GENERATORS

A common use for generators is to create graphic fill for travel matte effects. Just to be clear on the nomenclature, I'll remind you that "graphic fill" is any clip or graphic that has its edges defined by a matte. Got it? Great!

With a generator presiding as graphic fill, you can animate its parameters to make it appear as if it's playing inside of the text or any other travel matte. Filters and motion effects added to the generator can also make the fill more dynamic.

In the following section I'll show you how to make a standard highlight effect to fill text. Then I'll show you some alternatives methods. Working through these techniques should give you ideas about how to manipulate the graphic fill for any travel matte effect.

Creating a highlight effect for travel mattes

With the Highlight generator, you can create a highlight for your text or other travel matte effect. In a highlight, a bright, soft light appears to pass through the text. It's very simple to create a highlight for text. Just set it up like a travel matte

FIGURE 10-10

Set parameters for Angle, Width, Softness, and Color to customize your highlight.

FIGURE 10-11

The highlight glints across the text.

alpha effect, a technique you picked up in Chapter 8. I'll remind you of the process here.

1. Edit the background of your choice onto V1.

2. Edit a Text generator, such as Title 3D, onto V2. Use a bold font and a large size.

3. Edit the Highlight generator onto V3, and then load it into the Viewer by double-clicking on it. Set the keyframes for the Angle, Width, Softness, and Color of the highlight. The default horizontal setting for the Highlight generator is really not the way the effect should look. A soft, vertical or cambered band of color will create the look you'd expect (see Figure 10-10).

4. Set keyframes to animate the Center parameter so that the highlight travels across the text from left to right. Control + click on the Highlight generator and choose Travel Matte Alpha from the contextual menu. The highlight will then shine through the text as you play back the effect (see Figure 10-11).

5. Preview the effect and tweak it until you're satisfied. Render the effect when you're done.

The following exercise will acquaint you with techniques you can use to provide your clients with something fancier than a stock glint effect.

EXERCISE 10-3: CREATING A CUSTOM HIGHLIGHT FOR TEXT GENERATORS

Let's continue with another exercise for providing a simulated light source shining on some text. Although making a highlight effect, as in the last exercise, is acceptable, I prefer to make the light source sweep across the text like a searchlight. This exercise will also let you practice altering the anchor point of a clip or generator.

Get started by opening the Chapter 10 Exercise sequence and moving to the marker for Exercise 3. A background clip, "Waterside Boat," has already been added to V1 for you. Some music from Killer Sound (www.killersound.com) has been added as well.

1. Create the text and load it into the Timeline.

   a. Go to the Generator pop-up and choose Text → Text. Title 3D will work as well (more on Title 3D in Chapter 12).

   b. Click on the Controls tab and type "Bay Scene." Select the type by clicking in the Text Entry box and pressing Command + A.

   c. Choose a bold font. Size it up to fill most of the screen. I used Adobe's Magnesium Bold for my font.

   d. Edit your Text onto V2 using an Overwrite edit.

2. Go to the Generator pop-up menu and choose Matte → Color. The generator will load into the Viewer. Choose a dark color for the brighter light source to play against. I'm using a dark orange. I'll call this color matte the "light saber."

3. Edit the color matte onto V3.

4. Shift + Option drag the V3 color matte onto V4.

5. Load the V4 color matte into the Viewer. Click on the Controls tab and then choose a color for your light saber source. I chose a light orange.

6. Shape the light saber with a 4-Point Garbage Matte filter. To do this, perform the following steps:

   a. Since you're working in an OfflineRT sequence and need a garbage matte, it's helpful to nest the generator first (to change the order of the render pipeline), before working on the garbage matte. Select the V4 color matte and press Option + C. Name the nest "Saber_NEST" and click OK.

   b. You'll add a matte filter to the nest. Option + double-click on the Saber_NEST to simultaneously select it and load it into the Viewer. Go to Effects → Video Filters → Matte → 4-Point Garbage Matte.

   c. You need to make a thin, tall triangle with the matte. Points 1 and 2 will have the same values at the top-center of the Canvas. In the numeric field you can just enter the values X = 0 and Y = −120.

    d. Points 3 and 4 are equidistant and should play near the lower third of the frame. Set Point 3 at X = 25 and Y = 100. Point 4 should be X = –25 and Y = 100.

    e. Adjust the matte's parameters. Set Smooth to 2, Choke to 30, and Feather to 11. Choose Final in the View Mode menu.

7. You've got a nice light source going. Now you'll animate its movement. For this, you'll change the position of the anchor point and animate rotation.

    a. In the Motion tab, the coordinates for anchor point should be changed to X = 0 and Y = –120. Note that the anchor point and the garbage matte points at the top of the saber are precisely the same. Entering numbers ensures a precise effect.

    b. Move the playhead 2:00 forward from the beginning of the generator by holding down Shift, then tapping the Right Arrow twice.

    c. With the nest still selected, click on the Motion tab. Set a keyframe for Rotation. Make the value 90 and press the Enter key.

    d. Tap Shift + Right Arrow three more times to move the playhead ahead 3 seconds. In the numeric entry box for Rotation, enter –90. Smooth both of the Rotation keyframes.

    e. Preview the effect in the QuickView window at Quarter resolution. The saber should rotate from the top center of the Canvas in a natural sweeping motion.

8. Next, you'll duplicate this nest to make the saber have a bit more color.

    a. In the Browser, Control + click on the Saber_NEST sequence and choose Duplicate. The nested sequence will be duplicated. Click on the name of the nest and change the name to "Saber Point_NEST."

    b. Drag and drop the Saber Point_NEST onto V4 as an Overwrite edit.

    c. Double-click on the Saber Point_NEST to open it in the Timeline. Double-click on the color matte to load it into the Viewer, and then change it to a different color of your choice. I've chosen a saturated yellow-orange.

    d. Click on the Chapter 10 Exercise sequence tab in the upper-left corner of the Timeline.

tip

Paying special attention to the placement of your anchor point can add even more options for you to keyframe the movement of lines and shapes made with any generator.

New anchor point position

9. Unfortunately, even though the nest was duplicated, the filters and motion effects you added to it were not maintained. You can get them back with the Copy/Paste Attributes function.

   a. In the Timeline, click on the Saber_NEST to select it and then press Option + C. Click on the Saber Point_NEST and then press Option + V to launch the Paste Attributes dialog box.

   b. Click the Basic Motion and Filters checkboxes and then click OK. The motion and filter effects will be applied to the duplicate nest.

10. Select both nests and Shift + drag them upward so that the anchor points for both layers are now offscreen.

11. Distort the aspect of the Saber Point_NEST by first selecting it. Hold down the Shift key, then click the lower-right corner of the wireframe and drag it down and in. You'll scale and squeeze the light so that it plays inside the underlying light source. The scaling may feel a bit different since you're scaling from a different anchor point.

12. You'll join these two nests and the V2 color matte into one by selecting them and then pressing Option + C. These elements will be grouped into a nest so you can use it as graphic fill. Name the nest "Dual Sabers_NEST." Click OK.

13. Control + click on the Dual Sabers_NEST and choose Travel Matte Alpha from the contextual menu. The new light source will be inside the type and will rotate through it in an attractive manner.

14. If you wish, you can nest the Dual Sabers_NEST and the text. That way, you can add a drop shadow to the travel matte effect. Select the two layers and then nest them by pressing Option + C. Name the nest "Highlight Effect_NEST." Option + double-click on the nest and then click the Motion tab.

16. Adjust the Drop Shadow in the Motion tab.

17. Preview the effect and and render it once you like what you see. The text will have a lively animated highlight.

Customizing a graphic fill shows you're willing to go the extra mile to make a travel matte effect look even more impressive.

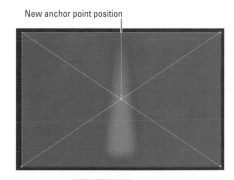

STEP 7
Change the coordinates for the light saber's anchor point.

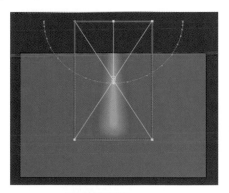

STEP 11
Distort the Saber by dragging the wireframe.

Image courtesy of Thinkstock Footage

STEP 17
Preview your effect and watch the highlight sparkle across the text.

Using Generators for Travel Mattes

In Chapter 8 you were introduced to travel matte luma effects created from a generator. I'd like to briefly revisit that idea. Now you'll combine techniques you've learned in earlier chapters to provide a greater variety of looks.

GENERATORS AS TRAVEL MATTE LUMA SOURCES

As you know, many generators are useful for providing the matte for a travel matte luma effect. Since FCP generators do not have alpha channels, you use the luminance information within the generator to create a travel matte luma effect.

Here's a list of generators you can use for travel matte luma sources:

- **Render generators:** Use Gradient, Custom Gradient, Highlight, Noise, or Particle Noise.

- **Shape generators:** These can really assist you in creating bold travel matte effects. These shapes can be keyframed, enlarged, or even placed partially offscreen for use in a travel matte effect. You can leave the edges soft for a vignette effect (see Figure 10-12), or make them razor sharp by moving the softness slider to the left.

- **Color Matte:** You can use a cropped color matte generator to make a source for a travel matte luma effect. Use a motion effect or add a filter to the cropped color matte to alter the look. You may have to nest the generator before adding effects.

FIGURE 10-12

For this vignette effect, an Oval generator was placed on V2, and slug placed onto V1. The two layers were nested so the matte could be moved (the Oval generator has no point controls). After the nest was placed on V2, Travel Matte Luma mode was applied to the graphic fill on V3.

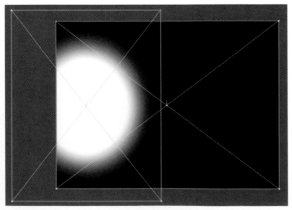

Image of girl courtesy of Thinkstock Footage (V0014650). Image of train courtesy of Getty Images, www.gettyimages.com (ev0137/Photodisc).

COMBINING SHAPES WITH MODES TO CREATE MATTES

In Chapter 9 you saw how composite modes blend clips to create entirely new imagery. Combining generators and composite modes can offer up new shapes for mattes. I'll explain the technique using two generators, but you can use more.

1. Stack two generators in the Timeline.

2. Apply a composite mode, such as Add, to the generator on the upper track. The new shape will now be apparent.

3. Select the two layers and type Option + C to nest them.

4. Place the clip you wish to act as graphic fill on the layer directly above the nest.

5. Control + click on the clip or generator that is the graphic fill. Choose Travel Matte → Luma.

The graphic fill will now appear to play inside the matte you made with the combined shapes (see Figure 10-13).

USING GRADIENTS TO CONTROL TRANSPARENCY

As you saw in Chapter 8, a gradient generator can control the transparency of a generator or clip when a travel matte effect is used. When making any backdrop or lower third, you can use this technique on a color matte or gradient instead of a video clip. If you keyframe the various parameters of the gradient, you can better control transparency.

Constructing elegant lower-third boxes

A lower-third effect is very common in broadcast video, especially in news programming. It's the "name plate" for identifying the person in a head-and-shoulders shot. Let's consider the box of color commonly used for the background of lower-third text.

Clips and generators that are used as backing in a lower-third text effect look more elegant when the colors gradually fade into the picture. You can have a separate text generator cast a drop shadow onto the backing — something you can't do with the standard Lower 3rd text generator.

1. Edit in your background element, such as a clip of a news anchor. I suggest you use a white color matte so you can see what's going on.

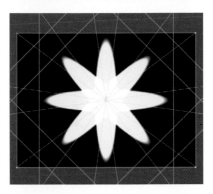

Images courtesy of Getty Images, www.gettyimages.com (ev0178/Photodisc; dv395013/ digital vision)

FIGURE 10-13

You can combine generators with modes, in this case Add. Here, I duplicated the original shape (top), and offset the layers with different Rotation values (center). Then I nested the stack and applied a Travel Matte Luma to the layer directly above the clip of the flower (bottom).

tip

Mattes that are keyframed from 100% black to 100% white make great transition effects.

2. Create your graphic fill element, which can be a color matte, gradient, imported background from LiveType, or video clip. Perform a mark clip and then edit the clip onto V3. Here, instead of using a simple gradient, I am using some blue rounded rectangles. Being nested, they provide a single source for the graphic fill.

> **tip**
>
> *After combined shapes are nested, you can add filters to the nest, such as Bulge, to further shape or distort the matte. Of course, you could also add a filter to any single layered generator that acts as a matte.*

3. Locate any generator that can make black and white colors. In the Timeline, mark the clip and then Overwrite Edit this clip onto V2. If you're using a strip of a color matte or a gradient as the graphic fill for the lower third, you may have to crop the matte on V2. (It's not necessary to crop your graphic fill.) In this example, the graphic fill is already constrained by an alpha channel because it was created from a matte shape.

4. Apply a travel matte luma composite mode to the V3 layer — your graphic fill — color matte or gradient. In my case, it's the nest of rounded rectangles (see Figure 10-14).

LiveType Textures as Travel Mattes

Livetype offers dozens of background textures. In addition to backgrounds, these textures can be used as fodder for travel matte effects. Textures with areas of high contrast are the best candidates. Regardless of the textures you choose, you'll probably need to desaturate the texture and adjust levels to maximize their potential as mattes.

Tunnel image courtesy of Getty Images, www.gettyimages.com (ev02369/Photodisc). Fence image courtesy of Thinkstock Footage (V0019922).

Here the LiveType texture Fog Machine will provide the matte. A color corrector has been added to adjust levels.

A background clip has been placed on V1, and a foreground clip on V3. The composite mode for the V3 clip has been set to Travel Matte Luma.

As the smoke undulates, the matte effect changes along with it, revealing different areas of the image.

Image courtesy of Thinkstock Footage (V0020023)

Here's the result of the travel matte effect on the rectangles. Note that the boxes on the right fade into the background due to the black areas of a linear gradient.

FIGURE 10-15

Elements such as a gradient and a drop shadow make this lower third stand out.

> **tip**
>
> *You can make source material for travel matte lumas in other applications, such as Adobe Photoshop or Boris RED, and then import them into Final Cut Pro.*

> **tip**
>
> *If I use a clip to provide the source for a Luma matte, then in almost every situation I'll apply a color corrector to it so saturation can be stripped and brightness levels adjusted.*

5. Nest your V2 matte and V3 graphic fill layers and then load the nest into the Viewer. Click the enable checkbox for Drop Shadow so your backing can cast a shadow onto the background. Once you've edited text onto the upper layer you can cast a drop shadow onto the lower-third backing.

You now have a lower third that's more elegant than the stock lower third (see Figure 10-15). It has a textured fill track, it fades into the background, and the text casts a drop shadow. Now that you have a simple recipe, try your hand at using a similar technique in the following exercise.

EXERCISE 10-4: CONTROLLING TRANSPARENCY WITH GENERATORS

Move to the Exercise 4 marker and let's get started. I've already added a base layer and a music track.

1. First, you'll duplicate and crop the gradient.

   a. Duplicate the gradient onto V3 by Shift + Option + dragging the copy of the gradient into place.

   b. Double-click it to load it into the Viewer.

   c. In the Controls tab, click the red "X" to reset the V3 generator to a standard black-and-white gradient.

   d. With the Crop tool, crop off everything but the bottom 1/5 of the screen, at a setting of 80 for Crop → Top.

2. Duplicate the V2 generator by Shift + Option + dragging it to V6. Crop the color matte so it has the same values as the V2 matte.

3. You'll now add the color mattes.

    a. Locate Matte → Color in the Generator pop-up menu. Edit the matte into V4 by overwriting it into place.

    b. Double-click the color matte and change the color to a chocolate brown in the Controls tab by clicking on the Color Control swatch. This color matte should be cropped until it is overlapping the cropped grayscale gradient underneath.

4. Shift + Option + drag the color matte clip to make duplicates on V5 and V7.

5. Load the color matte on V5 into the Viewer. You need to stylize this layer a bit to make it serve as a border with an open top:

    a. In the Motion tab, click the Reset button for Crop.

    b. Click on the Controls tab and then change the color to a royal blue.

6. You're going to shape this color matte with a shape matte filter. Go to Effects → Video Filters → Matte → Mask Shape. Click on the Filters tab and then change the settings to:

    Rectangle

    Horizontal Scale: 72

    Vertical Scale: 112

    Position: X = 0   Y = −40

7. Click the Invert button.

8. Next you'll set up the backing plate for the title.

    a. Double-click the color matte on V7 to load it into the Viewer.

    b. Working in the Canvas, press C to get the Crop tool and then re-crop the color matte to overlap the gradient on V6. Crop the right side of the color matte to clear the blue border on the right as well. It's OK if the underlying black gradient is sticking out.

9. For the V4 and V7 color mattes, change their composite mode to Travel Matte Luma to see the gradients work on their transparency.

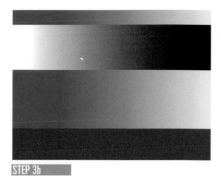

Image courtesy of Thinkstock Footage (V0016C18)

STEP 3b
Change the matte's color to a chocolate brown.

STEP 11
With the title added, your composite is complete.

10. From the Chapter 10 Clips bin, open the clip "Family Album WS," then overwrite it onto V2 in alignment with the rest of the generators. Double-click it to load it into the Viewer and set Scale to 60 and Center to X = 23, Y = 28. Crop off any blanking lines you see.

11. Click the Destination Button for V8 and then overwrite the title from the Chapter 10 Generators bin; it's called "Highlands Insurance." Your composite is now complete.

12. Select the V8 layer and then render the composition.

Although you've built an 8-layer composite, the final result looks clean and simple. If you use similar techniques, you'll come up with looks that are more elegant than using a plain gradient generator for a background. Strips of color that serve as lines of demarcation add to the appeal.

CREATING GEOMETRIC SHAPES WITH ALPHA CHANNELS

In motion graphics you want to have access to geometric lines and shapes for various reasons. Typically, you'll want these shapes to have an alpha channel so you can reveal background elements behind the shapes. Let's now talk about common ways to make lines and shapes in FCP.

Making a simple line is easy. All you need to do is crop a color matte or other generator. To make angled lines, rotate the cropped color matte.

FCP shape generators do not carry an alpha channel. No worries. You have the knowledge to construct a geometric shape with a fully controllable alpha channel.

Here are your choices for creating geometric shapes with alpha channels:

- **Make a travel matte luma effect.** This is your most flexible option. Start by constructing a travel matte with a white version of the shape on V2 as the matte. V1 is set aside for your background clip to play on. The graphic fill on V3 can be any clip, such as a color matte for a solid shape. An advantage of using a travel matte for shapes is controlling the size of the shape with one slider. It's also easy to feather the shape with the Softness slider. Just make sure your graphic fill will take up the area that will be feathered.

- **Add a luma key.** You could also add a luma key to a colored Shape generator. I usually don't go for this approach, as certain colors will begin to display transparency as you adjust the key.

- **Make the shape another way.** You could avoid using shape generators entirely and construct a shape by adding either a shape matte or a garbage matte filter to a color matte. You can use this approach to make shapes that aren't available in FCP, such as triangles and hexagons.

- **Use LiveType.** Another approach is to use LiveType and import the shape, either static or already affected. Shapes are brought into LiveType (or any standard text generator, for that matter) via the Character Palette (see Chapter 12 for more information). If you don't mind the preset shapes in the Character Palette, this is probably your most flexible choice for geometric shapes (see Figure 10-16).

- **Use fonts.** You can purchase font sets that are filled with geometric shapes. Use any text generator to deploy them in FCP. With this technique, you'll have the advantage of using the magnificent controls found in Title 3D.

- **Use a third-party plug-in.** My favorite option for this is Joe's Filters (www.joesfilters.com). You'll get shape generators of all types that have embedded alpha channels. Using this plug-in makes it quicker to create common shapes than applying a garbage matte to a color matte.

Knowing how to create the right geometric shape is very important to making broadcast design effects, which these days are peppered with geometric shapes.

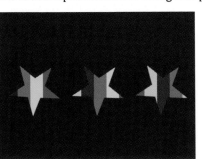

FIGURE 10-16

Import shapes from LiveType and then introduce a Travel Matte Alpha composite mode to the graphic fill layer.

Advanced Generator Effects

You can take generator use to a higher level when you combine the techniques you've learned in this chapter, such as creating travel mattes, tricking render order, adding filters to nested sequences, and other advanced concepts. Now let's look at another advanced technique: creating a Z-depth matte.

ADDING Z-DEPTH TO A COMPOSITE

Generally, 3D is the realm of third-party compositing applications, since a Z axis is not available in FCP. However, with a little know-how you can simulate a 3D look in FCP. This technique involves setting up a grayscale matte, separated by two identical layers of content (one sharp and one blurry), with a travel matte luma engaged. You'll then use the Distort tool to add perspective. It sounds complex, but it's really quite easy. Here we go.

EXERCISE 10-5: CREATING A Z-DEPTH MATTE

In this effect you'll fly multiple picture-in-picture layers across the screen, which you learned to do in Chapter 5. You'll then create a Z-depth matte to add interest. Open up the Chapter 10 Exercise sequence and move to the marker for Exercise 5. I've got some music from Killer Sound already edited into place.

1. In the Timeline, stack up copies of "Hip Girl," which is located in the Chapter 10 Clips bin. In my example I have seven copies of the clip stacked up. Scale down each clip to 50%. Use Copy/Paste Attributes to get this done quickly.

2. Trim the last 5 seconds of the stack. Move to the end of the stack and then press Shift + Left Arrow five times. Use the Double Blade tool to make a splice and then delete the excess footage to the right.

3. Use the Slip tool to slip each clip arbitrarily. This will make different content play back as the motion path moves.

Triangle Trick

To make a triangle shape, just add a 4-Point Garbage Matte to any clip or generator. Make sure at least two of the points have precisely the same X,Y values. Use a 4-point matte for a triangle? I can see that you're scratching your head. Here's how it works:

1. Edit a color matte into the Timeline.

2. Go to Effects → Video Filters → Matte → 4-Point Garbage Matte.

3. Set points 1 and 2 to be the same values. In my example, the values are X = 0 and Y = –100.

4. Use numeric entry boxes to set coordinates for points 3 and 4. The coordinates of the example are X = 70 and Y = 30 for point 3, and X = –70 and Y = 30 for point 4.

5. Scale each layer down to 50%.

6. To create a pattern, duplicate the layers and place them at equidistant X values in the Motion tab. You do the math and decide how far apart each triangle should be. I've set 90 pixels offset per layer. Also, every other triangle is rotated 180 degrees to complete the pattern.

7. The pattern can then be nested and treated as a group to make more complex forms.

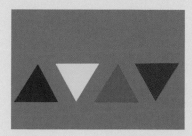

4. You'll now evenly space the clips across the Canvas and offstage areas. In the Timeline, load each clip into the Viewer, one at a time. Enter equidistant X values to space the clips vertically across the screen, as you did in the exercise in Chapter 5. Offset the clips by 200 pixels.

5. In the Timeline, select all of the layers and then drag them offscreen to the right in the Canvas in Image + Wireframe mode. Click the Add Motion Keyframe button in the Canvas.

6. Move the playhead to the end of the stack and then tap the Left Arrow key to put you at the head of the last frame to see what you're doing.

7. Shift + drag the wireframes offscreen to the left. The clips will now be set up to fly across the screen.

8. Nest the stack of clips by selecting the layers and pressing Option + C. Name it "Clear Stack_NEST."

9. Duplicate the nest. Shift + Option + drag the nest to V3.

10. Blur the nest on V1. Select it and then go to Effects → Video Filters → Blur → Gaussian Blur.

11. Option + double-click the nest and then click the Filters tab. Choose 18 for the Radius parameter.

12. You'll now need to place the matte on V2. Mark the clip and then load a Highlight generator into the Viewer by selecting Render → Highlight from the Gradients pop-up menu. Overwrite the generator into the Timeline.

13. You want the generator to be vertical, faded to white in the middle, and black on both edges. Double-click it to load it into the Viewer. Click the Controls tab and make the settings read as follows:

    Center: X = 0, Y = 0

    Highlight Angle: 0

    Highlight Width: 26

    Highlight Soft: 23

14. Select the Clear Stack_NEST in the Timeline, and solo it by pressing Control + S.

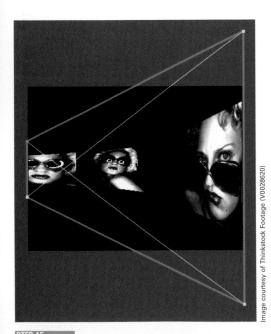

Image courtesy of Thinkstock Footage (V0028620)

STEP 15

Distort the V3 nest in the Canvas.

15. Use the Distort tool to distort the V3 nest. Working in the Canvas, Shift + drag the lower-right corner downward.

16. Copy the V3 nest. Turn on the other layers by toggling Control + S once more. Select the V1 and V2 layers and then paste attributes for Distort. All three layers will be distorted equally.

17. Control + click the V3 nest and then choose Travel Matte Luma from the contextual menu to finish off the effect. Note that if areas of the clip are dark in the same place as the matte, then that area of the comp becomes transparent as well. This could be remedied by nesting once more, but in this case leave the comp as is. Hey, it's a look, right?

18. As a final step, nest the clips and add a background.

    a. Select the clips and press Option + C to nest them. Name the nest "Z-Space Effect_NEST" and then click OK.

    b. Move the nest to V2.

    c. On V1, edit in the Space clip, located in the Chapter 10 Clips bin.

19. Step through your effect to make sure it is working. When you're satisfied, render the effect and enjoy.

Clips will now fly into the Canvas distorted and out of focus. The clips will then come into focus at a perceived depth, as the white part of the matte blocks out the transparency of the blurry layer. As clips continue to fly toward screen left, they again become blurry. Although you could keyframe blur for every layer, I like this variation since the blur effect seems a bit more organic and is fairly simple to set up.

Good going! You now have a blueprint to create cool-looking graphic effects from FCP's built in generators. With these building blocks, you can add accents of color, control transparency, and even add new dimensions to your composites.

STEP 19
Step through the effect to make sure it's working.

Troubleshooting

Many of the problems you'll encounter when working with generators are related to using them as both travel matte luma source and as graphic fill for the mattes. If you don't see your problem solved here, it's likely to be described in the Troubleshooting section of Chapter 8 or 9, as many concepts in these three chapters are interrelated.

A clip is not constrained by the matte shape

You probably applied the Composite Mode → Travel Matte Luma to the wrong layer. Make sure the grayscale object you want to use as the matte (your video "cookie cutter") lies on the track below the layer you want to use as your graphic fill. It's the graphic fill layer that's supposed to have the travel matte luma composite mode applied to it. If you still don't understand this, return to Chapter 8 for a more thorough explanation.

A Custom Gradient → Radial doesn't work well for a vignette effect

Many people reach for a Custom Gradient Generator → Radial for a round, soft-edged vignette effect (a portrait matte with soft edges) for travel matte source. Don't do this. You can't achieve a solid opaque center for a proper vignette effect this way, since white goes to gray immediately from the center of the gradient, leaving no solid white areas to preserve opacity.

In the section "Using Generators for Travel Mattes," I explained how to use the Oval generator for the travel matte luma effect. I like the Oval generator for this because you can adjust the slider to soften the edges, while the center remains totally opaque. The only trouble is that you can't move the oval from its centered position. If you alter its position with the Motion tab, your matte will be destroyed in the area previously occupied by the black area of the generator. That's why you need to add slug to a lower layer, and then nest the two layers to provide a new matte.

To make this effect really quickly, you could use the Mask Shape/Mask Feather filter combination. You do need to do a bit of tweaking with the Oval parameter to get a perfect circle. If you set the parameters at 60 for Horizontal Scale and 80 for Vertical Scale, you can get a nice circular shape to work with (40 and 50 if you want a smaller circle). After you shape your circle with the matte, you can add a Mask Feather to soften the edges. The Soft Edges matte filter also does a good job on squared-off vignette effects.

A clip that plays inside a travel matte is chopped off at the top

As long as you understand that your clip is graphic fill, you can easily solve this problem. Just reposition the clip to play inside the area defined by the matte.

If the clip isn't positioned and/or scaled properly inside the area defined by the travel matte, it will not fill the matte, and your effect will have the problem described above. If you do need to reposition the clip to fill the matte, try not to scale it up beyond 100%, since that will degrade the image. If your matte is traveling around the screen, nest the matte and fill layers prior to adding the motion effects.

Wrap-up

You now have a new perspective about how to use generators, and you've learned quite a few advanced techniques. I hope you've learned that there are many more purposes to generators than meet the eye.

Next up, we'll take a closer look at filter techniques.

WHAT'S IN THIS CHAPTER

- Creating mattes from channel effects
- Changing filter order and render order
- Discovering new uses for filters
- Advanced filter techniques
- Understanding the Displace and Bumpmap filters
- Adding filters to oversized nested comps

Filter 11
Techniques

Because there are so many filters in FCP, we'd be here until next Tuesday discussing each one. Then it would take another couple of weeks to talk about all of the scenarios where you'd use this filter or that filter. Therefore, this chapter will focus on techniques rather than feature descriptions or recipes. You'll learn how to control filters and how to combine them in novel ways. This chapter will also introduce you to the free filters that are included on the DVD.

How Filters Work

Having your head wrapped around how filters work is worth a bit of extra effort if you want to go beyond simply popping on a filter to create an effect. Knowing a little bit about RGB and alpha channels will help you select the proper filters — and apply the appropriate settings to them — to produce the effect you want.

A digital image has three *color channels:* red, green, and blue. These colors can be mixed to make any color in the visible spectrum. When you apply certain filters, they affect the information on each color channel.

You can look at the individual RGB channels in Final Cut Pro. Select an image in the Viewer's Video tab, go to View → Channels, and choose the channel you want to inspect. The channel information appears in shades of black, white, and gray. You might look at RGB channels when choosing the best channel for matte extraction or the like (see Figure 11-1).

The fourth channel is called the *alpha channel* (it's sometimes referred to as the *matte channel*). This is the channel that can be altered to make part of a clip transparent. The alpha channel is discussed in detail in Chapter 8; review that chapter if you need to refresh your memory.

Like the RGB channels, the alpha channel appears in shades of gray when you view it. These shades represent opacity and transparency: white is opaque, black is transparent, and gray is semi-opaque. When you capture a clip into Final Cut Pro, by default it has a fully white (100% opaque) alpha channel. You can alter an alpha channel by using motion effects (like Crop or Opacity) or filter effects (like Shape Matte or Chroma Keyer). See Figure 11-2.

You can view a clip's alpha channel by loading the clip into the Viewer, then going to the View Mode pop-up menu and choosing Alpha.

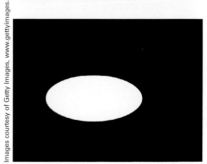

FIGURE 11-1

Evaluate each channel of a clip to see which one would be best to use for a matte. The original RGB image is shown at the top left. The Red channel (top right) is the strongest candidate for matte extraction. The Green channel (bottom left) and Blue channel (bottom right) are dark and don't have much contrast, and would be poor choices for making a matte.

FIGURE 11-2

The original clip is shown on the top left. In the second image (top right), a Mask Shape → Oval filter has been added. Once filter controls are adjusted, the mask creates transparency by altering the alpha channel, and knocks out the background. By viewing the alpha channel (or matte channel) on its own, you can plainly see that white is opaque and black is transparent (bottom left). In the final image (bottom right), the clip is moved to V2 and a background is added on V1 to complete the composite.

tip

You can invert an alpha channel by selecting the clip and going to Modify → Reverse Alpha.

note

Brightness and Contrast also play a role in channel effects. They control the overall brightness and darkness of all of the channels at once.

HOW FILTERS AFFECT CHANNELS

When you're creating effects, it's helpful to understand how you can influence the color and alpha channels with filters. Here are some examples of ways to affect channels using filter effects.

- When a filter affects all three color channels (RGB), it alters the entire image. The Tint filter is a good example.

- When you control one (or two) of the color channels, you can produce a matte or other compositing function. Telly's Channel Changer filter can do this. Just swap the alpha and red channels, and you've got an instant matte embedded in the clip.

- When you add filters to the alpha channel, you can affect the alpha channel's appearance by changing the look or shape of the matte. For example, if you blur a defined alpha channel with the Gaussian Blur filter, the edges of the matte will become softer. (This produces the same effect as Matte → Mask Feather.)

USING THE CHANNEL OFFSET FILTER

Before we move on, it's a good idea to get some hands-on experience with channel filters. You can use the Channel Offset filter to make a quick comp featuring the same clip in a four-way offset. This is a simple way to make a single video source look like four different ones.

1. Edit a clip into the Timeline and then crop a few pixels off of each edge of the clip to get rid of the blanking lines. Scale the clip to 105%. A bit of overscaling is acceptable to get a clean line once the point controls (crosshairs) are moved.

2. Select the clip and then nest it by pressing Option + C. Name the nest "Cropped Clip."

3. With the Cropped Clip nest selected, go to Effects → Video Filters → Channel → Channel Offset.

4. Make the following adjustments:
   Channel: Alpha + RGB
   Center Offset: X = 160, Y = 120
   Edges: Wrap

tip

Double the Center Offset value if you're working on footage with your own DV frame size.

You can keyframe the Center Offset or choose another channel for interesting variations. Edges → Repeat Edges can create some psychedelic effects.

EXERCISE 11-1: CREATING A MATTE BY SWITCHING CHANNELS

This exercise will show you how to create a matte, or transparency, in a clip. In the "Weights Butterfly" clip that's provided, the red channel is the strongest candidate for extracting a matte.

Before you get started, be sure that the Telly's FX plug-ins that came with this book are in your Plug-ins folder. (See Chapter 1 if you need instructions on installing Telly's FX.)

To get started, move to the marker for Exercise 1 in the Chapter 11 Exercise sequence. There are already two clips stacked up there: "Weights Butterfly" and "Clouds Above."

1. Select the "Weights Butterfly" clip on V2.

2. Go to Effects → Video Filters → Telly's FX → Telly's Channel Switcher.

3. Load the clip into the Viewer and click on the Filters tab to get access to the parameters.

4. You'll now swap channels to create transparency. To do this, use the menus to switch the channels:

    a. Set Alpha Source to R (for Red).

    b. Set the Red/Y Source to Alpha.

   You should now see Weights Butterfly blended with Clouds Above.

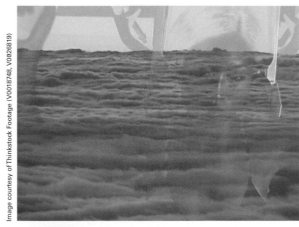

Image courtesy of Thinkstock Footage (V0018748, V0026819)

STEP 4
Swap channels to blend the two clips.

5. Next, you'll invert the alpha channel to reverse the matte. Go to Effects → Video Filters → Channel → Invert, and choose Alpha from the Channel menu.

STEP 5
Invert the alpha channel to make the effect more striking.

6. As an option, add a color corrector to adjust the clip's levels. Go to Effects → Video Filters → Color Correction → Color Corrector. Here, I've raised the Mids slider and lowered the blacks a bit. (I had to lower saturation, as they ventured into illegal areas. View → Range Check → Excess Chroma tipped me off. Levels and color are covered in Chapter 7.)

There you have it: a simple, organic-looking effect. In addition, you now know how to manipulate color channels to craft mattes.

Inspecting a Filter's FXScript

If you like to see what makes things tick, you can look at the code behind FCP's filters. Who knows? You might end up writing your own filters someday.

This code, called *FXScript,* is the basis for all native FCP filters. To take a look at the code behind a filter, follow these steps:

1. Select an FCP filter in the Effects tab.

2. Go to View → Effect in Editor. FXBuilder will launch and you'll see the filter's underlying code.

Writing FXScript is beyond the scope of this book, but you can learn it if you stick to your guns. If you want to develop custom plug-ins, a great ally in learning FXScript is Joe Maller, the founder of Joe's Filters. You can find lots of information about FXScript at www.joesfilters.com. Joe leaves all of the code for his filters "unlocked," so you can see how he has built them. Power to the People, Joe!

Applying Filters in the Right Order

As you've seen in the last several chapters, adding filters to clips is easy; you just drag and drop them from the Effects tab or add them from the Effects menu. You could keep adding filters until the cows came home, but you'd probably end up with quite a mess. Why? Certain filters work differently when you change either the order in which the filters are applied, or the order in which operations are rendered in a sequence. If you're applying multiple filters to a clip, you need to pay attention to both filter order and render order.

Free Filters Effects

Two questions: Who is "Telly"? And why is he giving me free effects?

The first answer: Telly is my nickname. The second answer: Because you need them.

Telly's FX is a collection of effects that's included with this book. It has plug-ins that I often found myself craving because they were available only in third-party applications. Why should I have to go to Adobe After Effects to apply a simple vertical blur? Other plug-ins were on my wish list because they were either missing from or not fully realized in FCP.

For a long time these plug-ins were only a pipe dream. Then I met Graeme Nattress, the programming wizard who made my dream a reality. Graeme's G Filters and G Film Look are some of the finest FCP add-on filters you can buy. He has also concocted plug-ins that convert NTSC to PAL and vice versa. You can check out all his plug-ins at www.nattress.com.

Telly's FX includes the following plug-ins:

- **Telly's Bumpmap and Telly's Displace:** These are distortion filters with Clip Control wells that play back maps in full motion.

- **Telly's Channel Switcher:** You can swap a color channel with an alpha channel for compositing, or create other color effects.

- **Telly's Directional Blur:** Choose the angle for the blur.

- **Telly's Horizontal and Vertical Blur:** Constrains the direction of a blur to either horizontal or vertical.

- **Telly's Radial Blur:** This circular blur can zoom or spin at any angle you choose.

- **Telly's FBM Noise:** Now you don't have to stack layers or blend modes to create noise.

- **Telly's Border:** This filter allows you to create a more malleable border that has composite modes.

- **Telly's Directional Blur Dissolve:** Choose the direction of the blur as two clips transition.

- **Telly's H & V Blur Dissolve:** A vertical or horizontal blur occurs as two clips transition.

- **Telly's FBM Noise Generator:** This generator provides a useful alternative to FCP's Noise generator.

- **Telly's Random:** This is a random text generator with changeable fonts and character types.

I hope you enjoy these effects as you use them in this chapter's exercises and in your own projects.

FILTER ORDER

Many people don't give filter order a second thought. But once you start stacking up filters in a clip, certain ones take on dominance in the overall effect, depending on where they are in the stack.

Blur filters are the most interesting ones to experiment with in this regard. When they lie at the bottom of the stack, they'll blur the effects of all filters that are on top of them. As you move a blur filter toward the top of the stack, it continues to blur other filters on top of it, but the filters underneath it are no longer affected by the blur. When placed at the very top of the stack, they blur only the image itself (see Figure 11-3).

Another order-sensitive group is the matte filters. To get the right matte effect, you often have to add more than one matte filter to the stack.

Before finalizing any effect that has multiple filters added to a single clip, try different filter orders for more interesting looks. To change filter order, simply drag a filter to a new position in the Filters tab.

Images courtesy of Getty Images, www.gettyimages.com (ev00141/Photodisc; ev00154/Photodisc)

tip

As every good compositor knows, applying just one filter rarely does the job when creating effects. Most of the time you'll need to add more than one filter — and have it in the right order — to get the desired result.

FIGURE 11-3

Here's an example of the importance of filter order. The image on the left has a Blur filter placed over a Border filter, and the border is still sharp. In the image on the right, the Border filter was placed over the Blur filter, and the border becomes blurred.

RENDER ORDER

FCP renders effects in a given order. Motion effects take precedence over filter effects when these two types of effects are combined in a composite. In certain cases, however, you do not want effects to be processed in this way. If you're familiar with a filter and it's not producing the expected effect after your piece is rendered, that's a telltale sign that it's been unduly affected by render order.

Fortunately, you can change the render order of effects to make a filter act on a motion effect, rather than the other way around. The solution is simple. Just apply the motion effect to a layer or layers, and then nest the layers. After you've nested the layer or layers, you can then add the filter to the nest. This reverses the render order, and you can continue building your effect. (This technique was explained in detail in Chapter 10.)

Well, so much for filter theory. Let's look at more tricks you can do with filters.

A Few Faves

tip

Lens-flare effects never seem to go out of style. For retina-burning lens flares, grab Knoll Light Factory 2 from Red Giant Software – www. redgiantsoftware.com.

It's not necessary for me to describe every filter in Final Cut Pro. You can try them out and see what they do. Instead, I'd like to point out special functions and features of some particularly useful filters.

BLUR FILTERS

Blur filters are probably the most widely used filters in Final Cut Pro. Sure, these filters can make images fuzzy, but their real power lies in your ability to animate them over time. For example, a Gaussian Blur can fake an in-camera rack focus. Gaussian Blur can also work on individual channels or on the luminance of a clip.

A key concept to keep in mind is that FCP's specialty blurs (Radial, Wind, and Zoom) all require what's called *post blur*. Post blur is necessary to prevent showing the "steps" (the multiple iterations of an image seen in the effect). To add a post blur, just add a Gaussian Blur with a low value for Radius.

Blur filters are quite a bit different from Motion Blur, which we looked at in Chapter 3. Blur filters are influenced by keyframes that you set. Motion Blur, on the other hand, is not a keyframable parameter, and is influenced by both the movement of the clip within a composite and the motion within the clip itself. The addition of Blur filters can intensify a Motion Blur effect.

A blur filter called Telly's Directional Blur, which is included with this book, is shown in Figure 11-4.

The Channel Blur filter is quite useful because you can actually blur the alpha channel with it. Use Invert to invert a color channel for a color effect, or to invert an alpha channel to reverse a matte, as you did in Exercise 11-1.

FIGURE 11-4

On the top is the original clip with Matte → Mask Shape → Diamond applied. On the bottom, Telly's Directional Blur is applied below the matte in the filter stack.

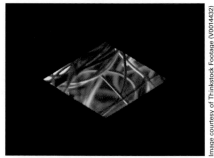

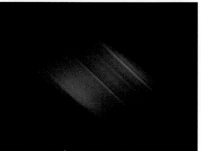

Channel filters have a more provocative function as well, which is deriving mattes and then compositing with them. Telly's Channel Changer simplifies that process. You can use it to make instant mattes from individual color channels.

COLOR CORRECTION FILTERS

Most people use these tools to correct an image's colors (see Figure 11-5). But you can also make the colors wildly incorrect, producing some insane color effects. Try tweaking the Limit Effects controls.

By pushing around the color balance wheels in either the Color Corrector or the Color Corrector 3-Way, you can derive some very interesting tints. I also use the color correction tools for adjusting levels. Review Chapter 7 for more cool things you can do with color correction.

tip

I use the Basic 3D filter to fake 3D movement for clips, nested sequences, and oversized LiveType layers within FCP. I call it my "motion control system."

FIGURE 11-5

On the top is a DV shot of Tokyo at night. I used the wrong camera setting, so the image is too light. On the bottom, a color correction filter has been applied, and levels and saturation are overdriven.

DISTORT FILTERS

When you change colors, lightness, or transparency with a filter (Posterize or Tint, for example), you're affecting channels. However, there are filters that serve a different purpose. Filters like Distort and Perspective mathematically redistribute the pixels on the Canvas.

You can have a little fun with FCP's Distort filters (see Figure 11-6). Many, like Fisheye and Cylinder, provide a "Hall of Mirrors" effect. The strongest filters in this category are Displace and Bumpmap. They are limited, however because they won't play back clips in the Clip Control wells. That's why the Telly's FX versions of these filters were created: to put this power back into your hands. We'll try these out a bit later in the chapter.

FIGURE 11-6

Distort clips can be used to distort facial features. Here, three Fisheye filters were used. Scary!

Clip courtesy of RobPongi.com

tip

With FCP's Border filters, the border affects only the full frame size of the clip, and does not affect the alpha channel. If you crop the clip, the border or bevel will not fit to the newly cropped edge. A third-party Bevel-Border Alpha plug-in can fix this. I use the one found in Joe's Filters (www.joesfilters.com).

Controlling Levels and Color in a Filter

Unfortunately, the Solarize filter has no color-control options. However, adding a color corrector filter to a Solarized clip will allow you to shift the hue and adjust levels and saturation, giving you more color options. Adding a color corrector to any filter or group of filters is a great way to add more control over the color and levels. For reliable results, make sure the color corrector filter lies at the bottom of a stack of filters.

Image courtesy of RobPongi.com

EXERCISE 11-2: OPERATING THE BLINK FILTER

Blink does more than meets the eye. This filter doesn't merely blink a single image on and off. You can use it much more creatively to strobe between two layered clips. I use this effect in music videos and other high-energy pieces.

If you don't know how to use the Blink filter with layered clips, an exercise is in order. Move to the marker for Exercise 2 in the Chapter 11 Exercise sequence.

1. Select the V2 layer that has already been placed in the Timeline.

2. Go to Effects → Video Filters → Video → Blink.

3. Load the V2 clip into the Viewer.

4. Click on the Filters tab and set the parameters as follows:

    On duration: 6

    Off duration: 3

    Opacity: 0

5. Preview the effect and make any necessary adjustments. If you like the results, go ahead and render it.

> **note**
>
> *It's not necessary to keyframe the Blink filter to get results — it will strobe between clips automatically. If you want the rhythmic pulse to increase, go ahead and keyframe these parameters.*

Now that you've seen the potential of the Blink filter, you can do other things with it, such as time keyframes to a musical beat or toy with opacity for a pulsing effect.

Advanced Filter Effects

Now it's time to delve into some more advanced ways to use filters. Here, you'll be combining filters, adding multiple copies of a filter to the same clip, rearranging filter order, and performing other sophisticated filter feats.

I'd like to start by exploring the lesser-known capabilities of the Emboss filter. Then we'll talk about techniques featuring distortion filters, the Extract filter, Basic 3D, and others.

USING THE EMBOSS FILTER

To get some mileage out of FCP's filters, you have to use them in unconventional ways. The Emboss filter is a good example.

On its own, the Emboss filter is nothing to write home about. It produces a gray, textured version of a clip. But if you combine it with a composite mode, you'll get some intriguing effects. I like to use Emboss on objects that have an alpha channel, such as text. This technique comes into play when creating a "bug," which is a semitransparent, embossed logo ID that's often found in the lower-right corner of the screen. You've seen them on TV. You'll create one in the following exercise.

tip

You can use the Quick-Time Color Tint filter to make a nice two-tone color effect. Just set Tint Type to Other and pick the two colors you'd like to replace as dark and light.

EXERCISE 11-3: EMBOSSED ALPHA EFFECTS

In this exercise you'll use a combination of techniques, including nesting to change FCP's render order. Get started by moving to the marker for Exercise 3. A background clip has already been added for you.

Note that this effect looks much better at full resolution. You may want to work with your own full-size DV footage for the best results.

1. Turn off the V1 clip by selecting it and pressing Control + B.

2. Go to the Generator pop-up menu and choose Matte → Color. A gray layer will appear in the Canvas. Drag and drop the clip onto V2. Trim it to the length of the V1 clip.

3. Select the color layer and then go to Effects → Video Filters → Matte → Mask Shape. Make the settings as follows:

     Rounded Rectangle

     Horizontal Scale: 40

     Vertical Scale: 17

     Center: X = 0, Y = 0

     Invert: Unchecked

You'll now have a gray rounded-rectangle shape.

4. Next, you'll copy and paste the matte filter you just made, which will cut a hole in the center of the color matte. Click on the existing matte filter and press Command + C and then Command + V. An identical filter will be added to the stack. Work on this filter at the bottom of the stack. Change the settings to the following:

> Rounded Rectangle
>
> Horizontal Scale: 35
>
> Vertical Scale: 12
>
> Center: X = 0, Y = 0
>
> Invert: Checked

(Double these values if you're working with full-size DV footage.)

STEP 4
You'll use this rounded rectangle to cut a hole in the matte.

5. Make sure the color matte's alpha channel is set to Modify → Alpha Type → Straight.

6. You'll now nest this single layer. This way, the emboss effect will work on the layer that already has the two matte filters applied.

   a. Select the layer.

   b. Press Option + C to nest it.

7. Name the nested layer "Embossed Back" and click OK.

8. Now that the layer is nested, you can apply the Emboss filter. It will act on the matte layer now. Select the nest and go to Effects → Video Filters → Stylize → Emboss. After loading the clip into the Viewer's Filters tab, make the following adjustments:

> Direction: −40
>
> Depth: 2
>
> Amount: 100

9. Change the composite mode to Overlay. Control + Click on the Embossed Back nest, and then choose Composite Mode → Overlay from the contextual menu.

10. You'll now work on another alpha object, a simple text generator. From the Generators pop-up menu, choose Text → Text. Edit the clip onto V3 and then load it into the Viewer. Click on the Controls tab to change the type.

    a. Type in the word "element."

    b. Choose a thick, bold font like Arial Black.

    c. Make the size 50.

    d. Set Origin to X = 0, Y = 8.

11. You can now use the Emboss filter from the "Embossed Back" nest on the type layer. Option + double-click on the nested layer and then click the Filters tab. Drag and drop the filter from the Filters tab onto the text layer.

12. Change the alpha type of the text layer to white. Go to Modify → Alpha Type → White. Change the composite mode to Overlay.

13. Select both layers in the Timeline, then position them in the lower-right corner of the comp.

14. Turn on the V1 clip by selecting the clip and pressing Control + B.

15. If you are experiencing any white fringe around the edges of either the text or the Embossed Back nest, you can add a Matte Choker, with Edge Thinning set to 15 and Softness set to 0.

16. Preview and then render out your effect.

Image courtesy of Thinkstock Footage (V0018652)

STEP 16

The finished product: an embossed overlay with a transparent background.

Great! You've made an embossed "bug." Now you can go forward with the Emboss filter and create fresh and interesting textured effects.

tip

If you have a freeze frame that's jittering, you can add a Video → De-interlace filter or Flicker Filter to make it hold still. By the way, you won't see jittering on the Mac's monitor; it shows up only on a video monitor.

tip

Don't forget that you can add filters not just to clips, but to stills, motion graphics, and text as well.

USING THE EXTRACT FILTER

The Extract filter is useful for making interesting looking blended effects. Essentially, you can take the brightness values of a given clip and then derive an alpha channel from those grayscale values. All you need to do is pull down the Copy Result parameter menu and select To Alpha and you will have your matte.

We covered mattes in Chapter 8, this is a more specialized use of the filter.

Saving Favorite Filters

Here's a technique you can use when you want to save a clip's filters in a single bin in your Favorites bin. This bin of ordered filters is referred to as a *Filter Pack.*

To save the compound filter effect, follow these steps:

1. Click the Filters tab and make sure that no filters are selected.

2. Press Option + F. A new bin with all of your saved effects will be created in the Favorites bin.

Name the bin something pertinent that will help you remember the combination of effects.

Filter order is vital to the creation of the effect. If you check the bin, you'll see that the filter order has been maintained. However, once you save and close your project, the filters will return to alphanumeric order. You can work around this by preceding each filter name with a number.

Now that you know how to save Filter Packs properly, here's how to use them. If you want to recreate an effect in a clip (or clips) in the Timeline, just select it and then drag and drop the bin of favorite filters. The Filter Pack will be applied to the clip.

When your system goes haywire, you often can solve issues by getting rid of a corrupted FCP Preferences file and restarting FCP. Alas, all of your saved favorites are instantly vaporized when you do this. Fortunately, you can preserve your favorites. Here's how:

1. Create a new project and name it Effects Favorites.

2. Open any current project. It will contain your favorites.

3. Drag and drop the entire Favorites bin into the Name Column of the Browser in your new project, instead of the Favorites bin in the Effects tab.

Your favorites will now be saved, just like any other clip or graphic. Even keyframes can be preserved this way. Pretty slick!

These favorites can now be subdivided, stored, and shared with all of your friends. Since it is a tiny file, your favorites can easily be electronically stored or distributed via e-mail.

EXERCISE 11-4: EXTRACT MATTE EFFECTS

This effect creates a stylish, monochromatic look with a surprising twist. To get started, move to the Exercise 4 marker in the Chapter 11 Exercise sequence. Two clips, a white color matte on V1 and "Businessman Single" on V2, have already been added.

1. Select the "Businessman Single" clip and then go to Effects → Video Filters → Matte → Extract to apply the filter.

2. Load the clip into the Viewer.

3. You'll now extract a matte created from the clip's brightness values. Click the Filters tab and change the parameters to the following:

   View: Final

   Threshold: 27

   Tolerance: 50

   Softness: 8

   Copy Result: To Alpha

   Invert: Unchecked

4. You've now created the matte, but to get the intended effect, you'll need to make the matte a solid red color. First, you'll place a solid piece of color onto the V3 video track.

   a. Shift + Option + drag the V1 color matte to the V3 track.

   b. Once in place, load the V3 color matte into the Viewer.

   c. Click the Controls tab and change the color to red by clicking on the Color Control chip and selecting red from the Apple Color Picker.

   d. To make the solid-colored matte effect, you'll need to designate the V3 color as graphic fill. This is the material that "fills in" the matte with the color. Control + click on the V3 color matte and choose Composite Mode → Travel Matte Alpha.

note

The Extract Matte effect was inspired by Philip Hodgett's "Great Visual Effects for Final Cut Pro" Training CD for advanced FCP effects. For more information about this CD, go to www.intelligent assistance.com.

Image courtesy of Thinkstock Footage (V0C18557)

STEP 4

Take the original shot (top) and apply a Travel Matte Alpha to fill the matte with a solid color (bottom).

5. To make a wild effect, you could choose a different item to use as graphic fill. For example, select Telly's Random generator from the Generators menu, Overwrite it onto V3, change its composite mode to Travel Matte Alpha, and apply the following settings:

Vertical Amount: 100

Horizontal Amount: 100

Character Color: Red

Character Type: Binary

Size: 5

tip

For steadying shaky hand-held shots, I head for the Stabilizer plug-in from Lyric Media (www.lyric.com).

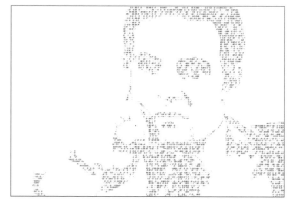

STEP 5

Experiment with different fills, such as the pattern of numbers shown here.

CGM DVE Filters

The amazing CGM DVE filter set that came with earlier versions of FCP is, unfortunately, no longer included in the FCP package. If you're upgrading from FCP 3, you can salvage these filters by Option + dragging them from the FCP 3 Plug-Ins folder to the FCP 4 Plug-Ins folder.

If you don't have the 1.0 version of the CGM DVE filter set, you can get the new version (CGM DVE 1+ offers the classic filters plus a couple of new ones) at www.cgm-online.com. They've been upgraded and now fully support YUV rendering. There is also a great set of filters called CGM DVE 2+. CGM DVE Volume 3 should be available by the time this book reaches you.

CREATING A BUMPMAP EFFECT

You can create a unique textured video effect with the Bumpmap filter. This effect uses one clip or graphic as the source for the texture that's applied to a second clip. For an effective bumpmap, select a clip that has strong luminance values (see Figure 11-7). You can pump up this strength by adding a color corrector filter.

Image courtesy of Getty Images, www.gettyimages.com (ev01399/Photodisc)

FIGURE 11-7

Here's a good candidate for a bumpmap. The image has already been inverted.

1. In the Timeline, select the clip you wish to apply the filter to. I am using the "Whirlpool" clip.

2. Load the clip into the Viewer and then click the Filters tab.

3. Choose Effects → Video Filters → Telly's FX → Bumpmap.

4. In the Browser, go to the clip you wish to use as the bumpmap and duplicate it by pressing Option + D. Control + click on the clip and choose Make Master Clip. Change its name to "Bumpmap."

5. Control + click on the clip and choose Open in New Viewer.

6. Apply a color corrector to the clip and make adjustments.

   a. Desaturate the clip by moving the Sat slider all the way to the left.

   b. Adjust the sliders for Blacks, Mids, and Whites to get a bumpmap with high contrast.

   c. Invert the bumpmap by going to Effects → Video Filters → Channel → Invert. You can achieve the best results by inverting Y, so choose that option from the filter's Channel menu.

7. Drag and drop the bumpmap into the Clip Control well.

8. Make adjustments in the Filters tab to make a texture you like. Here are the numbers I've chosen:

   Luma Scale: 3

   Direction: 110

   Outset: −80

   Repeat Edges: Checked

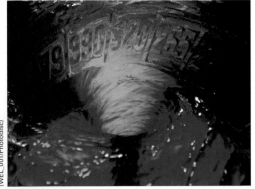

Image courtesy of Getty Images, www.gettyimages.com (WEL_001/Photodisc)

FIGURE 11-8

The bumpmap is now affecting the Whirlpool clip.

9 You may want to color correct the affected clip. In the example, I've adjusted both levels and saturation.

10. Now all you need to do is preview the effect and then render it (see Figure 11-8).

Next, you'll create a displace effect. After you've created a bumpmap and a displace effect, the differences between the two filters should become clear.

Bumpmap vs. Displace: The Nuances

A Bumpmap filter and a Displace filter produce similar effects. So what's the difference between the two?

Bump mapping merely adjusts a clip's brightness and contrast based on another image that's dropped into the Clip Control well. This creates the illusion of a light source by adding texture, highlights, and shadows. In the FCP version of the filter, the luminance values of the clip acting as a map are used to make this illusion.

Displacement mapping actually pushes pixels around. As with bump mapping, a channel could be used, but in FCP the clip's luminance is used to determine how the map affects the image.

With displacement mapping, you set a maximum amount for the pixels to be pushed horizontally and vertically. The image used for the displacement map is then lined up with the image being displaced, so that each pixel in the displaced image has a corresponding partner in the displacement map. How far the pixels in the displaced image are pushed around depends on the luminance of the pixels they're matched up with.

- If the displacement map pixel is white, the corresponding pixel in the displaced image is pushed the maximum amount in the positive direction (up/right).

- If the displacement map pixel is black, the corresponding pixel is pushed the maximum amount in the negative direction (down/left).

- If the displacement map pixel is 50% gray, pixels aren't pushed at all.

- Shades of gray above or below 50% gray cause pixels to be pushed some percentage of the maximum amount.

Understanding how to use these filters is very important to adding flowing textures and unique distortion to your composite.

EXERCISE 11-5: PUTTING DISPLACE TO WORK

In this exercise, you'll get practical experience creating an effect with a displace filter. You'll be using the Displace filter in the Telly's FX category.

To get started, move to the marker for Exercise 5. A clip called "Medical Tools" has already been placed in the Timeline for you.

1. Select the Medical Tools clip in the Timeline and then go to Effects → Video Filters → Telly's FX → Telly's Displace to place the filter onto the clip.

2. Load the clip into the Viewer, and then click on the Filters tab to get at the controls.

3. In the Browser, open up the Chapter 11 Clips bin. Duplicate the "Water Ripples" clip by pressing Option + D.

4. Control + click on the clip and choose Open Clip in New Viewer.

5. You'll now add a Color Corrector filter to the clip by going to Effects → Video Filters → Color Correction → Color Corrector. Change the sliders for the color corrector as follows:

   a. Move the Sat slider all the way to the left so the displacement map will have stronger luminance values.

   b. Since the map is a bit dark, move the Mids slider about a third of the way past the middle.

6. Let's save the clip as a separate, self-contained movie. First, export the clip as a QuickTime movie.

   a. Go to File → Export → QuickTime Movie.

   b. In the Save dialog box, check the box for Make Movie Self-Contained. Leave all the other options as they are. Before you click Save, make sure that the movie will be exported to your media drive. Name the clip "Ripples D-Matte" and click Save.

   c. Delete the duplicated Ripples D-Matte clip in the Chapter 11 bin to prevent confusion. Re-import "Ripples D-Matte.mov" into FCP and the Chapter 11 clips bin.

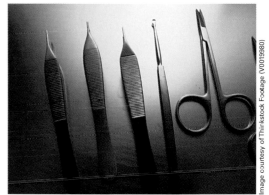

Image courtesy of Thinkstock Footage (V0019980)

STEP 1
Select the Medical Tools clip.

7. With the Filters tab open, drag and drop the Ripples D-Matte clip into the Clip Control well. Make the following changes to the parameters:

   a. Set Luma Scale to 3.

   b. Set the the Horizontal and Vertical Scale to 8 for each one.

   c. Make sure that the Repeat Edge checkbox is checked.

8. Preview and then render the effect.

The medical tools are now distorted by the luminance values from the water ripples. It should look like the tools are in a tub of water.

Image courtesy of Getty Images, www.gettyimages.com (WEL_014/Photodisc)

> **note**
>
> *There may be some "tearing" around the edges of the effect. This is normal. If you need to hide this edge, you can scale up the clip slightly.*

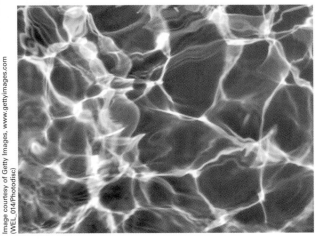

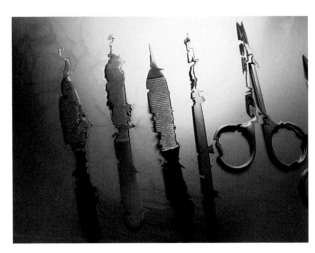

STEP 7

Drag the Ripples D-Matte clip (left) into the Clip Control well. When displaced, the tools should appear as though they're underwater (right).

USING FILTER EFFECTS ON OVERSIZED NESTED SEQUENCES

In Chapter 5 you learned how to create multilayered motion graphics compositions on oversized sequences. In this section I'll show you a similar technique that will enable you to expand the capabilities of certain filters.

With this trick, a clip can take on new shapes and features with the addition of a Distort, Perspective, or Basic 3D filter. In this exercise we'll use a Distort filter.

Oversized nested sequences and Distort filters

Distort filters create their effects by moving pixels to other parts of the Canvas. The filter's influence will not extend beyond the bounding box dictated by the size of the layer. To see this for yourself, add a Wave or Ripple filter to a clip and then scale it down a bit. The distorted form gets cut off on all four sides.

Because FCP treats any nested sequence as a single clip, you can trick it into thinking that a clip is laying on a larger layer (see Figure 11-9). To do this, you must create the nested sequence with a custom frame size that is larger than the original sequence. You'll practice this in the following exercise.

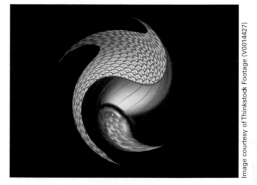

FIGURE 11-9

The Whirlpool filter can fully extend its "fingers" if the source clip lies within an oversized nested sequence and the filter is applied to the nest.

EXERCISE 11-6: FILTERS AND OVERSIZED SEQUENCES

In this exercise you'll practice applying filters to oversized sequences. You'll use the Ripple filter to create an interesting video pattern.

Move to the marker for Exercise 6.

1. Select the "Locomotive Gear" clip in the Timeline.

2. Nest the clip by pressing Option + C.

3. In the Nest Items dialog box, change the following items:

   Aspect Ratio: Custom

   Width: 1000 × 1000 (larger for DV frame size)

4. Name the sequence "Oversized Ripple_NEST." Click OK.

5. In the Browser, Control + click on the icon for the nested sequence and choose Settings. The Sequence settings dialog will launch. Go to Compressor → Animation. Click on the Advanced button and ensure that Millions of Colors + is engaged in the Depth menu of the Compression settings dialog. The "+" is important as it means "include alpha channel." Click OK.

6. Select the Oversized Ripple nest and then go to Effects → Video Filters → Distort → Ripple to apply the filter.

STEP 4

Here, the clip is not scaled down; it's merely centered within an oversized sequence.

7. Open the nest into the Viewer by Option + double-clicking on it in the Timeline.

8. Click the Filters tab and make the following adjustments:

    Amplitude: 38

    Wave Length: 11

    Horizontal Speed: −160

    Vertical Speed: −26

    Repeat Edges : Checked

9. In the Motion tab, scale the nest to 30.

10. Preview the effect and see if you'd like to make any changes to the parameters. As an option, you could keyframe them. Render the effect.

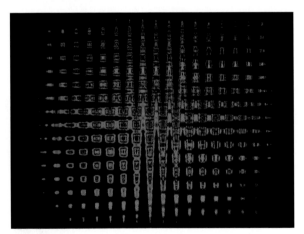

STEP 9

Preview the effect. The final pattern should look like this.

note

You are changing the compressor (or "codec") to Animation to accommodate the oversized sequence. DV sequences are meant to play back only the native frame size of either DV NTSC or DV PAL — no larger, no smaller. Although it renders in RGB, this codec is very reliable in effects building. It also causes no generational loss in quality to your graphics.

You've now created an interesting video pattern. Allowing the math to work on a clip over a larger grid will allow the effect to expand much further, providing even more options for your videographics. This technique should be useful for creating advanced video effects with FCP. Have fun with it!

Troubleshooting

There's not too much that can go wrong with any one filter, but here are a few problems that might crop up.

A filter doesn't produce the expected effect

You can get in a bit of trouble with filter order. Try switching the order in which you apply the filters. You can also reverse the proessing of effects by adding a motion effect, nesting the clip, and then adding a filter to the nest.

Favorite filters are lost when a corrupted Preference file is thrown away

Open a current project. It will contain your Favorites. Then, drag and drop the entire Favorites bin into the Name column of the Browser in your new project. Once this project is saved, you'll never have to worry about losing your favorites when your Preferences become corrupted.

Wrap-up

You've come a long way in understanding how to make effects work. I hope the exercises in this chapter will inspire you to work with ordinary filters in new ways, thereby creating extraordinary effects.

The nuts-and-bolts work is done, and now it's time to head into the rich world of titling and text effects.

04:00

00:22

00:14

1991 2026

Δ Φ

12

Titles and Motion Typography

Animated typography is a major component of any motion graphics composition.
Merely adding type to a layered composite
is not enough. You need to choose the
right fonts, artfully arrange words on the
screen, and then animate them in ways
that stand out from the crowd. Whether
you're creating a simple title or a fancy
layered animation, this chapter will show
you how to create eye-catching text treatments. You'll use Final Cut Pro's built-in
Title 3D text tool, as well as a fantastic
new application called LiveType.

Introduction to Titling

Before you get down to the nitty-gritty of pushing type around the screen, it's a good idea to have a basic understanding of titling terminology.

Here's a brief overview of Final Cut Pro's titling features.

- **Flying titles:** A flying title is a piece of text that moves through simulated 3D space. In Title 3D, this movement is achieved by keyframing parameters in the Controls tab, or with motion or filter effects. In LiveType, you move type by using preset effects or adding keyframes to an effects track and then altering parameters.

- **Motion path titles:** These are specialized flying titles that travel on paths (see Figure 12-1). This effect formerly eluded FCP users, but can now be created in LiveType.

- **Lower third:** This refers to text that's located on the lower one-third of the screen. This text might include the name or profession of a person who's being interviewed, providing news commentary, or the like (see Figure 12-2). A standard lower third has two lines of text that is separated by a line or a bar, and is set against a semi-opaque background such as a solid color or gradient.

FIGURE 12-1

With LiveType, titles can travel on motion paths.

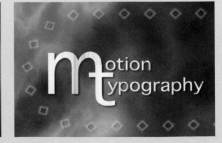

- **Roll:** At the end of a production you'll usually see credits move from the bottom to the top of the screen. You can also use a roll to create vertically scrolling graphic elements in a motion graphics piece.

- **Crawl:** In a traditional crawl, text scrolls across the screen from right to left. These days it's used — ubiquitously and often annoyingly — to parade a constant stream of information along the bottom of the screen during newscasts. Like a roll, a crawl can be used to move glyphs across the screen. (Title Crawl gives you a notch up on quality over the legacy Crawl generator because it uses vector text, so be sure to reach for that for your crawls.)

FIGURE 12-2

A Lower Third is commonly used to provide information about a person who's onscreen.

- **Reveal:** You can reveal text over time by animating the crop motion from one position to another on a large piece of text (see Figure 12-3). You can also use a mask shape to reveal text in a similar way. A soft edge makes this simple effect look even nicer, so you can feather the edge of a crop or add a Mask Feather filter.

FIGURE 12-3

You can reveal a word or line of text by animating a crop.

note

Mattias Sandström's "Too Much Too Soon" plug-in set includes a free Typewriter plug-in that you can download (www. mattias.nu) or grab from the Goodies folder of this book's DVD. With it, you can keyframe the speed of the letters rather than let the Typewriter generator dictate the speed. The BBC uses this style to type out breaking news stories — a very slick look.

■ **Bullet build:** A Bullet build usually consists of several layers of text, with each one flying in from offscreen on a separate motion path. Alternatively, you could reveal words one by one instead of flying them in.

■ **Type-on:** Use this effect to make a word appear on the screen letter by letter, as if it's being typed (see Figure 12-4). You'll be doing this in an upcoming exercise.

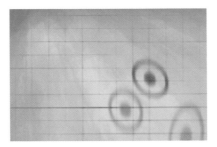

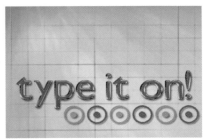

FIGURE 12-4
Here's a Type-On effect created in LiveType. The effect is automated; not a single keyframe was adjusted!

FCP's Titling Tools

When creating type with FCP, you have a number of options, each with its own advantages. You can choose from Title 3D, Title Crawl, and a new application called LiveType. These three tools provide a well-stocked arsenal that can tackle nearly every task related to motion typography

Title 3D and Title Crawl, which were incorporated into FCP 3 and are still around in FCP 4, offer substantial improvements over the program's original text generators. These tools were developed by Boris FX, and you'll sometimes see them referred to collectively as "Boris Calligraphy."

In FCP 4, the new type tool is LiveType. Despite its name, LiveType does much more than titling; it's a versatile compositing environment. This chapter will focus on the text-oriented features of LiveType. Some of its compositing tricks will be unveiled in Chapter 14.

FCP retains some legacy text generators, but the newer tools provide more options and better quality. You get better quality from Title 3D, Title Crawl, and LiveType because these tools use vector graphics instead of bitmaps, which means that type can be scaled up past 100% and still maintain a perfectly smooth edge.

With that knowledge in hand, let's next discuss how to decide which title tools to use when you've got some text movement tasks ahead of you.

USING TITLE 3D

You create and alter text in Title 3D's Text window, and apply animation settings in the Controls tab. You animate keyframes in the same fashion as you would in the Filters or Motion tabs.

In Title 3D you don't create text directly against your video background. You'll have to edit it into the Timeline first, evaluate it, and then come back and make changes if necessary. Despite this drawback, Title 3D is a very powerful tool. Let's start by taking a look at the Text window.

Title 3D's Text window operates like a word processor in which you can use rulers and tabs to help you position text. As you read this section, you might want to launch Title 3D so you can look at the Text window as I describe each tab. To launch Title 3D, press Option + Control + X.

The Text window

The Text window is divided into five tabbed sections (see Figure 12-5). You can get the most mileage out of Title 3D by digging in and experimenting with the various features of each tab.

- **Style tab:** Here's where you choose type sizes, fonts, and other type measurement and style choices. You'll get some experience with this tab in Exercise 12-1.

- **Page Wrap tab:** This tab is for choosing whether you want to "wrap" text or not. You could choose No Wrap to create a text crawl that could exploit the Controls tab parameters not found in Title Crawl. In most cases, however, you'll want to choose Wrap. Here you'll also find controls for setting margins and having text read in alternative directions, such as top to bottom.

> **note**
>
> FCP's legacy title generators still exist for a few good reasons. You may need them to restore an older project file that used those generators. The Lower 3rd generator comes in handy when you don't have time to construct a multilayered effect with Title 3D or LiveType. Finally, the Character Palette works with the generators, so you can create some quick fodder for travel matte effects.

> **tip**
>
> To kern text (widen or narrow the spacing between a pair of letters), position the cursor between two letters and press Option + Left Arrow to narrow the spacing, or Option + Right Arrow to widen it.

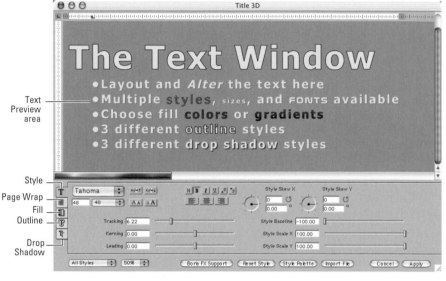

Text Preview area

Style
Page Wrap
Fill
Outline

Drop Shadow

FIGURE 12-5
You create and alter text in Title 3D's Text window.

- **Fill tab:** Here's where you choose the color and opacity for your text. You can also pick a gradient to fill the text.

- **Outline tab:** You can set up to five different outlines for your text here. Proficient use of the Outline tab can help you dramatically change the look of your text. You'll get to play with this feature a bit more in Exercise 12-1.

- **Drop Shadow tab:** This tab lets you apply shadows to text, including drop shadows and shadows cast at any angle. You can adjust shadow color, opacity, and softness to achieve the look you want (see Figure 12-6).

FIGURE 12-6
The Solid Shadow has a 3D extruded look to it.

There are a number of buttons at the bottom of the Text window. Here's what they do:

- **Boris FX Support** launches the Boris FX website.

- **Reset Style** button returns your text to the default style and color.

- **Style Palette** button will launch a special interface for text styles. (This useful palette will be discussed later in the chapter.)

- **Import File** allows you to import text documents — tabs and all — into Title 3D.

- **Cancel** closes the window without saving any changes to your text.

- **Apply** saves your text changes and loads the text into the Viewer.

There are also two menus at the bottom of the Text window: the Style Preview menu and the Scale menu.

- The **Style Preview** menu sets up the display of the Text Preview window. All Styles displays exactly how the text will look as you work, but it updates a bit more slowly than Basic Styles.

- The **Scale menu** is for setting the display size of the text in the Text Preview window. Reduce the scale if you've got a huge page of text that you want to see all at once.

Now that you have a basic understanding of the Text window, let's get started with the first exercise.

tip

If you need to animate a standard drop shadow to further sell the 2D to 3D perspective illusion, these controls cannot be keyframed. In that case, you may want to hold off adding drop shadows at this stage. In FCP, you can keyframe the drop shadow's movement, so that is the logical place to perform this feat.

tip

When you haven't altered any parameters in the Controls tab, Title 3D will play back in real time in most FCP systems.

Tabbed Text

Title 3D's Text window lets you set tabs to align columns of text. You can use this feature to set up different text sizes, colors, and styles, each in a separate column. Keeping all these text options on one page, rather than creating a new page for each one, will save you time when you create titles, bullet points, and other text effects.

To set up tabs in the Text window, click in the upper-left corner and then drag out a tab marker along the top of the ruler. This creates a tab marker. Double-click the marker to change it from left-justified, to right- or center-justified. If you reposition the marker by dragging it to a different place on the ruler, your aligned text will update on the fly.

EXERCISE 12-1: EDITING TEXT IN TITLE 3D'S TEXT WINDOW

Double-click the Chapter 12 Exercise sequence to get to work. Move the playhead to the beginning of the sequence. Note that I've already edited in a background and some music for you.

1. Go to the Generator pop-up menu and choose Title 3D, or use the keyboard shortcut Control + Option+ X. The Text window will launch.

2. Click in the Text Preview area and type "dj generica" (or "dj" and your name if you want to have more fun with it).

3. Select the text by pressing Command + A. Note that the character color is inverted. This is called the active selection.

4. In this step you'll use the controls in the Style tab to set up the text the way you want.

   With the text still selected, click in the Font Size numeric field. Clicking in this field — or any numeric field — causes your text to be passively selected (note the rectangle around the text) so you can monitor your changes on the fly. The text color is no longer inverted.

   a. Choose a text size. You can select a size from the drop-down menu, click the text-scaling buttons to the right of the menu, or type a number in the numeric field. For this exercise, type 110 and press Enter.

   b. Choose a sans serif font (say, Futura) from the font menu, and click the Bold ("B") style button.

   c. Center-justify the text by clicking the Center Justification button. (It's right below the Italic style button.)

STEP 3

In an active selection, colors are inverted.

STEP 4

In a passive selection, the text is surrounded by a rectangle.

5. Now you'll fill the text with a color.

   a. Click the Fill tab.

   b. With the text still selected and the Text Fill menu set to Color, click the Style Color swatch. Then choose a color from the Apple Color Picker and click OK. (Alternatively, you can also use the Eyedropper to select a color from the Color Ramp at the bottom of the Text Window or from any area of the FCP interface.)

6. You'll now add an outline to the text.

   a. Click the Outline tab.

   b. Make sure the type is still selected. (Select it with Command + A if necessary.) If the selected text is grayed out or is difficult to see, click in any numeric field to monitor the text.

   c. Check the box next to the T1 tab within the Outline tab to add a black border.

   d. From the Position menu, choose Outside. This will put the border on the outer edges of the text.

   e. Adjust the Edge Color, Width, and Opacity if you like.

7. Click the Apply button. Your edited text will update in the Viewer. Edit the text onto the V3 video track.

You should now be familiar with Title 3D's Text window. There are lots of controls to play around with here, so try out the different options in each tab.

Title 3D's Style Palette

A hidden secret of Title 3D is the Style Palette, which offers an amazing number of preset styles that you can use and alter (see Figure 12-7). You can even make your own styles that you can categorize and save. Here's how to use the Style Palette.

1. In Title 3D's Text window, enter some text, select it, and then click in any numeric field to keep the text selected. Add a style, such as Bold.

2. Click the Style Palette button at the bottom of the Text window. The Style Palette launches. The current style is displayed.

note

Before clicking the Apply button, you can still do an Edit → Undo in the Text window. You can't undo or redo your changes once you've clicked Apply.

tip

If you don't see your changes updating, make sure your text is selected in the Text Preview area of the Text window.

tip

If you're concerned about broadcast-safe levels for your titles, be sure to turn on the Range Check options for Excess Luma and Chroma values. See Chapter 7 for more on monitoring and changing levels. If you use pure white for titles, you'll quickly learn that these levels are most likely illegal.

tip

Let's say you're scaling a multi-line text page, and the text isn't scaling from the center. To remedy this, reset the anchor point if you're scaling text from the Motion tab, or the pivot point if you're using Title 3D in the Controls tab.

3. Click the Add Style button to add the style to the Palette.

4. Select the style and click the Rename Style button to give it a name. Type a descriptive name and click OK.

Now you can use the Style Palette to apply any of your styles to text in the Text window. Just select the text in the Text window and click the Style Palette button. In the Style Palette, choose the style you want and click the Apply Style button (or simply double-click the style). The style is applied in the Text window.

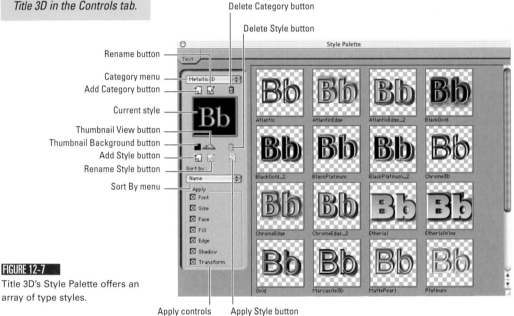

FIGURE 12-7
Title 3D's Style Palette offers an array of type styles.

You've Got Style

On the Boris FX website, you can find several style categories with dozens of options for you to choose from. It's free, but you do have to provide your FCP serial number. Go to www.borisfx.com/download/freebies.php to download almost a hundred new styles. Follow the instructions for installing the styles; they'll show up in Title 3D's Style Palette.

After you've loaded the preset styles, inspect how they are made in the various tabs of the Title 3D interface. You can learn a great deal about how to make titles by studying those made by the pros at Boris FX.

Title 3D's Gradient Editor

Introducing the Gradient Editor. It's located in Text window's Fill tab.

1. Click the Fill tab.

2. Choose Gradient from the Text Fill menu.

3. Click the Edit Gradient swatch to launch the Gradient Editor (see Figure 12-8).

4. Once in the Gradient Editor, you'll see the Shape menu. Choose a linear or a radial gradient. Use the controls to shape the gradient.

5. Click on a color stop (see Figure 12-9) and choose a new color, and then click OK.

tip

Perhaps you've heard that you shouldn't use serif fonts for video post-production, which is generally true. I'm a rebel, I guess, so I use them occasionally. However, I use larger sizes for serif fonts, as any portion of a letter that is less than one pixel wide will disappear.

Getting to Know the Title 3D Parameters

The parameters in the Controls tab are different from the ones in the Text window. For one thing, the Controls tab parameters are "global," so by altering them you're changing the entire text page, not just selected characters or words. Therefore, the Controls tab is where you animate parameters for Title 3D. Keep in mind how you want to use these controls to influence perspective with positioning, scaling, and distortion.

- **Scale:** Great for scaling text above 100%. Uncheck the Lock to Scale X button to distort text.

- **Distance:** This is a Z-space scale effect for your text. It will dramatically fly text toward or away from your audience.

- **Tracking:** Move letters together or apart — over time.

- **Tumble, Spin**, and **Rotate:** These controls for offer perspective and Z-space motion possibilities.

- **Pivot:** You can animate a pivot point once you unlock it, which is very useful for creating patterns of flying text.

- **Letter Skew:** This control distorts text along the X or Y axis.

- **Letter Scale:** These sliders scale individual characters in a block of text.

- **Letter Spin, Tumble,** and **Rotate:** These controls move a character around its baseline's X, Y, or Z axis, respectively.

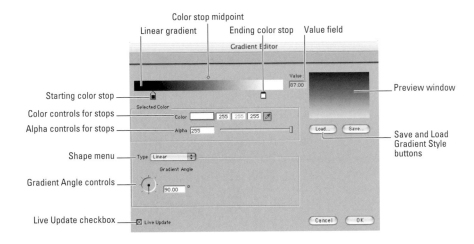

FIGURE 12-8

The Gradient Editor is located in Title 3D's Fill tab.

Color stop midpoint

Linear gradient · Ending color stop · Value field

Starting color stop

Color controls for stops

Alpha controls for stops

Shape menu

Gradient Angle controls

Live Update checkbox

Preview window

Save and Load Gradient Style buttons

FIGURE 12-9

Select a color stop and then adjust the Alpha slider to change its level of transparency.

A gradient has two *color stops:* one for the starting color (black by default) and another for the ending color (white by default). Click a color stop to select it, and then adjust its color (see Figure 12-9). You can change either the start or stop color — or both. You can also add more color stops if you wish. It's easy to do; just click between existing color stops and a new color stop will appear. To remove a stop, click it and drag downward. You can also adjust the position of a color stop's midpoint by clicking and dragging it.

You should spend a little time playing around with the Gradient Editor. You can build up a library of gradients by clicking the Save button after you've composed a particularly nice one. Reload the gradient style by clicking the Load button.

Animating type in Title 3D

You've set up the text in the Text window and tried out a few style options. Now it's time to animate some text.

Title 3D's animation controls reside in the Controls tab. You animate type much as you would any other effect.

1. Create your text and stylize it in the various tabs of the Text window.

2. Save the changes to the title by clicking the Apply button.

3. Edit the Title 3D clip into the Timeline, and then double-click it to load it into the Viewer.

tip

Drag the Gradient Editor and the Text window so they're side by side, have the text passively selected and the Live Update box checked in the Gradient Editor, and you can see changes to gradient fills as you make them.

4. Click on the Controls tab to get at the parameters for Title 3D. You can see that there are 18 animatable controls in this window.

5. Keyframe the parameters as you wish.

Now that you're familiar with the controls in Title 3D, it's time to jump into an exercise to give you some hands-on experience.

EXERCISE 12-2: FLYING TITLES IN TITLE 3D

In this exercise you'll fly some type around the screen. You'll gain experience with the Title 3D controls and with adding filters to text generators.

Double-click on the Chapter 12 Exercise sequence to get to work.

1. Copy the piece of text you made in Exercise 12-1.

2. Move the playhead to the first marker in the music track, just past the marker for Exercise 2. Option + click the V2 Auto Select button, and then paste the title onto V2. Your title will come in on the musical downbeat.

3. Now that your title is edited into the Timeline, park the playhead on the stack of clips. Double-click the clip and then click the Controls tab. You're now going to stylize your text.

   a. In the Controls tab, click on the large gray square that says "Click for Options." The Text window will launch.

   b. Select the text and change the font to Futura Condensed. (If the Bold style button is enabled, disable it now.)

STEP 3b

Choose the Futura Condensed font.

tip

When you apply a gradient, every letter will be filled with the gradient individually, instead of the gradient as a whole showing through the entire word or phrase. To do the latter, you'd create a travel matte effect with a Gradient generator to be used as graphic fill.

tip

If you're using the Eyedropper tool to pick colors in the Gradient Editor, you can click on the color ramp in Title 3D or anywhere on the screen.

tip

You can change the look of a linear gradient by dragging the color stops closer to or farther away from each other. Dragging two color stops close together in a linear gradient makes for a nice highlight.

note

The X,Y position coordinates are different in Title 3D and FCP. FCP places the (0,0) position in the center of the Canvas. In Title 3D, the (0,0) position is in the upper left portion of a standard video frame. This may cause you some trouble if you're trying to calculate position values across platforms. For situations like this, use your calculator or just position the text with the point controls.

STEP 3c
Launch the Gradient Editor.

c. In the Fill tab, choose Gradient from the Text Fill menu. Then click on the Edit Gradient swatch to launch the Gradient Editor.

d. In the Gradient Editor, use the Eyedropper to grab shades of green from the clip in the Canvas for your color stops. Make the dark green darker and the light green lighter with the color controls. Click OK when you're satisfied with the new fill.

e. Click the Apply button.

4. You're now going to animate the text. Click on the Timeline and place the playhead at the beginning of the title. With the text clip deselected, type +201 and press Enter to move the playhead 2:01 forward.

a. Load the clip into the Viewer and click the Controls tab. Set keyframes for Position, Scale, Spin, Tracking, Letter Tumble, and Letter Spin, but do not change their settings.

b. Click on the Timeline and then tap the Up Arrow key to move the playhead back to the beginning of the Title 3D generator. You're going to set the keyframes that will make the type fly in.

tip

You can save a Title 3D clip as a Favorite, even after it's been keyframed. Double-click it in the Timeline to load it into the Viewer. Go to Effects → Make Favorite Effect, and the Title 3D clip will go into the Favorites bin. Go there and name it something appropriate.

STEP 4
You'll scale, spin, track, and tumble your text.

c. Set the Position X/Y parameter to X = 160 and Y = 50 to raise the title a bit.

d. Set the Scale X parameter to 30.

e. Set Tracking to 140 to spread out the letters.

f. Set Spin to 90.

g. Set Letter Tumble to −45.

h. Set Letter Spin to 45. The text will now appear as if it is flying for the first 2:01 of the effect.

5. Now you'll animate the word a bit further down the Timeline.

a. With the clip deselected, type +215 and press Enter.

b. Set a keyframe for the regular Spin (not Letter Spin) parameter by clicking its Insert Keyframe button.

c. With the clip deselected, move the playhead forward another 1:15 and then type −360 in the Spin parameter to set an automatic keyframe.

d. Also set a keyframe for Tracking, but do not change its value.

e. Move the playhead to the end of the clip and change the parameter for Tracking to 4. The letters will move apart as the clip plays.

6. Click on the Timeline and tap the Up Arrow key to place the playhead back at the beginning of the clip. You'll now add and animate the drop shadow.

a. Click the Motion Tab and then click the Drop Shadow checkbox. Click the disclosure triangle and then set keyframes for Offset, Softness, and Opacity; don't change any values, though.

b. With the clip deselected, type +201 to move forward 2:01.

c. Change the Drop Shadow settings to:

Offset: 2

Softness: 1

Opacity: 30

7. You'll now duplicate the title. Select the V2 clip and then Option + Shift + drag the clip up one track. You'll now have two identical clips in the Timeline.

tip

You can change the color or the transparency of a color stop. This is more powerful when you take a second look at that feature. Making certain colors semi-opaque allows objects on lower video tracks to be seen behind the text, only within that color. Yes, it's cool!

tip

When you're learning to use Title 3D, play around with different combinations of settings. Use two at first, and then work up to multi-parameter settings to get a feeling for the kinds of movement you can create with these controls.

8. You'll now alter the copied clip.

    a. Load the clip into the Viewer and in the Controls tab, click on the Title 3D gray box to launch the Text window.

    b. In the Style tab, select the text and then type the word "presents."

    c. In the Style tab, set the point size to 58 and Tracking to 10.

    d. In the Fill tab, choose Color from the Text Fill menu, and select a light gray.

    e. Change the Outline to 1 pixel in the Outline tab and then click the Apply button to apply the changes.

9. You need to adjust a couple of keyframes to make the second title support the main text.

    a. With the clip deselected, type +201 to move the playhead ahead 2:01 to the second marker in the audio track.

    b. Double-click the "presents" title clip and then click the Controls tab and change the keyframe settings for Position X/Y to X = 230 and Y = 195. Step through the effect and see how the two titles are flying.

    c. Go to the Spin parameter and then click twice on the right keyframe navigation button until you reach the −360 keyframe. Type 360 in the numeric field. The new title will now spin in the opposite direction.

    d. Trim both titles so they're 7:00 in duration and then remove any In or Out points.

 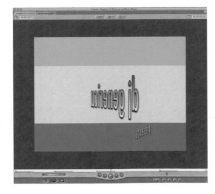 

STEP 9

Now you'll spin the text in the opposite direction.

10. Select the two Title 3D generators and then press Option + C to nest them. Name the nest "dj generica_NEST" and then click OK. The titles will collapse into a nest.

11. Preview and then render the effect.

12. Save the project.

You've now created an animated type effect that takes advantage of a number of Title 3D's parameters. Nice going!

Creating Type Effects with LiveType

One of the greatest innovations that Apple has brought to Final Cut Pro is an awesome program called LiveType. This application is more than just a standalone titler; it's a compositing environment and a motion graphics tool. Once you get the hang of it, it's very easy and fun — even addictive — to compose motion graphics with this program. In this section we'll hit the highlights, and then you'll launch into a series of exercises using LiveType. (LiveType will make another appearance in Chapter 14.)

LIVETYPE HIGHLIGHTS

With so many features that can benefit effects artists, LiveType boggles the mind! Here are some key features:

- LiveType imports anything QuickTime can understand, with alpha channels. It exports to any QuickTime format, so you can export to Compressor, FCP, or another application, all with different frame sizes.

- It includes more than 150 pre-keyframed motion effects — including fades, zooms, blur, and jitter — for type, objects, and imported images (see Figure 12-10).

Why Not Use Wireframes?

Although dragging a text block's wireframe around the Canvas is easy, in most cases you'll have more control over scale and position if you use Title 3D's motion parameters instead.

For example, if you create some huge text and then move its wireframe, parts of the letters will be chopped off. If you move the text with the Position X/Y controls in the Controls tab, the letters will remain intact. In this case, the frame remains static; you're just repositioning the elements within the frame.

There are exceptions to this rule. For example, you can't control the scale or position of a nested title sequence with Controls tab parameters. They must be controlled by Filters and Motion tab parameters.

If you create oversized text and move the wireframe, letters outside the frame will be cut off.

Millennium font from from Digital Juice: www.digitaljuice.com

Nesting and Duplicating Title Sequences

After all your layered title elements are edited onto the Timeline, you should get into the habit of nesting them. Select the layers, press Option + C, and then name the nest.

There are a number of important reasons for nesting titles:

- Opacity fades, scaling, and cropping can be controlled for multiple text layers if they're nested first.

- You can create compound text effects. Use Title 3D's controls to spin, track, and rotate the text. Then, after nesting them, you can apply further effects to the nest in the Filters or Motion tab.

- You can save time by duplicating a nested sequence to make an effects template. Let's say you make a flying title effect. Duplicate the nested title sequence and open it in the Timeline to make changes. Make the changes in Title 3D's Text window and click the Apply button, and you've got a new title with the same animation as the original.

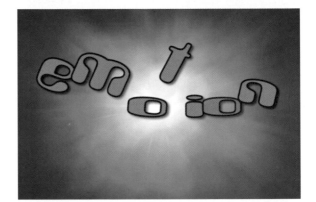

FIGURE 12-10

Here's LiveType's preset Turbulence effect.

- A new animated type media called *LiveFonts* performs a number of preset tricks and easily keys over video (see Figure 12-11). You can even make your own LiveFonts if you have the gumption!

- Animated previews of wireframes for motion effects and LiveFonts help you plan out your effect.

- You can do a Lo-Res render preview, which is great for quick quality-control checks.

- You can import markers from FCP to hit beats and make motion type events happen with precision.

- LiveType includes more than 350 Textures and Objects to use as backgrounds, graphic elements, and fill for type (see Figure 12-12).

- You can use Mattes and Objects, which carry alpha channels that can be exploited throughout LiveType and FCP.

- Because LiveType treats every letter as an individual layer, you can scale, move, or rotate characters individually or as a group.

- You can bend and shape Bézier tracks to provide motion paths for text.

- A Travel Matte feature lets you put video in type.

- LiveType can output multiple frame sizes, including custom ones. This means that oversized HDTV frames in LiveType can be manipulated with FCP's motion controls in Standard Definition frame size.

- You can group tracks together to move different chunks of text as a single unit in the Timeline. Great for fine-tuning multilayered effects.

- Templates are provided for motion graphics treatments, bullet text builds, and other titling effects.

- You can save and share custom effects across projects.

Drop Shadows and Text Perspective

Adding a drop shadow to type provides perspective and improves legibility. Here are some rules of thumb:

- If the text is to be perceived as far from the surface of the background, then the drop shadow should be offset a good distance. The shadow should be soft and somewhat transparent. (Conversely, to appear close to the background, a shadow should be offset just a bit, and be hard and opaque.)

- If you want a piece of text to look like it's moving from high above the background to near the background, keyframe the drop shadow's offset, softness, and opacity from soft and transparent to hard and opaque.

- If you want a simulated light source that moves around the text, keyframe the direction of the drop shadow.

Image courtesy of 12 Inch Design, www.12inchdesign.com

Here the text appears to be some distance from the background.

tip

It's a good idea to name your titles so they can be easily identified in the Timeline. For individual title generators, choose the title by clicking on it and then pressing Command + 9. The Item Properties for the title will launch, and you can rename it. Also, remember to carefully rename duplicated nested title sequences and nests so you don't confuse them with the originals.

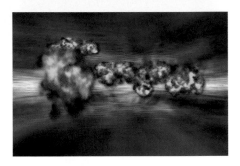

FIGURE 12-11

Here LiveType's LiveFonts have been combined with System fonts for a striking effect.

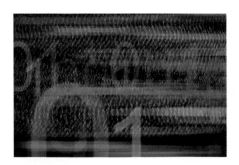

FIGURE 12-12

LiveType includes hundreds of Textures and Objects that can be used in type or graphics effects.

- Used in tandem with Title 3D, LiveType can create lavish title treatments.

- LiveType can be used to animate objects as well as text (see Figure 12-13).

Whew! Now that you're aware of some of the amazing things LiveType can do, let's get started with an exercise.

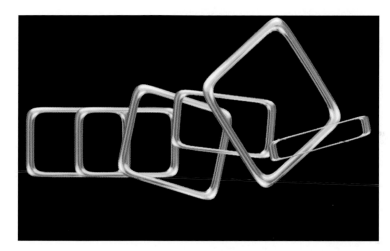

FIGURE 12-13
Don't confine yourself to letters and numbers when animating with Livetype.

EXERCISE 12-3: CREATING A TYPEWRITER EFFECT IN LIVETYPE

In this exercise you'll create an automated "type-on" effect. You'll use all of LiveType's palettes, in addition to the Character Palette.

Open the Chapter 12 bin in the Effects Project. Click the LiveType icon in your Dock or double-click it in the Applications folder. Let the fun begin!

1. After LiveType has launched, you must set the LiveType Preferences correctly. Go to Edit → Project Properties.

   a. In the Project Properties dialog box, choose NTSC or PAL and the appropriate frame size from the Presets menu. Leave Upper First unchecked.

   b. Raise the Opacity slider for Background, and then choose any color you like by clicking on the color swatch.

2. Save the project and name it "Countdown Type On." Save this file to the same place you keep your Documents folder → Final Cut Pro Documents → LiveType Projects. (Make a LiveType project folder if you don't have one yet.)

Text-entry boxes

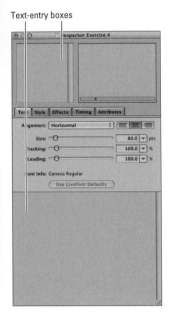

Click in one of the Inspector's
text-entry boxes.

Click the Character Palette icon in
the Toolbar and select Show Character Palette.

3. You'll now locate the characters by first opening the Character Palette, which provides vector-based imagery for use in LiveType.

    a. In LiveType, click in one of the text-entry boxes in the Inspector. This will set a place for the characters you choose from the Character Palette.

    b. Activate the Character Palette by going to Apple menu → System Preferences → International and clicking on the Input Menu tab. Check the box for Character Palette, and close the International window.

    c. You should now see the icon for the Character Palette in your Mac's Toolbar. Your Character Palette will remain there until you uncheck the box in the System Preferences → International window. I leave mine checked at all times.

    d. Click the Character Palette icon and choose Show Character Palette.

4. You'll now be working with the Character Palette and LiveType.

    a. Choose Roman from the Character Palette's View menu.

    b. Click the Character Palette's By Category tab.

    c. Choose Digits from the categories on the left side of the Character Palette (you might have to scroll down to see it).

    d. Click the white, circled "10" glyph in the character set on the right, then click the Insert button. The character appears in LiveType's text-entry box.

    e. Repeat step d for characters 1-10, entered in descending order. After you're through, close the Character Palette.

5. You'll now add effects to this track. You'll make the type fly on, do a few tricks, and then "hammer" off.

    a. Select the track by clicking it in the Timeline. Drag the right end of the track so that it is 4:00 in duration.

    b. Click the Effects tab in LiveType's Media Browser. Choose Mechanical from the Category menu. Scroll down a bit and choose Type from the Name column, and then click the Apply button.

    c. In the Timeline, click the Frame Ruler where the text track ends to place the playhead there. Tap the Left Arrow and press O.

   d. Click the Play button in the Canvas to load a RAM preview of this effect. You'll see that it typed on the numbers very uniformly.

6. The next effect will make the text scale up and down quickly.

   a. Click and drag the playhead to 1:10. The Timecode will update in a tool tip next to the playhead to help you find your place. Press the I key to set an In point.

   b. Go to the Effects tab's Category menu. It should still be set to Mechanical. Choose Click On from the list of effects in the Name column. Click the Apply button. A new effect now appears in its own track.

   c. Click the Apply button two more times. You'll now have three new effects, and tracks for each.

7. You'll now move the effects down the Timeline. Zoom in a bit by clicking on the Zoom control in the lower-left portion of the Timeline.

   a. Click anywhere in the light-purple area of the first Click On effect, and then drag it down the Timeline to the In point.

   b. Move the playhead to 1:20 and press the I key to mark where you'll drag the next Click On effect. Repeat the previous step to drag the effect to the playhead.

   c. Move the playhead to 2:00 and press the I key. Move the third Click On effect and align it with the In point you just set.

8. Next, you'll do a type-on effect called "Hammer" to make your text disappear.

   a. Park the playhead at 2:15 and set an In point.

   b. Still working in the Mechanical category of the Media Browser's Effects tab, select Hammer, and then click the Apply button. The effect will now be applied to your track.

   c. Drag the effect to the In point.

   d. Click and drag the end of the effect to align it to the end of the text track. The text will now "hammer" offscreen.

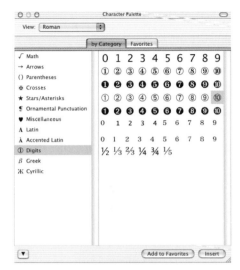

STEP 4d

Select a character from the Character Palette and click Insert.

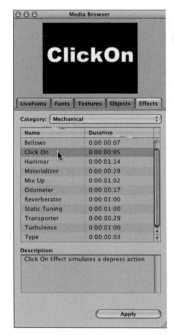

STEP 6b

In the Media Browser's Effects tab, choose Click On from the list of Mechanical effects.

A purple light indicates an active parameter for the keyframe

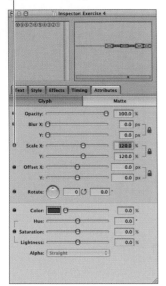

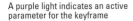

Set the Scale slider to 120. Note the purple light next to the slider.

9. In this step you'll modify a keyframe for one of the Click On effects to change the animation behavior for all of the numbers on the track.

a. Select the track in the Timeline.

b. Click the diamond-shaped keyframe on the third Click On effect.

c. Click the Inspector's Attributes tab to access the parameters. Slide the slider for Scale to 120.

d. Set In and Out Points around the three Click On effects, and then RAM preview that section. Note that the effect you just altered scales up instead of down for that brief moment.

10. You'll now preview the entire effect.

a. Move the playhead to the end of the Hammer effect. Tap the Left Arrow key and then mark an Out point.

b. Press Option + Left Arrow once or twice to move the playhead to the beginning of the sequence. Set an In point.

c. Click the RAM preview Play button to load your effect into RAM and play it back in real time.

11. You'll now render your creation.

a. Choose File → Render Movie or press Option + Command + R. Name the movie "Countdown Type On," making sure that the Render Background box is unchecked. Navigate to your media drive.

b. Leave Render Only Between In/Out Points checked, and then click Save.

c. After the render is finished, a window will pop up, allowing you to play through your effect. (The Play button is in the lower left corner of the window.)

d. After you check out your render, close the window.

12. Save the project and then close it by pressing Shift + Command + W or by going to File → Close Project.

Congratulations! You've just animated some text using LiveType. As you can see, this tool makes it easy to do a relatively complex effect. Now let's look at some other effects you can create with LiveType.

Animating Type on a Motion Path

One of the most popular type effects is to fly it on a curved path. You already know how to make motion paths in FCP. The process is quite similar in LiveType, except that you shape the tracks as if they were paths. The other difference is that instead using a Pen tool, you use a pointer to shape the tracks into Bézier paths.

Here's a quick exercise so that you can get going creating a basic path for text.

EXERCISE 12-4: PLACING TEXT ON AN OPEN PATH

In LiveType you need to be familiar with manipulating tracks in the Canvas. Note that there's a blue line in the Canvas that can be shaped according to where you want your text to fly.

1. Open LiveType. Save the Project and name it "Exercise 4." Reduce the Canvas size to 50%.

2. Drag the End points of the track off of the Canvas. Note that by holding down the Shift key you can constrain the horizontal and vertical movement of the End points. After you've done this, you're free to resize the Canvas to 100%.

3. You'll now reshape the track to provide the path for the text.

   a. Control + click somewhere near the middle of the track. Choose Add Control Point from the contextual menu.

   b. Click on the control point and Shift + drag it downward just a bit.

4. Control + click on the control point and choose Curve In from the contextual menu. Do this once more, this time choosing Curve Out.

5. You've now got a Bézier handle that you can adjust. Click the handle's end point and drag it to reshape the curve.

6. Type "pair of dice" in one of the text boxes. You'll see immediate feedback in the Canvas.

7. You'll now animate the text. Make a new effect for the track by pressing Command + E.

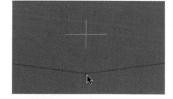

STEP 3b
Click on the control point and Shift + drag it downward.

STEP 5
Drag the Bézier handle to reshape the curve for your text path.

8. Drag the edges of both the track and the effect to 4:00. Press Option + Right Arrow, then press O to set an Out point.

9. Click on the last keyframe in the effect to select it (it darkens when you do) and then click on the Effects tab in the Inspector.

   a. Select Slide from the Parameter menu.

   b. Click the + button to add the parameter to the effect.

   c. In the Active Parameters pane, double-click on the word "Slide." Enter −70 in the dialog box that appears, and then click OK.

10. Click on the first keyframe and then double-click on the word "Slide" once more. Enter 70 and click OK.

11. Click the Play button in the Canvas to load the effect into RAM. Evaluate it as it plays back and make adjustments if you wish.

12. Now you'll change your System font to a LiveFont and adjust its color.

   a. Select the text in one of the text boxes and then click on the LiveFonts tab in the Media Browser.

   b. Double-click on Pulse in the list of LiveFonts.

   c. The LiveFont has been applied, taking the place of the font you added earlier. However, the duration changed to 1:00, which is the duration of the LiveFont. Adjust the duration by clicking on the Timing tab, entering 4 in the Loop parameter, and pressing Enter. This cycles the LiveFont effect four times and returns the duration to 4:00.

   d. Click on the Attributes tab in the Inspector. With neither keyframe selected, click on the color swatch and choose a green color.

   e. Click on the Text tab and change the font size to 90.

13. Press Command + E, and then resize the track so it matches the others. Select the first keyframe and then click the Style tab in the Inspector. Click the Glow tab and then click the Enable checkbox. Set Opacity to 0.

14. Move the playhead midway through the effect. Take the Opacity slider back down to 0. This sets an automatic keyframe for Glow.

15. Tap the Right Arrow key twice to move two frames forward. Slide the Opacity slider to 100% to set another keyframe.

> **note**
>
> If you like LiveFonts, you can find more at www.screencaffeine.com or www.livetypecentral-.com. The DVD that came with this book includes a free LiveFont from Live-typecentral. You'll find it in the Goodies folder.

STEP 12d
Choose a shade of green for your text.

STEP 20d
Scale up the "P" in the Canvas.

16. With the Timeline selected, tap the Right Arrow twice again to move the playhead. Slide the Opacity slider for Glow back down to 0.

17. Do a RAM preview on the effect. Now it momentarily glows as the text flies by.

18. Since the glow flicks on and off too quickly, you can adjust the keyframes a bit to lengthen the duration of the glow effect. In the effect, click and drag the first diamond shaped keyframe a bit further to the left. Click and drag the last keyframe a bit further to the right.

19. Set In and Out points around the Glow effect and then do another RAM preview until you are satisfied with the glow effect.

20. You'll stylize the text now.

    a. Drag the playhead to the middle of the Timeline so you can see the text.

    b. Select the track and the effect by clicking anywhere on it in the Timeline.

    c. In the Inspector, select the letter "P" in the Text window.

    d. Drag the letter up in the Canvas to work on it. Click and drag with the Shift key held down in the upper right corner of the blue bounding box to scale it up a bit.

    e. Drag the letter back into place and then click and drag in the upper left of the bounding box to rotate the "P" to match the other letters.

f. Repeat the process for the letter "D," but this time just click and drag the glyph's wireframe in the track. Select the word "dice" in the Inspector and reposition it by clicking and dragging in the Canvas.

g. Shift + drag the entire track to center it on the Canvas. While the Track is selected, tap any of the Arrow keys to nudge the track in any direction.

21. Render the movie by doing the following:

a. Go to File → Render Movie. Save your LiveType renders onto your media drive in the proper folder.

b. In the Save dialog box, make sure the Render Background box is unchecked. Render Only Between In/Out Points should be unchecked in this case. Name the movie "Pair of Dice."

c. Click Save to begin the rendering process.

Good going! You just made a custom effect with LiveFonts. Go to Track → Save Effect to store it in the Media Browser for future use.

CLOSED-PATH TEXT

Now that you've made an open-path text effect, it's time to move on to a slightly more difficult endeavor: creating a closed motion path. As you know from the work you did in Chapter 4, a closed motion path starts and finishes in the same place. Let's get going with an exercise right now.

EXERCISE 12-5: PLACING TEXT ON A CIRCULAR PATH

This exercise is similar to the last one, but here you'll be concentrating on creating the right shape for the track. This exercise is similar to the one in Chapter 4 where you made a circular motion path by tracing a circle generator with the Pen tool. If you can make a good-looking circle, you can do just about anything!

Get started by launching LiveType.

1. After you've opened LiveType, save this file with your other LiveType project files. Call the project "Exercise 5."

2. Go to Edit → Project Properties and make the background opaque by sliding the Opacity slider in the Project Properties dialog box. Click OK.

3. Click in either text-entry box. In the main Toolbar, click the Character Palette icon and choose Show Character Palette from the menu.

4. In the Character Palette, choose Roman from the View menu. In the By Category tab, choose Miscellaneous. Choose the glyph that looks like an audio-tape reel and then click the Insert button. After you're through, close the Character Palette.

5. With the Canvas at 100% size, Shift + drag the track (the blue line) downward until the reel glyph is positioned in the center of the Canvas. With the Title Safe overlays on (from View → Title Safe), there's a crosshair showing where the center of the Canvas lies.

6. Click the Attributes tab in the Inspector and then click in the numeric field for Scale. Type 650 and press Enter to set the scale of the glyph. The glyph should now appear much larger in the Canvas.

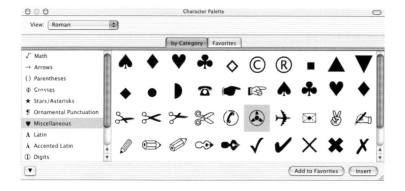

STEP 4

In the Character Palette, choose the character that looks like a tape reel.

STEP 5

In the Canvas, Shift + drag the track's blue line downward.

7. Now you'll make a new track in the Canvas. This is for tracing the tape reel glyph to create a circular track. Click on the Canvas or Timeline and then press Command + T. Another track comes into the Timeline and on the Canvas.

8. Shift + drag the new track to the bottom of the Canvas so that the tape glyph is resting on it.

9. Control + click directly on the center of the track and choose Add Control Point from the contextual menu. A large blue dot appears in the track.

10. Control + click again and choose Curve In. A Bézier handle is added to the track. Control + click one more time and choose Curve Out. You'll now have two Bézier handles in the center of the track, which appear as smaller blue dots. Don't drag the handles yet.

11. Control + click on the track's left end point and choose Curve Out. Do the same for the end point on the right, but choose Curve In.

12. Drag the right end point to the top-center of the circular glyph. The Title Safe overlay will help you position the handle.

13. Click and Shift + drag the Bézier handle for the right end point to the right until you hit the Title Safe line on the right side of the frame.

New Tracks are created in the Canvas and the Timeline

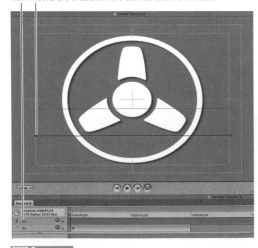

STEP 7
Press Command +T to create a new track.

Drag the new track to here

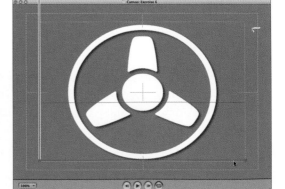

STEP 8
Shift + drag the new track to the bottom of the Canvas.

14. You'll now position the left end point to mirror the right end point.

    a. Drag the left end point to the top-center of the circular glyph. You should see them "lock" together with just a small movement.

    b. Control + click on the overlapping end points and choose Link End Points. This will make your type fly around this shape continuously.

    c. Shift + drag the Bézier handle to the left until you hit the Title Safe line.

15. Work on the center control point at the bottom of the circle. Shift + drag each handle to the Title Safe border to get a good head start on the circular path. Shift + drag each handle inward a bit to get the track to hug the edge of the tape glyph toward the bottom of the circle.

16. You'll now have to adjust the Bézier handles to get the track closer to the edge of the glyph.

    a. Before you work on the handles, you may want to zoom into the Canvas a bit more. A setting of 200% will do. Use the scroll bars to put the right Bézier handle into view.

    b. Start with the upper-right Bézier handle and drag it downward and inward a bit. You'll start to see the track get closer to the tape reel glyph.

    c. Repeat the process for the left Bézier handle.

    d. Zoom the Canvas out once more to 100% to inspect your circular track and make adjustments to the bottom Bézier handles to match the edge the glyph.

17. You're now going to make some text to surround the tape glyph in this track.

    a. Click in either text-entry box and type "dj generica • dj generica • ". (Make the black dot by typing Option + 8.) Put a space between the dots. In the text-entry box, copy and paste the words so you have "dj generica" repeated four times.

    b. In the Text tab of the Inspector, set the size to 32. Set the Tracking to 138.

Newly added Bézier handles

STEP 10
Add Bézier handles to the track.

note

LiveType does not have a "Show as Square Pixels" option, so when you work with round shapes thye're slightly distorted on the computer screen. Don't worry. It will look OK on the video monitor.

    c. In the Attributes tab, unlock the Offset Y parameter by clicking on the lock next to it. Adjust the slider to 32 to make the text hug the outer edge of the circle.

    d. Set a font by selecting the track and then clicking the Fonts tab in the Media Browser. Scroll through the fonts and when you see one you like, click the Apply button.

    e. Fine-tune your Tracking adjustment to fit the words around the circle. If you change the font style, you'll generally have to adjust tracking.

18. Your next feat is to animate these two tracks with a simple rotation effect. First work on the circle of text.

    a. Select the "dj generica" track in the Timeline.

    b. Add a new effect to the track by pressing Command + E.

    c. In the Timeline, click and drag the right edge of the track and the effect so that that they are both 5:00 in length. Once you've dragged them there, mark an Out Point by pressing Option + Right Arrow and then O.

    d. Repeat steps a through c for the "Tape Glyph" track. Both tracks will now have effects applied to them

    e. Click on the "dj generica" effect's final keyframe. Don't be concerned if the type disappears here.

    f. Click the Effects tab in the Inspector and choose Slide from the Parameter menu.

STEP 17d

Choose a font in the Media Browser's Font tab.

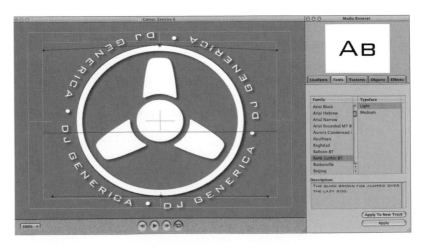

g. Click on the + sign to add the effect.

h. Double-click the word "Slide." A dialog box will pop up. Enter –65 in the numeric field and click OK.

i. Check the Wireframe preview in the Inspector. You'll see the text begin to travel in a circle. If the preview does not show this, your end points may not be linked. Control + click on the end points once more and choose Link Endpoints from the menu.

Damaged Text

There are a lot of ways to stylize your text to make it look at bit more aggressive, lively, or urban. In motion graphics circles, this is known as "grunging" or "damaging" text. You can achieve this look by smudging, blurring, and colorizing text and then animating it, usually in random, rapid movements.

Here are the ways I like to "grunge" up text:

- The easiest way to get grungy text looks is to buy specially made fonts that already have rough edges and grungy fill. You can find a good selection of grungy (and non-grungy) fonts at www.fontshop.com.

- FCP and LiveType both offer blur effects.

- You can grunge up your text by changing its composite mode. I often go for a combination of Add mode and Blur for a "burned in" look.

- Try some filters in the following categories: Blur, Channel, Distort, Matte (to control areas of visibility), Stylize, Perspective, and Video.

- You can change the fill of text by constructing a Travel Matte Alpha effect. You can also use Textures from LiveType or FCP generators like Noise and Particle Noise.

- Using a Distort filter (like Telly's Displacement Map, a free plug-in that comes with this book), you can make text warp according the luminance of a matte layer.

Making text look grungy is only half the battle. It must also *move* like grunge text in brisk, angular motions. It's fairly time consuming to keyframe this kind of text movement by hand in FCP, so stick with LiveType, which has motion presets for making text bop around the screen.

tip

You can add a damaged look to text by layering identical copies in the Timeline and then distorting, blurring, and adding modes to the background copy.

19. Now you'll animate the "Tape Glyph" (I'll call it that from this point forward).

    a. Click on the Tape Glyph effect's final keyframe.

    b. Click on the Attributes tab in the Inspector.

    c. Next to the Rotate dial, enter in –1 for the number of revolutions and then press Enter.

You should now see the Tape Glyph spinning in your Wireframe preview window.

20. You're already set up to do a RAM preview. Click the Play button to load the effect into RAM. Once it plays back, see if you'd like to make any adjustments.

21. You'll now render these elements. Go to File → Render Movie. Make sure the Render Background box is unchecked.

22. Save and close the project.

You've now mastered both open- and closed-path text effects. Nice work!

tip

If you really want to understand Title 3D, Title Crawl, and LiveType, you must get Philip Hodgetts' "Killer Titles" CD package, which has more than 40 tutorials. Check it out at www.intelligentassis-tance.com/killertitles. Philip has placed a sample tutorial on this book's DVD in the Goodies folder.

EXERCISE 12-6: INTEGRATING TITLE 3D, TITLE CRAWL, AND LIVETYPE

In this exercise you can practice integrating all of the type tools. This richly layered text treatment is a popular look you can incorporate into your own projects.

You'll be working in Final Cut Pro for this exercise.

1. Make a bin (Command + B) in the Chapter 12 bin and call it "LiveType Imports." Import the "Countdown Type On" clip from Exercise 12-3 from your Live Type Renders folder by Control + clicking on the bin and choosing Import → Files. Import the "Tape Glyph" and "Pair of Dice" clips into the same bin using the same method.

2. Now that you've got your title elements gathered, it's time to set up the composite. For this, you'll be using the titles you created in the previous exercises.

    a. With Snapping engaged, move the playhead to the first marker in the audio track until it snaps into place.

    b. In the Timeline, select "djgenerica_NEST" (from Exercise 12-2), and then Option + drag it to the playhead.

3. Drag and drop the Tape Glyph clip next to the "Pair of Dice" clip on V2. Trim the glyph to the marker.

4. You'll now stylize the glyph by adding a composite mode and a filter and then placing it in another area of the Canvas.

   a. Up the grunge factor a notch by changing the composite mode for the Tape Glyph clip. Park the playhead on the clip and choose a mode from the contextual menu. You're free to choose your own mode. Here, Add is used.

   b. With the Tape Glyph clip selected, go to Effects → Video Filters → Image Control → Sepia. From the Timeline, load the clip into the Viewer and then click the Filters tab. Use the Eyedropper tool to pick a color from the Canvas, and then adjust the color as you see fit.

   c. Blur the clip to lend perspective. Select the clip and then go to Effects → Video Filters → Blur → Gaussian Blur. Keep the setting for Radius low (2 to 4 is fine) so that the glyph and letters are still somewhat legible.

   d. Turn on Clip Overlays by pressing Option + W. Drop the Opacity to 50% by dragging down the adjust line. With the Pen tool, set a keyframe about 10 frames into the clip. Click and drag downward with the Pen tool at the beginning of the clip to set another keyframe. The clip will now fade up nicely.

   e. With Image + Wireframe mode engaged in the Canvas, and the clip selected, drag the wireframe partially offscreen to the left, as shown.

STEP 4a

Apply a composite mode to the clip. Add mode is used here, and Overlay mode in the figure below.

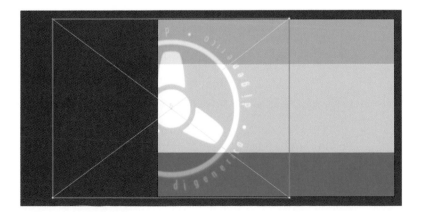

STEP 4e

Drag the wireframe partially offscreen in the Canvas.

5. You'll now add the Countdown Type On clip onto V3 as an Overwrite edit, in the same place as the Tape Glyph clip. To see the track more easily, you may have to reduce your track size. With the Timeline selected, use the Shift + T shortcut to toggle the height.

   a. Park the playhead on the Countdown Type On clip and then select it. Click and drag the wireframe to the upper half of the colored stripe at the top of the composite. As you drag the clip in the Canvas, it's helpful to have the playhead parked near the middle of the clip so you can see most of the characters.

   b. With Overlays → Title Safe on, position and scale down the clip's wireframe. Then, reposition the wireframe to push the image into the Action Safe region in the upper-right portion of the Canvas.

   c. As with the Tape Glyph clip, change the composite mode and add a tint and a blur to the clip to grunge up the type a bit.

6. At this point you'll need to make an additional element in Title 3D.

   a. Open Title 3D by pressing Control + Option + X.

   b. Type "on sale now."

   c. Choose the Futura font and size it to 40 points. Pick a light green color from the Canvas with the Eyedropper tool. Click the Apply button.

   d. Edit the title onto V4. Align the beginning of the title with the beginning of the Countdown Type On clip.

   e. Double-click the title to load it into the Viewer. In the Canvas, click and drag to position the wireframe beneath the Countdown Type On clip.

   f. Grunge up this piece of text as you did with the other background text elements. Use a composite mode and a touch of Blur.

7. Now you're going to stylize the "on sale now" text on V4.

   a. In the Timeline, move the playhead to the fifth marker: "Music Hit."

   b. Option + click the Auto Select button for V4, and then make an Add Edit in the clip. You can do this by clicking with the Razor Blade tool where the playhead lies or by pressing Control + V.

   c. With the latter half of the newly spliced clip selected, click the Add Motion Keyframe button in the bottom-right corner of the Canvas.

d. Move the playhead forward 1:00 by pressing Shift + Right Arrow. Make another Add Edit at this location.

e. Select the spliced section of the title by clicking on it. Press the Left Arrow key to see the clip in the Canvas as you crop.

f. Press C to select the Crop tool. In the Canvas, click and drag the wireframe along the left side of the clip all the way to the right (a blue line representing the crop will guide you). The text is now quickly cropped offscreen with the Crop Left keyframe automatically set.

g. Moving back to the first section of the clip, select it and then go to Effects → Video Filters → Video → Blink. Load the clip into the Viewer and then click on the Filters tab. Change the Blink settings as follows:

> On Duration: 10
>
> Off Duration: 3
>
> Opacity: 0

8. You'll now add the main title element using Title Crawl in FCP.

a. Click the Viewer's Video tab. In the Viewer, click on the Generator pop-up menu and choose Title Crawl. The Text window will launch.

b. Click on the Page Wrap tab and make sure the parameter for Text Wrap is set to No Wrap. After you've done that, click the Style tab.

c. Type "dj generica" in the Text window's Text Preview area. Set the size to 104 points. In the ruler at the top of the window, click on an area a few spaces beyond the end of the text line. A tab marker will then be set at that position.

d. Press the Tab key. The cursor will snap to where you set the tab marker. Type "dj generica" once more.

e. Press Command + A to select the text and then passively select it by clicking in a numeric-entry box. Choose the Futura Condensed font.

f. You'll now add an outline to the text. With the text still selected, click the Border tab. Check the Border Style checkbox.

g. Click the Fill tab. With the text still selected and the Text Fill menu set to Color, click on the Eyedropper next to the color control swatch. Click on the light-green stripe in the Canvas. Click the Apply button and the changes you made will update in the Viewer.

h. Edit the Title Crawl generator into the Timeline on the V5 track. As with the other clips, just drag and drop the clip as an Overwrite edit. Make sure to align it with the other clips in the stack. You can trim the title to the end of the music if you wish.

i. You'll now animate the crawl. Load the clip into the Viewer and then click the Controls tab. First, click on the 1:2:1 Deflicker checkbox to prevent interlace flicker. Then, choose Crawl from the Animation Style menu.

9. You'll now add identical Title Crawl Generators to V4 and V3. To do this, just add duplicates of the V5 generator.

a. Select the Title Crawl generator on V5 and then Shift + Option + drag the clip upward to V6.

b. Repeat the process, but this time Shift + Option + drag the clip upward to V7.

10. Stylize the V7 Title Crawl generator. Before you get started, you may want to turn off the V6 clip's visibility by selecting it and pressing Control + B. After you're set, you can start stylizing the clip.

a. Load the V7 Title Crawl generator into the Viewer. Click the Controls tab and then click on the gray box that says, "Click for options." Title Crawl's Text window will launch.

b. In the Text window, click inside the Text Preview area. Press Command + A to select the text, and then the Delete key to remove it. Set the point size to 40 and Tracking to 2.

c. Type some new text, talking up how cool the new "dj generica" album is. It doesn't really matter what you type, as it won't be terribly legible in the end.

d. In the Border tab, uncheck any border style. A border will not be necessary for this line of type.

e. Click the Fill tab and then click on the color control swatch. Make the color a lighter green by dragging the lightness slider upward in the Color Picker. Click OK.

f. In the Text window, click the Apply button to apply your changes.

g. You'll need to reposition the text. Click on the Point Controls button in the Controls tab. Working in the Canvas, click and drag the point controls to an area slightly above the dark green stripe, so you can clearly see the lettering.

h. With the clip still selected, go to Effects → Blur → Gaussian Blur. Double-click the clip to load it into the Viewer and then click the Filters tab and set the Radius parameter to 2.

i. Change the composite mode to Overlay.

11. You'll want to change the look for the V6 Title Crawl generator as well. Turn on its visibility and then get started on adding styles.

a. Double-click the Title Crawl generator to load it into the Viewer.

b. Click the Controls tab and then click on the gray Text Entry and Style box. The Text window will launch.

c. Click in the Text Preview area. Press Command + A, and then press Delete.

d. Set the point size to 25, and type more hype! This time, type even crazier stuff about "dj generica" and how amazing the new recording is.

e. With the text passively selected, click the Fill tab and then click on the color control swatch. This time make the color lighter by adjusting the main slider in the Color Picker. Click the Apply button.

f. In the Border tab, uncheck any border style. Click Apply.

g. Adjust the point controls in the Controls tab to set the position of this text within the dark green stripe.

h. You need to blur this title out to make it illegible. With the clip still selected, go to Effects → Blur → Gaussian Blur. Double-click the clip to load it into the Viewer. Click on the Filters tab and adjust the parameter for Radius. Set it to 1.

i. You can change the composite mode for this text layer as well. Mine is set to Add mode, completely "blowing out" the exposure of the text.

12. Stylize the background. You can use a clip from the Chapter 12 Clips bin to mix with the green-and-white background. You'll have to step into the nest for the background to work on this.

a. Double-click the "Background Chapter 12" nest to open it in the Timeline. You should now see a new Timeline with three layers of color mattes.

b. The clips in the bin are not long enough for the background, so you'll need to do a Fit to Fill edit to span the time. Click the V4 Destination

> **tip**
>
> In LiveType, the default color of a System font is black, so the Hue and Saturation sliders will not change the font. Lightness will change only its grayscale value. To change a font's color, use the Color parameter instead. For LiveFonts, you should use the HSL sliders or the Color parameter.

STEP 12c

Apply composite modes such as Hard Light (top), Overlay (center), or Screen (bottom) to radically alter the look of your clip.

button. Park the playhead anywhere on the stack of clips and perform a Mark Clip (press the X key). Drag and drop the clip of your choice onto the Fit to Fill Canvas Overlay to perform the edit.

c. Alter the clip as you wish. Blurs or composite modes are good choices.

d. Click the Chapter 12 Exercise sequence tab and then see how your clip looks when it's blended with the type and the background.

e. Fade up the opacity of the three newly added Title Crawl generators. To do this, select the Tape Glyph clip in V2 and copy the clip. Select the Title Crawl generators on V5, V6, and V7 and press Option + V to launch the Paste Attributes dialog box. Click the Opacity checkbox, and then click OK. Drag up the latter part of the adjust lines so that the opacity for the text fades up to 100% rather than 50% for each clip.

f. Set keyframes with the Pen tool to fade out the Tape Glyph clip.

g. Fade the stack of clips to black. Load slug into the Viewer by choosing it in the Generators menu. Edit 15 frames of slug onto the end of the sequence on V8. With the Pen tool, fade up the opacity of the slug. This fades the stack to black. You can use the Pen tool to fade out the audio as well.

13. Preview the effect and then render it.

14. Save the project to disk. Play back the effect and enjoy.

Troubleshooting

If you have trouble with any of FCP's text and titling tools, the following tips might help.

FCP crashes when styles are loaded

If you're experiencing any problems with newly installed Title 3D Preset Styles in FCP 4, you may have corrupt Preferences, or the styles themselves may have problems. I had this problem myself and remedied it by throwing away the Title 3D 1.1 Preferences file and reinstalling Title 3D 1.1. The Preferences file is located in your Home → Library → Preferences → Title 3D 1.1 Preferences. The download for the Title 3D 1.1 Installer is available at www.BorisFX.com.

A drop shadow doesn't show up

If you've added a drop shadow to some text and don't see it in the Canvas, check to see if Drop Shadow is checked in the Motion tab. If you're using the Title 3D or Title Crawl Text window in Title 3D and don't see your drop shadow, make sure that the enable checkboxes are checked in the Drop Shadow tab. If you don't see a drop shadow as you adjust the sliders in the Drop Shadow tab, you probably don't have the text selected.

Text looks jagged in the Canvas after it's rendered

Your text may look a bit jagged after rendering because it must now display in the codec of your sequence. Computer monitors don't display the true quality of rendered graphics.

If you're still having trouble, you might not be properly monitoring video. Your video monitor will show you the true quality of your text, which will vary between pretty darned good and absolutely brilliant, depending on whether you're using the Apple DV-DVCPRO codec and a DV system or 10-bit codec installed in a higher-end FCP system.

Text that's rendered in the DV codec may not be acceptable for broadcast, so you may need to output in an uncompressed format. For most corporate video and certain cable television outlets, DV compressed text will be fine.

Wrap-up

Now that you've completed this chapter, you have a wide variety of options for creating text effects. My hope is that you'll go on to create titles that can stand alone as works of art.

WHAT'S IN THIS CHAPTER

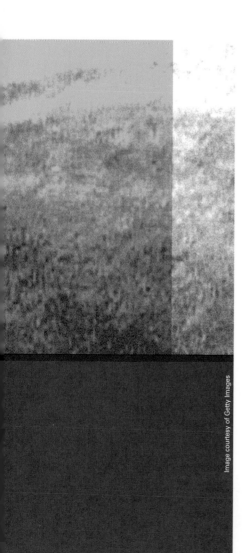

13

Speed Effects

As an effects junkie, one of the first things you'll want to do is alter the speed at which clips play. Final Cut Pro won't let you down: you can make clips slow down, speed up, or freeze, as well as create time-remap speed effects like those you see in feature films. Although FCP makes these effects easy to accomplish, there are some subtleties you'll want to understand and some pitfalls you'll want to avoid. That's where this chapter comes in.

Speed Overview

You can perform a number of basic tasks to affect the speed of a clip:

- Speed up a clip to create time-lapse effects

- Slow down a clip to produce a slow-motion effect

- Freeze a clip to make a video still or freeze frame

Let's consider some instances where you'd use a speed effect.

WHY USE SPEED EFFECTS?

There are lots of reasons for slowing down and speeding up clips. Here are a few common scenarios:

- You're working on a music video and have used all of your B-roll except for one shot. There's a hole in your sequence, but the remaining shot is too short to fill it. You could make the short clip fill the gap by slowing it down with a Fit to Fill edit.

- You have a shot of people walking down a busy street and want to slow down the clip to show details of the busy people in constant motion. You'd create this type of slow-motion effect with the Speed dialog box.

- You locked down an hour-long shot on a moonrise and want to speed up the clip to make the moon move across the sky in just a few seconds. For this-time-lapse effect, you can also use the Speed dialog box.

- You're working on a snowboarding piece and want to have the boarder's mid-air trick be slo-mo and the landing be high speed. This is a time remap (or variable-speed) effect.

We'll look at each of these speed effects in this chapter.

Speed Controls

Final Cut Pro offers several basic tools and techniques for altering a clip's speed. Controlling speed effectively boils down to using the right tool for the job. Let's first look at the tools.

- **Fit to Fill edit:** A clip's speed is determined by the duration between the set In and Out points in the Viewer and the In and Out points in the Canvas (see Figures 13-1 and 13-2). This is a great way to fill any gaps with B-roll, like areas between beats in a music video.
- **Speed dialog box:** This is the yeoman's way to create speed effects. Here you can enter precise percentages and durations to control constant speed, as well as make a clip play in reverse.
- **Time Remap:** This is FCP's killer set of speed controls (new in FCP 4), which includes a tool that helps you variably control a clip's speed (see Figure 13-3).
- **Freeze frame:** You can create a freeze frame with either the Modify menu or by time remapping.

Image courtesy of Getty Images www.gettyimages.com (ev02117/Photodisc)

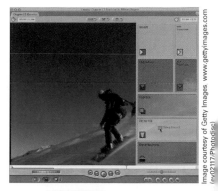

FIGURE 13-1
The Canvas Edit Overlay displays the green Fit to Fill edit area where you can drag and drop a clip.

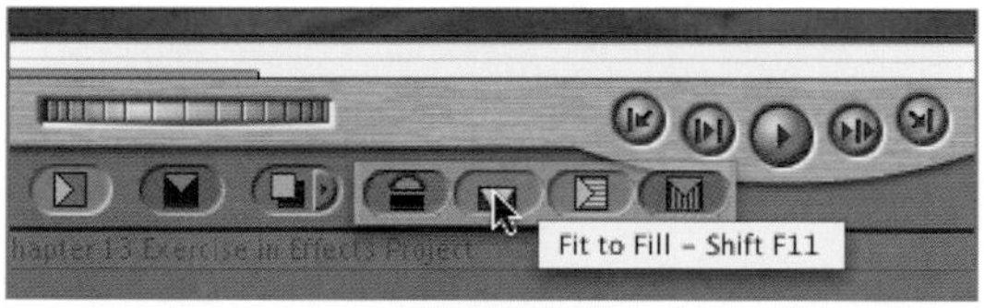

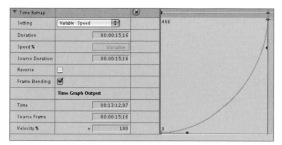

FIGURE 13-2
Click the tiny arrow next to the Replace Edit button in the Canvas and hold down the mouse button. Additional choices pop up, including Superimpose and Fit to Fill.

METHODS OF SPEED CONTROL

FCP gives you two main methods of speed control: constant and variable.

- **Constant:** A clip slows down, speeds up, or plays in reverse at a fixed speed. The clip will have a new duration, depending on whether frames were added (as in a slow-motion effect) or subtracted (as in a sped-up effect).

  You can enable constant speed control in a few different ways:

  - Use a Fit to Fill edit to automatically create a constant speed effect.
  - Use the Speed dialog box.
  - In the Time Remap section of the Motion tab, use the Setting menu to select Constant Speed.
- **Variable:** The duration of the clip does not change, but source frames are remapped to frames earlier or later

FIGURE 13-3
Here's the Time Remap section of the Motion tab.

tip

If you're in Constant Speed mode and smooth just one of the time remap keyframes, you'll have an instant variable-speed effect.

than the original. The resulting frames are stretched out over time. There are three main places to work on a variable-speed effect:

- The Timeline: You can use the Time Remap tool in the Timeline to create a variable-speed effect.

- The Keyframe Editor: Use the Time Remap, Pen, or Selection tool to precisely adjust the effect (see Figure 13-4).

- The Time Graph in the Motion tab: You can work on the velocity of a variable-speed effect in the Motion tab. Use the Pen tool to set keyframes.

Now we'll touch on the tools individually, with exercises for each one to get you more familiar with the various speed techniques. You'll first work on the simplest way to affect speed, Fit to Fill.

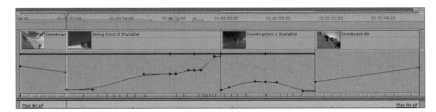

FIGURE 13-4
The Keyframe Editor is a great way to work with variable-speed effects.

FIT TO FILL

tip

You can smooth keyframes for speed effects in the Keyframe Editor or the Time Graph in the Motion tab. Just Control + click on the keyframe and choose Smooth.

Our first stop on the speed roadmap is the Fit to Fill edit. This is an editing function where you pick In and Out points in both the Viewer and the Canvas.

A Fit to Fill is easy to do, as the edit function itself decides just how fast or slow your clip will become. Because Fit to Fill does the calculations for you, you'll never get an "insufficient content" warning or the like. The duration of the set In and Out points in the Viewer and Canvas determines just how the speed effect will be applied. Here are a couple of typical scenarios:

- A short duration in the Viewer and a long duration in the Canvas will result in the clip being slowed down.

- A long duration in the Viewer and a short duration in the Canvas will result in the clip being sped up.

Performing a Fit to Fill edit

It's easy to make a Fit to Fill edit for a speed effect:

1. Mark In and Out points both in the Viewer and the Canvas.

2. Drag and drop the clip into the green Fit to Fill Canvas Overlay or press Shift ⏐ F11.

3. The clip will then be added to the Timeline with a speed effect determined by the Fit to Fill edit.

Let's now do a quick exercise to get you up to speed (pun intended) with this tool.

EXERCISE 13-1: PERFORMING A FIT TO FILL

In this exercise you'll be doing Fit to Fill edits to choose the precise visual content you want to show for each musical phrase.

I'll show a cool trick I use to cut music to the beat. You'll also learn how to alter a Fit to Fill edit once it's in place. This technique of placing Add Edits (also called "splices") on the fly is a fast way to set boundaries for Fit to Fill and Replace edits for cranking out music videos and musical montages. The end result is cutting to the beat with the option of speed effects (Fit to Fill) or regular speed (Replace Edit).

Open the Chapter 13 bin and then the Chapter 13 Sequences bin. Double-click on the Chapter 13 Exercise sequence. Move to the Exercise 1 marker. I have some music and some color mattes already edited into the sequence.

1. From the Chapter 13 Clips bin, load the "City Flight" clip into the Viewer and press the X key to mark the clip.

2. Turn off the Auto Select buttons and then park the playhead in the first gap in the Timeline and tap the X key once more to mark the duration of the gap. You now have four points set for the edit.

3. Set the video track location for the edit by clicking the appropriate Destination button, in this case V1.

4. Press Shift + F11 or drag and drop the "City Flight" clip onto the green Canvas Overlay that says "Fit to Fill." The clip now fits into the gap.

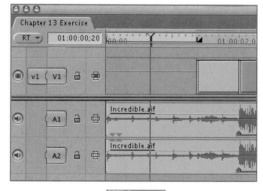

STEP 2

Park the playhead in the first gap in the Timeline and press X.

5. Zoom in on the clip on the Timeline and note the new Speed percentage for the clip. Mine says 725%, so it will not play back in real time. On all but the most powerful Macs, anything over 200% may have to be rendered.

6. Next, you'll do a Fit to Fill edit by simply parking the playhead in the gap and performing the edit. This is generally the fastest way to slam in a speed effect.

   a. Remove edit points in the Timeline by pressing Option + X.

   b. Park the playhead on the first gap in the Timeline.

   c. Load the "Tunnel Vision" clip into the Viewer. Don't set In or Out points.

   d. With the Destination button still engaged to V1, press Shift + F11 to execute the Fit to Fill.

7. Now you'll learn how to use Fit to Fill to quickly change the contents of a clip while adding a speed effect at the same time.

   a. Remove any edit points on the Timeline by pressing Option + X.

   b. Park the playhead anywhere on the first color matte.

   c. Load the "NYC Drive" clip into the Viewer. Don't set In or Out points.

   d. Press Shift + F11 to do the Fit to Fill edit. This makes for another high-speed effect.

8. Repeat the process for the next color matte in the Timeline. This time, however, you'll mark In and Out points in the source.

   a. Load the "NYC Peds" clip into the Viewer.

   b. Find the section of the clip where the people are crossing the street (about 5:00 into the clip) and mark an In point.

   c. Press Shift + Right Arrow to move forward 1:00 and set the Out point.

   d. Press Shift + F11. Since the 1:00 duration was shorter than the color matte it replaced, this is a slow-motion effect.

9. The final step of this exercise will show you how to apply Add Edits on the fly to the musical beats on a dummy video track — in our case, the last color matte in the sequence.

   a. Perform a mark clip for the color matte by parking the playhead on it and pressing the X key.

b. Be sure you're set to loop playback by checking he View menu. If Loop Playback isn't checked, select it in the menu or press Control + L.

c. Play back this section of music a couple of times and tap your foot to get into the rhythm.

d. Hold down the Control key and begin tapping the V key every 4 or 8 beats — your choice here. Make two or three Add Edits. Add Edits are now displayed in the Timeline wherever you marked them on the fly.

e. For each section, perform a Fit to Fill for any of the newly spliced color mattes using any of the methods you've learned so far. Use clips from the Chapter 13 Clips bin. Set the In and Out points from the Viewer to make both slow and fast motion effects.

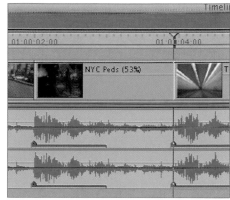

STEP 8d

Press Shift + F11 to do a Fit to Fill edit.

10. You'll now tidy up the edits you just made. To turn on Audio Waveforms (keyboard shortcut Command + Option + W), you can use one of two methods:

   - Align the edit to an audio waveform by using the Roll tool. Click the edit point and then drag the edit to the desired waveform.

   - Scrub the playhead to find the actual beat, select the edit and then tap the E key to extend the edit to the edit point.

     If you don't have enough handle to perform either of these trims (which occurs if you mark the entire source clip in the Viewer), you can mark new In and Out points in the Timeline that more precisely match the beat. With the playhead parked on the clip, press F to match-frame the original clip back into the Viewer. Redo the Fit to Fill to fill the new duration by pressing Shift + F11.

11. Render your sequence and then check it out.

So there you have it! A full understanding of how a Fit to Fill edit works and a new technique to help you cut to the beat and make music videos. Let's move on to another great way to make speed effects, using the Speed dialog box.

SPEED DIALOG BOX

Next to a Fit to Fill edit, the Speed dialog box is the simplest way to add a speed effect. There are a couple of "gotchas" that could foil the uninitiated, but I'll point those out. You should first know how to make a speed effect using this method:

1. Select the clip in the Timeline.

2. Go to Modify → Speed or press Command + J. The Speed dialog box launches.

3. In the box, choose the speed percent or duration you want.

4. Click OK to apply the speed effect.

Speed dialog behavior

Making a speed effect using the Speed dialog box has the same result as an Insert edit, in that the duration of the sequence will be affected. After you've built your background track, synched sound elements to visuals, and are building effects vertically, you'll want to avoid this "rippling" behavior, as it can throw off the timing of those synched events (see Figure 13-5).

In the upcoming exercise you'll learn a couple of ways to tame this rippling behavior.

FIGURE 13-5

Here's the Timeline before the slow-motion effect (top). Note the marker that is spanning precisely 5:00. After a slow-motion effect, the adjacent clip is "rippled" to the right down the Timeline (bottom). The adjacent clip now extends beyond the marker.

Speed dialog options

Before we jump into the next exercise, let's take a look at some of the options in the Speed dialog box (see Figure 13-6).

- **Constant/Variable Speed menu:** Here you can set the speed to constant or variable.

- **Duration:** This is great when you need to give your clip a precise duration.

- **Speed percent:** This option allows you to choose the precise percentage of speed to apply to a clip. A percentage less than 100% will make a slow-motion effect, while a percentage greater than 100% speeds up the clip. The new speed percentage also affects the duration of the clip. For example, if you had a :20 source clip and set it to run at 200%, the duration would end up being :10. If you set the same clip to 50% speed, the duration would be :40.

- **Frame Blending:** When you're doing a slow-motion effect, checking this box will make the motion look smoother as it plays back.

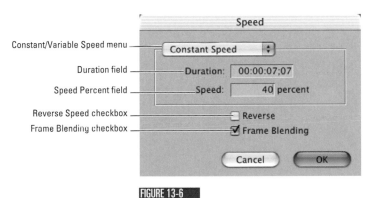

FIGURE 13-6

The options in the Speed dialog box are shown here.

tip

Frame Blending will give you a real-time preview on your video monitor. However, you shouldn't judge any speed effect's quality until you render it at a high-quality setting.

tip

If you experience any anomalies with your speed effect, try adjusting the percentage to a variable of your base time. For NTSC, this would be a multiple of 30, like 60% or 300%. PAL users should use a multiple of 25, like 50% or 500%.

What Is Frame Blending?

Frame blending occurs when you apply a slow-motion (or reverse slow-motion) effect to a clip. New frames must be added to preserve the duration of the effect. If you do not have Frame Blending enabled, these frames are simply duplicated, creating a choppy look.

Frame blending softens the slo-mo look by creating new fields of frames from a blend of the adjacent frames. This behavior is called *interpolation*. The drawback of frame interpolation is that this makes the overall picture softer and "smearier." You have to take that into account when making the choice between smooth or stuttery motion.

To soften a stuttery look you could add a touch of motion blur. I find the best looks are created with high sampling (32) and lower percentages of blur (less than 100), but you can adjust either to taste. Keep in mind that the more sampling you have, the more time you should allow for rendering. Clips slowed down below 20% will especially benefit from a touch of blur. Motion blur can take a long time to render, so just render small sections as you perfect your effect.

You could also use a third-party filter to soften a stuttery effect; see Chapter 14 for details.

EXERCISE 13-2: USING THE SPEED DIALOG BOX

In this exercise you'll get some practice using the Speed dialog box. Double-click on the Chapter 13 Exercise sequence and move to the marker for Exercise 2.

1. Select the "BART Walk By" clip, which has already been placed the Timeline. Note the position of the "BART escalator" clip next to it, extending to the end of the marker.

2. Press Command + J or go to Modify → Speed. The Speed dialog box will launch.

3. In the Speed Percent box, enter 50% and then click OK. As you can see, the effect rippled the other clip down the Timeline.

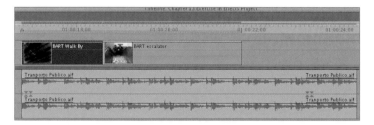

STEP 1

Note the position of the clips in the Timeline.

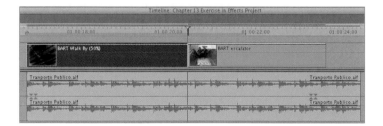

STEP 3

With the first clip slowed down, the other clip has rippled down the Timeline.

Going for a Choppy Look

When applying speed effects, beginning artists often leave Frame Blending checked. However, you might consider unchecking the box if you want to go for a distinctive jittery look.

Filters can also help you enhance a stuttery look. For example, the Strobe filter displays fewer frames per second as it plays in real time. The longer the duration, the choppier the effect. Try it with or without Motion Blur for two different flavors of strobe.

4. Mark In and Out points around the two clips and play In to Out (Shift + \). The clip will play in real time, since its speed is less than 200% of the original.

5. Command + click on the clip "BART Escalator" and choose Speed from the contextual menu to launch the Speed dialog box.

6. Uncheck Frame Blending and then click OK.

7. Render the effect. Note the changes on your video monitor (you won't be able to discern the difference on your computer monitor). You'll see that the effect is a bit choppier.

8. With the clip selected, press Command + J to launch the Speed dialog box.

9. This time, click both the Frame Blending and Reverse checkboxes and then click OK. Play back this real-time effect from In to Out.

10. Return to the Speed dialog box and enter 100% for the Speed Percent. Uncheck the Reverse checkbox. Leave the Frame Blending checkbox checked. Your clip now returns to its normal state.

This completes a basic tour of the Speed dialog box.

EXERCISE 13-3: TAMING RIPPLING BEHAVIOR

In the previous exercise you saw that using the Speed dialog box can cause events to ripple down the Timeline. This exercise will help you avoid this behavior. Open up the Chapter 13 Exercise sequence and move to the marker for Exercise 3.

1. In the Timeline, click on the "Bike Single Track 2" clip to select it.

2. Shift + drag the clip to a video track where there are no other clips in either direction. Here I've placed it on V3.

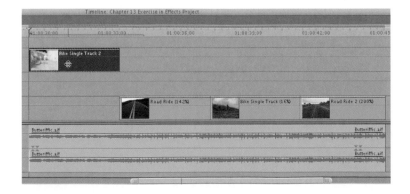

STEP 2

Drag the clip onto a track that has no other clips in it.

3. Lock all other video tracks by Option + clicking the lock on the V3 track.

4. Select the clip and choose Command + J to launch the Speed dialog. Set the Speed Percent to 200% and then click OK. The clip will resize in the Timeline.

5. Unlock all tracks by Option + clicking on the V3 lock once more.

6. Drag the speed-affected clip back into V1. Now you can either move the other clips from the right to close the gap or fill the gap with another clip. Since all of the other clips are synched to the music, it's better to fill the gap.

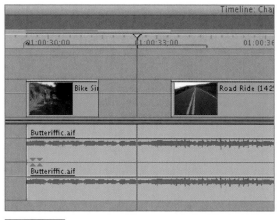

STEP 6

Use a Fit to Fill edit to fill the gap.

7. Load the "Roller Blader CU" clip from the Chapter 13 Clips bin and then set an In point right before her head comes into the frame.

8. Park the playhead in the gap and do a Fit to Fill edit by pressing Shift + F11. Play back your sequence to check it.

There's another way to make a speed change to a clip without affecting its duration or having to drag the clip up to another video track. This is the method I usually use.

1. Tap the Up Arrow to go to the beginning of the clip.

2. Click on the "Bike Single Track" clip (the fourth clip) in the Timeline.

3. Remove any In or Out points (Option + X).

4. Click the Match Frame button in the Canvas, or press the F key.

5. Press Command + J to launch the Speed dialog box. Type 50 for the Speed Percent and then click OK. Your master clip has now been slowed down.

6. In the Viewer, press Shift + I to move the playhead to the In point.

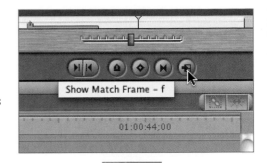

STEP 4
Click the Match Frame button in the Canvas.

7. Press F11 or click the Replace Edit button to Replace Edit the speed-affected clip back into place.

8. Play back the sequence and note that the change did not require moving the clip to another track. Your sequence is still exactly the same duration.

9. If you wish, you can return your master clip to its original speed in the Speed dialog. Click on the Viewer and then press Command + J. Set the Speed Percent back to 100% and click OK.

Being aware of these two simple techniques will put you in command of speed effects, particularly if you're adjusting speed after editing a clip into the Timeline.

Time Remapping

Time remapping, also called *variable speed,* is a welcome addition to Final Cut Pro 4. With time remapping, you can make a clip play back at different speeds at various points in the clip. You can also *dynamically* change the speed of a clip by adding and then smoothing time remap keyframes with Bézier handles. These time remap keyframes are special kinds of keyframes, which I'll explain in detail in just a bit.

Here's a simple time remap scenario: a clip could start playing at regular speed, speed up for a moment, play in slow motion for a few seconds, and then speed up rapidly to the end of a clip. This example describes the classic time remap effect, which you'll get experience with in an upcoming exercise.

tip

If you're not satisfied with the speed-affected content displayed in the Canvas, you can load it into the Viewer and slip the footage by Shift + dragging either In or Out point with the Selection tool or by clicking and dragging either point with the Slip tool.

Feature Request: Time Remapping

During the dog days of FCP 1.01, people were hankering for a new breed of speed effect that started to pop up in movies. Even corporate clients would ask, "Um, Kevin, could you do that speed effect, like... in *The Matrix?*"

Yes, I could. But before FCP 4 it was necessary to use third-party plug-ins, additional applications, or a kooky workaround with the Razor Blade tool I'd rather forget.

How did the folks at Apple know that FCP users wanted this feature? Because they monitor feature-request bulletin boards on the Net.

You, too, can make a feature request. Just log on to one of the Final Cut Pro bulletin boards on the Web. The Los Angeles Final Cut Pro User Group (www.lafcpug.org) presents a yearly poll that's always interesting. The FCP-centric www.2-pop.com/feature-requests.html has a discussion board for feature requests. And there's www.apple.com, which is probably the best place to leave your comments. Go to www.apple.com/support and then go to Discussions. Click Final Cut and then Final Cut Pro. At the top of that page is a Feedback forum where you can submit suggestions and feature requests.

HOW TIME REMAPPING WORKS

With time remapping, you're changing the timing relationship of a source frame as it relates to other frames in a clip. When this timing change occurs, the original frames on either side of the keyframe must be played either faster or slower. The simple process of moving one source frame to an earlier or later time is what sets a time remapping effect in motion (see Figure 13-7).

It's important to understand exactly what you are affecting before you go dragging time remap keyframes up, down, left, and right. Time remap keyframes are a different kind of beast, and the results can be unpredictable if you don't know just what you're doing.

Time remapping and duration

Recall that in constant-speed effects, the duration of the clip is affected. A slow-motion effect will extend the sequence and make the clip longer, while a fast-motion effect will make it shorter.

In any variable-speed effect, you can make as many speed changes as you wish, but the clip's duration will never change. For example, if you wanted to slow a clip down in a certain section, it *must* be sped up elsewhere because all frames must be displayed by the time the clip finishes playing.

There are a number of ways to work on a time remap effect, so before you get going, you need to understand how to read the Time Graph.

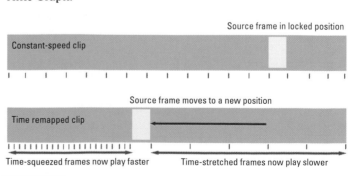

FIGURE 13-7

Original frames either bunch up and play quickly or spread out and play slowly around the source frame's new position.

Viewing the Time Graph in the Motion Tab

You can view the Time Graph in two places: in the Motion tab's Time Remap section and in the Keyframe Editor. Click on the Motion tab and click the triangle next to Time Remap in the Name column to see the graph along with the associated controls (see Figure 13-8).

You'll see controls for some familiar items:

- **Setting:** You can change a constant-speed effect to a variable-speed one with this drop-down menu.

- **Duration:** This is the duration of the clip as displayed in the Timeline.

- **Reverse:** Make a clip play in reverse by checking this box.

- **Frame Blending:** Check this box for a smoother look when playing back slow-motion effects.

You'll also see informational readouts for the following:

- **Speed Percentage:** This shows the speed percentage at the current position of the playhead. It's grayed out if set to Variable Speed.

- **Source Duration:** Displays the original duration of the clip.

- **Time:** This is the current sequence time at the current playhead position.

- **Source Frame:** This is the timecode readout of the source frame that's displayed at the current playhead position.

- **Velocity Percentage:** Shows the rate of speed as a clip changes from one speed to another. This kicks in after you've smoothed the keyframes.

tip

You may have noticed that when you use the Setting menu to change a clip's speed from constant to variable and then play back the clip, no speed effect occurs. This is normal. As a rule, a variable-speed effect cannot occur until you alter at least one Time Remap keyframe.

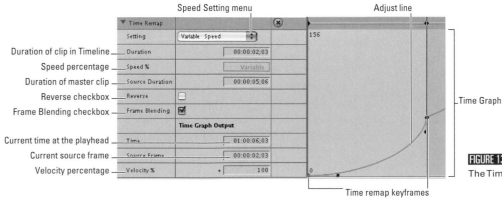

FIGURE 13-8

The Time Graph in the Motion tab.

Viewing the Time Graph in the Keyframe Editor

It's easier to see the variable-speed adjustments you make to clips if you set and adjust Time Remap keyframes with the Time Remap tool in the Timeline's Keyframe Editor. After you've got the process down, you can work more confidently in the Motion tab.

To open the Keyframe Editor, follow these steps:

1. Double-click the clip to load it into the Viewer.

2. Click on the Motion tab and turn down the disclosure triangle next to the Time Remap effect. You'll see the Time Graph and the other controls and readouts. The "gotcha" here is that you *must* have this area open in order to see your Time Graph in the Keyframe Editor.

3. Click the Clip Keyframes control button in the lower-left corner of the Timeline.

4. Control + click the button to see all the displays of the Keyframe Editor. Choose Video → Select All.

5. Widen the Keyframe Editor area by clicking and dragging in the Keyframe Editor column, located to the right of a track's Auto Select button (see Figure 13-9).

6. Control + click in the Keyframe Editor and choose Time Remap → Time Graph. The Time Graph will appear.

With the Selection tool, click and drag in the Keyframe Editor Column to adjust the Keyframe Editor's work area

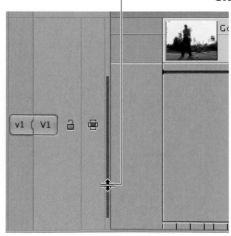

FIGURE 13-9
You can expand the Keyframe Editor's work area.

With the Time Graph up in the Keyframe Editor, you'll get visual cues — in the form of overlays and tool tips — that show you what's going on with the clip as you make your adjustments. The Time Remap tool also constrains vertical and horizontal movement of the source frame's time remap keyframe to help keep keyframe movement precise.

You can also see the distribution of the Speed Indicator tic marks, which indicates how fast a clip is playing back at various points in time. The closer the tic marks are spaced, the faster a clip plays; the farther they're spaced, the slower it will play. If the tic marks are red, that means the clip is playing back in reverse (see Figure 13-10).

Creating speed effects in the Time Graph

Working in the Time Graph in either the Motion tab or the Keyframe Editor, you can begin to shape your time remap effect. Moving a Time Remap keyframe to a new position will automatically make a variable-speed effect.

Two scenarios could arise regarding the positioning of a source frame:

- If a source frame is to be displayed earlier than its original position, the remaining frames in the clip must be stretched out, playing in slow motion until the clip's Out point is reached. The frames before the original source frame must now play faster in order to be through in time to display the frame chosen by the newly set keyframe.

- If a source frame is to be displayed later than its original position, the remaining frames in the clip must be bunched up until the clip's Out point is reached. The frames before the original source frame must now play more slowly to fill up the time before displaying the source frame chosen by the time remap keyframe.

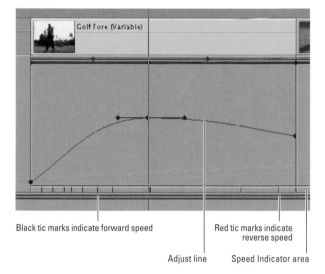

FIGURE 13-10

The Time Graph in the Keyframe Editor.

Black tic marks indicate forward speed

Red tic marks indicate reverse speed

Adjust line

Speed Indicator area

Understanding the Time Graph

The dominant feature of the Time Graph is its adjust line. It's blue in the Keyframe Editor and green in the Motion tab.

Unlike other adjust lines, the Time Graph's adjust line is displayed at a 45-degree angle, extending from left to right. You should also see two keyframes — representing the first and last frames of your clip — already set in place as a default. If your clip has been trimmed or captured with handles, you'll have four time remap keyframes.

In a time remap effect, the adjust line changes angles and directions with each adjustment you make to the time remap keyframes you add.

Look on the left side of the Time Graph (see Figure 13-11). The vertical rise in the graph represents the individual frames of the clip. You should see the first-frame and last-frame numbers here. The horizontal run represents the frames in the sequence.

tip

Hold down the Command key as you drag the Time Remap tool if you want to engage "gear down" behavior to make precise adjustments.

note

Just to get the nomenclature straight, source frames are the actual video frames, and time remap keyframes are the items that control the frames' movement over time. It follows that every source frame has the potential of carrying a time remap keyframe.

When you drag a Time Remap keyframe up or down, you're moving the source frame at that position to another position. If you move the keyframe left or right, you're moving the time position of that source frame.

As you view time remap effects, it's crucial to note that the angle and the direction of the Time Graph adjust line indicates that — in that section of the clip — a clip is playing normally, slower, faster, forward, in reverse, or is frozen.

This may make better sense to you observing the angle of the adjust line right in the Keyframe Graph, so I'll touch on that in a minute. First, let's get down to the business of adding time remap keyframes to source frames and then moving them to adjust the speed effect.

Adding time remap keyframes to source frames

As you now know, you need to move source frames of a clip to a different place to create a time remap effect. How? You must first emblazon them with a time remap keyframe. Each time remap keyframe represents a place in *sequence time* for one of the source frames in your clip.

Here's how to add time remap keyframes to your source frames:

- You can add time remap keyframes in the Timeline with the Time Remap tool by first locating the frame, and then clicking directly in the clip. (See Figure 13-12.)

- In the Keyframe Editor or Motion tab, click on the Time Graph's adjust line with the Pen tool.

tip

If you hold down the Shift key while using the Time Remap tool, you can scrub through the clip to more accurately find the source frame you want to affect.

This Time Remap keyframe represents the placement of the final source frame of the clip on the sequence.

This time remap keyframe represents the first source frame of the clip.

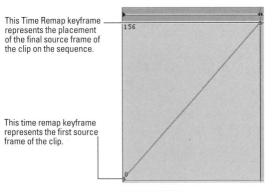

FIGURE 13-11
Click on the adjust line to add Time Remap keyframes.

FIGURE 13-12
The Time Remap tool provides a readout in the Timeline.

Moving time remap keyframes

Now that you know how to add time remap keyframes to source frames, let's turn to moving them to another place in sequence time, which is vital for controlling the speed effect. There are two ways to do that: you can either move a source frame from another time to the playhead or move a source frame to a new time. Let's look at both of these methods.

To move a source frame from another time to the playhead, move the time remap keyframe up or down at that point in time. A new source frame is "slipped" through that point in the sequence time (at the current position of the playhead), kicking the original source frame — which used to be at the playhead position — to an earlier (up) or later (down) sequence time.

You can move the keyframe in a couple of ways:

- Click and drag the keyframe up or down with the Pen or Selection tool. A tool tip will show the source frame's position offset (see Figure 13-13).

or

- Click the Time Remap tool and then drag left or right. The keyframe will move up and down in the Time Graph. Helpful tool tips and overlays will tell you what's going on with the position of the source frame (see Figure 13-14).

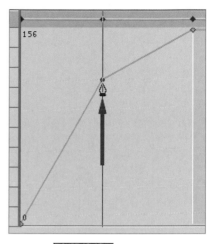

FIGURE 13-13

With the Pen tool, click and drag upward to make the time remap keyframe represent a later source frame.

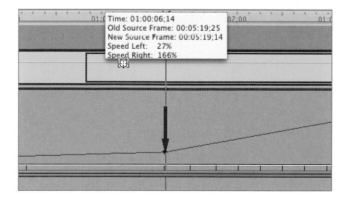

FIGURE 13-14

Click and drag to the left to make the time remap keyframe move down to represent an earlier source frame.

To move a source frame to a new time, you'll move the source frame left or right to a new place in the sequence time. There are a couple of ways to do this:

- Click and drag the keyframe left or right with the Pen or Selection tool. I recommend holding down the Shift key as you drag to see both the frame number and the source frame's position offset.

- Hold down the Option key and then click the Time Remap tool at the keyframe position. Drag left or right, and the keyframe will move left or right along with the playhead. (See Figure 13-15.)

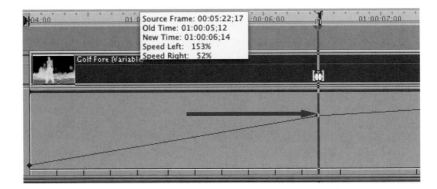

FIGURE 13-15
With the Time Remap tool, you can move the keyframe to the right to make a source frame appear at a later sequence time.

Adjusting the speed of a time remap effect

After adding a time remap effect to a clip, you'll invariably have to tweak it. For this, you'll need to work in the Time Graph. Typically you will want to adjust at least one of two time remap keyframes to make a clip play back a bit faster, or slower.

- To make a clip play faster between two time remap keyframes, raise the second one a bit, so that the adjust line is between 0 and 45 degrees in the Time Graph. That portion of the clip will now play faster. However, there is a new source frame at the second keyframe, and the remainder of the clip will play slower after that keyframe.

- To make a clip play slower between two source-frame keyframes, lower the second one until the adjust line is between 45 and 90 degrees. That portion of the clip will now play slower. However, there is a new source frame at the second keyframe, and the remainder of the clip will now play faster after that source-frame keyframe.

- To adjust a speed effect that plays in reverse, you'll apply the same principles as above, but you'll be setting the adjust line to be between 90 and 180 degrees.

- If you want a speed effect that freezes on a source frame, you'll need to make sure that they are at the same value between keyframes and that the adjust line is perfectly horizontal at 90 degrees.

Therefore, if the Time Graph Line is

- **0 to 45 degrees:** The clip plays back at faster-than-normal speed.

- **45 degrees:** The clip plays back at normal speed.

- **45 to 90 degrees:** The clip plays back in slow motion.

- **Straight line:** The clip plays back as a freeze frame.

- **90 to 135 degrees:** The clip plays back in reverse in slow motion.

- **135 to 180 degrees:** The clip plays back in reverse in fast motion.

tip

If you click and drag up or down on the adjust line between any two time remap keyframes, the source frames can be changed to earlier or later source frames at those positions by their relative amounts.

Sharp vs. smooth time shifts

In time remapping, you have the choice of using keyframes that are either corner points or smooth. If you use corner-point keyframes, the shifting of time is abrupt. If you smooth a time remap keyframe (do it just as you would with any other keyframe), you can make the speed of objects moving through the frame shift gradually.

EXERCISE 13-4: TIME REMAP EFFECTS

In this exercise you'll create two time remap speed effects. The first is the "bullet time" effect like the one you've seen in Hollywood features such as *The Matrix*, on broadcast television, and coming soon to a corporate video near you. In the second effect, the clip plays forward and then backward. You'll also take a shot at smoothing, or *ramping*, the speed of the effect. These clips have been slowed down in camera, so you'll be performing additional speed effects on them.

Open the Chapter 13 Exercise sequence and move to the marker for Exercise 4. A clip and some audio are already edited into the Timeline.

1. Open the Keyframe Editor by clicking on the Clip Keyframes button. If necessary, widen the window by clicking and dragging upward in the Keyframe Editor column.

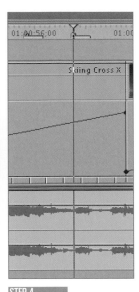

STEP 4
Place the playhead on the "Downbeat" marker.

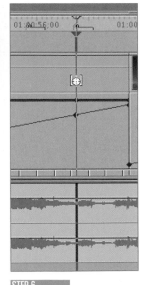

STEP 6
Set the keyframe for the source frame.

2. When you first open the Keyframe Graph, you won't see the Time Graph until you set your first keyframe. However, it's possible to see the Time Graph in the Keyframe Editor before setting a keyframe. Do this with the two clips you'll be working on, as follows:

   a. Load the "Skiing Cross X" clip into the Viewer.

   b. Click on the Motion tab.

   c. Turn down the triangle for Time Remap.

   d. Control + click in the Keyframe Editor and choose Time Remap → Time Graph. The graph for the clip will appear in the Keyframe Editor.

   e. Repeat the process for the adjacent "Snowboarders 1" clip.

3. Play the Exercise 4 sequence and listen for the first two obvious musical cues, the "bass stop" (about 5:18 into the music) and then the "downbeat," where the guitar comes in the second time (about 6:20 into the music). Make two markers in the Timeline to note these cues. Name them "Bass Stop" and "Downbeat."

4. You'll be concentrating on the "Skiing Cross X" clip first. Place the playhead on the "Downbeat" marker. The skier has finished his trick and is now out of the picture.

5. Select the Time Remap tool in the Tool Palette or type S + S + S.

6. Click the Time Remap tool at the playhead position to set the keyframe for the source frame.

7. Click and drag to the left to bring the second skier back into the middle of the screen. (You just slid the source frame to an earlier time.)

8. Perform a mark clip and then play back this real-time effect from In to Out.

9. Now you'll make that "bullet time" effect, where the clip plays at regular speed, slows for a bit, and then speeds to the end. You could make this effect in a couple of different ways, but the method you'll use here will first move the time remap keyframe to the "Bass Stop" marker. You'll then set a second keyframe in the next step. You're doing it this way to get experience with both moving a source frame to the playhead and moving the keyframe to another time.

   a. Hold down the Option key.

b. Using the Time Remap tool, click and drag the clip so that the time remap (source frame) is newly aligned to the "Bass Stop" marker.

c. Once the keyframe is lined up with the marker, let go of the mouse button.

10. Now you'll add another time remap keyframe back where you started. You're doing this to readjust the source frame back on the "Downbeat" marker. Move the playhead there now.

11. With the Time Remap tool, click and drag to the left once more. The keyframe will move downward in place. In the Canvas, the new frames pass through the playhead position as you drag. Choose a new source frame for the "Downbeat" marker. In this case, bring the skier back into the frame.

12. Play In to Out and evaluate your "bullet time" effect. To fine-tune the effect, Control + click on each keyframe and set it to Smooth. Make the speed change gradually rather than abruptly. I think you'll notice the difference right away. I suggest you make the Keyframe Editor a bit wider to make more precise adjustments.

13. Move the playhead to the next clip, "Snowboarders 1." You'll do another time remap effect here. With the Selection tool, double-click on the clip to load it into the Viewer.

14. This time you'll work in the Viewer to complete the effect. Click on the Motion tab to get rolling. In the Motion tab, note that the clip has been trimmed, and that there are four keyframes already in the Time Graph by default. This is normal for a trimmed clip.

15. In the Timeline, scrub the playhead in the Time Ruler to find a beat in the music about midway through the clip. Leave the playhead in place to mark the beat.

16. In the Motion Tab, click on the adjust line with the Pen tool to set a time remap keyframe. You can adjust this keyframe's vertical position just a wee bit, to frame 50. This is where the snowboarder comes close to the camera, matching the beat of the music.

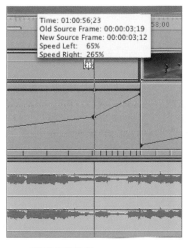

Time: 01:00:56;23
Old Source Frame: 00:00:03;19
New Source Frame: 00:00:03;12
Speed Left: 65%
Speed Right: 265%

STEP 7
Click and drag to the left.

Skiing Cross X

00:00:03;19

Image courtesy of Getty Images, www.gettyimages.com/ev02128/Photodisc

STEP 11
In the Canvas, the new frames pass through the playhead position as you drag.

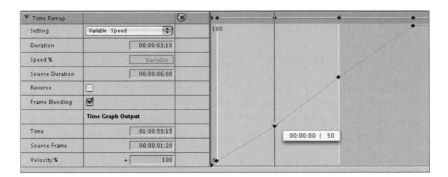

Adjust the time remap keyframe's position in the Keyframe Graph.

17. With the Pen tool, drag the last time remap keyframe downward until the keyframe represents the first source frame. A tool tip will pop up when you engage the Shift key while dragging. Careful there! It's possible to set errant keyframes if you drag even a bit to the left or right. If that happens, perform an Edit → Undo and drag the keyframe down once more.

18. Mark In to Out and then play back the clip from In to Out by pressing Shift + \ (backslash). The snowboarders should move forward and then backward. Note that the entire clip did not display and that the remainder of the clip's frames were compensated for beyond the trim points. This is how you can mold a time remap effect to do precisely what you want.

19. After you've played In to Out, return to the Keyframe Graph and smooth the time remap keyframes. Then preview the clip once more. You should see the time shifting gradually, rather than abruptly. See which flavor of time shifting you like best. There are two more clips here that you can use to try out more speed effects if you wish.

20. Save the project. You're done.

Good going! You've made two time remap speed effects.

Video looping effect

You can make a groovy VJ scratching, looping video effect with the "Play forward/Play reverse" technique you learned in steps 15-17 above. There, you moved through every frame forward and then backward as the clip played. For the VJ scratching effect you'd do the same thing, except you'd go back and forth between some action within the clip, much like a hip-hop DJ would scratch a record.

tip

If you're still having trouble understanding the concept of time remap keyframes, reread the above section and continue experimenting on your own. If the light doesn't go on immediately, that's completely normal. My suggestion? Walk away from your computer — go catch a movie and it will hit you like a ton of bricks at e bus stop on the way home. Worked for me!

You can create a very similar effect as follows:

1. Choose a clip that has some sort of action in it that you'd like to loop. Load it into the Viewer if you wish to work in the Motion tab.

2. Working in the Keyframe Editor's Time Graph or in the Motion tab, set a keyframe where the action you'd like to loop begins. You can use the Pen tool to get this done quickly (see Figure 13-16).

3. Play forward until you see the action end and then click on the adjust line with the Pen tool (see Figure 13-17).

4. Move the playhead forward the amount of time you'd like to elapse before you'd like to see the beginning of the action again.

5. With the Pen tool, click and drag the adjust line downward until you reach the original source frame.

6. Repeat this process to have as many loops, or "VJ scratches," as you desire.

FIGURE 13-16
Set the first keyframe where the action begins. The martial artist is about to leap.

FREEZE FRAMES

The freeze frame is the unsung hero of speed control. Here are a few uses for freeze frames:

- A still frame with a bit of Gaussian Blur can be used as a background for titles or for a DVD menu.

- A still frame can be exported to another program, such as Adobe Photoshop, for further effects application and masking.

- You can use the still in a "freeze-come-to-life" effect where, for example, a subject moves across the frame, is frozen for a moment, and then continues on.

With FCP 4, you now have two ways to make a freeze frame. Let's look at those methods right now.

FIGURE 13-17
Make another time remap keyframe at the end of the action. Here the martial artist has finished his move and landed.

Making a freeze frame with the Modify menu

You can easily make a freeze frame out of any frame of video. Here's how:

1. Park the playhead on the frame you want to freeze.

2. Go to Modify → Make Freeze Frame, or press Shift + N. The freeze frame loads into the Viewer.

3. You're now free to edit the freeze frame back into the Timeline.

Scrub Speed Effects

Back in the eighties, we used to make speed effects by rolling the source tape deck more slowly or quickly and then recording the resulting signal on the record deck. Yes, you needed *at least* two tape decks to do speed effects in linear editing. Pretty clunky, considering that now all you have to do is press Command + J or change some time remap keyframes in Final Cut Pro!

The idea behind the technique I'm about to share with you is along the same lines, except you use FCP's Timeline as your source deck.

The plan here is to record Timeline playback while "scrubbing" the Timeline. After you've recorded your Speed-Scrub effects, you just Log and Capture the piece back into FCP. Sounds weird? Just try it! This is a very cool technique you can add to your arsenal, and there are lots of variations to try.

- **Scrub Forward or Reverse:** You can add a more random look to your speed effects by scrubbing from right to left on the Timeline. Scrub either slow or fast, in forward or reverse, smooth or jagged, logarithmic or linear. Mix it up — you get the idea. This looks a lot different than time remapping because it has a much more "random" feel to it.

- **Hyper-Montage:** You can create a montage of images that fly by at blinding speed. Just put as many images as you can in the Timeline, zoom way out, and then scrub rapidly, yet as smoothly as possible.

- **Scrub "Scratching":** When you click and drag to an interesting portion of the Timeline with the playhead, move your wrist back and forth to make a quick reverse and forward movement you can repeat. This is akin to "scratching" a record like a hip-hop DJ.

- **Loop:** Scrub to a section of the Timeline, then click back to where you originally started dragging on the Timeline Ruler and scrub to the same ending point.

- **Video Stutter:** Tap the Left and Right Arrow keys to move one frame at a time forward or reverse. The Up and Down Arrow keys will move you from edit to edit as you record.

- **Super Slo-Mo:** If you zoom in on you clip in the Timeline, you'll have more control over a single image when slowly scrubbing to do a slow-motion effect.

Using time remapping to create a freeze frame

You can also make a freeze frame with time remapping:

1. In the Timeline, locate the frame you want to freeze with the playhead.

2. Set a time remap keyframe at that position.

3. Move the playhead forward as far as you want the freeze frame to last.

4. With the Pen tool, click and drag the Time Graph adjust line until it is horizontal. The source frames for the two time remap keyframes should be exactly the same.

5. Trim off the frames that are not freeze frames.

6. Close any gaps in the Timeline if you need to.

7. Load the clip into the Viewer, go to the Time Remap section, and turn off frame blending. This should sharpen up the frame.

Troubleshooting

When working with speed effects and stills, you may experience a few common maladies. These are all easy to work through, as you're now familiar with the inner workings of speed effects.

Control + clicking in the Keyframe Editor didn't bring up the Time Graph

Turn down the disclosure triangle in the Motion tab first. Then you should be able to select the Time Graph from the Keyframe Graph's contextual menu.

A freeze frame looks great on the computer monitor but is shaky on a video monitor

This is probably the most common problem with making stills that have significant motion in them. The reason this jittering happens is that the freeze frame is a really a still frame made from duplicated, interlaced fields. If there is significant motion in the original footage, the fields may jitter when viewed on a video monitor. Since you can't see interlaced playback on a computer monitor, the jitter is undetectable unless you're monitoring your work as you go or when it's too late and you've mastered your show to tape. Another great case for monitoring your work as you go.

Do the following for a quick fix:

1. Select the clip in the Timeline.

2. Go to Effects → Video Filters → Video → De-interlace.

3. Load the clip into the Viewer by double-clicking on it.

4. In the Filters tab, choose Lower (Even) from the Field drop-down menu.

5. Re-render the freeze frame.

6. Output again.

There's a "hitch" when a clip goes into or comes out of a freeze

If you see a hitch when a clip goes into a "freeze-come to life" effect, just trim the edit back one frame to the left on the outgoing side. If you see one when the clip begins playing again after the freeze, trim the incoming side one frame to the right. Loop around the edit to make sure that it plays back without any hitches. Another way to beat this problem is to do this effect with time remapping.

Time remapping causes a portion of a clip to slow down

Let's say you want to speed up a clip from 0% to 600% over time, but time remapping makes you slow the clip down in another place to compensate. You don't want to do this, and you need to use all of the footage in the clip. Is there any way you can accelerate the clip from beginning to end without worrying about slowing it down somewhere else?

Technically, you can't. However, it is possible to compensate the other side of the time remap keyframe with a freeze and then trim it off once you've reached your 600% speed requirement. If you understand the way time remapping works, this should make sense. You're going to move the source frame representing the clip's final frame to an earlier place in the clip. This will automatically speed up playback.

Here are the steps for working in the Motion tab:

1. In the Motion tab, click and drag the final time remap keyframe to the very top of the Time Graph.

2. Begin sliding this time remap keyframe — which represents the final frame of the clip — to the left, making the adjust line steeper. This leaves behind a straight line — which represents a freeze — as you drag.

3. After you've reached the velocity you want, just trim off the rest of the clip (which is a freeze frame) with any of the trim tools. Close any gaps if necessary.

The Time Remap tool can also perform these functions. A good reason to use it is to view the helpful tool tips that pop up, including a readout showing the percentage for velocity.

As you can see, in time remapping the duration of the speed effect must be the same length as the clip, but it can be trimmed after the fact.

Slow-motion frames are choppy, even when Frame Blending is off

You can add a bit of motion blur to make up for not having enough frames to simulate an in-camera slow-motion effect (where more frames are cranked through the camera than the native speed). If you still aren't satisfied, you can buy a third-party plug-in like BCC Optical Flow, Twixtor, or ReTimer to help you create a much better slow-motion effect. See the next chapter for information on plug-ins.

Wrap-up

With speed effects under your belt, you can now work with just about any effect imaginable in Final Cut Pro. There's only one more major skill to learn before you become really solid in your effects creation capabilities, and that's the ability to integrate other applications in your effects workflow. Let's move on to the final chapter.

WHAT'S IN THIS CHAPTER

- Using Adobe Photoshop with Final Cut Pro
- Using third-party applications with Final Cut Pro
- Adding unique effects using plug-ins

14
Integrating Other Applications with FCP

You're now aware of all the awesome effects you can create with Final Cut Pro. But you've also learned that FCP can't do everything. Fortunately, you can extend FCP's functionality tenfold by adding filters called plug-ins, which allow FCP to perform feats it can't do by itself. You can also enhance FCP's capabilities by integrating files created in programs like LiveType, Adobe Photoshop, and Boris RED. Let's get going with some techniques that will expand your effects-creation repertoire.

Using Photoshop for Video Effects

When you're creating effects in Final Cut Pro, you can take advantage of an amazing compositing tool for still images: Adobe Photoshop. With Photoshop, you can create an array of looks for video stills, graphic elements, lower-third elements, and the like. You can also create mattes, perform color correction, and create tints. This section will give you some tips for incorporating elements from Photoshop into your FCP effects creations.

The current version of the program is called Photoshop CS. This version of the software offers some niceties for the video editor, including support for non-square pixels, text on a Bézier path, 16-bit image support, and color matching capabilities.

Because many video graphics professionals own a copy of Photoshop, this chapter will present techniques for incorporating Photoshop graphics into Final Cut Pro projects. If you don't own Photoshop, skip ahead to the sections that describe other applications you can use to extend FCP's capabilities.

IMPORTING A FREEZE FRAME INTO PHOTOSHOP

You can export a video still, or freeze frame, from FCP into Photoshop, apply filters or layer effects, and then bring it back into FCP. Here's how:

1. In Final Cut Pro, park on the frame you wish to export. Press Shift + N to load the freeze frame.

2. Go to File → Export → Using QuickTime Conversion, and then choose Still Image from the Format menu.

3. Click the Options button to choose the format for your still frame. I recommend Photoshop or PICT. Name and save the still to an appropriate folder. Don't worry about any of the other options right now; just click OK.

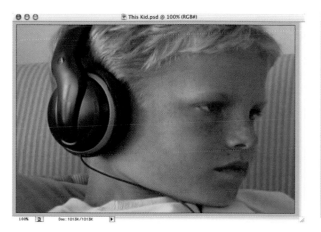
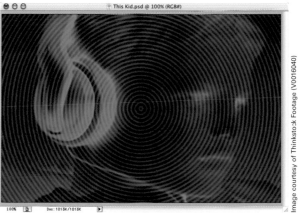

Image courtesy of Thinkstock Footage (V0016040)

Image courtesy of Thinkstock Footage (V0016040)

4. Name the file, choose a folder to save it to, and then click the Save button.

5. Drag and drop the file onto the Photoshop icon. (If you're not working in Photoshop CS, the image will look a bit squished, but don't worry — this is the way the frame is supposed to look when you look at it in a square-pixels file.)

6. Create the effect of your choice in Photoshop (see Figure 14-1).

7. Go to File → Save As and name the file.

8. Import the copy back into Final Cut Pro and place your new freeze frame into the Timeline.

Now let's look at another trick you can do with Photoshop: making an alpha channel for your video still. With an alpha channel, you can create transparency behind your freeze frame to change the background. In the following exercise you'll learn how to make an embedded alpha channel.

FIGURE 14-1

The original frame that was exported from FCP is shown on the left. On the right, a filter has been added in Photoshop to create an effect.

note

If you don't own Photoshop, you can try out a version at www.adobe. com/products/tryadobe/ main.jhtml.

EXERCISE 14-1: CREATING AN EMBEDDED ALPHA CHANNEL IN A FREEZE FRAME

Locate the Chapter 14 Sequences bin in the Chapter 14 bin, and open the Chapter 14 Exercise sequence. A clip has been loaded into the Timeline for you. Park the playhead on the first frame of the sequence.

1. In Final Cut Pro, park on the frame you wish to export — in this case, the first frame of the "Kid Rock" clip. Press Shift + N to load the frame into the Viewer.

2. Export the freeze by performing steps 1 through 5 of "Importing a Freeze Frame into Photoshop."

tip

An excellent online resource for Photoshop video techniques is www.kenstone.net. Ken has a great library of resources and tips about using Photoshop and FCP.

tip

If you're not happy with your original selection, press Command + D to deselect it.

3. Once the still is in Photoshop, you can create an alpha channel to knock out the background. With the Magic Wand tool, click on the blue couch; you'll see the "crawling ants" show up in all areas that are a similar blue. Shift + click a different area of the couch, and continue to select the rest of the blues on the couch.

4. Shift + click in the area underneath the headphones to select that area as well.

5. Change the Tolerance parameter from 32 to about 8, and then Shift + click the wall areas. (You changed the tolerance so that you could select the color of the wall, but not the boy's light-colored hair.)

6. The "crawling ants" tracing the boy indicate a mask selection. To save the selection in order to define an alpha channel, click the button at the bottom of the Channels palette.

7. Click on the Channels palette. You'll see that in addition to an image in each of the Red, Green, and Blue channels, there's a new one called "Alpha 1." This is the alpha channel you just created. To see how your alpha channel looks, click on the eyeball (indicating layer visibility) in the palette next to the alpha channel layer. It should show up in red.

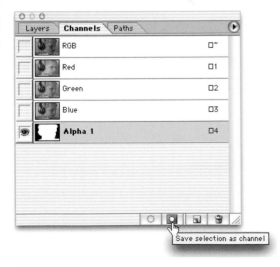

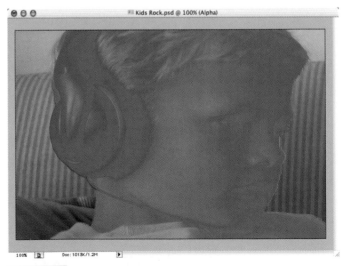

STEP 6
Click this button in the Channels palette to save the selection and define an alpha channel.

STEP 7
Click the eyeball icon. The alpha channel shows up in red tones.

8. Press Command + D to deselect the mask.

9. In the Channels palette, turn off the visibility eyeballs for the Red, Green, and Blue channels, leaving only the alpha channel's eyeball turned on. The image should be black-and-white. The alpha channel is the reverse of what you need, so select the channel by clicking on its name and then press Command + I to invert it.

Press Command + I to invert the alpha channel.

10. With the alpha channel still selected, you'll now use Photoshop's Paintbrush tool to touch up some rough edges and holes in the matte.

    a. Locate the areas of the matte you need to work on by zooming in on the image with the Zoom tool.

    b. Turn on the visibility eyeballs for the RGB channels, but do not select any of the channels.

11. Click on the Paintbrush tool to select it. Paint with black or white to touch up the matte until you've smoothed any rough edges around the boy's mouth and around the back of his head near the headphones.

12. After you're satisfied with your paint job, you'll need to save your selection again to make a second, improved alpha channel.

    a. Click the Save Selection as Channel button once more. An alpha channel called "Alpha 2" will appear in the Channels palette.

    b. Click and drag the Alpha 1 channel into the trash at the bottom of the Channels palette. Alpha 2 will now be the presiding alpha channel.

note

Painting on the alpha channel while viewing the RGB channels can be disorienting at first. Black paint appears as red, and white paint seems to erase black. Don't worry; you'll get used to it. The red (sometimes called "rubylith") is supposed to assist you in making a better matte. You can change the color and opacity of the rubylith by double-clicking on the Quick Mask icon.

tip

When you work with non-square-pixel files in Photoshop CS, you'll see your image in a simulated square-pixel representation. This mode does not provide an accurate view of aliasing, so if you're doing detail work such as painting a matte in the alpha channel, you can temporarily work with the simulation preview turned off. Go to Image → Pixel Aspect Ratio → Square.

STEP 14
Import the image into FCP and create a composite there.

13. Go to File → Save As to save a copy and leave the original intact. Name it "Image Alpha" or the like.

14. Import the graphic into FCP and place it on a layer above a bold graphic background.

PRESERVING PHOTOSHOP LAYER STYLES

You'll want to use the full complement of layer styles in Photoshop's Layers menu. However, you might be confounded when you import Photoshop layers into FCP and find that the styles disappear.

Here's how to preserve the layer styles:

1. Apply the layer styles you wish to any or all of the layers in your Photoshop comp.

2. Save the file and name it "My Layer Effects_Original."

3. Click the New Layer button at the bottom of the Layers palette to add a new layer for every layer that has a layer effect. Place each new layer directly beneath the previous affected layer.

4. Working from the top layer down, select an affected layer and then click the Link icon next to the blank layer below it.

5. From the palette's shortcut menu, choose Merge Linked. Each pair of layers will be merged into a single layer.

6. Repeat this process until all the affected layers are merged.

7. Go to File → Save As and name the copy "My Layer Effects_Merged." The layer styles are now ready to be imported into FCP.

8. Import the file into a bin in FCP, and then drag and drop the nested sequence into the Timeline. You'll see that the layer styles have been preserved.

tip

If you'd like your Photoshop matte (alpha channel) to have uniformly feathered edges, go to Select → Feather, and then choose the pixel radius from the Feather Selection dialog box. To feather a section of the alpha channel, use a lightly feathered brush or a smudge or blur tool. Zoom in to work with precision.

Adjusting Images for Non-square Pixels

Photoshop CS deals with non-square pixels in a different way from Photoshop 7 and earlier versions. Here's how to work in Photoshop CS when you're creating a still frame or frame or multilayered file that you'll import into FCP:

1. Go to File → New to open the Image Size dialog box.

2. Choose an image size from the Preset Sizes menu to match the native frame size of your FCP sequence (720 x 480 for DV NTSC, for example). You should also choose a preset for title-safe and action-safe guides.

3. If you want to import a freeze frame, then choose File → Place.

4. Save the image and import it into FCP.

The image will now play back in real time in your FCP sequence.

If you're using a pre-CS version of Photoshop, you'll need to start with an adjusted frame size that differs slightly from your native-sized DV or 601 frame:

Format	Native Frame Size	Adjusted Size
NTSC DV	720 x 480	720 x 534
NTSC 601	720 x 486	720 x 540
NTSC DV 16:9	720 x 480 (anamorphic)	864 x 480
NTSC 601 16:9	720 x 486 (anamorphic)	853 x 486
PAL	720 x 576	768 x 576
PAL 16:9	720 x 576 (anamorphic)	1024 x 576

After you've completed your creation in Photoshop at the adjusted size, you'll need to squeeze it to the native frame size. Follow these steps:

1. After saving the image, go to Image → Image Size.

2. In the Image Size dialog box, uncheck Constrain Proportions.

3. Resize the image by entering the dimensions for native frame size.

4. Save this image as a copy and import the result into FCP.

Now you'll have much more predictable results when importing multilayered Photoshop creations into Final Cut Pro.

APPLYING A PHOTOSHOP FILTER TO AN FCP IMAGE SEQUENCE

You can apply a Photoshop filter to a series of FCP stills called an *image sequence*, which you can then play back as a video sequence in FCP. In the following exercise, you'll start in FCP and export an image sequence to Photoshop, where you'll apply a Photoshop filter to the frames via a batch process called an *action*. You'll then import the sequence back into FCP and play it back in real time.

EXERCISE 14-2: APPLYING A FILTER TO AN IMAGE SEQUENCE

Open the Chapter 14 Exercise sequence and move to the Exercise 2 marker. A clip, "Bubble Girl," has been added for you.

1. In Final Cut Pro, perform a Mark Clip function for the "Bubble Girl" clip and then go to File → Export → Using QuickTime Conversion.

2. Now you'll save the image sequence.

   a. In the Save dialog box's Format menu, choose Image Sequence and then click the Options button. The Export Image Sequence Settings dia-log box will appear.

   b. Choose Photoshop from the format menu, and then click OK. You'll be back at the Save dialog box.

   c. To avoid messing up the Desktop with dozens of icons, you should save your image sequence into a folder. Create a new folder and name it "Bubble Girl_SEQ."

   d. Click the Save button. The frames will be placed in the folder.

3. Press Command + H to hide FCP. Open the Bubble Girl_SEQ folder and take a look at all of those frames! You'll need to use a representative frame to test out your filter.

   a. Press Command + D to duplicate the first file (Bubble Girl 001.psd), and then drag it out of the folder and onto the Desktop. This will be your test frame for Photoshop.

   b. Drag and drop the duplicate frame onto the Photoshop icon.

4. Choose a filter or group of filters that you'd like to apply as a batch to your test frame. After trying a few filters, click on the History palette and click where it says "Open." This resets the image.

5. To apply the filter to all the frames in the sequence, you'll need to make a Photoshop action, which will record what you do to your test frame. After the action is recorded, you can apply it to all the frames in the folder.

   a. Go to Window → Actions tab to view the Actions palette, or just click the Actions tab.

   b. Click on the button in the upper-right corner of the Actions palette, and choose New Action from the menu that appears. In the Actions dialog box, name the action "Graphic Pen." Click the round Record button to begin recording your action.

   c. Go to Filter → Sketch → Graphic Pen. The Graphic Pen controls dialog box will appear. Make any adjustments you like, and then click the OK button.

   d. Click the square Stop button in the Actions palette. Now you've created a simple action for the selected frame.

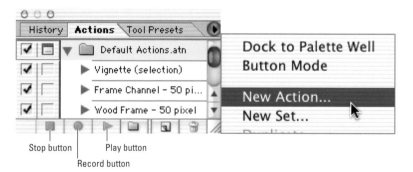

Stop button | Play button
Record button

Add the Photoshop Graphic Pen filter to the still, and record that action in Photoshop's Actions palette.

Photoshop Transfer Modes

Photoshop has its own set of composite modes called *transfer modes*. You set up transfer mode effects the same way as you do in FCP, by stacking up layers and applying a mode to the layer on top of the stack.

Many of these modes are identical to FCP's composite modes, and will come through when a Photoshop image is imported into FCP. If FCP has no equivalent mode, you'll need to merge the mode-affected layer into a blank layer (precisely the same way you preserved layer styles). Flattening the entire image is another way to work around unsupported modes.

6. You'll now apply the action to all the frames in the folder.

    a. Go to File → Automate → Batch. The Batch dialog box will appear.

    b. Make sure the Graphic Pen action is selected in the Action menu.

    c. Make sure that Folder is selected in the Source menu. Click the Choose button and select your Bubble Girl_SEQ folder.

    d. In the Choose a Batch Folder dialog box, click the Choose button.

    e. In the Destination menu, choose Save and Close to overwrite the original images.

    f. Click OK. The action you created will be applied to each image in the folder.

7. After the batch of images has been processed, you'll need to import it into FCP.

    a. In FCP, press Option + Q to open the User Preferences dialog box.

    b. Change Still/Freeze Duration to :01 (one frame).

8. In the Chapter 14 bin, make a new bin called "Bubble Girl." Go to File → Import → Folder. Then navigate to your new image sequence. Click the Choose button to place the frames into the bin.

9. You can now export this series of frames as a self-contained QuickTime movie.

You've now made an FCP movie with a Photoshop filter applied to it! I hope you're beginning to see that you can use Photoshop for much more than making title elements or lower-third graphics. With a little effort, you can use it as an image-processing tool.

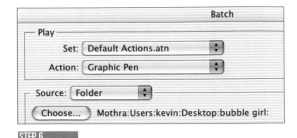

STEP 6

Use the Batch dialog box to apply the action to all the frames in the sequence.

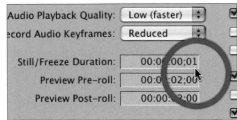

STEP 7

In FCP's User Preferences dialog box, set the Still/Freeze Duration to one frame.

STEP 9
The Graphic Pen filter has been applied to all of the frames in the image sequence.

USING FCP'S EXTERNAL EDITORS FUNCTION

Final Cut Pro's External Editors function enables you to launch an external application such as Photoshop from within FCP, edit a still graphic in that application, and have the changes show up in the image in FCP.

1. In FCP, go to Final Cut Pro → System Settings. The System Settings dialog box will appear.

    a. Click the External Editors tab. The External Editors window will appear.

    b. Click the Set button next to Still Image Files (see Figure 14-2). The Choose a File dialog will appear.

    c. Navigate to the Photoshop icon in your Applications folder. Click Choose.

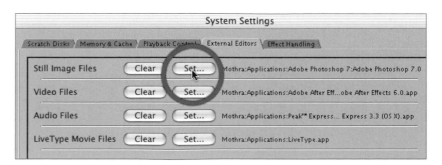

FIGURE 14-2
Use FCP's External Editors window to select Photoshop as your editor for still images.

tip

Adobe Studio Exchange (www.studio.adobe.com) is a great resource for Photoshop users. There you'll find all sorts of helpful actions, brushes, droplets, templates, styles, and scripts.

2. Now that your External Editors settings will launch Photoshop for still images, you can apply this function to a still image in the Timeline. Control + click on any image created in Photoshop and choose Open In Editor to launch Photoshop.

3. In Photoshop, edit the Photoshop file as you see fit, but don't delete or rename any layers.

4. Press Command + S to save the Photoshop file. Once you begin working in FCP once more, the file will update to reflect the changes you made in Photoshop.

LiveType Integration

Although LiveType is included with Final Cut Pro, you can treat it like a third-party application in most respects. You can import footage into LiveType, create an effect with the footage, and render it for import back into FCP.

TRAVEL MATTE TYPE EFFECTS IN LIVETYPE

tip

Any shape, movie, texture or Photoshop graphic imported into LiveType via the File → Place command will show up as a black dot in the text window. If you need multiple copies of this clip or graphic on the track, you can Copy/Paste the item as many times as you wish. You can shape the path, as well as change the Text Size, Text Tracking, and Scale properties to alter the orientation of the copies in relation to each other. You can also matte movies or textures to these glyphs.

You can create two kinds of travel matte effects in LiveType. You can either have the entire track "stencil" through a background to reveal the graphic fill, or have the fill attached to individual characters.

Go to the Inspector and click the Attributes tab, and then the Matte tab, where you'll find a menu with matte choices:

- Matte to Background is the "stencil" effect, where type punches through an intermediate background to reveal a graphic fill.

- Matte to Movie or Image maps a movie or still image individually to each character on the track.

- Matte to Texture lets you choose a LiveType texture to map to each character.

Matte to Background

In this effect, the text "stencils" a layer on a lower track to reveal whatever layer (or layered composition) lies below the Background Bar. In this case, whatever is below the Background Bar does not move with the text; the background moves behind the text.

The background for the graphic fill can actually be built out of several layers. This is similar to using a nested sequence as the fill track for a Travel Matte Alpha effect in Final Cut Pro.

1. In LiveType's Text Entry box, create your title with a bold, sans serif font (not a LiveFont).

2. Add a background from the Textures tab to the Timeline.

   a. Scroll through the textures in the Media Browser's Textures tab. Once you've found a good one, click the Apply to New Track button.

   b. Drag the texture above the Background Bar, but below the Text track.

   c. Select the Text track; it should be at the top of the stack.

   d. In the Attributes tab, click on the Matte button to bring up the Matte pane. In the Matte pane, choose Background from the Matte To menu. The text will now punch through the Texture below the Text Track.

3. Turn off Track 01 and Track 02 by clicking their Disable buttons. You'll now work on the background.

4. Click the Apply to New Track button. Once it's in the Timeline, drag the texture or object below the Background Bar. Create what you want to see within the stencil by choosing a texture from the Textures tab or an object from the Objects tab.

   Another option is to turn off the tracks below the Background Bar to leave the graphic fill blank. After rendering the effect, the area defined by the text will carry the alpha channel. In this scenario, you could add the graphic fill in FCP.

5. Render the movie.

Now let's look at the other two options for making matte effects in LiveType.

Matte to Movie or Image and Matte to Texture

Matte to Movie or Image and Matte to Texture are similar, in that the graphic fill resides within each individual text character.

By default, when you matte a movie, image, or texture to a track, each character will carry an image. But if you click on the glyph in the Canvas, you can then choose a different movie, image, or texture for each glyph in the Matte tab.

> **tip**
>
> *You should look into bringing in Photoshop files into LiveType. With Photoshop CS, you can run an automated process called a script to export a layer into a folder as a PSD file. At the very least, this will help you keep track of the proper order once you import the layers into LiveType individually. Go to File → Scripts → Export Layers to Files, and then choose the destination where you'd like to keep the files and select the file type as PSD. Be sure to check the Maximize Compatibility checkbox. You can now rebuild your layered PSD in LiveType.*

These effects are easy to set up. You simply locate a movie or texture and apply it. There's no need to slap it into the Timeline first. The following exercise will show you how it's done.

EXERCISE 14-3: CREATING MATTE TO MOVIE EFFECT IN LIVETYPE

In this exercise you'll apply a movie to a series of glyphs to create some amazing flying picture-in-picture effects. Start by opening LiveType.

1. Save the LiveType file and name it "Matte to Movie." Click once in either text box.

2. Launch the Character Palette and pick out a diamond shape. (I found mine in View → Roman → Miscellaneous.) Select the shape and then click the Insert button. Now close the Character Palette.

3. In the Attributes tab of the Inspector, set the Scale for the diamond shape to 225%.

4. Make four more diamonds. To do this, select the small black diamond in the text box and copy and paste it four times. After you've got your diamonds, spread them out and resize the text. Click on the Text tab and change the Size to 80 and Tracking to 180.

5. Now that you've got your diamonds set up, you can matte a different movie to each one. In the Canvas, click on the diamond on the far left.

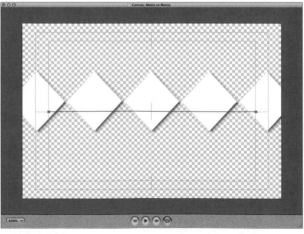

STEP 4

Make four more diamonds by copying and pasting the original.

6. In the Attributes tab, click the Matte button to bring up the Matte pane. In the Matte pane, from the Matte To menu, choose Movie or Image, and then click Choose.

7. In the Open dialog box, choose a movie or image from your list of clips, and then click the Open button.

8. Your movie or texture will now be in the diamond character. You have a few choices to control the graphic fill in the Matte pane.

   a. Use Scale to resize the image within the glyph. If you need to precisely position the graphic fill, use the Matte to Background function instead.

   b. Use Speed to set how fast the movie plays within the glyph.

   c. Use Sequence to offset the timing of the background movie for each glyph on the track.

9. After you're satisfied with the movie, click on the next glyph and fill it with a different movie. Fill the rest of the glyphs on this track with different movies.

10. If you like, you can tint each movie with the Color parameter in the Attributes tab, add a background from the Textures tab, apply a glow from the Style tab, add a motion effect, and so on.

11. Ensure that your Project Properties are properly set and then render this composite.

Now that you've completed this exercise, you can see new and interesting ways to integrate Live Type elements with clips originally captured in Final Cut Pro.

> **note**
>
> *If you want the same movie or texture applied to all of the glyphs, select the track in the Timeline instead of an individual glyph in the Canvas.*

> **note**
>
> *LiveType automatically exports files using the Animation codec, with an alpha channel included.*

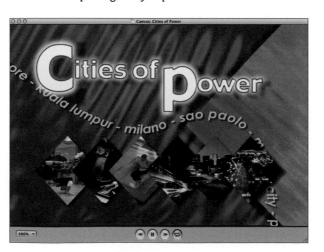

STEP 10
Stylize your effect with the options in LiveType's many tabs.

Third-Party Applications

As a video graphics professional, you have to be a jack-of-all-trades. Your skills should include knowing how to use Adobe Photoshop and at least one or two additional compositing programs. In addition, you might need to use additional graphics applications or plug-ins to accomplish tasks that aren't in Final Cut Pro's bailiwick. These tasks might include the following:

- **Matte Creation.** Still and motion mattes for blending images in a composite.

- **Rotoscoping.** Create a matte for a subject that moves over time.

- **Motion tracking.** Track an object and derive keyframe data as it moves. The keyframes can then be copied and pasted into another effect.

- **Image stabilization.** Steady a shaky hand-held shot as if it were on a tripod.

- **Corner pinning.** Place a flat object on a plane and have it maintain perspective as the camera moves.

- **Vector painting.** Paint on video frames. You can add handwriting or a painterly pattern, or eliminate dirt and scratches.

- **Cloning.** Multiply existing objects. Fill a stadium with fans made from a single group of people.

- **Wire removal.** Clone pixels on either side of a narrow anomaly lying in frame, such as a wire on an actor flying across a green screen.

- **Creating 3D layers.** Move clips, objects, cameras, and lights in 3D space.

- **Moving virtual cameras and lights.** Change the viewpoint of the comp by moving simulated cameras and lights around a virtual stage.

- **Performing 3D extrusion.** Add a three-dimensional perspective to two-dimensional elements.

Exporting FCP Footage into Other Applications

In order to work with Final Cut Pro footage in other applications, you've got to export it properly. In Chapter 2 you learned how to export a QuickTime movie for use in another application. Remember, if you've cropped a clip, added a matte, or altered the alpha channel and want to preserve these effects in a third-party program, you must export a lossless codec like Animation or None. You must also remember to set the color depth to Millions of Colors + when you export the file.

- **Controlling effects with expressions.** Have the controls of one effect drive the parameters of another effect.

- **Particle generation.** Create sparks, smoke, confetti, or the like.

- **Applying specialty keyframes.** FCP has rudimentary keyframes, but there are whole bunches of behavioral keyframes available in other programs.

THIRD-PARTY APPLICATIONS OVERVIEW

You've already seen how to augment FCP's capabilities with Photoshop. In this section we'll look at some additional helpful applications.

Boris RED 3GL

Boris RED, from Boris FX (www.borisfx.com), is an amazing video compositing application that bridges the gap between standalone compositing applications and FCP plug-ins. RED lets you create advanced motion graphics without having to exit FCP, which is a big selling point.

Boris RED 3GL is the latest version. The "GL" refers to OpenGL, which is a protocol for speeding up video display. Boris RED 3GL can do many of the tasks listed earlier in this section: motion tracking, stabilization, corner pinning, rotoscoping, matte generation, multilayered effects, generators, and titling, to name a few. In addition, it accepts just about every Adobe After Effects third-party plug in — even those that are not compatible with FCP.

Boris RED meshes well with FCP. It shows up as a filter in FCP's Effects menu. Applying RED as a filter opens the Boris RED interface, which allows you to create your effect and then return to FCP for rendering (see Figure 14-3). When RED is applied this way, as many as seven additional video tracks are available for compositing within the Boris RED interface.

In addition to being available as a filter, Boris RED appears as a generator in the Generators tab as well.

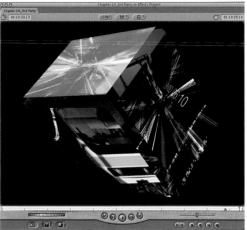

FIGURE 14-3

Make a composite in RED and then click the Apply button. Your composite will show up in FCP, ready to render.

Adobe After Effects

Final Cut Pro editors like to use Adobe After Effects for a lot of different purposes: motion graphics, visual effects, Web graphics, and even traditional animation. This program integrates exceedingly well with Adobe Photoshop and Adobe Illustrator (a vector-based drawing and painting program), offers 3D layers, virtual

note

Boris RED's documentation warns that transitions will render in RGB color space rather than in YUV color space, giving rise to the possibility of color shifts. The manual recommends rendering in RGB color space if you use a Boris RED transition. The RGB-YUV inconsistency isn't a problem if you use Boris RED as a filter in FCP, because FCP performs the conversion back to YUV color space.

tip

I like the Boris RED window called the Library Browser, which is like LiveType's Effects tab on steroids. By inspecting the preset effects, you can figure out how they were originally created. This provides a great learning tool for the beginning compositor.

cameras and lights, is savvy with expressions (where one animated control moves another control), and includes specialized keyframes. You can even rotoscope moving objects.

You can export FCP files to After Effects by creating either a self-contained or a reference movie (see Chapter 2 for details). The QuickTime method has a drawback, however: it brings in a "flattened" movie that's devoid of layers.

Using a plug-in called Automatic Duck Pro Import (www.automaticduck.com), you can preserve FCP layers and other elements. Your FCP Timeline will be duplicated as an After Effects Timeline. Some FCP effects will be transferred, but titles and most transitions will not transfer.

Once your FCP files are in After Effects, you can use that program's tools to add effects to them. To bring your After Effects comp back into FCP, you'll need to render the file. There are two scenarios for returning rendered QuickTime files to FCP from After Effects or other applications:

- If you want to preserve alpha channel transparency from your rendered composition (see Figure 14-4), you should render in the Animation codec, specifying Millions of Colors +.

- If you do not wish to re-render the comp within FCP, you can export using the same codec and settings found in the FCP sequence where you'll be placing the rendered comp (most likely the DV codec).

FIGURE 14-4
This After Effects composite has been imported back into Final Cut Pro, with its alpha channel retained for further compositing tasks in FCP.

Pinnacle Commotion

Commotion Pro, from Pinnacle Systems (www.pinnaclesys.com), does a number of compositing tricks, including tracking, painting, masking, and rotoscoping. Rotoscoping is its number one strength. You can also use it for post-production tasks, such as painting out analog video dropouts or extraneous items like boom poles.

Apple Shake

Apple Shake (www.apple.com/shake) is a powerful compositing application that you can use to work on multilayered composites. Shake excels at keying, motion tracking, compositing in linear and log space, and distributed rendering (using more than one computer to render files).

If you want to get your hands on Shake right now, I suggest you pick up *Shake 3 Professional Compositing and Special Effects,* by Marco Paolini (Peachpit Press). The book includes a 30-day license that allows you to use Shake with your own footage.

Discreet Combustion 3

Combustion, a sophisticated compositing application from Discreet (www.discreet. com/combustion) offers a jam-packed tool set for motion graphics, visual effects, or film work. The program combines paint, animation, and 3D compositing tools. Combustion's strong suits include particle generation, morphing, keying, feathering, color correction, and motion tracking.

Macromedia StudioMX

Macromedia StudioMX (www.macromedia.com) provides some great tools for bringing your FCP motion graphics creations to the Web, PDA devices, and even cell phones. The StudioMX package combines Dreamweaver, Freehand, Fire-works, and Flash, all now available as "MX" (or professional) applications.

The link between StudioMX and FCP is QuickTime, which can fully understand the .fla file format. The .fla format is the default movie made by Macromedia Flash, MX's core motion graphics delivery application.

To get FCP video into Flash to deploy it to the Web, you have to export it as a QuickTime movie and then optimize it for Flash.

note

Although some third-party plug-ins for After Effects work in FCP, the native After Effects plug-ins do not, so don't attempt to load them into your FCP Plug-Ins folder. They simply won't show up.

tip

Curious about Adobe After Effects? Adobe offers a 30-day tryout version at www.adobe.com/products/ tryadobe/main.jhtml.

tip

Macromedia Fireworks files come into FCP as layered comps. Just make sure to use the Export function instead of Save, and then choose .PSD for the export file type.

3D Integration

You've seen 3D animation in its familiar form, but were you aware that 3D applications are also great for generating images for motion graphics compositions? My favorite application for this purpose is Maxon's Cinema 4D XL. I suggest you give it a try. A free try-out version is included in the Goodies folder on the DVD.

Plug-Ins

tip

You can export motion graphics that you create in Flash to FCP. However, vector graphics will be rasterized and may be compressed. To keep images from looking chunky or grainy, keep rotation to a minimum and add a bit of motion blur once you get your source animation into FCP.

A great way to expand FCP's capabilities is to add third-party filters to your stock collection. These add-on filters are called *plug-ins*. Plug-ins can do anything from changing the speed at which a clip plays to adding a film look or a unique texture. When you install plug-ins, they end up in Library → Application Support → Final Cut Pro System Support → Plug-Ins.

PLUG-IN COLLECTIONS

Plug-ins often come in sets. Here are some of my favorite collections:

- **Boris Continuum Complete 2.** BCC 2 (www.borisfx.com) is my favorite set of filters. The package includes more than 100 filters, and some generators and effects as well (see Figure 14-5). (Many of BCC 2's plug-ins are included with Boris RED.)

- **CGM Filters Volumes 1 and 2.** CGM Filters Volume 1 was included with Final Cut Pro 3, and you can use these filters with FCP 4 if you upgraded from FCP 3 and still have the filters available. Notable among these is the excellent Film Dissolve transition. If you don't have the original CGM filters, you can purchase updated versions at www.cgm-online.com. The CGM filters have been optimized for the G5 and RT Extreme, and they render very quickly.

FIGURE 14-5

Boris Continuum Complete 2 has a multitude of filters you can put to creative use. Here, I've placed flames in front of a building.

- **Joe's Filters.** Another versatile package is Joe's Filters (www.joesfilters.com). These plug-ins include Adjustments, Alpha Effects, Blur, Noise, Soft Effects, Stylizing, Video, and Time, as well as a Shapes and Ellipse generator. The filters are optimized for RT Extreme. As a bonus, you can open them in the FX Script Editor and modify them. Among my favorites in this collection are Joe's Soft Spot, a circular diffusion filter for blurring inside or outside a circular area, and Joe's Color Glow, which creates colored auras.

  - **Eureka!** Eureka! was one of the first plug-in sets created for FCP, and it has returned as a useful, low-cost set of filters. Check it out at www.kafwang.com. The collection includes some outstanding transitions as well, including Film Dissolve and Flash Cross.

■ **Final Effects Complete.** This is a versatile collection of lighting, motion, and particle-generation effects, as well as generators. While other plug-ins may duplicate some of Final Effects functionality, nothing comes close to Mr. Mercury, which turns your video into wonderful blobs that ooze and shimmer like quicksilver (see Figure 14-6). For more information, go to Media100's website at www.media100.com/fec.asp.

■ **Sapphire.** Sapphire, from GenArts, offers a set of blurs, generators, and more than 200 effects. (The filters work in After Effects as well as in FCP.) Sapphire is not cheap, but it's one of the best effects packages available. Check it out at www.genarts.com.

■ **G Filters.** G Filters offers a unique collection of useful plug-ins for FCP. New from G Filters are Standards Conversion filters, which convert video between NTSC to PAL and from PAL to NTSC and from 29.97 to 24P and back. Way cool! Filter Set 1 and 2 provide excellent dissolves, levels, lines to create travel mattes, and even some unusual effects like earthquakes and bug eyes. The G Film plug-ins excel in film look, too – more on this in a bit. Check out these filters made by Graeme Nattress, who also is the genius behind my own plug-in set, "Telly's FX." Go to www.nattress.com to pick up all the offerings from G Filters.

■ **Lyric Motion Tracking Plug-in Kit.** Until this package was released, the only way to achieve stabilization and corner pinning within FCP was to use an applicaton such as Boris RED, Adobe After Effects, Commotion, Combustion, Curious gFX, or Shake. This plug-in kit is good bang for the buck. Check it out at www.lyric.com.

Media100's Mr. Mercury plug-in offers a unique way to distort your clips.

SPECIALTY PLUG-INS

If you have specialized needs for your motion graphics creations, don't overlook the many specialty plug-ins available for Final Cut Pro. These plug-ins are often one-trick ponies, but they do their tricks very well. They range from 3D effects to photorealistic backgrounds. Here are a few of my favorites.

Conoa 3D

One of the more interesting plug-ins is Conoa 3D (www.conoa.com), which allows you to map clips to any of twelve three-dimensional shapes (see Figure 14-7). You can then manipulate the resulting 3D images in X, Y, and Z space. As in 3D modeling applications, you can adjust camera position, lighting, material, reflections, textures, and reflectivity.

Psunami

Psunami, from Digital Anarchy (www.digitalanarchy.com), simulates seascapes with amazing realism. You can control everything from the swell size to wind speed and direction. You can create lighting effects and apply colors to the water and the sky. Best of all, you can fly virtual cameras around the seascape (even underwater!). You can also "float" graphics on the surface of the water (see Figure 14-8).

FIGURE 14-7
The Conoa 3D plug-in allows you to map an image to a shape such as a sphere.

FIGURE 14-8
Psunami can be combined with FCP to create motion graphics floating on the surface of the water.

Knoll Light Factory 2

You can use Knoll Light Factory 2, from Red Giant Software (www.redgiantsoftware.com), to add finishing touches to your effects. This package includes more than 20 lighting-effect filters that range from simple lens flares to photon torpedoes. You can purchase it at www.digitalanarchy.com.

ReelSmart Twixtor and ReTimer

Do you use FCP's Time Remap feature in a lot of your work? If so, you may have found yourself wanting more accurate time remapping, in particular for super-slow-motion effects. Two plug-ins are particularly useful for time remapping:

- ReelSmart Twixtor is a time-remapping plug-in from RE:Vision Effects (www.revisionfx.com). You create a slug that's of the duration you want for the time-remapped clip, and then drag the clip to the Color Source well. It can take a little trial and error to determine the best settings for Frame Interpolation and Motion Vectors, depending on the amount and nature of movement within the frame.

- RealViz ReTimer is distributed by Digital Anarchy (www.digitalanarchy.com). ReTimer functions in the same way as Twixtor, by having you drop the input sequence into the well.

Whichever time-remapping plug-in you use, you'll be able to achieve smoother motion than you would by using FCP's Time Remap function.

Grain Surgery

Have you ever tried to rescue a poorly lit night shot, or match a scene where you had to turn up your camera gain to the extent that your image was grainy? Or maybe you'd like to add some graininess for a stylized effect or a film look (see Figure 14-9). Grain Surgery 2 (www.visualinfinity.com) performs those tasks with ease, allowing you to remove, match, or add grain.

FIGURE 14-9
You can use Grain Surgery to create a grainy film look.

Film Look Plug-ins

To make your digital video look like it was shot on film, you can either export your video to Adobe After Effects and apply a film look, or use a plug-in. An excellent plug-in set called Standards Conversion, from Graeme Nattress, offers conversion from 29.97 fps NTSC or 25 fps PAL sequence to 24P (progressive scan) and back. Check it out at www.nattress.com.

The Eureka! (www.kafwang.com) and Sapphire (www.genarts.com) plug-in collections include film-look effects as well. Sapphire allows you to match the color characteristics of specific 35mm or 16mm film stock, something that FCP editors coming from a film background will appreciate.

Digital Film Tools' Digital Film Lab provides an extensive collection of modifiable film-look presets, which are defined by look rather than by stock. Their other plug-in, Digital Film Tools 55mm, simulates various optical filters you'd place on a camera lens. If you did not shoot with a ProMist filter (something I don't recommend for shooting HD) and your talent looks too harsh, then 55mm is the package that will be the perfect fit for many of you. Their Dissolve Factory plug-in creates a cinematic dissolve. You'll find more information at www.digitalfilmtools.com.

Additional Plug-ins

Here are some additional specialty plug-ins that you can use to achieve just the right effect in Final Cut Pro.

- **Artmetic Filters** (www.artmetic.com) is a diverse collection of plug-ins.

- **Boris Graffiti 2** (www.borisfx.com) offers titling tools and effects.

- **Color Theory,** from Theory LLC (available from Digital Anarchy, www.digitalanarcy.com), helps you choose the right colors for your creations.

- **Composite Suite,** from Digital Film Tools (www.digitalfilmtools.com), includes lighting filters for compositing.

- **dvMatte Pro,** from dvGarage (www.dvgarage.com), is chroma keying application that improves on FCP's Chroma Keyer filter.

- **Effects Essentials** from Buena Software (www.buenasoftware.com) offers a variety of color filters.

- **Fields Tool Kit,** from RE:Vision Effects (www.revisionfx.com), is an excellent interlacer/deinterlacer.

- **Moving Picture 4,** from Stage Tools (www.stagetools.com), enables you to pan and zoom in a still image. **Moving Parts** lets you animate individual layers in a comp.

- **Profound Effects Swim** (www.profoundeffects.com) produces a wiggly, oozing morph.

- **Reel Smart Motion Blur, Reel Smart Smooth Kit,** and **Reel Smart Video Gogh** (www.revisionfx.com) offer motion blurs and trails, Gaussian blur, and oil-painting effects, respectively.

- **Text Anarchy** (www.digitalanarchy.com) is a collection of cool text effects.

- **Trapcode Shine** (www.trapcode.com) is considered by many to be the best way to create radial lighting effects. Most effects are keyframable. **Trapcode Starglow** adds a glow to objects' edges.

- **Ultimatte AdvantEdge,** from Ultimatte (www.ultimatte.com), is a chroma keyer plug-in.

- **Virtix Filters** (www.virtix.com) is a diverse collection of plug-ins.

There are many more third-party plug-ins that function well in FCP. For a more exhaustive list of plug-ins, go to my website: www.fcpworld.com.

Wrap-up

With the completion of this chapter, you should be pretty good at making effects with Final Cut Pro. That's not to say that you've learned everything there is to know about creating effects and motion graphics in FCP. I'm still learning new things every day, and you can as well. I hope the techniques and exercises in this book have inspired you to experiment on your own, and to try out new techniques to expand your skills. Before long, you'll be creating effects you never dreamed possible (see Figure 14-10).

I've enjoyed writing this book, and I hope you've enjoyed reading it. If you'd like to continue learning about effects creation, or want additional updates and tips, be sure to visit my website at www.fcpworld.com. Good luck in all your creative endeavors!

FIGURE 14-10
Stay creative, and good luck!

Index